Passions of the Tongue

Studies on the History of Society and Culture

Victoria E. Bonnell and Lynn Hunt, Editors

1. *Politics, Culture, and Class in the French Revolution,* by Lynn Hunt
2. *The People of Paris: An Essay in Popular Culture in the Eighteenth Century,* by Daniel Roche
3. *Pont-St-Pierre, 1398–1789: Lordship, Community, and Capitalism in Early Modern France,* by Jonathan Dewald
4. *The Wedding of the Dead: Ritual, Poetics, and Popular Culture in Transylvania,* by Gail Kligman
5. *Students, Professors, and the State in Tsarist Russia,* by Samuel D. Kassow
6. *The New Cultural History,* edited by Lynn Hunt
7. *Art Nouveau in Fin-de-Siècle France: Politics, Psychology, and Style,* by Debora L. Silverman
8. *Histories of a Plague Year: The Social and the Imaginary in Baroque Florence,* by Giulia Calvi
9. *Culture of the Future: The Proletkult Movement in Revolutionary Russia,* by Lynn Mally
10. *Bread and Authority in Russia, 1914–1921,* by Lars T. Lih
11. *Territories of Grace: Cultural Change in the Seventeenth-Century Diocese of Grenoble,* by Keith P. Luria
12. *Publishing and Cultural Politics in Revolutionary Paris, 1789–1810,* by Carla Hesse
13. *Limited Livelihoods: Gender and Class in Nineteenth-Century England,* by Sonya O. Rose
14. *Moral Communities: The Culture of Class Relations in the Russian Printing Industry, 1867–1907,* by Mark Steinberg
15. *Bolshevik Festivals, 1917–1920,* by James von Geldern
16. *Venice's Hidden Enemies: Italian Heretics in a Renaissance City,* by John Martin
17. *Wondrous in His Saints: Counter-Reformation Propaganda in Bavaria,* by Philip M. Soergel
18. *Private Lives and Public Affairs: The Causes Célèbres of Prerevolutionary France,* by Sarah Maza
19. *Hooliganism: Crime, Culture, and Power in St. Petersburg, 1900–1914,* by Joan Neuberger
20. *Possessing Nature: Museums, Collecting, and Scientific Culture in Early Modern Italy,* by Paula Findlen

21. *Listening in Paris: A Cultural History,* by James H. Johnson
22. *The Fabrication of Labor: Germany and Britain, 1640–1914,* by Richard Biernacki
23. *The Struggle for the Breeches: Gender and the Making of the British Working Class,* by Anna Clark
24. *Taste and Power: Furnishing Modern France,* by Leora Auslander
25. *Cholera in Post-Revolutionary Paris: A Cultural History,* by Catherine J. Kudlick
26. *The Women of Paris and Their French Revolution,* by Dominique Godineau
27. *Iconography of Power: Soviet Political Posters under Lenin and Stalin,* by Victoria E. Bonnell
28. *Aestheticized Politics: Fascism in Italy, 1919–1940,* by Simonetta Falasca-Zamponi
29. *Passions of the Tongue: Language Devotion in Tamil India, 1891–1970,* by Sumathi Ramaswamy

A

Philip E. Lilienthal

Book

The Philip E. Lilienthal imprint
honors special books
in commemoration of a man whose work
at the University of California Press from 1954 to 1979
was marked by dedication to young authors
and to high standards in the field of Asian Studies.
Friends, family, authors, and foundations have together
endowed the Lilienthal Fund, which enables the Press
to publish under this imprint selected books
in a way that reflects the taste and judgment
of a great and beloved editor.

Passions of the Tongue

Language Devotion in Tamil India, 1891–1970

Sumathi Ramaswamy

UNIVERSITY OF CALIFORNIA PRESS
Berkeley · Los Angeles · London

University of California Press
Berkeley and Los Angeles, California

University of California Press, Ltd.
London, England

Library of Congress Cataloging-in-Publication Data

Ramaswamy, Sumathi.
Passions of the tongue : language devotion in Tamil India, 1891–1970 / Sumathi Ramaswamy.
p. cm.—(Studies on the history of society and culture ; 29)
Includes bibliographical references and index.
ISBN 0-520-20804-8 (cloth : alk. paper).—
ISBN 0-520-20805-6 (pbk. : alk. paper)
1. Ramaswamy, Sumathi—Knowledge—Dravidian languages. 2. Language and languages—Study and teaching—United States. 3. Critical pedagogy—United States. 4. India—Languages—Political aspects. 5. Language and culture—India—History. 6. Nationalism—India—History. 7. India—History—British occupation, 1765–1947—Historiography.
I. Series.
PL4758.9.R3528P37 1997
494'.811'0954—dc21 96-52441

Printed in the United States of America
9 8 7 6 5 4 3 2 1

The paper used in this publication is both acid-free and totally chlorine-free (TCF). It meets the minimum requirements of American Standard for Information Sciences—Permanence of Paper for Printed Library Materials, ANSI Z39.48-1984.

Contents

Illustrations

Acknowledgments

This book would not have been possible without the assistance of several individuals and institutions. Funding for its research and writing was provided by a U.S. Department of Education Fulbright-Hays DDRA Fellowship; a Charlotte W. Newcombe Doctoral Dissertation Fellowship from the Woodrow Wilson National Fellowship Foundation; a Rockefeller Residency Fellowship at the Institute on Culture and Consciousness in South Asia, the University of Chicago; and a Research Foundation grant by the University of Pennsylvania. I am grateful to all these institutions, as well as to the Departments of History and South Asia Regional Studies, University of Pennsylvania, for their financial and intellectual support over the past few years.

I owe an immense debt of gratitude to numerous individuals across Tamilnadu who have been gracious with their time and advice since the beginning of this project in 1990: Professors A. A. Manavalan, P. Kothandaraman, I. Maraimalai, and R. Ilavarasu; K. Sivathamby and A. Alagappan; Dr. M. S. S. Pandian; Ganapathy Stapathi; Gurusami Stapathi; Mr. T. N. Ramachandran; Mr. R. Muthukumaraswamy, managing director, the South India Shaiva Siddhanta Works Publishing Society; and Mr. S. Ramakrishnan, director, Cre-A Publications. I am also indebted to Dr. Cilampoli Chellappan, Mr. P. S. Mani, Mr. P. K. Kothandapani, and Mr. L. K. Ramanujam for lending me books from their personal collections; and to *Kaviaracu* Mudiyarasan for so graciously sharing his unpublished memoirs. Finally, I owe special thanks to Dr. A. R. Venkatachalapathy, fellow historian, for his valuable insights on

Tamil literature and politics; and to B. Krishnamoorthy and Dora, for their hospitality, for sharing their wonderful collection of Tamil books and journals, and for reminding me so much about the pleasures of doing research in Tamil.

This study would not have been possible but for the painstaking assistance of librarians in three different countries: the staff of the Tamilnadu Archives, Madras, and in particular Mr. Sivakumar and Mr. Loganathan; Ms. Geeta Jayanthi at the Maraimalai Adigal Library; Ms. Shyamala at the Periyar Library; Mr. Sundararajan at Anna Arivalayam; Mr. T. Padmanabhan at the Tamil University Library; Ms. Sengamalam at the Bharatiar Memorial Library; Mr. Kanakaraj of the Bharatidasan Memorial Library; Mr. Sankaralingam at the Roja Muthiah Research Library; and the staff of the U. V. Swaminatha Aiyar Library, the International Institute of Tamil Studies Library, the Theosophical Society Library, the Madurai Tamil Sangam Library, and the Karanthai Tamil College Library; Meera Dawson at the India Office Library, London; James Nye at Regenstein Library, University of Chicago; and David Nelson at Van Pelt Library, University of Pennsylvania.

This book is based on my doctoral dissertation in history from the University of California, supervised by Eugene Irschick, Thomas Metcalf, and Robert Goldman, to all three of whom I owe enormous gratitude for their encouragement, thoughtful advice, and suggestions. George Hart and Kausalya Hart cheerfully put up with all my translation needs, as did Sam Suddhananda and Vasu Renganathan: I am immensely grateful to them. Numerous others generously offered advice on various aspects of this work: Benedict Anderson, Arjun Appadurai, Carol Breckenridge, Dipesh Chakrabarty, Valentine Daniel, Nicholas Dirks, David Gilmartin, Ruqayya Khan, Alan Kors, C. S. Lakshmi, David Ludden, Michelle Maskiell, Pamela Price, Mytheli Sreenivas, Carroll Smith-Rosenberg and Romila Thapar. I owe special thanks to Franklin Presler for sharing his field notes and experiences with me and to Paula Richman who, way back in the spring of 1991, encouraged me to pursue this study and has since then shared many insights and sources. To Sandy Freitag, I owe more than mere gratitude for being a great mentor, wonderful critic, and supportive friend. Last but not least, I would like to thank Valentine Daniel, two anonymous reviewers, and Lynn Hunt, for their valuable advice on a penultimate draft of this book; and Lynne Withey, Sheila Levine, Dore Brown, and the production staff at the University of California Press for all their assistance.

My greatest personal debts are to my family: my parents, who over the years have cheerfully encouraged my preoccupation with history and Tamil literature and have always provided a loving and intellectually stimulating home for me to return to; my siblings, whose own academic achievements have set the standards for mine; my mother-in-law, who has been a source of immense joy and comfort; and, above all, my husband, whose critical advice on my scholarship has contributed in innumerable ways in shaping my vision, and whose love and friendship have given me the strength to pursue that vision.

Note on Transliteration

Because this is a book about the cultural politics of language, albeit one written in a tongue different from its subject matter, I have chosen to use transliterated forms of Tamil terms, phrases, and names of texts, wherever appropriate. My transliteration follows the University of Madras Tamil Lexicon scheme. For the sake of readability, however, I have not transliterated proper names of individuals, deities, castes, institutions, and places, but have instead used the most recognizable Anglicized form. Unless indicated otherwise, all translations from Tamil are mine.

Preface

"BETWEEN HOMES, BETWEEN LANGUAGES"

It is only appropriate that a book about passions of the tongue ought to have a confession about my own passion for languages, or, more truthfully, a confession about an embarrassing lack of attachment to any particular one. I grew up in a home in New Delhi surrounded by numerous languages and multiple cadences. It was, linguistically at least, a mongrel household—a hybrid formation, in today's fashionable parlance. I heard Tamil spoken by my mother and, after a fashion, by my father as well, although he appeared to be more comfortable in Kannada, which I heard him use in conversations with his siblings, and for formal transactions with many colleagues of his Bangalore-based firm. To this day, my father, a child of Tamil-speaking parents who grew up in Bangalore, counts in Kannada and insists he even dreams in it. As happens in many a Brahman household, I also heard a lot of Sanskrit in the context of prayers I was made to learn from the time I was six. And as is true of the life trajectory of so many young girls who grow up in post-independence India in bourgeois families burdened with the task of preserving "Indian tradition" even while aspiring to be "modern" and "Westernized," I was started on classical Indian music lessons—in my case, Carnatic music—when I was seven. This exposed me to the sounds of Telugu which I learned without comprehending, and it is even today a language I continue to passively hear when I listen to my tapes. There were two other languages which found a prominent place in my life-world: (Indian) English, the principal language of all my formal schooling, of my private pleasures of reading, and of public discourses with family and friends alike; and Hindi, a language I used in the marketplace, and for the consumption of movies and songs, a passion I hold on to, albeit in a truncated fashion, to this day. Unbeknownst to me then, but something I recognize now, these very "Hindi" movies, as well as everyday life in Delhi, familiarized me with the sounds of Urdu, a language with which Hindi speakers of today share an intimate and recent past. So, what was the place of Tamil, this putative "mother tongue" of mine, in this constellation of languages in which I moved? I had no formal schooling in it, nor could I read it. I did not speak it, or hear it spoken, in public. We used it liberally at home, but freely interrupted by English and Hindi; and I can tell from having a specialist's knowledge of it today that it was heavily Sanskritized.

While I may appear as some kind of exotic polyglot creature to those who have grown up in environments that are predominantly monolingual, my (multi) linguistic experience, I would insist, is something that many who live in the subcontinent, especially in urban bourgeois India, would readily recognize as their own, even if the specifics may vary with each personal story. In turn, my polyglot habits echo a deeper history of multilingualism on the subcontinent produced by the displacement and resettlement of populations in areas where their languages were confined to the home and the family; and they are a consequence of a national education policy which, however haphazardly implemented, ideally expects every Indian citizen to formally study at least three languages: her "mother tongue" (or "regional language"), Hindi, and English. Yet, as my example illustrates expediently, this official linguistic hope has more often than not foundered on issues of how to define the "mother tongue" and encourage its active use in an environment where English and Hindi rule as languages of prestige, profit, and power; of how to promote the study of English against the forces of nationalism that identify it as the language of the (colonial) West; and of how to ward off protests that Hindi, the putative "official" language of India, is but the tongue of one region masquerading as the language of the nation. These linguistic battles are very much part of my personal history that have fostered my interest in the cultural politics of languages in modern India.

While my multilinguality is quite the norm for a person of my class, caste, and educational background in India, what is perhaps less usual is the intellectual turn I made towards studying Tamil, a language which, its official status as my "mother tongue" notwithstanding, was after all on the margins of the linguistic economy in which I functioned. Today, my mother proudly insists that the seeds of my future intellectual interest were sown in my fifth grade when I came home one day, from my Hindi- and Punjabi-speaking school environment, and apparently demanded in my childish Tamil, "nampellām tamiḻā?" (Are we Tamilians?). My own memory of my curiosity about Tamil, however, is tied in with a fairly subversive desire, in my teens, to figure out the contents of the frequent letters addressed jointly to my entire family from my grandmother in Madras. These letters, which were bilingual, were, it seemed to me, curiously coded. Their opening lines in English were usually formulaic inquiries about our health and welfare. The really juicy news that make up the everyday texture and pleasures of family life in India were always, however, in Tamil, and therefore beyond my illiterate reach. Determined to have access to this tantalizing knowledge of family politics that made strategic use of linguistic politics, I learned the Tamil script when I was fifteen and, slowly but surely, was able to read those wonderful letters to my curious siblings who remain, to this day, illiterate in Tamil. I also learned something then that I am able to theorize about today: the proliferation of multiple languages, whether in the family or in the nation, allows for the strategic deployment of linguistic resources to practice "intimate" politics in one's "own" tongue that shuts out the unfamiliar, the foreigner.

My intellectual interest in the histories and cultures of Tamil-speaking India were piqued for the first time when I went to college, first for my bachelor's degree at Delhi University, and then for my master's and master of philosophy degrees at Jawaharlal Nehru University, New Delhi. Although I studied Indian history at two of India's finest institutions and with some of its best historians, whose teaching continues to stand me in good stead today, I was soon troubled by the remarkable lack of disciplinary interest in southern India in the nation's capital, itself only an echo of geopolitical realities. At the same time, as a Brahman wanting to learn Tamil in the aftermath of a powerful anti-Brahman movement in the state, I did not expect my interest in the language or its history would be welcomed in its putative home, Tamilnadu. These factors among others brought me to the United States, first to the Department of Anthropology at the University of Pennsylvania, and then later to the Department of History at the University of California, Berkeley. And it is perhaps a fitting end to this quixotic history of my relationship to Tamil that I finally formally learned the language, this troubled "mother tongue" of mine, in a land far away from both my home and my mother.

I grew up then with not just a singular identity that defined itself around the speaking of one language, but used to the luxury—or is it a burden?—of having multiple, albeit partial, identities that I could deploy in various ways in different contexts. At its worst, this has meant that I have frequently felt between languages, between homes; at its best, I have also experienced the pleasures and possibilities as well as the contradictions of being at home in many languages and many places and among many peoples. It is this kind of life which has cultivated in me attitudes which resonate with what the Italian-born, Australia-raised, French-educated feminist philosopher Rosi Braidotti has characterized as "nomadic consciousness." In her 1994 monograph *Nomadic Subjects,* she proposes that such a consciousness "entails a total dissolution of the notion of a center and consequently of originary sites or authentic identities of any kind," even as it resists "settling into socially coded modes of thought and behavior" and thwarts "assimilation into dominant ways of representing the self" (Braidotti 1994: 5). In contrast to the exile or the migrant whose thoughts are fissured by loss, separation, and longing for homes left behind, a nomad's relationship to the world around her, she suggests, is one of "transitory attachment" and "cyclical frequentation." The nomadic style, then, is without a nostalgia for fixity, authenticity, or singularity. Linguistically, the condition of nomadism goes hand in hand with polyglottism: just as a nomad is always in transit between places, a polyglot is "in transit between languages." As such, the nomad-as-polyglot "has some healthy skepticism about steady identities and mother tongues." "Is it because the polyglot practices a sort of gentle promiscuity with different linguistic bedrocks, that s/he has long since relinquished any notion of linguistic or ethnic purity?" she asks (Braidotti 1994: 8, 28).

I may not agree with everything Braidotti has to say about nomadism as the paradigmatic form of consciousness for the end-of-this-millennium critical thinking, nor do I explore here the full theoretical implications of her provocative suggestions. But her work has re-alerted me to the critical possibilities—rather than to the paralyzing ineffectualities—of being between languages and between homes, a condition that increasingly characterizes so many transnational subjects in a postcolonial era. Nomadic consciousness has made me wary of the "renewed and exacerbated sense of nationalism, regionalism, localism that marks this particular moment of our history," even as it has enabled me to "think through and move across established categories and levels of experience: blurring boundaries without burning bridges," as Braidotti puts it aptly (1994: 4, 12). Certainly, constructions of cultural essences and authenticities have been important strategies for the reempowerment of the disenfranchised in many parts of the world, especially under colonial regimes. But my nomadic consciousness also urges me to ask who determines which authenticities are legitimate, which essences retrograde. Under what circumstances? Most important, why and how is it that cultural possessions, be they language or religion or that most sacred entity of all, the nation, assume an enormous materiality and fixity, and ultimately end up by possessing the possessor(s)?

Like my life, this book, too, has had its share of nomadism. The research that has gone into it, and into the doctoral dissertation on which it is partly based, was done across cultures and continents (as all nomadic projects are) in India, England, and the United States. Parts of the book came into being in Madras; others in Berkeley, Chicago, and Philadelphia, very different intellectual and cultural sites, "American" though they may all be. Today, I have come to believe that my "India pages," as I refer to them privately, inject the passion and sense of urgency that I have felt to be necessary counters to the rarefied existence I lead in the U.S. academy. At the same time, I am all too aware that my position in that academy has allowed me the luxury of continuing my nomadic lifestyle, with all the critical de-centering possibilities that entails. The writing of history, we have been told many times, especially in recent years, is an act that is complexly entangled with writing the nation; the most authentic histories, it follows, are those written from within the space of the nation. Yet this history that I write straddles nations, just as it is between languages and between homes. Ultimately, though, its actual production site is far away from the people and the nation(s) which are its subjects. Even while I am aware of the complex consequences of this for the contents of this work, as well as for its reception and reading, I prefer to think, with Salman Rushdie, that if the purpose of critical thought is to find new angles with which to enter our historical realities and to unsettle established certitudes, then my geographical displacement and my critical nomadism offer me a certain purchase. Or perhaps, as he wryly notes, this is simply what I must think in order to go on with my work.

CHAPTER ONE

Introduction

Language in History and Modernity

It was a quiet, cool January dawn in the South Indian city of Tiruchirapalli in the year 1964. A can in his hand, a man named Chinnasami left his home—leaving behind his aging mother, young wife, and infant daughter—and walked to the city's railway station. On reaching there, he doused himself with its contents and set himself on fire, shouting out aloud, "inti o̱lika! tamil̠ vāl̠ka!" (Death to Hindi! May Tamil flourish!). Chinnasami's example was not lost. A year later, to the date, history repeated itself but not necessarily as farce: five other men burned themselves alive "at the altar of Tamil." Three others died just as painfully—not in a raging blaze, but by swallowing insecticide—also for the sake of Tamil, they declared in their own last words. These dramatic acts were reported by the mainstream news media in India, sometimes in a matter-of-fact fashion, sometimes with derision, but invariably as yet another example of the "frenzy" and "fanaticism" that speakers of Tamil habitually display when it comes to their language. American newsmagazines like *Time* and *Newsweek* briefly noted the acts, translating them for the benefit of their readers by reporting that "in the style of Vietnamese monks," these men had "turned [themselves] into human funeral pyre[s]." The Vietnam analogy came home to roost in South India: the monks immolated themselves for their religion, but no one had yet burned themselves for their language, it was suggested. That pride of place goes to speakers of Tamil. *Uṭal maṇṇukku, uyir tamil̠ukku,* "body to earth, life for Tamil": in stories and poems about these men which have circulated since, so is their "sacrifice" for their language commemorated.

How do I, a late-twentieth-century historian, make sense of these deaths? Disciplined by history, I would naturally demand, What is it that led so many men and women to proclaim that they would live and die for their language? Why did they so passionately confess that a life without Tamil is not worth living, that they would forsake material gains and worldly pleasures, even the ambrosia of the gods, for its sake? Trained by my discipline to always historicize, these deaths—as indeed the lives of these women and men—have nonetheless taught me to appreciate the hubris of the historical will to elucidate, as they have laid bare the inadequacies of the very language of history itself to write about matters such as these. Yet historicize I must, if only to rescue these men and women from charges of "frenzy" and "fanaticism." And so I will return to their stories, later, but only after resorting to history.

And yet it would seem that history as a discipline has no place for acts such as Chinnasami's or, for that matter, for the language for which he sacrificed himself. While it is hardly news that languages have histories, "the odd thing about the *questione della lingua* [the language question] is how rarely historians ask it," Gramsci's attempt to theorize it notwithstanding (Steinberg 1987: 199). This is especially true for colonial and post-colonial India where the language question—that complex of issues relating to language, politics, and power—has hardly been interrogated by disciplinary history despite its obvious importance for the political cultures of the emergent nation-state. The historian is a rare presence in scholarly debates on the national language crisis, the internal partitioning of the nation into linguistic states, or the pedagogical dilemmas of multilingualism.[1] This is partly because of a (Orientalist) preoccupation with caste and religion, those two gatekeeping concerns of South Asian studies on identity politics (Ramaswamy 1993: 684–85). But just as clearly, it seems that because our historical conceptions come to us in and through language, historians have tended to treat it, the linguistic turn notwithstanding, as a transparent medium of communication of information rather than as an ideological formation that itself has a politics which has to be historicized.

Yet, even as I try to make a case in this study for (Indian) historians to take the language question seriously, I do so with the troubled knowledge that disciplinary history has been complicit in the Europeanization of alternate life-worlds and imaginations. For the knowledge procedures and institutional practices of history have universalized the European historical experience as the desirable norm, against which all other histories, Indian included, appear inadequate and incomplete (Chakrabarty 1992). Nevertheless, as Dipesh Chakrabarty insists, we cannot give up on history, for it is one of the fundamental modalities of our times, "in the establishment of meaning, in the creation of truth regimes, in deciding, as it were, whose and which 'universal' wins." What we can—and must—do instead, as Meaghan Morris recommends, is to resist the writing of histories of places like India "as a known history, something which has already happened elsewhere, and which is to be reproduced, mechanically or otherwise, with a local content" (quoted by Chakrabarty 1992: 17–20). Histories which seek to corrode the universalizing imperative of Europe's knowledge practices ought to heed all those "scandalous" moments of "difference" which "shock" and "disrupt" the homogenizing flow of history-as-usual:

> Subaltern histories, thus conceived in relationship to the question of difference, will have a split running through them. On the one hand, they are "histories" in that they are constructed within the master-code of secular History and use the academic codes of history-writing (and thereby perforce subordinate to themselves all other forms of memory). On the other hand, they cannot ever afford to grant this master-code its claim of being a mode of thought that comes to all human beings naturally, or even to be treated as something that exists out there in nature itself. Subaltern histories are therefore constructed within a particular kind of historicized memory, one that remembers History itself as a violation, an imperious code that accompanied the civilizing process that the European Enlightenment inaugurated in the eighteenth century as a world-historical task.
>
> (Chakrabarty 1995: 25)

The "unassimilable," the "untranslatable," the "different"—these then are the stuff of histories written in a post-colonial moment. The goal is not the illusory quest for the authentic, but a narrative refusal to seek recognition through collapsing the "difference" of India's histories into the "sameness" of Europe's. And so, when I raise the *questione della lingua,* and demand that Indian historians heed it, I do so with the full realization of its European origins. And yet, the work of colonialism and modernity has ensured that this is no longer a question that just belongs to Europe but is also a dilemma for the worlds that it colonized. To ask the language question, but to answer it and write it differently for a colonial and post-colonial context—these then are the burdens of this book.

LANGUAGE AND DEVOTION

How then do I write *differently* the (hi)stories of Chinnasami and his fellow speakers who claimed a willingness to die for Tamil? Although Chinnasami's immolation by itself is a spectacularly singular act, defying easy translation into universal categories, the attitudes that produced it could be conveniently assimilated into the metanarrative of nationalism, as yet another instance of "linguistic nationalism." Indeed, this is typically how the few scholarly works that deal with the question of Tamil, if only tangentially, gloss it—as "Tamil nationalism," or its variant, "Tamil revivalism," and as such, an entity that is forged in the shadows of metropolitan Indian nationalism, itself declared a "derived" version of the normative European form (Chatterjee 1986).[2] It would be hard to deny the importance of ideologies of nationalism, derived or not, for much that happens in late colonial and post-colonial India. We hear repeatedly in the words of many a speaker of Tamil, from at least the later decades of the nineteenth century, the logic of Herder, Fichte, and other prophets of (European) linguistic nationalism:

> Language is breath;
> Language is consciousness;
> Language is life;
> . . . .
> Language is the world;
> Without language, who are we?
> (Bharatidasan 1978: 132)

That the cunning of Europe ensures that Herder & Co. speak in such clear Tamil tones only reminds us of the regimes of repetition and mimicry that colonialism sparked among subject populations. Yet, as Homi Bhabha observes, colonial mimicry is marked by a profound ambivalence, for "in order to be effective, mimicry must continually produce its slippage, its excess, its difference." Mimicry in the colony, "on the margins of metropolitan desire," is always "a subject of difference that is almost the same, but not quite" (Bhabha 1994: 85–92). But how do we narrate the lives of those who lived in the colony so as to keep alive this ambivalence of mimicry, this tension between the "almost the same" but the "not quite," which dismembers European norms and forms, as Bhabha reminds us? Equally crucial, how may we write their stories so as to displace the universal narrative of nationalism, a narrative whose normative "silent referent" is always (western) Europe, that paradigmatic site of the modern nation-state (Chakrabarty 1992)? For inevitably in such a narrative, "Tamil" nationalism is a (distorted) variant of something that has already happened elsewhere, but reenacted with local content.

This is not the only problem with the analytic of nationalism for writing a different history. Even as the nation-state has become so ubiquitous in this century that, as Benedict Anderson (1983: 14) observes, "everyone can, should, will 'have' a nationality, as he or she 'has' a gender," there has been a tremendous surge in scholarly works on nationalism. Indeed, that single term, "nationalism," has become theoretically overburdened, rendering it incapable of capturing the many incommensurable differences that separate the story of one nation from another. And yet, nationalisms "do not work everywhere the same way: in a sense they must work everywhere in a *different* way, this is part of the national 'identity' " (Balibar 1989: 19). This is especially true when it comes to the complex nexus between linguistic identity and nationalism. Herder, Fichte, and others may have declared that "those who speak the same language . . . belong together and are by nature one and inseparable whole" (Kedourie 1961: 69). But nationalism is not everywhere predicated on linguistic passions, nor does language loyalty necessarily or always induce a singular nation-state, if we recall the Swiss in the very heart of Europe, modern Latin America as it emerged from the former Spanish and Portuguese empires, or even Arabic in parts of its diaspora, to cite a few random examples (Seton-Watson 1977). In other words, passions of the tongue do not readily map onto the passions of the nation. As Prasenjit Duara has recently suggested in his *Rescuing History from the Nation,* "although nationalism and its theory seek a privileged position within the representational network as the master identity that subsumes or organizes other identifications, *it exists only as one among others* and is changeable, interchangeable, conflicted, or harmonious with them" (1995: 8, emphasis mine). In this book, I hope to "rescue history from the nation" by displacing the latter as the locus of this particular history I write, and by refusing to subordinate, all too quickly, the sentiments and notions of all those who lived and died for Tamil under the rubric of "nationalism." Which is why I propose a new analytic to theorize the discourses of love, labor, and life that have coalesced around Tamil in this century, discourses which can only be partially contained within a metanarrative of nationalism, or even a singular conception of the nation, as we will see.

My access to this analytic—and hence to a different take on the language question—is through a Tamil word, *paṟṟu,* which speakers of

Tamil routinely use in their talk about the language. Typically, the term appears with the word *tamiḻ* in the compound *tamiḻppaṟṟu,* the hinge on which hangs the structure of affect and sentiment that develops around Tamil. So, its speakers are told to cultivate *tamiḻppaṟṟu,* to demonstrate *tamiḻppaṟṟu,* and to not sacrifice *tamiḻppaṟṟu* for worldly gains. Those who practice *tamiḻppaṟṟu* are *tamiḻar,* "Tamilians"; by the same token, anybody who does not show *tamiḻppaṟṟu* is not a Tamilian. The lexical meanings of *paṟṟu* include adherence, attachment, affection, support, love, and devotion. Out of these, I have chosen "devotion" to gloss *paṟṟu,* and the term "Tamil devotion" to denote *tamiḻppaṟṟu,* as well as other similar sentiments that Tamil speakers express for the language: *aṉpu,* "affection"; *pācam,* "attachment"; *kātal,* "love"; *ārvam,* "passion"; and the like.

This then is a book about the poetics and politics of *tamiḻppaṟṟu,* "Tamil devotion"—those networks of praise, passion, and practice centered on Tamil. And it is about the lives of those women and men who declare themselves to be *tamiḻppaṟṟāḷar* or *tamiḻaṉpar,* "devotees of Tamil." I analyze how the language has been transformed into an object of devotion in the course of the social mobilization and political empowerment of its speakers. I explore the consequences of this for the ontology of Tamil, as well as for the formulation of cultural policies around it. And I consider how language devotion produces the modern Tamil subject—*tamiḻaṉ,* the "Tamilian"—an entity whose subjectivity merges into the imagined self of Tamil. *eṅkum tamiḻ, etilum tamiḻ,* "Tamil everywhere, everything in Tamil": this is the leitmotif of *tamiḻppaṟṟu* at its climactic moment. "If we live, we live for Tamil; if we die, we die for it," declared one of its devotees (Puthumai Vanan 1968: 7). Another insisted, "[Our] mind is Tamil; [our] entire body is Tamil; [our] life is Tamil; [our] pulse is Tamil; [our] veins are Tamil; [our] flesh, muscle, everything is Tamil; everything in [our] body is Tamil, Tamil, Tamil" (S. Subramanian 1939: 15–16).

Body, life, self: all these dissolve into Tamil. Devotion to Tamil, service to Tamil, the sacrifice of wealth and spirit to Tamil: these are the demands of *tamiḻppaṟṟu* at its radical best.

As we will see, there are considerable differences among Tamil's devotees over the meaning of their language, and over how best to practice *tamiḻppaṟṟu.* Nonetheless, I consider them as members of one singular community because they all agree upon one foundational certainty: the natural and inevitable attachment between Tamil and its speakers, an attachment that is repeatedly presented in devotional talk as inviolable, eternal, sacral. The goal of this study lies not so much in exposing the illusory nature of this certitude as in illustrating how, and in what manner, *tamiḻpparru* is able to generate and sustain it in the first place. What ideological devices and strategies of persuasion are deployed by Tamil's devotees to convince their fellow speakers of the natural and unshakable bond(s) between themselves and their language? What are the institutional practices through which such a certitude is disseminated among Tamil speakers so as to appear self-evident and commonsensical? What are the ways in which its logic is used to mount resistance against putative foes, and to garner power? And finally, how is this certitude deployed to produce the modern Tamilian, whose subjectivity is anchored by Tamil and has no existence independent of it?

My use of *tamiḻpparru* to interrogate the language question thus is not a nativist gesture, for I make the concept do theoretical work for me in ways which exceed the many tasks that speakers of Tamil have themselves assigned to it in their prolific discourses. Neither is it meant to alienate non-Tamil-speaking readers, despite its alterity (heightened no doubt by the diacritical marks that grace its English transliteration!). Nevertheless, its frequent presence in these pages marks the difference accompanying the ideologies of Tamil that cannot be readily assimilated into preexisting categories such as nationalism. By leaving it untranslated in many instances, and by glossing it in English in others, I seek to remind the reader (and me) of the ironies of writing about Tamil devotion in English, as I wish to draw attention to the inevitable hybridity that accompanies academic exercises like this one, which are conducted between cultures, between languages. But above all, following the cue of many who have written on the politics of translation, *tamiḻpparru* allows me to "inscribe heterogeneity" in these pages, even as its assertions betray, as we will see, the colonial and post-colonial space which it inhabits (Niranjana 1992).

So, what kind of theoretical work does the analytic of devotion perform in this study? Most obviously, by hijacking it from the domain of religion to which it has been conventionally confined in South Asian studies, I wish of course to suggest that devotion is not solely directed towards deities and religious personages in India. Instead, piety, adoration, and reverence have routinely centered on sovereigns and parents; more recently, on politicians, movie stars, and other figures of popular culture; and most distinctively in our time, on the nation. Remarkably, through the intervention of its supporters, Tamil, too, joins their ranks, and even subversively displaces them—so much so that, as *tamiḻpparru* gathers strength as the century wears on, it is increasingly asserted that Tamil alone ought to be the sole and legitimate focus of the unconditional devotion of its speakers. This indeed is the dream, and demand, of the most fervent of its adherents. The analytic of devotion allows me to demonstrate how sentiments that accumulate about Tamil among its speakers resonate with attitudes expressed towards deities, sovereigns, and parents. In fact, central to the work of *tamilpparru* is the wholesale annexation of genres of praise, vocabularies of reverence, and habits of adulation which have been conventionally reserved for such notables.

Further, the analytic of devotion enables me to track the myriad micronetworks of statements and practices through which Tamil has been transformed, over time, in specific historical, political, and social circumstances, into an object of passionate attachment. Despite what its devotees might claim, Tamil (or for that matter, any language) does not have an inherent, natural, even God-given capacity to generate loyalty, love, longing; it is made to do so, and to serve specific ends. Such structures of sentiment that tie a language to its adherents are crucial to the politics of its empowerment. Yet they are too hastily passed over by a social science scholarship that has its sights set on demonstrating how languages have been used as agents of social and political mobilization, or as catalysts for nationalist activity. In such analyses, we learn little about how specific languages are transformed into sites of such loyalty, reverence, and love. How indeed do they acquire the capacity which *enable* them to act as symbols or catalysts, or, just as crucially, *disable* them from doing so? To remember Chinnasami, once again, *how* does Tamil acquire the power to move him to burn himself alive in its name?

The politics of language empowerment, however, are never independent of its poetics, those rhetorical norms and strategies of persuasion through which its adherents attempt to convince their fellow speakers about the glories of their language, the urgency of its cause, and the need to surrender their wealth, bodies, and souls for it. Such networks of talk are especially crucial for *tamilpparru,* for the hold that Tamil appears to exercise over its devout follows not least from the deployment of the persuasive power(s) of the language itself. Its devotees repeatedly confess to the joys of hearing the very sound of Tamil, and comment on its *menmai* (softness), *inimai* (sweetness), *nunmai* (fineness), and so on. The potency of Tamil devotional talk lies not just in the scholarly breadth it displays or in the logic of its arguments, but just as crucially in its strategic use of alliterative phrases, affective figures of speech, catchy idioms, rhetorical flourishes, and the like. My analysis of Tamil devotion therefore follows the suggestion that "linguistic practice, rather than simply reflecting social reality, [is] actively . . . an instrument of . . . power. . . . Words [do] not just reflect social and political reality; they [are] instruments for transforming reality" (Hunt 1989: 17).

Attention to linguistic practices is particularly necessary in colonial situations where new language hierarchies emerge to displace older ones, as European languages, linguistic forms, and literary genres capture prestige, profit, and power (Cohn 1985; Fabian 1986; Rafael 1988). As elsewhere in the British empire, Tamil devotion, too, paradoxically relies on English to stimulate *tamil̲ppar̲r̲u,* a reliance that noticeably diminishes by the 1920s and can rightfully be seen as one of its more visible successes. The attitudes of Tamil's devotees towards English, the language of their colonial masters, are quite equivocal and contradictory. While many of them—as is typical of bilinguals spawned by colonial systems—are clearly at ease in going back and forth between the two languages, there are many differences in the structure and logic of arguments, the representational devices, and the strategies of persuasion they deploy in doing so. Rather than reflecting some essential qualities inherent to either language, such differences are themselves traces of the different ideological work performed by the two languages, Tamil and English, within *tamil̲ppar̲r̲u.* All this of course only reminds us that linguistic practices such as these are never just about languages. Instead, our choice of languages and the myriad ways in which we use them are intimately reflective of our sense of selves and the worlds in which we live, the economies of prestige and power within which we function, and the politics of our beings.

Finally, I turn the lens of devotion on *tamil̲ppar̲r̲u* itself, to reveal how despite the claims of Tamil's devotees, there is no singular, homogeneous language that consolidates itself as the focus of their love and adulation; there is no singular, homogeneous community that emerges in their imaginings; and there is no singular path to practicing what they praise and preach. Its apparent singularity as a sentiment notwithstanding, *tamil̲ppar̲r̲u* itself is multiple, heterogeneous, and shot through with difference.

LANGUAGE, COLONIALISM, AND MODERNITY

Tamil's devout have been quick to assimilate Chinnasami and his fellow self-immolators into a pantheon of devotees which stretches back into the hoary mists of time and includes mythical sages, legendary kings, even the gods themselves. For like the nation, that other entity produced in modernity, *tamiḻppaṟṟu,* too, is driven by the imperative to clothe itself in timeless antiquity, so that devotion to Tamil appears to be as ancient as the language itself. Yet Tamil devotion—in the sense in which I have identified it as networks of praise, passion, and practice through which the language is transformed into the primary site of attachment, love, and loyalty of its speakers—is a more recent phenomenon whose foundations were laid in the nineteenth century with the consolidation of colonial rule in what was then the multilingual Madras Presidency. Writing the Tamil question differently also therefore means a resistance to assimilation into a nativist antiquity. For, continuities with the past notwithstanding, Chinnasami's act, and the stories of his fellow devotees who proclaimed their willingness to place their life and limb at the service of the language, has to be located within new regimes of imagination, institutional practices, and technologies of meaning production that were ushered in, however skewed, with colonialism and modernity. And what were some of these?

First, although it has been transformed into a subject of sustained devotion fairly recently, Tamil attracted praise from at least the second half of the first millennium C.E. But much of this praise was episodic, scattered, even oblique. The language was rarely the primary subject of such eulogies, for the fundamental concern of even its most ardent admirer was with ensuring the literary worth of its poetry, or the salvational potential of its hymns, rather than with Tamil per se. Indeed, it is only in the latter half of the nineteenth century that Tamil emerges as an autonomous subject of praise (Krishnan 1984). Further, in the pre-nineteenth-century verses of praise, the power of the language was complexly entangled with the power(s) of divinities and extraordinary beings, rather than with the power of "the people." Tamil was eulogized, but not because it ensured communication between its speakers, enabled the schooling of the citizenry, or facilitated the governance of the populace. Instead, it was held in awe for its demonstrated ability to perform wondrous miracles and command the all-powerful gods (Ramaswamy 1996).

This is not to say, in a reworking of the old secularization argument, that an enchanted world in which Tamil was divine and salvational gave way, with modernity, to a disenchanted one in which it is bureaucratized and rationalized. On the contrary, the language continues to be assigned a salvational task within the regimes of Tamil devotion, as we will see. Yet the terms on which Tamil is rendered salvational vary, as does the logic. In *tamilpparru,* the ideological work done on the language places the people who speak it at the very center of the project, as an imagined community. It is the task of ensuring that Tamil commands the adulation and veneration of its speakers, rather than the attention of the gods, which consumes its modern devotees. We get a glimpse of this new people-centered ideology in the Tamil-speaking region from around 1879:

> Tamil gave birth to us; Tamil raised us; Tamil sang lullabies to us and put us to sleep; Tamil taught us our first words with which we brought joy to our mothers and fathers; Tamil is the first language we spoke when we were infants; Tamil is the language which our mothers and fathers fed us along with milk; Tamil is the language that our mother, father, and preceptor taught us. . . . [T]he language of our home is Tamil; the language of our land is Tamil.
>
> (Vedanayakam Pillai 1879: 285)

As we will see later, the imagining of Tamil as the favorite of the gods lingers on well into this century, but it has to contend with a new sentiment ushered in with modernity in which languages are seen as the personal property of their speakers (Anderson 1983: 66–69). Hence the insistent use of collective pronouns, such as "our" and "their," in modern discourses on language. This people-centered ideology of modernity inaugurates a *patrimonial* imagination in which language is constituted as a tangible, material possession that is transmitted from one generation of its speakers to another who relate to it as a property-owning "collective individual" (Handler 1988: 140–58). Since it is their patrimony, its speakers are enjoined to ensure the well-being of their language, for in this lay the future of the community whose very existence is now predicated on its possession. Propelled by such a logic of possession—of language as personal property—*tamilpparru,* too, declares that speakers of Tamil "have" a language; it renders them the new masters of Tamil, masters who are called upon, ironically, to "serve" the language with their body and life.

Chinnasami and his fellow devout also lived and operated in a world in which print culture had become normalized (Venkatachalapathy 1994). This was a hybrid culture; put in place in the seventeenth and eighteenth centuries by sundry European missions and colonial establishments, it then bloomed prodigiously after 1835 with the legalization of Indian ownership of presses. From around 1812, the College of Fort St. George in Madras, with its coterie of British administrator-scholars and their Tamil-speaking subordinates, began to publish Tamil grammars, editions of ancient literary works, prose translations and commentaries, and so on (Zvelebil 1992: 159–64). By the 1890s, when *tamiḻppaṟṟu* began to manifest itself, it was quite clear that print and prose were fundamental technologies through which it would be practiced. Well into the next century, the devout struggled to find funds for their printing presses, subscribers for their journals, and readers for their books. But they did not give up their confidence in this new miraculous technology that allowed them to circulate their ideas about their language among the populace, however limited its literacy. Speeches made in Tamil revival organizations and literary academies, at public rallies, even street poetry and processional songs, were invariably translated into print. Print helped in the standardization and homogenization of Tamil, and granted it a visible continuity with an ancient remote past that it resurrected. It ushered in new discursive styles, modes of punctuation and syntax, genres of literature, transformations in script, and new ways of relating to the language—as something seen and read, rather than merely heard. Like the modern nation, the devotional community was at its core a print community, a network of Tamil speakers who were also now readers and consumers of the language, "connected through print" (Anderson 1983: 47–49).

Finally, as Tamil emerges as a subject of devotion in the late nineteenth century, it also becomes a subject of history. In 1903, V. G. Suryanarayana Sastri (1870–1903) posed a novel question—"What is the history of a language?"—and then replied: "The emergence of sounds to express thought, and the formation of words; speech and its development into language; alphabets and their use in writing; grammatical conventions and language formation; word conventions and textual traditions—these are the contents of the history of a language" (Suryanarayana Sastri 1903: i–ii).

Recognizing the existence of such histories in Europe, Suryanarayana Sastri appropriated the new European sciences of comparative philology and historical linguistics to publish his *Tamiḻmoḻiyiṉ Varalāṟu* (History of the Tamil language), arguably the first secular history of the language in Tamil.[3] A little prior to this, M. Seshagiri Sastri had published a philological analysis of the language (1884). Indeed, comparative philology elicited much admiration among the devout. As one of them, D. Savariroyan (1859–1923), declared:

> The science of Comparative Philology—the invention of German writers enables one to understand the secrets of languages, their points of resemblance or divergence. It discloses as in a mirror, the origin and growth of a language, its primary and secondary stages, its manifold transformations, its word-formation and its grammatical structure. The cultivation of such a study confers innumerable benefits on the languages and without doubt we also shall be partakers of these advantages according to the degree to which we cultivate it.
>
> (Savariroyan 1899–1900: 39)

This fascination with comparative philology and historical linguistics was clearly compensatory, a response to colonial comments on the absence of "historical," "comparative," and "scientific" work in India prior to the arrival of European technologies of knowledge. So, the missionary Robert Caldwell (1814–1891), author of *A Comparative Grammar of the Dravidian or South-Indian Family of Languages* (1856), acknowledged the "earnestness" and "assiduity" with which "native" grammarians had hitherto studied their languages, but observed with regret that they did not have the "zeal for historic truth" that is the "special characteristic of the European mind":

> They have never attempted to compare their own languages with others—not even with other languages of the same family. They have never grasped the idea that such a thing as a family of languages existed. Consequently the interest they took in the study of their languages was not an intelligent, discriminating interest. . . . Their philology, if it can be called by that name, has remained up to our own time as rudimentary and fragmentary as it was ages ago. Not having become comparative, it has not become scientific and progressive. . . . If the natives of southern India began to take an interest in the comparative study of their own languages and in comparative philology in general . . . [t]hey would begin to discern the real aims and objects of language, and realise the fact that *language has a history of its own, throwing light upon all other history.*
>
> (Caldwell 1875: x–xi, emphasis mine)

The "comparative" study of languages, the genealogical links between languages of the same "family," the "history" of language, and the "progress" of language: these provided the agenda for the numerous linguistic studies carried out in colonial India, "the happy hunting ground of the philologist," from the late eighteenth century. Colonial ideologies were driven by the assumption that "mastery" of India's languages would secure the "mastery" of India; it would enable British "command" and "native" obedience; and it would ensure "the vast and noble project of the Europeanization of the Indian mind." The "grand work" of British rule was thus inevitably accompanied by the colonization of Indian languages, a project involving "descriptive appropriation" and "prescriptive imposition and control" (Cohn 1985; Fabian 1986: 76). India's numerous languages were collected, classified, standardized, enumerated, and thus dramatically transformed from "fuzzy" and "uncounted" entities into neatly bounded, counted, and mapped configurations (Kaviraj 1992). The result was an arsenal of grammars, manuals, dictionaries, and glossaries culminating in the grand, multivolume authoritative *Linguistic Survey of India* (1903–28). Caldwell's *Grammar*—the most-cited English-language narrative in Tamil devotional discourse—belonged to this arsenal and authorized many of the founding assumptions of Tamil devotion. It popularized the key term "Dravidian" (based on the Sanskrit word *drāviḍa,* itself a transmutation of *tamiḻ*) as the umbrella category for Tamil and the other languages of South India whose origins and structure, as demonstrated using the "scientific" principles of comparative philology, were quite different from Sanskrit and its "Indo-European family of tongues" of the North. Partha Chatterjee (1993: 7) has recently suggested that the modernization and standardization of Bengali from the mid-nineteenth century was carried out by an emergent bilingual intelligentsia "*outside* the purview of the [colonial] state and European missionaries." Yet India's languages, Bengali included, were (re)appropriated by their speakers only after they had been incorporated into a colonial economy of distinctions, hierarchies, and meanings. Thus Tamil's devotees waged their battles on a colonial (and colonized) terrain where Sanskrit loomed loftily as a "classical" tongue, and Tamil was reduced to a mere "vernacular"; where Sanskrit was the language of the "fair" and "noble" Aryans, Tamil the tongue of the "menial" and "dark-skinned" Dravidians; and so on. Colonial knowledges of India were certainly "dialogically" produced through interactions with "native" categories, traditions, and informants. In the process, however, many a "native" notion was fundamentally altered in meaning as well as in use, the modern concept of "Dravidian" being an excellent case in point (Irschick 1994).

Above all, the colonization of language meant its historicization: language has a history of "its own," a history that, like many others in the nineteenth century, was imagined organically. So languages are born, grow, produce literatures, spawn civilizations, and even die, if not tended to appropriately. The histories of various languages were laid out in linear narratives which sequentially charted their evolution through time. Produced as they were in a colonial context, many such narratives about India's languages were steeped in the rhetoric of decline and degeneration. A glorious past was inevitably followed by the dismal present; under the aegis of the British and enlightened "natives," India's languages could be rescued, "revived," and "improved," paving the way to a bright future. This logic of decline and of improvement drives Tamil devotionalism as well, which attempts to historicize Tamil by locating its "origins," "development," and "spread." Such a historicization is invariably accompanied by a comparison of its "progress" with that of other languages; not surprisingly, it culminates in the lament that Tamil was utterly doomed, and that something had to be done to save it. When this historicizing imperative converges with the patrimonial imagination about Tamil, an entirely novel horizon of sensibilities crystallizes that I characterize as *modern*. The life of the language is now perceived as inextricably intertwined with the lives of its speakers as an imagined community: their pasts, present, and futures are inseparable. So declared one of Tamil's devotees in 1915: "O Tamil pandits! O Tamil people! Be warned! Guard your language. Language is the life of its community of people. If the Tamil language is destroyed, the excellence and glory of the Tamilians, too, will be destroyed. . . . Let your tongues only speak Tamil; let your quills only write Tamil; let your hearts only desire Tamil" (Subramania Siva 1915: 202).

It is because Chinnasami and his fellow devout are subjects of such an imagination that their stories inevitably differ from those of any speaker of Tamil who loved and praised the language prior to modernity.

LANGUAGE AND GENDER

The globalization of the nation form and its cultures of modernity enabled the universalization of the concept of language as "mother tongue," the site where culture becomes nature. The mother tongue is a construct that emerged at a particular historical moment in the complex transformation of Europe's linguistic landscape from the middle of the second millennium, as Latin was progressively withdrawn from the public domain and the "vernacular" was elevated as the language first of the state and then eventually, by the nineteenth century, of the nation (Seton-Watson 1977). The historicity of the construct, however, has scarcely been explored. Consider the following statement by the American literary critic Walter Ong:

> Why do we think so effortlessly of the first language we learn as our "mother" tongue? . . . The concept of "mother" tongue registers deeply the human feeling that the language in which we grow up, the language which introduces us as human beings to the human life world, not only comes primarily from our mother, but belongs to some degree to our mother's feminine world. Our first language claims us not as a father does, with a certain distance that is bracing . . . but as a mother does, immediately, from the beginning, lovingly, possessively, participatorily, and incontrovertibly. Mother is closer than father: we were carried in her womb. In her and from her we were born. Our world is a fragment of hers.
>
> (Ong 1977: 22–23)

Yet neither Ong nor other scholars who routinely use the term "mother tongue" interrogate the historical conditions under which the "first language" comes to be so "effortlessly" attached to "our mother's feminine world," from philology to pedagogy. Why in so many contemporary societies whose patriarchal foundations have been only further updated with modernity, and where everything from property inheritance to the generational transmission of one's very name is reckoned through the father, does the figure of the mother come to be associated with language? The association seems especially surprising given the importance accorded in modernity to language as the essence of the national spirit. Even for feminist theorists of language, this has not been a matter of concern (Cameron 1990), nor has it been one for scholars of South Asia. This is particularly striking because the category of the "mother tongue"—and its equivalent in Indian languages—appears to have gained salience only from the second half of the nineteenth century in the subcontinent, but has since become ubiquitous. Today, speakers of Tamil invariably use this term, and its Tamil gloss, *tāymoḻi* (lit., "mother language"), to refer to their language. Consider how one of its admirers defines Tamil as *tāymoḻi:* "Tamil is the *tāymoḻi* of the Tamil community. The newly born child calls the woman who gave birth to it, '*ammā*' [mother]. She, too, coos over her child and calls it '*kaṇṇē*' [precious one]. So, because Tamil is the language with which the mother is hailed, and it is the language which the mother herself uses, it is our *tāymoḻi*" (Sivagnanam 1970: 2).

The echoes here of Ong's statement from the other side of the world are loud and clear. As we will see, Tamil's devotees, as indeed others in India, struggled to secure official recognition, from the colonial state, of their language(s) as "mother tongue." What was at stake in doing so? Why does the new people-centered ideology of language and the patrimonial imagination ushered in with modernity resort to the figure of the mother? In attempting to answer such questions for Tamil, this study opens up for critical scrutiny the feminization of languages in modernity, a feminization that has been so naturalized as to have sealed off the "mother tongue" from history.

Tamil devotion would remain simply a rehearsal of Europe's linguistic history if all that happens to Tamil in the course of being drawn into various structures of modernity is its recasting as "mother tongue," *tāymoḻi.* Yet this is not the only kind of feminization that the language undergoes within the regimes of *tamiḻppaṟṟu.* For lurking in the shadows of the "mother tongue," but frequently disrupting its hegemonic claim on Tamil, is Tamiḻttāy (lit., "Mother Tamil"), the apotheosis of the language as goddess, queen, mother, and maiden. Indeed, in the discourses of Tamil's devotees, there is a ready slippage between *tamiḻ;* Tamiḻttāy; *tāyppāl,* "mother's milk"; *tāy,* "mother"; and *tāymoḻi,* "mother tongue," all of which over time come to be synonymous with each other. Like other figures of difference, Tamiḻttāy operates subversively to disrupt the flow of hegemonic discourses and ideologies, compelling the "mother tongue" to reveal the convergence between "language" and "motherhood" that has come to be so naturalized. The work of Tamiḻttāy thus offers a striking illustration of the displacement and disarticulation of European notions at the very site of their colonial deployment.

My first introduction to Tamiḻttāy came in 1988 when I chanced upon an anthology of poems called *Moḻiyaraci,* "Queen language." Its very first selection, drawn from an 1891 play, *Maṉōṉmaṇīyam,* by P. Sundaram Pillai (1855–97), represented the earth as a woman whose beautiful face is *paratak kaṇṭam* (India) and whose radiant brow is the southern peninsula. The *tirāviṭa nāṭu* (Dravidian land) adorns that brow as an auspicious *tilakam* (sacred mark). The poem then declared:

> O great goddess Tamil (*tamiḻ aṇaṅku*)!
> Like the fragrance of that *tilakam,* your fame spreads in all directions, and delights the whole world.
> Spellbound in admiration of your splendid youth and power, we offer you our homage.

The poem went on in this vein for several more verses (Velayutam Pillai 1971: 1–3). My interest in it was further piqued when I discovered that its first verse was institutionalized in June 1970 as the Tamilnadu state's "prayer song." The government's reasons for doing this are telling:

> It is observed by Government that many prayer songs are being sung at the commencement of functions organized by Government or attended by Ministers. In order to ensure uniformity in the singing of prayer songs, the Government have been for some time considering whether a theme might be chosen for being rendered as a prayer song, which will have no religious or sectarian association. After very careful consideration, the Government have decided that the piece containing six lines from Thiru. [Mr.] Sundaram Pillai's "Manonmaneeyam" which is an invocation to the Goddess of Tamil, would be an appropriate theme for being rendered as a prayer song.[4]

In his reminiscences, M. Karunanidhi (b. 1924), the Tamilnadu chief minister who ordered the institution of the prayer song, observes that there were orthodox Tamilians who objected to this official recognition accorded by the state to the "Goddess of Tamil."[5] Yet despite this, the government stood by its decision. Soon after, in April 1971, the adjoining union territory of Pondicherry, the predominantly Tamil-speaking former French colony, also instituted an anthem in praise of Tamiḻttāy based on a 1939 poem by the well-known poet and native of Pondicherry, Bharatidasan (1891–1964) (Krishnamurthy 1991: 139–40).

Over the next couple of decades, both governments faced many problems in implementing their orders and getting their constituents to sing these songs correctly. Many Tamilians do not even realize that Tamiḻttāy is the embodiment of the language they speak when they invoke her in these songs. Nevertheless, what intrigues me is that the governments of both these Tamil-speaking regions chose to make Tamil devotion into an everyday public and performative act in this way. Why personify the language, and why resort to the female figure? How is the female body deployed in devotional discourse(s), and to what ends? Why does the figure of the mother come to dominate from among a whole range of female subject-positions?

Just as intriguing to me has been the virtual lack of recognition accorded to Tamiḻttāy by scholars. Elsewhere, I have suggested that this may be due to the many ambiguities that surround the figure in the intellectual and cultural discourses and practices of the region (Ramaswamy 1993: 687–90). But it is precisely because it is a figure—of speech, worship, and identity—which manifests itself episodically that I am intrigued by the cultural, political, and ideological work to which Tamiḻttāy has been put by her devotees. How does one write the history of a concept that is not ubiquitous, consistent, or immediately apparent? Fellow scholars in Tamilnadu frequently expressed incredulity and even skepticism over my interest in Tamiḻttāy. "There is no such thing

as Tamiḻttāy," one of them told me; "she is only a figment of our imagination," another assured me. I found it difficult to reconcile such statements with my innumerable encounters with her in essays, poems,
songs, textbooks, newspaper reports, and public speeches. If Tamiḻttāy
is so inconsequential, why did these texts dwell in such loving detail
and at such length on her various attributes, marvel over her many past
achievements, and lament over her current state of decrepitude? If she
is only a figment of the imagination, how would we account for the
colorful posters and newspaper cartoons which have made visible what
is arguably a mere metaphor? And what about her wooden and stone
statues and metal images which have transformed literary imagination
into material substance? Coming of age as a historian at a time when
the clarion call of my discipline has been to make the hidden, the submerged, and the suppressed "visible," I asked myself how one writes
the history of something that is visible but not seen.

For her devotees, Tamiḻttāy is a singular figure with her own unique
biography, a repertoire of deeds that cannot be reproduced, and a range
of powers unfathomable. There is literally no one like her. Yet it is clear
that she joins a pantheon of comparable female icons of the nation such
as Bhārata Mātā, "Mother India"; Britannia of England; Marianne of
France; Guadalupe of Mexico, and the like (Agulhon 1980; Gutwirth
1992; Mosse 1985; Ryan 1990; Sarkar 1987; Warner 1985; Wolf
1958). Some other Indian languages have been similarly feminized
(King 1992). Nevertheless, because she is a figure who cannot be easily
assimilated or translated into a ready-made narrative of language-and-
nationalism organized around the founding concept of "mother
tongue," Tamiḻttāy allows me to interrogate and write the language
question differently. So, in spite of her interstitial and episodic presence
in the narratives of her own devotees, Tamiḻttāy emerges as one of the
principal protagonists of this book.

PREVIEW

Tamil's devotees tell numerous stories about their language. The many
variations and differences in these stories are informed, however, by
one foundational narrative, which goes like this. Once upon a time,
long long ago, Tamiḻttāy had reigned supreme, lavishly patronized by
great Tamil kings. That had been an age of peace, prosperity, and happiness. There had been no inequities based on caste, creed, or gender.
Learning, culture, and civilization had flourished. Today, however,

ignored by her "children," "Tamilttāy has been cast into prison. . . . [S]he has several ailments. She languishes away, devoid of the fine food of poetry. . . . How many wounds, how many scabs, how many boils, how many pustules, how many scars, plague our mother! Tamilttāy's beautiful body—her glorious form—is now riddled with bloody wounds. And what of her heart?" (Kalyanasundaranar 1935: 30–31).

Her devotees identify their land and community with the body of Tamilttāy: "O Mother! Your land shrinks! Your sons diminish! Your body, too, shrinks!" (Suddhananda Bharati 1936: 10). In turn, the salvation of the body politic lies in ridding the body of Tamilttāy of its wounds, scars, and centuries of neglect. Her devotees repeatedly insist that if Tamilttāy prospers, so too will Tamilians, and so too will their land and community. In the mystical poet Suddhananda Bharati's utopian vision of a new Tamil homeland restored to the reign of Tamilttāy and Tamil learning:

> There is gold and greenery everywhere;
> The smile of our illustrious queen who reigns over the cool Tamil grove, is like the glow of the morning light that destroys darkness . . . [!]
> Countless poets sing their songs!
> The cuckoos fill the air with sweet Tamil music!
> . . . .
> The land holds high its head; our own arts and sciences shoot up like mountains! . . .
> The parched land is now a pleasant grove!
> . . . .
> Holding her auspicious scepter, our mother reclines gloriously on her priceless throne of knowledges. . . .
> And celestials pray for her long life thus, "Long live Tamil sweeter than nectar! . . .
> May you grace us so that Tamil learning flourishes and the entire world flourishes with it!"
>
> (Velayutam Pillai 1971: 80–81)

This narrative of the golden past of Tamil, its degenerate present, and its utopian reign in the future provides the driving imperative for Tamil devotional practice, which draws its strength from the desire to restore Tamil and Tamilttāy's lost honor and pride. This imperative manifests itself in the repeated plea that Tamil speakers should wake up from their centuries of "sleep" and, filled with a new consciousness (*uṇarcci*), bring about the "improvement" (*vaḷarcci*) of Tamil. Only thus could they fulfill their filial debt to their language/mother and reestablish the rule of Tamil (*tamiḻ āṭci*) (Kothandaraman 1986).

Clear as this agenda may appear, it was constrained from the start by the multiple and often countervailing conceptions that prevailed about the language among its devotees, and it is these that I first detail in chapter 2. I follow this, in chapter 3, with an analysis of Tamiḻttāy, a figure that appears on the surface to bring unity to the multiple imaginings about Tamil, but that on closer scrutiny dissolves into the contrary images of goddess, mother, and maiden. My aim in this chapter is to demonstrate that just as Tamil is multiply configured, and Tamiḻttāy is multiply imagined, so too is language devotion multiply manifested, as religious, filial, and erotic, all struggling for prominence and domination. From love, I move to questions of labor in chapter 4. Here, I explore how the differing agendas of the various imaginations about Tamil come into play in public policies and politics, and I track the many dilemmas that trouble its devotees as they translate their "talk" of *tamiḻppaṟṟu* into *tamiḻppaṇi,* "service" and "work" for Tamil. And then at last in the penultimate chapter 5, I turn to the lives and stories of those devotees, which are offered as models of emulation for all good and loyal Tamil speakers. My concern here is to chart the production of what I characterize as the "devotional subject," an entity wrought in the cauldron of Tamil devotionalism whose history is the story of the language, and whose life cannot be imagined independently of Tamil. At the turn of this century, the devotional subject is one among a large number of possible subject-positions occupied by speakers of Tamil. By the middle of this century, not least because of the myriad activities of *tamiḻppaṟṟu,* there is a dramatic shift: the devotional subject is the only legitimate subject, for to be Tamilian meant that one *has* to be a devotee of Tamil; there is no other subject-position possible or desirable for its speaker, in the view of the ardent enthusiast. I explore this at some length in my concluding chapter 6, where I consider how the "Tamilian" becomes a subject of Tamil as the language itself becomes subject to *tamiḻppaṟṟu.*

Love, labor, and life as these are articulated in the discourses of Tamil devotion around the figure of Tamiḻttāy: these, then, are the primary concerns of this study. It is with the help of Tamiḻttāy and the practices of *tamiḻppaṟṟu* that coalesce around her that I set out to explore the language question in Tamil India differently—as a history that appears almost the same, but is not quite.

CHAPTER TWO

One Language, Many Imaginings

In his important reflections on language and nationalism, *Imagined Communities,* Benedict Anderson concludes evocatively: "What the eye is to the lover . . . , language—whatever language history has made his or her mother tongue—is to the patriot. Through that language, encountered at the mother's knee and parted with only at the grave, pasts are restored, fellowships are imagined, and futures dreamed" (1983: 140).

In this statement, as elsewhere in the vast scholarly literature on nationalism, languages are assumed to have singular, homogeneous, and stable identities that their speakers carry with them from mother's knee to the grave. Yet this in itself is perhaps one of nationalism's lasting myths, installed by its own strategies of rationalization and standardization of language. The many adventures of Tamil within the discourses of *tamilpparru* suggest rather that attachment to a language is rarely singular, unanimous, and conflict-free. A language may carry a singular name—its "proper" name—but this does not necessarily translate into a singular body of sentiments that connect it to its speakers. Instead, as languages are subjected to the passions of all those interested in empowering them, they attract multiple, even contrary, imaginings. The power that they exercise over their speakers is correspondingly varied, multiplex, and historically contingent.

The putative unity suggested by the name "Tamil" notwithstanding, there is no monolithic presence which reigns in the regimes of Tamil devotion that so assiduously transform the language over time into an object of adulation, reverence, and allegiance. Instead, it is imagined in different ways in different contexts by different devotees. In four such regimes of imagination—the "religious," the "classicist," the "Indianist," and the "Dravidianist"—Tamil is variously conceived as a divine tongue, favored by the gods themselves; as a classical language, the harbinger of "civilization"; as a mother tongue that enables participation in the Indian nation; and as a mother/tongue that is the essence of a nation of Tamil speakers in and of themselves. *Tamil̲ppar̲r̲u* is thus not a static monolith, but evolves and shifts over time, entangled as it is in local, national, and global networks of notions and practices about language, culture, and community.

What follows in this chapter, then, is a discursive history of Tamil from the 1890s to the 1960s. By "discursive history" I mean the history of the discourses that gathered around Tamil as it became the focus of talk and practice. "Discourse" has become one of the most frequently used but casually understood terms of our times. My own sense of it has been influenced by Foucault's. Although I do not necessarily agree with many aspects of his work nor explore all its consequences, I do follow his assumption that discourses are "practices that systematically form the objects of which they speak," and I agree with his insistence that production of discourses (= "knowledges") cannot be divorced from the work of power (Foucault 1972: 49). Accordingly, I focus on statements not primarily to analyze their truth-value, their accuracy, or the extent to which they correctly reflect the "beliefs" of their producers; instead, my concern is to consider how propositions are advanced and arguments built; to uncover the ideological devices used and conceptual moves made in this process; and to determine how certain notions about language, culture, community, and history acquire a hard materiality with the circulation and recirculation of such utterances through talk as well as institutional practices. For devotees of Tamil, undoubtedly, *tamil̲ppar̲r̲u* is a state of mind, an exemplary habit, a way of life—indeed, the only possible condition of being. It may be all these, but I analyze it as a network of discourses which forms, and reforms, the focus of its attention, the Tamil language.

Further, I also treat *tamil̲ppar̲r̲u* as a network of competing "projects." The concept of "project," too, has been much used but little defined in recent scholarship. Like Nicholas Thomas, I find the concept useful, for it draws our attention "not towards a totality such as a culture, nor to a period that can be defined independently of people's perceptions and strategies, but rather to a socially transformative endeavor that is localized, politicized, and partial, yet also engendered by longer historical developments and ways of narrating them" (1994: 105). As Thomas writes,

> A project is neither a strictly discursive entity nor an exclusively practical one: because it is a willed creation of historically situated actors it cannot be dissociated from their interests and objectives, even if it also has roots and ramifications which were not or are not apparent to those involved. And a project is not narrowly instrumental: the actors no doubt have intentions, aims, and aspirations, but these presuppose a particular imagination of the social situation, with its history and projected future, and a diagnosis of what is lacking, that can be rectified. . . . This imagination exists in relation to something to be acted upon . . . and in tension with competing . . . projects, yet it is also a self-fashioning exercise, that makes the maker as much as it does the made. And projects are of course often projected rather than realized.
>
> (N. Thomas 1994: 106)

Not least of the reasons I find such a notion of the project attractive is because it allows me to consider Tamil's devotees not as mute ciphers but as interested beings grappling with the many new ideas—and some old ones—about their language ushered in with modernity, even as it draws attention to the discursively situated contexts of their articulations and practices.

RELIGIOUSLY TAMIL: THE LANGUAGE DIVINE

Through much of the nineteenth century in many parts of India, the quest for foundational principles for the "reform" of society in the aftermath of colonial conquest led to a retreat into "religion" and "tradition," imagined as sites outside the sphere of the colonial state, and hence pure and untouched. What followed was a fundamental redefinition of religious identities, the polarization of communities on religious principles, and the yoking of religious traditions to the various political and cultural projects of modernity (K. Jones 1989). These came to pass in the context of a colonial regime which singled out religiosity as the essential, inherent, and eternal trait of the Indian, just as materialism and science were the province of the West. For India, therefore, true modernity "would lie in combining the superior material qualities of Western cultures with the spiritual greatness of the East" (Chatterjee 1986: 51).

Living as they did in the crosswinds of colonial modernity, many of Tamil's devotees, too, fell victim to the assumption that religious fundamentals would provide salvation to a populace imagined in decline. The means to such a salvation lay in divine Tamil, "the tongue vouchsafed by God to fulfill his purpose in this world" (Devasikhamani 1919: 24). (Re)assertions of Tamil's divinity (*teyvattaṉmai*) accompanied a wave of religious revivalism which surfaced in the Madras Presidency in the closing decades of the nineteenth century, primarily centered around a reworking of Shaivism, declared the most ancient and authentic religion of those Tamilians who were not Aryan Brahmans. Neo-Shaivism, as I shall refer to this reformulated religion, began to make its presence felt from around the 1880s through the publishing and organizational activities of some its principal exponents, such as P. Sundaram Pillai, J. M. Nallaswami Pillai (1864–1920), P. V. Manikkam Nayakar (1871–1931), K. Subramania Pillai (1888–1945), Nilambikai Ammai (1903–45), and, most prolific of all, Maraimalai Adigal (1876–1950). These reformers typically hailed from the ranks of the new elites spawned by colonialism everywhere in India: they were educated, urban, middle-class, upper-caste "non-Brahman" professionals and government employees. They may have disagreed with each other on finer points of terminology or doctrine, but they were unanimous in their demand for the removal of "polytheistic" religious practices, claimed to have been introduced into a pristine Shaivism by Aryan Brahmans from the North through their linguistic vehicle, Sanskrit. Their program was puritanical and elitist as well in its advocacy of vegetarianism and teetotalism, and in its call for the excision of "irrational" customs and rituals (animal sacrifices, the worship of godlings, and the like) which were the very stuff of village and popular religion. For the true "Tamil religion" (*tamiḻar matam*), they insisted, was the monotheistic, "rational" worship of Shiva using pure Tamil rituals based on Tamil scriptures performed by Tamil ("non-Brahman") priests through the liturgical medium of divine Tamil (Alarmelmankai 1914; Maraimalai Adigal 1930a, 1974b; K. Subramania Pillai 1940; Swaminatha Upatiyayan 1921).

Neo-Shaivism emerged to counter what was perceived as the disparagement of Dravidian beliefs in colonial narratives, as well as in neo-Hindu formulations produced primarily in northern India. Numerous internal contradictions and changes through time notwithstanding, British colonialism operated on the fundamental assumption that India was primarily Hindu, and that Hinduism, in turn, was made up of at least two principal streams which were historically, philosophically, and racially different from each other. On the one hand, there was the high and morally uplifting religion of the "Aryans" locked away in ancient Brahmanical texts written in Sanskrit, which a whole century of Orientalist research had construed as authentic and pure Hinduism. On the other, there were the "aboriginal," "barbaric," "material demonologies" of the "pre-" or "non-"Aryan tribals, village folk, and uneducated masses, which, by the 1880s, were increasingly identified by many as "Dravidian." Dravidian religion was generally caricatured as "fear-ridden," "hideous," and "wholly degrading, intellectually, morally, and spiritually" (e.g., Elmore 1915: 149–52; Whitehead 1921: 152–58). It was deemed "primitive" because of the absence of recognizable scriptural or philosophical traditions such as those possessed by the "civilized" Aryans, and because of its reliance on shamanistic rituals, animal sacrifices, and animistic ceremonies involving petty village deities and bloodthirsty mother-goddesses.

Such colonial speculations also generated an evolutionary theory of Indian religious history (Inden 1990: 117–20). The dark, feminine, materialistic, and sensual religion of the aboriginal Dravidians was conquered by the philosophically and intellectually advanced, virile, white gods of the Aryans. Over the centuries, it was conceded, the two religions did intermesh, the influence of the superior Aryan modifying the "crude animism" of the primitive Dravidian for the better. This had not happened, however, without taking a toll, for latter-day Hinduism reveals the extent to which a pristine Aryan religion had itself come to be eroded by the superstitious and animistic practices of the Dravidian "sub-stratum" (Caldwell 1856: 518–28; Elmore 1915; Whitehead 1921). Nevertheless, "whatever be their present-day union or interminglement, it is difficult to imagine any original connection of the Aryan Brahmans and their subtle philosophies, with the gross demonolatory of the Dravidian peoples who surround them" (Government of India 1912: 51).

Such a theory was extremely useful for a body of thought that we now identify as "neo-Hinduism," which struggled to salvage Hinduism from a colonial scrutiny that savagely denounced some of its aspects, while lavishing praise on others. Like colonialism in whose shadows it was forged, nineteenth-century neo-Hinduism, too, reduced "India" to a Hinduism whose pure and authentic manifestations were limited to the Sanskritic scriptural tradition characterized as "Aryan" (Halbfass 1988: 197–262; K. Jones 1989). In many a neo-Hindu narrative, the progressive admixture of the aboriginal Dravidians had caused the "fall" of Hinduism from its glorious Aryan beginnings, a decline that was only further exacerbated with the invasions of the Muslims. Although not all neo-Hindus or Indian nationalists unanimously participated in the denigration of the Dravidian, they nonetheless shared a lasting conviction that India could be saved by returning to the imagined purity of a pristine Sanskritic Aryanism (Leopold 1970).

By the turn of this century, several neo-Hindu organizations had established themselves in the Madras Presidency; one of the most influential among them was the Theosophical Society, which moved its headquarters to Adayar in 1882–83. The society was heavily patronized by English-educated Tamil Brahmans who found its validation of scriptural and Aryan Hinduism, appropriately scientized and modernized, particularly satisfying (Irschick 1969: 26–54; Suntharalingam 1974: 290–311; Mani 1990).[1] While Brahmans all across India generally prospered under colonial rule, Tamil-speaking Brahmans had especially reaped rich rewards. Barely 3 percent of the population, they disproportionately dominated the bureaucracy and various professions such as education, journalism, law, and medicine, as well as associational politics, into the 1920s, primarily by getting a head start in English and university education (Visswanathan 1982). But even more perniciously, Brahman domination was ensured by a colonial legal culture which institutionalized Brahmanical social theory as the very foundations of the Raj (Derrett 1968: 225–320; Washbrook 1989: 241–44). As a consequence, all those caste Hindus who were not Brahman—almost three-fourths of the populace of the Presidency—were unilaterally considered "Shudra," the lowest of the Sanskritic fourfold hierarchy. Such a characterization came to be increasingly resented by the later decades of the nineteenth century by upper-caste "non-Brahman" landholding and merchant elites, growing numbers of whom, especially among Chettis and Vellalas, were also acquiring English education and competing for urban jobs, as well as for political privilege, within a colonial state structure that was undergoing increasing bureaucratization and centralization (Barnett 1976: 22–27; Washbrook 1976: 280–87).[2] So P. Sundaram Pillai, one of the founding fathers of neo-Shaivism, complained thus in 1896 to a fellow Vellala, Nallaswami Pillai:

> Vellalas who form the flower of the Dravidian race have now so far forgotten their nationality as to habitually think and speak of themselves as Sudras. . . . In fact to tell them that they are no more Sudras than Frenchmen and that the Aryan polity of castes was the cunningly forged fetters by which their earliest enemies—the Aryans of the North—bound their souls which is

worse than binding hands and feet, might sound too revolutionary a theory, though historically but a bare fact.

(quoted by Nallaswami Pillai 1898–99: 112)

Many a Brahman intellectual was quick to respond to such charges. M. Srinivasa Aiyangar, amateur historian and litterateur, countered:

> Within the last fifteen years, a new school of Tamil scholars have come into being, consisting mainly of admirers and castemen of the late lamented professor . . . Mr. Sundaram Pillai. . . . Their object has been to disown and to disprove any trace of indebtedness to the Aryans, to exalt the civilization of the ancient Tamils, to distort in the name of historic research current traditions and literature, and to pooh-pooh the views of former scholars, which support the Brahmanization of the Tamil race.
>
> (M. Srinivasa Aiyangar 1914: 46)

Not least of the consequences of the turn-of-the-century culture wars between these elite products of the "new" education and of the colonial bureaucratic and professional systems was that by the 1920s Brahmans as a community were declared enemies of Tamil and of its speakers. Manickam Nayakar, a devotee of Tamil who also claimed that "his best and tried friends are mostly Brahmans," was compelled to declare in 1917 that "the general disposition of many a Brahmin is to disown his kinship with the rest of his Tamil brethren, to disown his very mother Tamil and to construct an imaginary untainted Aryan pedigree as if the Aryan alone is heaven-born. . . . [T]heir general trend is to assume that they are themselves Aryans and not Tamilians, and to take as an axiom that Tamil and Tamils owe everything to Sanskrit" (Manickam Nayakar 1985: 75). Indeed, as we will see, although individual Brahmans continued to proclaim their *tami̲lppar̲r̲u* into the 1920s, their devotion was always suspect, tainted as it was by their community's support of Sanskrit, increasingly deemed alien to Tamil and its culture.

In such a charged climate, the ascendancy of the Brahman-dominated Indian National Congress in the early 1900s, and the entry of the Theosophical Society into nationalist politics from 1913, only fueled the growing fears of the Vellala and Chetti elite that under the guise of "nationalism," Brahmans would hijack the nation and turn it into a Sanskritic, Aryan, and above all Brahman domain. In such a nation, Tamilians who were not Brahmans would continue to be ritually and socially denigrated as "Shudra," "the sons of concubines" (Maraimalai Adigal 1963, 1974a: 44–45). It is thus not surprising that the earliest efforts to constitute an alternate non-Aryan, non-Sanskritic, and non-Brahmanical religion as the embodiment of all that was truly and originally Tamil were most actively sponsored by these Vellala and Chetti elites. Synecdochically representing the entirety of the "non-Brahman" populace of the region, they vigorously argued that it was only such a "Tamilian religion" that would stem the continuing empowerment of an Aryan-Sanskritic-Brahman Hinduism which inevitably spelled doom for Tamil and its speakers in the emergent nation. In turn, these "non-Brahman" elites received the support of the colonial state, itself seeking allies to counter the growing influence of the Congress. The consequence was an informal alliance between them and the colonial administration, which is reflected in the pro-British stance of the Justice Party (founded in 1916–17 to represent "non-Brahman" interests) and in the eulogies of British rule and English that surfaced within neo-Shaivism (Maraimalai Adigal 1967a, 1974a: 45–46).

THE POLARIZATION OF TAMIL AND SANSKRIT

So, from the turn of this century, neo-Shaivism engaged in a complex set of maneuvers. On the one hand, it had to counter the damaging caricatures of Dravidian religion in colonial narratives. On the other, these very texts also contained much ammunition that could be deployed for its battle against neo-Hinduism and its surrogate, Indian nationalism: the declaration that Dravidian religion far preceded Aryan arrival, not just in the Tamil-speaking country but all over India; the suggestion that Tamil-speaking Brahmans had never participated in this religion; the pronouncement of ancient Tamilian society as egalitarian, untainted by the hierarchical and oppressive caste system of the Aryans; and above all, the possibility that that most important Hindu deity, Shiva, might be Dravidian in origin (Elmore 1915: 13–14; Gover 1871: 1–15). Neo-Shaivism appropriated such colonial propositions, fused them with statements drawn from pre-colonial Shaiva narratives, and proposed the following tenets of the emergent "Tamilian religion," *tamiḻar matam* (also called by some, "Dravidian religion," *tirāviṭa matam*): Shaivism is the true and original religion of all Tamilians who are not Brahman. It is also the most ancient religion of India, predating Sanskritic Hinduism by many centuries. Its principles are enshrined in the devotional and philosophical texts of divine Tamil, and it would be in vain, therefore, to seek it in the demonistic rituals of the populace (as the colonials were wont to). Further, it was not the Dravidians who corrupted a pristine Hinduism (as neo-Hindus were inclined to suggest); on the contrary, it was Brahmanism and Aryanism that had debased the original Tamilian religion and diverted it from its hallowed path of monotheism, rationalism, and egalitarianism into the "gutters" of polytheism, irrational rituals, and unjust social hierarchies (Maraimalai Adigal 1930a: vii–viii; Savariroyan 1900–1901: 269). The removal of such impurities brought in by Sanskritic Brahmanism would lead to the retrieval of pristine Shaivism, the restoration of a pure Tamilian subjectivity, and the growth of self-respect and pride among speakers of Tamil. And it is for this project that Tamil was enlisted by neo-Shaivism, its divinity reemphasized and popularized in the process. Cleansed of its Sanskritic impurities, the divine language would be the beacon that would throw light on all that was originally Tamil/Dravidian. It would sift and separate the pure Tamil Shaiva texts from all those masquerading as such.

The writings and speeches generated by neo-Shaivism show that this was not an easy or consistent project, not least because there was little agreement over what constituted the original Shaivism, and because it was difficult—in certain cases impossible—to dismantle the complex linkages that had developed between Tamil and Sanskrit over the centuries of their coexistence from the early first millennium C.E. In the early decades of neo-Shaiva activity, from around the 1880s to around 1905, there were few explicit statements against Sanskritic Hinduism per se. The focus instead was on countering the negative characterizations of Dravidian religion by asserting its distinctiveness, its uniqueness, its rootedness in high philosophy, and its parity with the Sanskritic tradition. "Moderate" neo-Shaivism, therefore—as exemplified by the writings of J. Nallaswami Pillai, for instance—envisioned Tamilian religion as part of a larger Hindu complex, but oriented around divine Tamil and its scriptures rather than around Sanskrit.

Gradually, however, such assertions gave way to overt antagonism towards Sanskritic-Brahmanical-Aryan Hinduism, and even to calls for a complete break from the latter by the 1920s. This transformation took place in the context of changes in the curriculum of Madras University, which, starting in 1906, became the site of an acrimonious debate over the compulsory study of Sanskrit and the elimination of the "vernaculars"; the growing demand for "Home Rule" by the Besant-led factions of the Congress, beginning in 1915; the British promise of "self-government" by stages in 1917; the many attempts after that by the colonial state to play off the "non-Brahman" against the Brahman in electoral politics; and finally, the iconoclastic atheism of E. V. Ramasami (1879–1973) and his followers (Irschick 1969; Nambi Arooran

1980: 35–139; Washbrook 1976: 274–87). In the "radical" neo-Shaivism that crystallized in response to these events, and is perhaps best exemplified by the later religious writings of Maraimalai Adigal, a Tamil-speaking Dravidian "non-Brahman" Shaiva community was clearly posited against Sanskritic, Brahmanical, Aryan Hinduism (Maraimalai Adigal 1930b, 1974b; K. Subramania Pillai, 1940: 45–47). Talk of parity between Tamil and Sanskrit gave way to assertions of the superiority of the former. Legends and stories that had accumulated over the centuries about Tamil's divine powers were recycled and embellished, and the very legitimacy of Sanskrit was questioned in this process.

One such story, based on an incident in the life of the nineteenth-century mystic Dandapanisami, is especially popular in neo-Shaiva tellings. When challenged by a Brahman who invoked the superiority of Sanskrit because the *Veda*s were in that language, Dandapanisami declared that unlike them, the Tamil scriptures did not advocate the sacrifice of goats and the consumption of meat. The argument between the two notables continued for a while, and it was finally decided to settle the matter by calling upon the deities. They placed in front of the spear of Lord Murugan three chits with the following messages: "Tamil alone is eminent," "Sanskrit alone is eminent," and "Both are eminent." A virgin maiden was asked to choose among the chits and she picked out the one that declared, unambiguously, "Tamil alone is eminent." Dandapanisami rejoiced, brushed his eyes reverentially with the chit, and then placed it in his mouth. Subsequently, he composed his famous verse on Murugan which praised him as the lord who himself had declared Tamil's superiority over Sanskrit. He then went on to write the *Tamiḻ-alaṅkāram,* a hundred-verse eulogy of Tamil recounting its various miraculous abilities and supernatural powers (Velayutam Pillai 1971: 124–61).[3] In the same vein, another of Tamil's admirers, years later, narrated a story his mother had told him about one of his ancestors who had had the power to cure the sick and the dying with the help of Tamil hymns. One day, a cobra, with its hood raised, wandered into the room where he sat, offering his prayers in Tamil. It drank some milk and slithered away, leaving him unharmed. "Is it not clear from this that Tamil has supernatural powers!" he asked rhetorically of his readers.[4] Such stories, of which there are many, reminded Tamil speakers that the Tamil scriptures were infinitely superior in their moral and ethical content, and in their salvific potential, to the Sanskrit *Veda*s. It was a Brahmanical conspiracy that denied the divinity and ritual efficacy of Tamil, designated it as a "Shudra" language, and appropriated all its treasures, including the mighty Shiva himself, for Sanskrit (Maraimalai Adigal 1936a: 105–6; K. Subramania Pillai n.d.: 15–17).

By the time radical neo-Shaivism was under full steam in the 1920s, it was declared unequivocally that Tamil, and not Sanskrit, was the *only* appropriate ritual language for all pious Tamilians. Indeed, Tamil is the world's first divine language, and the religion it expounds the most eminent: "In the whole wide world, there is no greater god than Paramashivam [Shiva]; no religion loftier than Shaivism; no land more superior to the Tamil land; no language more divine than Tamil . . . and no people more auspiciously pure than Tamilians" (Swaminatha Upatiyayan 1921: 20).

Taking advantage of the technologies and communication possibilities generated in the colonial milieu, neo-Shaiva associations and publications took this message of Tamil's divinity to the public. They urged Tamil speakers to make divine Tamil the center of their renewed religious lives, the core of their (recast) beings. Prior to the neo-Shaiva revival, the cause of divine Tamil and of Shaivism had largely been the purview of religious specialists, temples, and monasteries. Now, lay intellectuals and activists—who were career bureaucrats, lawyers, academics, and even civil engineers—established societies for propagating the message of neo-Shaivism in various cities and towns across the Tamil-speaking parts of the Presidency. They published books and journals, conducted religious and Tamil classes, arranged conferences, and ran local libraries (Nambi Arooran 1980: 20–21; Ramaswamy 1992b: 84–89). Many of these societies as well as their journals were short-lived, and suffered throughout their careers for want of support and subscription. Yet there are success stories as well, such as the Tirunelvēli Teṉṉintiya Caivacittānta Nūṟpatippuk Kaḻakam, founded in 1920.[5] Both this organization and its journal *Centamiḻc Celvi* (founded in 1923) continue to exist today, albeit not without their share of problems. Although neo-Shaiva organizations eschewed direct participation in associational politics, they threw their influence behind many causes dear to *tamiḻppaṟṟu* such as the demand for education in Tamil, the numerous protests against Hindi, and the movement for renaming Madras state as Tamilnadu, the land of Tamil.

BEING RELIGIOUS, THE TAMIL WAY

Movements for religious reform in colonial India have been extensively studied, and a recent volume clearly shows that spoken, rather than scriptural, languages were the sites of some of the most intense debates and discussion in this regard (K. Jones 1992). Yet, while we have a growing understanding of the recastings of religious doctrines, practices, and conceptions of community, the changes undergone by the languages through which such reconfigurations were attempted have been left largely unexamined. *Tamiḻppaṟṟu*'s divinization of Tamil to authenticate its project(s) reminds us that the medium itself has to be empowered in order to empower the message, to invoke an overused but nevertheless appropriate cliché. Neo-Shaivism declared that Shaivism and divine Tamil are the two "eyes" with which modern Tamil speakers would regain their lost vision and be redeemed. Divine Shiva and his divine Tamil go together, hand in hand, and cannot be separated: each lends power and authority to the other.

Neo-Shaivism emerged to counter what was perceived as the recasting of India as predominantly Aryan, Sanskritic, Brahmanical, and Hindu by both colonialism and neo-Hinduism. Such a countering was necessary because of the fear that "non-Brahman" Tamil speakers would inhabit such an India only in the fissures: ritually denigrated, socially demoted, and symbolically cast out, as "Dravidians" and "Shudras." Yet speakers of Tamil had once been the dominant people of the subcontinent, a preeminence they had lost with the arrival of Sanskritic Aryan Brahmanism. In Maraimalai Adigal's version of this imagined history, "the religion of the land, that is Shaivism, underwent a marked change." Yet, he wrote, this was a change that was limited to the "outer rim," for "in its center, it remained as pure as crystal and as impenetrable as a hard diamond. What is bound and true to its core, what is perfect and complete in itself, requires no change, requires no improvement" (Maraimalai Adigal 1930c: iii).

Neo-Shaivism attempted to recover this imagined pure center and use it as the foundation on which to (re)constitute a true Tamilian religious subjectivity untouched by Brahmanism, Aryanism, Sanskrit, and Hinduism. Cleansed of its Sanskritic impurities, Tamil, the language in which its pure and original scriptures were deemed written, was the means through which this center could be reached. The language had perforce to be (re)divinized for this project, for it had to take on and counter the power of divine Sanskrit. Other religious groups in earlier times had advocated the divinity of Tamil, but not always at the expense of Sanskrit, and not in such a sustained and prolific manner using the modern technologies of print and communication (Ramaswamy 1996). In the changed circumstances of the late colonial period, when a devolving state rewarded communities that could establish their timeless distinctiveness and religious autonomy, there was much to be gained by claiming the existence of a unique Tamilian/Dravidian community, bonded together from time immemorial by its own distinctive religious traditions that were embodied in its own sacred language. Such a claim necessarily called for a de-legitimization of Sanskrit and a radical distancing from its scriptures and tradition. Such a project also perforce needed the projection of Tamil as divinity, the ranking favorite of the gods themselves.

CIVILIZING TAMIL: THE LANGUAGE CLASSICAL

The search for authentic first principles as the foundation on which to rebuild a modern community did not lead all of *tami̱lppaṟṟu* towards religion and Shaiva scriptures. Instead, with the help of the secular sciences of comparative philology, archaeology, ethnology, and history, a new source for these was located in ancient Tamil heroic and love poems of the so-called Caṅkam age of the early centuries C.E. Hitherto completely outside the horizon of contemporary scholarly awareness, these poems were "discovered" and published between the 1880s and 1920 primarily because of the efforts of C. W. Damodaram Pillai (1832–1901) and U. V. Swaminatha Aiyar (1855–1942).[6] The story of this "discovery" in all its fascinating detail has yet to be told, but it is important to register some of its manifold effects on *tami̱lppaṟṟu*.

Most immediately, with this "discovery," the antiquity of Tamil literature, dated up until then in colonial histories to the late first millennium, was now pushed back, at the very least, to the early centuries C.E., and in the writings of some devotees to the beginning of time itself. These poems not only deepened the antiquity of Tamil literature, but quite as crucially, within a few years of their being made public, they came to be valorized as the repositories of an ideal and perfect Tamil society, prior to its colonization by either the British or, more enduringly, by the Brahmanical Aryans from the North. They were combed to generate nostalgic portrayals of an ancient Tamil people who were adventurous and heroic; who roamed the high seas in pursuit of gold and glory; who were "hospitable and tolerant in religion," "egalitarian" and "rationalist," fun-loving but contemplative and philosophical as well (Kanakasabhai 1966). Most significantly, these poems were tangible proof that Tamilians were speakers of the only "living" "classical" language and the proud possessors of a great "civilization," the most ancient in the world. Devotional narratives, regardless of their ideological differences and political commitments, are saturated with the pride that their authors experience in being the modern-day inheritors of this ancient literature. In his memoirs, S. Ilakuvan (1910–1973), a Tamil college teacher who was imprisoned in 1965 for his participation in the anti-Hindi protests, has this to say about the effect on his young mind when he learned in college about the antiquity of Tamil and the wealth of its literature:

> The glories of the ancient Tamil land and the eminence of Tamilians captured my heart. I became convinced that classical Tamil (*uyartan̲ic cemmol̲i*) had to have been the mother of all the languages of the world. I was saddened that our great and glorious Tamil country has today lost its name, and languishes away as a small part of Madras [Presidency]. I resolved that my life's mission lay in restoring the rights of the Tamil land, and the preeminence of Tamil. The battle for Tamil is the battle of my life.
>
> (Ilakuvanar 1971: 91).

Similarly, M. P. Sivagnanam (1906–1995), who hailed from an indigent working-class family and could afford only a primary school education, studied these poems on his own when he was in a colonial prison in the early 1940s. He writes of his experience on reading one of the anthologies of the Caṅkam corpus, the *Pur̲anān̲ūr̲u:*

> I gained consciousness of belonging to a community called Tamilian when I first read the *Pur̲anān̲ūr̲u*. Before that, I knew I was a Tamilian. But it was only on reading the *Pur̲anān̲ūr̲u* that I realized that the Tamil-speaking people had their own unique history, their own unique customs, their own distinctive political traditions, and their own nationality. Tamilians have had their own unique motherland (*tāyakam*) and its name is Tamilnadu, I realized. Tamilnadu had been ruled for thousands of years by Tamilians. It struck me that no empire from the North had ever subjugated Tamilnadu or Tamilians during the Caṅkam period. When I learned that men and women lived as equals in those days, my heart rejoiced. I forgot myself when I read the poems about the heroism of the mothers who sent off their young, innocent sons to the battlefield thronging with spears. I thanked God with all my heart for the good fortune of being born in such a Tamil land.
>
> (Sivagnanam 1974: 250)

Again and again, there are similar examples of the wonder and admiration that the poems of this ancient literary corpus elicit from Tamil's devotees. They have been invoked as models for personal belief and behavior, as inspiration for public and political action, and as the founding charter for an ideal society of the future in which Tamil would reign supreme, once again.

THE TYRANNY OF CIVILIZATION

An undiluted enchantment with the Caṅkam age undoubtedly floods the entire devotional community. But its poems were of special interest to a particular regime of *tamiḻppaṟṟu* that I characterize as "counter-Orientalist classicism." This regime's fundamental agenda lay in securing acknowledgment—from the world at large, but especially from the colonials and from the Aryan North—of the "civilizational" status of Tamil culture. It went about this task by demanding recognition of an ancient truth that had been grossly overlooked by Orientalism, colonialism, *and* metropolitan nationalism: namely, that Tamil, too, like Sanskrit, was glorious, polished, and perfect. It is *centamiḻ*, "refined Tamil." Yet Orientalism and the colonial state had classified it as a "vernacular," as a corrupt derivative of Sanskrit, and denied its great texts the status of "literature." Classicism thus sought to rescue Tamil from its current lowly status as a mere "vernacular" (*uṇṇāṭṭu moḻi*) and to have it reinstated in all its glory as a "classical" language (*uyartaṉic cemmoḻi*) that was, like Sanskrit, Greek, and Latin, the vehicle for a lofty, unique, and refined literature, culture (*paṇpu*), and civilization (*nākarīkam*) (Suryanarayana Sastri 1903: 132–34). The historian Nambi Arooran (1980: 70–110) has skillfully charted the growing demand among Tamil scholars and politicians from the early decades of this century for recognition of Tamil as a classical language on par with Sanskrit (and Arabic and Persian) in the curriculum of Madras University. I would suggest that there were other gains to be made in securing such a recognition, besides ensuring the victory of "non-Brahman" (Tamil) over "Brahman" (Sanskrit) in the struggle for power in the region. A less tangible, but nonetheless potent, consequence lay in the possibility that Tamil speakers, too, might now demand membership to that select club of "civilized" cultures of the world whose languages had been deemed "refined" and "classical."

It has been suggested that "the colonies of the European empires were in the nineteenth and early twentieth centuries the context of a new and doomed efflorescence of European discourse about virtue, race, and civilization, even while that discourse was in a process of radical reconsideration in Europe as the alternative ontology of 'political economy' advanced" (Kelly 1991: 11). Tamil devotionalism as conducted in the classicist idiom offers one striking illustration of such an efflorescence, although I will reserve judgment (for now) on whether this was necessarily "doomed." Unlike neo-Shaivism, which retreated into the domain of an (imagined) uncolonized religion to conduct its project of resistance and renewal, classicism took its battle right into enemy territory. For the concept of "civilization" was no innocent classificatory device through which Orientalist and colonial knowledges neatly organized the messy world of culture(s). Instead, it was a fundamental technology of rule in which colonial dominance was secured by institutionalizing a hierarchy of differences, not only between the "West" and the "Orient," but between the various regions, cultures, and communities of the subcontinent as well, on a developmental scale ranging from savage barbarism to civilized perfection. Language was one tangible index by which such differences of cultural and moral worth were measured. The "inflectional" Indo-European, representing the summit of linguistic (and racial) achievement, was the standard by which the "tonal," "isolating," and "agglutinative" languages that were not Indo-European were evaluated: the latter were declared incapable of expressing complex, abstract, refined thought. Correspondingly, their speakers were "primitive," "barbarous," and morally deficient (Curtin 1964; Metcalf 1994; Spadafora 1990).

Such notions were embedded in numerous discourses on language, race, and progress that came to the attention of Tamil's devotees. Consider the following unflattering portrayal of the "Turanians," a linguistic and racial group into which, through much of the late nineteenth century, many colonial narratives placed Tamil speakers:

> We may say generally that a large number of them . . . belong to the lowest Paleozoic strata of humanity[,] . . . peoples whom no nation acknowledges as its kinsmen, whose languages, rich in words for all that can be eaten or handled, seem absolutely incapable of expressing the reflex conceptions of the intellect or the higher forms of consciousness, whose life seems confined to the glorification of animal wants, with no hope in the future and no pride in the past. They are for the most part peoples without a literature and without a history[,] . . . peoples whose tongues in some instances have twenty names for murder, but no name for love, no name for gratitude, no name for God.
>
> (quoted in Gover 1871: vii–viii).

And consider the response by one of Tamil's devotees, Nallaswami Pillai, to such a characterization:

> Did we not all read in our school-days that the Tamilians were aborigines and savages, that they belonged to a dark race, a Turanian one, whom the mighty civilising Aryans conquered and called Dasyus, and that all their religion, language and arts were copied from the noble Aryan. Even a few years

> ago, a great man from our sister Presidency held forth to a learned Madras audience how every evil in our society, whether moral, social or religious, was all due to the admixture of the civilized Aryan with the barbarous Tamilian.
>
> (Nallaswami Pillai 1906–07: 29)

Classicism, like neo-Shaivism, thus set out to contest all such claims—Orientalist as well as metropolitan Indian—that denigrated Tamil speakers as "barbaric" and "primitive," and that unilaterally declared that the "civilized" Aryan was inevitably superior to the "aboriginal" Dravidian. This battle, however, was fought not on the ground of religion but on the terrains of "literature" and "history," those domains whose very possession spelled the difference between peoples who led moral and civilized lives and those who barely subsisted on immoral "animal wants." In this war, the weapon was the "classicality" (*uyarttaṉiccemmai*) of Tamil with which its devotees would demonstrate the originality, autonomy, and antiquity of their culture and history; the distinctiveness of their language from Sanskrit; its crucial role as a parent of many languages; and its status as the fount of an ancient civilization as glorious as, if not more glorious than, the Sanskritic one (Maraimalai Adigal [1948]; Suryanarayana Sastri 1903).

Like neo-Shaivism, classicism, too, was an oppositional discourse that was conducted largely by an educated, urban, and professional middle class, attracting academics (historians, litterateurs, philologists, and Tamil scholars), schoolteachers, lawyers, and bureaucrats. Unlike neo-Shaivism, however, a number of Brahman admirers of Tamil, among them V. G. Suryanarayana Sastri, T. R. Sesha Iyengar (1887?–1939), and U. V. Swaminatha Aiyar, joined the ranks of devotees who were nominally Christian, such as D. Savariroyan and G. Devaneyan (1902–81), as well as upper-caste "non-Brahmans" like P. Sundaram Pillai, Maraimalai Adigal, and Somasundara Bharati (1879–1959), and those of Sri Lankan origins such as Damodaram Pillai and V. Kanakasabhai (1855–1906). Like neo-Shaivism, classicism primarily conducted its activities through literary and historical societies, the most famous among them (which continue to exist today, although fairly truncated) being the Maturait Tamiḻc Caṅkam, "Madurai Tamil Academy," founded in 1901 (henceforth Madurai Tamil Sangam); the Karantait Tamiḻc Caṅkam, "Karanthai Tamil Academy," founded in 1911 (henceforth Karanthai Tamil Sangam); and the Shaiva Siddhanta Kazhagam. Like their neo-Shaiva counterparts, with whom they frequently shared members, their contrary views of Tamil notwithstanding, these associations promoted the cause of Tamil in educational institutions, petitioned for the establishment of a Tamil University, encouraged the battle against Hindi, and so on. But most of all, they focused upon editing and printing ancient manuscripts, publishing periodicals and books, holding literary festivals, running libraries, and conducting classes for the study of classical Tamil. As such, they represent the antiquarian and scholastic aspirations of *tamiḻppaṟṟu.*

THE CONTEST WITH SANSKRIT

Classicism, too, was concerned, like neo-Shaivism, with demonstrating the antiquity (*toṉmai*) and primordiality (*muṉmai*) of Tamil, as well as its uniqueness (*taṉimai*) and purity (*tūymai*). These were not established, however, by linking Tamil to the world of the gods, as in neo-Shaivism. Instead, it was argued that Tamil is the first language of the first humans to flourish on the face of this earth, prior to the emergence of any other language or people (Devaneyan 1966; Maraimalai Adigal 1948). Indeed, classicism drew upon the secular science of comparative philology to dispute ancient religious stories (which neo-Shaivism had revived) about the divine origins of Tamil, insisting instead that the language was not bestowed upon the world by Shiva, but emerged to fulfill the need for human communication (P. T. Srinivasa Aiyangar 1985: 13–15; Suryanarayana Sastri 1903: 51–57).[7]

In all such matters, classicism, too, of course contended with the hegemonic influence of Sanskrit, not so much as a "divine" language but as India's paradigmatic classical tongue. A century of colonial linguistic practice had only reinforced the ancient Sanskritic dogma that all languages (of India) are corruptions of a primordial, eternal Sanskrit. British scholar-administrators and their Brahman teacher-assistants based in Calcutta's Asiatic Society and College of Fort William had declared Sanskrit as the fount of Indian "vernaculars," the sole generator of high Hindu civilization, and the only language worthy of comparison with the lofty Greek and Latin. This is a story that has been already told many times (Kejariwal 1988; Kopf 1969).

What has been less noted is the resistance to such formulations that arose almost from the beginning of colonial rule among British administrators and missionaries based in South India. Skeptical about the clubbing together of the languages spoken in "their" part of the subcontinent with the northern tongues, these men were especially critical of the characterizations of Tamil or Telugu as "vulgar derivatives" of Sanskrit.

This skepticism was first voiced in Alexander Campbell's *Grammar of the Teloogoo Language* (1816) and in Francis Ellis's introduction to that grammar. Tamil and Telugu, it was argued, form "a distinct family of languages, with which the Sanscrit has, in latter times especially, intermixed, but with which it has no radical connection" (Ellis 1816: 2). In the 1840s and 1850s, other philological analyses reinforced such assertions, frequently referring to Tamil in this process as "copious," "elegant," "refined," and "cultivated" (Asher 1968; Singh 1969: 78–88). In 1855, Tamil was even declared "a rival of the ancient Sanskrit" (Bower 1855: 158). All such scattered observations were consolidated in 1856 in Robert Caldwell's *Comparative Grammar of the Dravidian or South-Indian Family of Languages,* which used the word "classical" to characterize *centamil̲,* "correct Tamil" (Caldwell 1856: 31); authorized the name "Dravidian" to refer to the "family of languages" of South India, distinct from Sanskrit and its Indo-European family of tongues (28–37); insisted that Tamil "can dispense with its Sanscrit altogether if need be, and not only stand alone but flourish without its aid" (31); and suggested that prior to the arrival of Aryan Brahmans, the "elements of civilization" already existed among the Dravidians (77–79).

Tamil's devout found much that was flattering in Caldwell's *Grammar,* which lent the authority of comparative philology (and the West) to the claims of autonomy and distinctiveness of Tamil made in its precolonial texts that *tamil̲ppar̲r̲u* resurrected. Yet Caldwell's hallowed status notwithstanding, all his ideas were not wholeheartedly embraced, pace recent scholarly evaluations of the missionary's impact on Tamil cultural politics (Dirks 1995, 1996; Ravindiran 1996). Indeed, many devotees resented his claim that the term *tamil̲* had derived from the Sanskrit words *draviḍa* or *drāviḍa* (Chelvakesavaroya Mudaliar 1929: 9; Damodaram Pillai 1971: 3–6, 34–35; R. Raghava Aiyangar 1979: 4–13). Others objected to his attempts to establish affinity between the Dravidian and "Scythian" families of languages, insisting instead that the former was completely distinctive and autonomous (T. Chidambaranar 1938: 5; Devasikhamani 1919: 26). Many also set aside his suggestion that Dravidians had migrated into India, proposing instead an autochthonous origin which placed them in the subcontinent from the beginning of time (T. Chidambaranar 1938: 10). Finally, there were even those who resisted Caldwell's classification of Tamil as a "Dravidian" language, insisting that the word *draviḍa* had been used in the past for Tamil-speaking Brahmans alone (Damodaram Pillai 1971: 34–39;

Devasikhamani 1919: 9; Somasundara Bharati 1912:1). Their resistance is not surprising, for in spite of some eulogistic portrayals of Dravidian culture in the writings of some colonials (like C. D. Maclean and Gilbert Slater), which the devotees found useful to invoke, the dominant colonial image of the Dravidian, as created through census records, administrative manuals, and district gazetteers, is captured in this unflattering picture of the 1891 *Census:*

> This was a race black in skin, low in stature, and with matted locks; in war treacherous and cunning; in choice of food, disgusting, and in ceremonial, absolutely deficient. The superior civilisation of the foreigner [the Aryan] soon asserted itself, and the lower race had to give way. . . . The newcomers had to deal with opponents far inferior to themselves in civilisation, and with only a very rudimentary political organisation, so that the opposition to be overcome before the Arya could take possession of the soil was of the feeblest.
>
> (Government of India 1893: 123)

In such statements, which were also picked up by many a metropolitan nationalist narrative to pursue the agenda of salvaging Indian pride by taking refuge in Aryanism, the white, virile, civilized, energetic, and superior Aryan is starkly contrasted with the dark, feminine, menial, and aboriginal Dravidian. Correspondingly, the latter's language, too, is "aboriginal," uncivilized, and inferior. So the 1901 *Census of India* observed: "In India, the Indo-Aryan languages—the tongues of civilization . . . —are continually superseding what may, for shortness, be called the aboriginal languages such as those belonging to the Dravidian, the Munda, or the Tibeto-Burman families. . . . [I]t may be added that nowhere do we see the reverse process of a non-Aryan language superseding an Aryan one" (Government of India 1903: 248–49). This particular statement in the *Census* was authored by George Grierson, who headed the ambitious *Linguistic Survey of India* project for the colonial state (published 1903–28). It is telling that the underlying premise of this authoritative survey was that the "civilized" Aryan languages are inherently superior to the "aboriginal" non-Aryan. So, commenting on the progressive shrinkage in the spread of Dravidian languages, Grierson noted, "Aryan civilization and influence have been too much for [them]" (Government of India 1903: 279). And in the *Linguistic Survey,* although the "importance" of Tamil is recognized, and the antiquity of its literature noted, it is not unambiguously adorned with the mantle of classicality and civilization, as is Sanskrit (Grierson 1906: 298–302).

All the same, slowly but cautiously from the 1920s on, the colonial state began to concede the antiquity and "copiousness" of Tamil, and its status as a "cultivated" language. Dravidian speakers of today, the *Census of 1931* admitted, have "a culture of very great antiquity[;] . . . speakers of Dravidian languages [were] the ancient inhabitants of Mohenjadaro and perhaps the givers of culture to India" (Government of India 1933: 454–55). The *Census* was here alluding to the recently discovered archaeological remains of the Indus Valley in Mohenjadaro and Harappa, which pointed to a sprawling prehistoric urban civilization rivalling Mesopotamia and Egypt. To the delight of many a Tamil devotee, this prehistoric civilization was declared to have been possibly Dravidian by some colonial archaeologists. Thus Maraimalai Adigal quoted John Marshall in 1941:

> They (the orientalists) pictured the pre-Aryans as little more than untutored savages (whom it could have been grotesque to credit with any reasoned scheme of religion or philosophy). Now that our knowledge of them has been revolutionized and we are constrained to recognize them as no less highly civilized—in some respects, indeed, more highly civilized—than the contemporary Sumerians or Egyptians, it behoves [*sic*] us to re-draw the picture afresh and revise existing misconceptions regarding their religion as well as their material culture. . . . The Indus Civilisation was Pre-Aryan and the Indus language or languages must have been Pre-Aryan also. Possibly, one or other of them . . . was Dravidic.

Maraimalai then proceeded to overwrite Marshall's tentative conclusion with the following sweeping pronouncement:

> If Sir John Marshall had had a first hand knowledge of the Tholkappiam and some other ancient classics of Tamil, he would have easily shown in corroboration of what he stated as regards the pre-Aryan antiquity of one of the Dravidian languages, that *Tamil, alone, and not any other, as he vaguely affirmed, must have been the language spoken and cultivated by the pre-Aryan inhabitants of the Indus Valley.*
>
> (Maraimalai Adigal 1974a: 11–13, emphasis mine)

Maraimalai Adigal was not alone in making such a bold assertion. More than a decade earlier, in the late 1920s, soon after Marshall's report on the Indus Valley excavations was first published, fellow devotees T. R. Sesha Iyengar and M. S. Purnalingam Pillai had already insisted that "future discoveries and dispassionate researches" would confirm Dravidian authorship of the Indus civilization and "the remote antiquity" of Tamil culture (Purnalingam Pillai 1945: 26; Sesha Iyengar

1989: 32–61). They were able to make such assertions confidently, emboldened as they were by the many claims of classicism which challenged the dominant Orientalist wisdom about Tamil's place in India's past, and which proceeded to write an alternate script in which history began not in the North with the Aryans, but in the South with the Dravidians.

OPPOSING ORIENTALISM

Classicism's status as an oppositional discourse is most apparent in the frequently expressed lament that the achievements of Tamil speakers in India's history had been totally ignored by scholars, especially those based in the North. As Sundaram Pillai dramatically declared in 1897: "The history of Indian Civilization is the old story of the Giant and the Dwarf. The victories in it are the victories of the vaunting Aryan, while the wounds are the wounds of the bleeding pre-Aryan" (quoted by Nallaswami Pillai 1898–99: 113).[8]

The first step lay in overthrowing this "Aryan bigotry and pride" and rewriting the script of India's history so as to show how "Dravidian forebears enriched, strengthened and improved the culture of Aryan India" (Sesha Iyengar 1989: 63). Two basic strategies were adopted for such a rewriting. In the one that I call "compensatory," the aim was to demonstrate that "Hindu" or "Indian" civilization had emerged from a "harmonious commingling of the cultures of the Dravidian and the Indo-Aryan" (Sesha Iyengar 1989: 63). Tamil, it was insisted, "was quite as classical" as Sanskrit, and its literature "is no less ancient, noble, and vast."[9] Tamil and its literature were thus validated by espousing a parity with Sanskrit, whose value was never questioned. Neither is the divide between "Aryan" and "Dravidian," seen as distinctive but complementary halves of "India," nor the legitimacy of the Brahman. As can be expected, compensatory classicism was a strategy that was favored typically, though not always, by devotees who were nominally Brahman, such as R. Raghava Aiyangar (1870–1946), M. Raghava Aiyangar (1878–1960), T. R. Sesha Iyengar, and Swaminatha Aiyar. Their commitment was to a syncretic Indian civilization jointly produced by the "genius" of Tamil and the "genius" of Sanskrit, both of which are necessary and complementary (P. T. Srinivasa Aiyangar 1985: 85).

From the start, but especially by the 1920s, this strategy was challenged by another that I call contestatory, paradigmatic examples of which may be found in the writings of Suryanarayana Sastri, Savariroyan Pillai, M. S. Purnalingam Pillai, Maraimalai Adigal, G. Devaneyan, K. Appadurai (1907–89), and K. A. P. Viswanatham (1899–1994), among others. Contestatory classicism asserted the superiority of Tamil over Sanskrit, rather than the parity of the two. Sanskrit, after all, was a "dead" language in contrast to the everlasting Tamil (*kaṉṉittamiḻ*). The "barbarian" Aryans had developed into "civilized beings" on coming into contact with the "highly civilized Dravidians" rather than the other way around. For in the ancient past, Tamilians were settled agriculturists, whereas the Aryans had been mere nomadic pastoralists. Tamilians lived in splendid cities and traded with distant lands, while Aryans were still grazing herds. Tamilians were monotheistic and philosophical, whereas Aryans were polytheistic and ritualistic. Tamil had not evolved from Sanskrit, as the Orientalists maintained; on the contrary, classical Sanskrit itself developed under the influence of Tamil (Maraimalai Adigal 1963, 1966; Purnalingam Pillai 1985: 4–5).

Thus contestatory classicism reversed Orientalism's claim that the true genius of India lay in its Aryan past, asserting instead that it is to Tamil and Tamilian culture that Indian civilization owes all, for, in Sundaram Pillai's words, "what is ignorantly called Aryan philosophy, Aryan civilization, is distinctively Dravidian or Tamilian at bottom" (quoted by Nallaswami Pillai 1898–99: 112). In the logic of contestatory classicism, Aryan Brahmans had not only been responsible for bringing about the end of the Dravidian golden age, but they had also stolen all that was originally and truly Tamil and passed it off as their own (Maraimalai Adigal 1963, 1966; Savariroyan 1900–1901). Misinformed by such crafty Brahmans, Western scholars had got India's history all wrong. So instead of beginning in the North and with "the Aryan Conquest," Sundaram Pillai suggested that the "scientific historian" should begin his study in the South, which was after all, "India proper" (quoted by Nallaswami Pillai 1898–99: 113).

TAMIL AND THE NOSTALGIA FOR CIVILIZATION

From early in this century, Tamil's classicist devotees went about the task of setting the record straight. The result has been a new—and, from the devotee's perspective, an infinitely more satisfactory—script for the Tamil (and Indian) past. In "the hoary past" (going back millions of years ago, in many accounts), there had been an ancient megacontinent (consisting of present-day Australia, Africa, and southern

Asia) where Tamil had flourished. This was the land referred to as "Kumarikkaṇṭam" in ancient Tamil texts and attested to as "Lemuria" by Western scientists. Classicism offered brief but nostalgic portrayals of Kumarikkaṇṭam, imagined as the home of the first two Tamil academies that produced countless literary masterpieces. This state of prelapsarian bliss came to an end with a series of floods, which destroyed the original Tamil civilization and which compelled Tamil speakers to fan out and civilize different parts of the world, taking their language with them. "Traces of this wide dispersion are found in Palestine, Egypt, Italy, Scandinavia, and far-off Erin in the names of places with the suffix *ur,* in the modes of life pursued, in the resemblances of the Tamilian myths to those of Greece and to the northern sagas" (Purnalingam Pillai 1945: 4). So, the urban remains of the Indus Valley and the great poems of the Caṅkam age were only the later remnants of a much more ancient Tamilian civilization, established at the very beginning of time. Orientalism had thus got wrong not only the history of India, but that of the world as well, for it was the Tamil-speaking land which was the "cradle" of the "whole human race" and of "human civilization" (K. Appadurai 1975; Devaneyan 1966; Somasundara Bharati 1912).

The consolidation of industrial modernity in the West has frequently sparked nostalgia for a life in nature, away from city lights and urban sprawls, amid fresh fields and rolling pastures. *Tamiḻppaṟṟu,* I have insisted, is a discourse of modernity. But it was conducted in the milieu of a colonial culture whose own ideology of the civilizing mission deemed that the natives lacked "culture" and "civilization." Tamil's modern devotees, therefore, yearn not for nature but for culture and for civilization. The archaeological remains of the Indus Valley and the poems of the Caṅkam age, not to mention the antediluvian continent of Lemuria, enabled them to claim that Tamil speakers, too, had "civilization," just "like the Greeks," but even earlier. In 1967, C. N. Annadurai (1909–69), a devotee of Tamil who was also the chief minister of the state of Tamilnadu, gave a speech at Annamalai University in Chidambaram in which he extolled the virtues of the Caṅkam poems and the antiquity of "Dravidian civilization." He then called upon the students to carry "the message that our classics contain to the entire world and declare that what was *the most ancient here is what is being introduced today as the most modern*" (quoted in Ryerson 1988: 141–42, emphasis mine). Reversing the logic of Europe's civilizing mission, *tamiḻppaṟṟu* thus claimed that Tamil speakers did not need to be granted civilization, for they had possessed it all along, long before any one else, and indeed had bestowed it upon the rest of the world. But such a claim has come with its own costs. For in its anxiety to secure membership in the select club of the civilized, *tamil̲pparr̲u* reinforced Europe's civilizational model of the world. So, ironically, the "uniqueness" of Tamil and its "civilized" state is claimed by demonstrating its similarity with other "civilized" cultures, by insisting Tamil speakers were, after all, "the Greeks of the East" (Purnalingam Pillai 1985: 5–6).

LANGUAGE AND THE NATION: INDIANIZING TAMIL

In the 1890s, around the same time that neo-Shaivism and classicism emerged, a third imaginary also surfaced in the discourses of *tamil̲pparr̲u,* which I call "Indianist." Over the next few decades, it moved from strength to strength, gathering reinforcement from metropolitan Indian nationalism as well as compensatory classicism at home. By the 1930s, however, this regime had to contend with the assertions of both radical neo-Shaivism and contestatory classicism against Hinduism, Brahmanism, and Sanskrit, all of which Indianism deemed necessary to Tamil devotion. More contentiously, it locked swords with the Dravidianist regime of *tamil̲pparr̲u* that was provoked by the Madras government's attempt to institute the compulsory study of Hindi in 1937–38. Dravidianism introduced into Tamil devotion the political and cultural philosophy of E. V. Ramasami, C. N. Annadurai, and their populist Dravidian movement, which the Indianist regime branded as contrary to the spirit of Indian nationalism and hence illegitimate.

In contrast to neo-Shaivism and classicism, however, both Indianism and Dravidianism were overtly political projects concerned with transforming the nature of power relations in the Tamil-speaking region. But here the similarity between the two ends. For Indianism, it was British colonialism and English that had to be replaced by the Indian nation with its family of "national" languages, of which Tamil would be the language of the region, while Hindi would be the "official" language of communication with other Indians. For Dravidianism, on the other hand, "India" itself occupied the space vacated by the colonial, whose legitimacy was only ambivalently questioned. Indeed, the Dravidianist's scathing denunciations of the "imperialism" of India (identified with the North, Aryan Brahmans, Sanskrit, and Hindi) were as passionate as the Indianist's attacks on colonialism. This important distinction notwithstanding, both the Indianist and the Dravidianist are critically concerned with Tamil as the language of politics, and not merely as the language of religion and ritual, or literature and civilization. Their agenda was to ensure that Tamil ruled (again) within *tamiḻakam*, "home of Tamil." Therefore, it was not enough to establish learned academies and publish books which proclaimed the glories of divine or classical Tamil. In addition, its devotees had to fight for its institutionalization as the language of government, education, and everyday public communication. As T. V. Kalyanasundaram (1883–1953) demanded in 1924, "What is the condition of our mother tongue, Tamil, today? Where is Tamiḻttāy? Does she adorn the seat of government? Does she preside over our associations? Does she flourish in our legislative chambers? Can we at least see her in our schools and colleges? Can we spot her in those political bodies that claim to fight for our rights? At the least, is there a place for her in Tamil newspapers?" (Kalyanasundaranar 1935: 19).

Rather than relying on religious or literary revivalism, as did neo-Shaivism and classicism, these regimes therefore encouraged Tamil enthusiasts to aggressively engage state structures and institutions, and to intervene in political processes, for it was in and through politics that Tamil could be empowered. And in turn, empowered by the claims of Indianism and Dravidianism, many devotees of Tamil went on to become state legislators; members of various government committees on language, education, and cultural policies; even chief ministers by the late 1960s. With Indianism and Dravidianism, *tamiḻppaṟṟu* finally enabled its practitioners to secure power, privilege, even profit.

Indianism's prime exponents in the devotional community were V. O. Chidambaram Pillai (1872–1936), especially before the 1920s; T. V. Kalyanasundara Mudaliar prior to the 1940s; V. Ramalinga Pillai (1888–1972), R. P. Sethu Pillai (1896–1961), and M. P. Sivagnanam; and Brahmans like C. Rajagopalachari (1878–1972), V. V. Subramania Aiyar (1881–1925), Subramania Sivam (1884–1925), Suddhananda Bharati (1897–1990), and of course, the most paradigmatic of them all, Subramania Bharati (1882–1921). Generally from upper-caste, middle-class, middle-income families—Sivagnanam is a striking exception here—they were professional journalists, lawyers, teachers, litterateurs, poets, and politicians; and in their private lives, they were reformed but devout Hindus. In contrast to Dravidianists, who imagined (away) India in very Tamil terms, these devotees framed their concern with Tamil in terms of India. India, in turn, was sometimes an abstract territorial space; at other times, it was personified, like Tamil, as the goddess and mother, Bhārata Mātā, "Mother India." So, the opening lines of one of Subramania Bharati's most popular poems on Tamil incorporates the phrase *vande mātaram* (homage to [our] mother) from the famous hymn that the Bengali Bankim Chandra Chatterjee had composed in honor of Bhārata Mātā:

Long live the glorious Tamil!
Long live the fine Tamil people!
Long live the auspicious Indian nation !
. . . .
Vantē Mātaram! Vantē Mātaram!
(Bharati 1987: 50)

It is not accidental that the "mother" whom this verse reverenced is not Tamiḻttāy but Bhārata Mātā, for Indianism was driven by the terrible anxiety that *tamiḻppaṟṟu* would lead Tamil speakers to forget India. Thus Tamilians were chastised in a poem by Ramalinga Pillai first published in 1922:

Intiyattāy [Mother India] languishes in sorrow, and you speak of your own community!
That is disgraceful!
O Tamilian, break the chains that enslave that venerable woman . . . !
Long live the Tamil land!
May our Tamil language flourish, so that our Intiyattāy who supports us may find fulfillment.
(Ramalinga Pillai 1988: 29)

Negotiating gingerly between loyalty to Bhārata Mātā and devotion to Tamiḻttāy, between the shoals of pride in the nation (*tēṣāpimāṉam*) and pride in their language (*pāṣāpimāṉam*), Indianism reminded Tamil speakers that the liberation of Tamil would have to proceed in tandem with the liberation of India. In his reminiscences, the mystic-poet Suddhananda Bharati recalls how as a young man, his passions were directed as much against the emergent Dravidian movement as against the British, and how he and his young friends countered the cry of "Down with Brahman Rule" with the alternate cry of "Vantē Mātaram." When we are enslaved to the British, what is the point of saying that we are slaves to Aryanism? he asks. "Relinquishing our home to a foreigner, siblings fight with each other over food. Meanwhile, the foreigner seizes all our food and goes away, leaving us with our squabbles" (Suddhananda Bharati 1950: 143–46). In the Indianist vision, therefore, Tamil speakers had to work together with their Indian "siblings" to throw off the shackles that fettered both Bhārata Mātā and Tamiḻttāy, instead of fighting with each other. Swayed by the impassioned rhetoric of the Dravidian movement, they ought not to forget that this was their primary goal, Sethu Pillai reminded them on the very eve of Indian independence: "In fifteen more months, we are going to rule over our own nation. India is going to belong to Indians. Similarly, is there any doubt that Tamilnadu will belong to Tamilians? . . . Tamil̠ttāy in all her former glory and splendor will reign in our hearts" (Sethu Pillai 1968: 1–2).

Not surprisingly, Indianism launched few attacks on Brahmans, Aryanism, or Sanskrit. On the contrary, it produced sympathetic accounts of Brahman contributions to Tamil and its culture, many of whose authors were not Brahmans (Kalyanasundaranar 1935: 37–38; Ramalinga Pillai 1953: 44–48; Sivagnanam 1979: 96–101). Some of its proponents even cast aspersions on (colonial) neologisms such as "non-Brahman" and "Dravidian," whose very legitimacy and historicity they questioned (Bharati 1988: 229, 263; Ramalinga Pillai 1947, 1953: 40–51; Sivagnanam 1979: 63–68). Further, there was always a place for Sanskrit within Indianism's economy of sentiments about Tamil: "In Tamilnadu, Tamil ought to be preeminent. All over India, may Sanskrit flourish, as it always has. To accomplish the unification of our Indian nation, everyone should know Sanskrit. Nonetheless, in Tamilnadu, Tamil should flourish with great eminence" (Bharati 1988: 229).

Given this linguistic division of labor, some even recommended that Sanskrit should be the national language of India (Nuhman 1984: 57–59; Padmanabhan 1982a: 274–76; Rajagopalachari 1962: 51). Correspondingly, Indianist prose was also heavily Sanskritized, especially in the hands of its Brahman practitioners. This lack of hostility towards Sanskrit extended to other Indian languages as well. In the Indianist vision, India is a land where, "along with the glorious Tamil, there flourishes Sanskrit and Urdu and Persian, the unique Telugu, Kannada with its sweet words, lofty Marathi, and fine Malayalam, Gurjaram [Gujarati], Hindi, and eighteen such languages" (Venkatesvara Ayyar 1918: 3). This congenial vision, of course, was severely tested after independence with the struggle over linguistic states and the securing of borders with neighbors, as well as over the Indian state's Hindi policy in the 1950s and 1960s, as we will see.

But in general, Indianism's strategy was to gloss over all internal sources of contention and difference in favor of closing ranks against the real enemy, the English-speaking colonial. Tamilians were reminded, repeatedly, that it was English—rather than Sanskrit or Hindi or any other Indian language—which was responsible for the current sorry state of their beloved Tamil. Kalyanasundaram thus rebuked the Anglophiles who discarded Tamiḻttāy and worshipped Āṅkilattāy (Mother English) instead. "Their birth mother starves; the other mother is well-fed. What a sign of our times!" (Kalyanasundaranar 1935: 21). In his autobiography, Suddhananda Bharati writes that from early in his life, he had to resist pressures brought upon him by his Brahman family to study English. He asked of them, "Why should I study English in order to be a servant to someone else? I am a Tamilian. I will only study Tamil." His resistance to English was fostered partly in response to an environment in which he saw so many young men mortgage their family homes and property to chase after an English education, only to wander around jobless afterwards. What did they acquire, he asks, "by giving up their mother and running after the other woman?" All they can say proudly is "'I do not know the *Gītā,* but I do know Gibbon. . . . ' Is Tamil not enough for the Tamilian?" (Suddhananda Bharati 1950: 54–69; see also Bharati 1988: 180–85).

The Indianist dilemma is quite apparent in Suddhananda Bharati's story, however. He tells us that his youthful resistance to English soon gave way to an appreciation for its necessity for Tamilians if they wanted to be citizens of the world (Suddhananda Bharati 1950: 94). Indeed, he soon became "infatuated with English"; he often gave public lectures in it, and even taught English to schoolchildren. Even the most anti-English of devotees was aware that English was necessary not just for learning the ways of the West, but also for communicating with other Indians until a suitable national language had been selected. As that latter project ran aground on the reefs of "Hindi imperialism," many devotees who in their early years wrote passionately against English, like Kalyanasundaram and Rajagopalachari, became its advocates, albeit reluctantly, from the 1940s.

In attempting to persuade Tamil speakers that "India" or its languages would not harm Tamil, Indianism came to rely heavily on the emotive metaphor of the mother. Consider the following statement:

> The sons of Bhārata Mātā speak several languages. . . . Our Indian sons adorn their Intiyattāy [Bhārata Mātā] with these languages. In adorning her thus, is their unity harmed or affected? Those who say that the existence of so many languages is harmful speak from ignorance. Born from the womb of India, these brothers may speak various languages but are united by the same spirit of love and devotion for their nation. . . . Therefore, the existence of so many languages in the nation is a sign of excellence.
>
> (Venkatesvara Ayyar 1918: 2–3)

The Indianist logic was the logic of the family, itself reconstituted as the foundational site of unity, cooperation, and harmony. Could siblings, born from the same mother's womb and reared on her milk, harm each other? So Ramalinga Pillai reminded his fellow speakers that they should not forget: "However many languages there are in the Indian nation, for several thousands of years, the Indian people have been drinking the same mother's milk, and are members of the same culture" (Ramalinga Pillai 1953: 53).

Indianism, of course, presented Tamil speakers with two mothers, Tamiḻttāy and Bhārata Mātā. It was not a choice between one or the other, as Dravidianism would have it. Instead, in the Indianist imagination, while Tamiḻttāy's womb and milk unites all Tamil speakers as *Tamilians,* the womb and milk of Bhārata Mātā transfigures them into *Indians,* and ties them with other Indians in webs of sibling solidarity. It is through sharing Bhārata Mātā's womb and milk that Tamilians, the children of Tamiḻttāy, symbolically become part of the Indian body politic.

It is also the logic of the family and of motherhood that generated that very crucial notion that Indianism (and Dravidianism) popularized among Tamil speakers: namely, that Tamil is their *tāymoḻi,* "mother tongue," the language of their home and mother. Part of the challenge that Indianism faced, of course, was to reconcile Tamil's homely status as "mother tongue" with neo-Shaivite attempts to promote its divinity, and classicist efforts to secure its classicality, a task that was not all that easy.

INDIANISM AND DIVINE TAMIL

Like neo-Shaivism, but unlike classicism or Dravidianism, the Indianist regime was willing to accept that Tamil is a divine language (Bharati 1988: 117; Ramalinga Pillai 1953: 13–18). Unlike neo-Shaivism, however, this did not lead it to question the legitimacy of Sanskrit and of Aryan Brahmanical Hinduism. Consider how Tamiḻttāy introduced herself in one of Bharati's poems published in 1919:

> The primordial Shiva gave birth to me;
> The Aryan son Agastya saw me and took delight;
> That Brahman endowed me with a grammar, complete and perfect.
> (Bharati 1987: 529)

All the same, even if Indianism thus upheld Tamil's divinity, it did not make this into a fundamental part of its own agenda, as did neo-Shaivism. For there was concern that dwelling on Tamil's divinity would hinder its transformation into a modern language of governance, education, public communication, and politics. As early as 1892, one of its devotees—T. Saravana Mutthu, librarian of the Presidency College, Madras—demanded, "How does it benefit Tamil if we vehemently in-sist that God created Tamil?" (1892: 3–4). The educationist P. Sivaswami Aiyar similarly suggested in 1917 that "instead of relying on the belief that Tamil was a divine gift and that its vocabulary was copious and its diction rich and self-contained, serious attempts should be made to incorporate into Tamil, from other languages, if necessary, terms that were easy to understand" (Irschick 1969: 304). Recognizing the growing skepticism among many about Tamil's abilities to communicate the modern sciences of the West, Bharati's Tamiḻttāy observed to her "children" in 1919:

> "Tamil will die a slow death
> The languages of the West will triumph in this world."
>
> So says the simpleton;
> Alas! what an accusation!
> Go forth in all eight directions!
> Bring back here the wealth of all learning!
> By the grace of my father, and the penance of our learned scholars, this great taint will be effaced,
> With lofty fame I shall last forever in this world!
>
> (Bharati 1987: 531)

It is perhaps not surprising that Bharati saw the task of modernizing and scientizing Tamil as a joint enterprise, made possible through Shiva's grace and human scholarship, for as he insisted elsewhere, Tamil's divine origin was not just fantasy but historically attestable (Bharati 1988: 117). Like Bharati, Indianism was ultimately ambivalent about Tamil's divinity, an ambivalence that is also reflected in its attitude towards religion. As did so many "secular" nationalists in colonial and post-colonial India, devotees of Indianist persuasion upheld the inherent equality of all Indian religions. All the same, Hinduism in particular—in its reformed new "universalist" version which condemned caste hierarchies and irrational rituals, and recommended an action-oriented practice of spiritual truths—received special attention. For Bharati, as indeed for others like him, Hinduism was the best religion of the world and Tamil speakers its most eminent practitioners. Correspondingly, a true devotee of Tamil was not exclusively Shaivite (as in neo-Shaivism), nor polemically atheistic (as in Dravidianism), but clearly and proudly a "Hindu." As Bharati insisted in 1917:

> A man who has pride in Tamil (*tamiḻapimāṉam*) is one who embraces Hinduism (*hintu tarmam*). That alone will illuminate the path of the devotee of Tamil. For the man who does not care for the *Tēvāram*, the *Tiruvācakam*, the *Tiruvāymoḻi*, the *Tirukkuṟaḷ*, and the *Kamparāmāyaṇam* has no claim to be a devotee of Tamil. One who knows these texts will realize that it is through Hinduism that this world will find salvation.
>
> (Thooran 1986: 257)

Thus in contradistinction to radical neo-Shaivism, which adopted an oppositional stance towards Sanskritic Aryan Hinduism in the name of a "Dravidian" Shaivism, Indianism linked the cause of Tamil to an inclusivistic neo-Hinduism (Halbfass 1988: 403–18; Ramalinga Pillai 1953: 39). Indeed, to counter Christian missionary influence in schools (and later, the Dravidian movement's atheism), Indianism advocated a thorough grounding in Tamil and Sanskritic scriptures for Tamil children as part of its "national education" (*tēciya kalvi*) scheme.

All the same, such an embrace of religiosity brought its own share of problems for Tamil's devotees, as it did for others in modern India. Indianism did celebrate the existence of diverse religious beliefs among Tamil speakers, although it employed a distinctly Hindu idiom in such a celebration (Bharati 1937: 35–36; Ramalinga Pillai 1988: 28–29). Nonetheless, there was also considerable anxiety that such a diversity itself could, and did, give rise to sectarian divisiveness and tensions. Not surprisingly, in these circumstances, Indianism placed its hopes in Tamil as the bond which would tie together all Tamil speakers, be they Hindu, Muslim, or Christian. In a public speech that he gave in 1928, Kalyanasundaram pointed out: "If we wish to bind the people born in this [Tamil] nation in the net of unity, there is only one instrument, and that is the Tamil language. . . . We may be attached to different religions, but we cannot forget we are all Tamilians" (Kalyanasundaranar 1935: 25–26).

Kalyanasundaram was able to say this with confidence because he and his fellow devout were simultaneously creators as well as subjects of the founding certitude of *tamiḻpparru:* in contrast to caste and religion, which divided one Tamil speaker from another, their language, especially in its incarnation as "mother tongue" and as Tamiḻttāy, bonded them together in the "net of unity," as firmly and surely as the love of their mother(s).

INDIANISM AND CLASSICAL TAMIL

In the same manner that it affirmed Tamil's divinity, Indianism also confirmed its classicality, especially because the burgeoning classicist scholarship was so convincingly demonstrating to Tamil speakers that while their "mother tongue" might not yet be "scientific," it was certainly more ancient and venerable than English or any other European language being paraded around as a paragon of modernity. So Bharati (1937: 62) declared in 1919 that he had read and appreciated "the exquisite beauties" of Shelley, Victor Hugo, and Goethe, but no "modern vernacular of Europe can boast of works like the *Kural* of Valluvar, the *Ramayana* of Kamban and the *Silappadhikaram* (Anklet Epic) of Ilango."

Like the other regimes of *tamiḻppaṟṟu,* the Indianist, too, represented the age of the Caṅkams as free of sectarian strife and caste oppression, when the philosophy of "all towns are our towns, and all men are our kinsmen" had reigned (Kalyanasundaranar 1935: 28–36; Ramalinga Pillai 1953: 57–59). Its concern with these poems as with other works of Tamil literature, however, was not so much antiquarian as it was utilitarian. The hope was that these would help modern Tamil speakers liberate themselves from their enchantment with English. If they were exposed to the greatness of their past through the medium of their own language, they would truly appreciate the value of Ilango and Kamban, instead of lauding Shakespeare and Tennyson (Bharati 1937: 62; C. S. Subramaniam 1986: 252–60; Kalyanasundaranar 1919: 122–26). Accordingly, many of Tamil's Indianist devotees, like Subramania Aiyar, Chidambaram Pillai, and Sivagnanam, undertook the publication of accessible (and in many instances Sanskritized) interpretations of ancient Tamil works, which were also popularized through literary conferences, street plays, and movies (Sivagnanam 1970: 97–104, 109–15).

While there was a general consensus that it was important to stress Tamil's classicality so as to bolster the pride and self-respect of its speakers today, there was also concern that an excessive emphasis could detract from the equally urgent task of transforming it into a modern language of rule, education, and everyday communication. And this utilitarian thrust to the Indianist project led it to rebuke, even denigrate, "panditic" and scholarly Tamilians who, it was claimed, resisted efforts to help change Tamil into a useful contemporary language, in their single-minded pursuit of its classicality (Bharati 1987: 527–28; Nuhman 1984: 16–33; C. S. Subramaniam 1986: 264–65). For Indianism, a true Tamil devotee was one who made Tamil suitable for school textbooks, and one who would ensure that it was the language used by its speakers in their assemblies and associations. "The Tamil devotee (*tamiḻapimāṉi*) is one who produces new knowledges, new literatures, and new life in Tamil," in Bharati's words (Thooran 1986: 256–57). The absence of modern, scientific literatures in Indian languages, devotees like Bharati insisted, perpetuated Indian enslavement to English through dependence on the Western mastery of the sciences. The aim therefore was to learn as much as possible from English, in order to displace it from its throne and replace it with Tamil, suitably modernized and scientized. Their faith in the inherent greatness of Tamil notwithstanding, many of its devotees wondered about its ability to communicate modern, scientific thought. From the turn of this century, these enthusiasts had to face Anglophile critics who claimed that "wallowing in sentimentalism," supporters of Tamil were sacrificing the youth of the country to their "superstitious beliefs in the vernaculars."[10] A contributor to the *Educational Review* in 1916 insisted, "The fact is that our vernaculars are in a most crude state so far as scientific exposition is concerned. It is no answer to say that we have very good poetry and some grandiloquent prose, in the vernaculars. A language that is well equipped for poetic expression is not necessarily so for a scientific thesis. Kalidasa and Bhavabhuti may well feel handicapped if they were set to translate a modern elementary textbook of science" (quoted in Irschick 1969: 304–5). The challenge therefore lay in scientizing Tamil, in transforming it from a language of great poetry and piety into one of modern science and technology.

A similar challenge was faced by language reformers and modernizers in other parts of the subcontinent, as indeed in other regions of the world (Fishman, Ferguson, and Dasgupta 1968). But in Tamil India, those committed to the creation of scientific vocabularies had to contend not only with all the problems of colonial modernity (such as borrowing from the West without sacrificing pride in the indigenous, embracing the secular without surrendering the religious, and so on), but also with the many languages that rivalled for attention as the reservoir from which to draw for "improving" Tamil—English, Sanskrit, and classical Tamil being the principal contenders. By the 1930s, devotees of Indianist persuasion came to clash with others on this matter because in their logic, Sanskrit was the one language that had the power to displace English, a contention that gave rise to considerable ire, as we can imagine.

This was not the only problem that Indianist devotees faced, for they also sought to ensure that in the process of modernizing and scientizing Tamil, they authorized a language that could easily be used by "the people," its principal consumers. Indianism's clarion call, as captured in Bharati's exhortation "to write as one speaks," meant that the Tamil used in textbooks, newspapers, and political speeches ought to be understood, in the words of V. Ramaswamy (1889–1951), by the rickshaw-puller on the street. So Bharati's preface to his famous 1912 poem *Pāñcāli Capatam* (The vow of Panchali), insisted: "Simple words, a clear style, easy rhythms that can be readily comprehended, and simple tunes that the common folk will appreciate—he who composes a poem along these lines today will be breathing new life into our mother tongue" (quoted in Nuhman 1984: 92). Yet the modern Tamil authorized by Indianism in the name of "the common folk" continued to be Sanskritic in its lexicon, betraying both the upper-caste and upper-class prejudices of its practitioners, as we will see.

INDIANISM AND THE "MOTHER TONGUE"

In all these struggles—to counter the excessive influence of Tamil's divinity and classicality, to wean Tamil speakers away from their infatuation with English, to create new vocabularies for use in scientific education and modern government, to fashion a language that would be understood by "the common folk"—Indianism relied extensively on Tamil's status as "mother tongue." In the Indianist regime, as indeed in Dravidianism, the speaker's relationship to Tamil is cast in the intimate and familiar terms of a child's interactions with its mother, rather than with some distant abstraction called "the classical tongue" or "the divine language." Early in this century, Bharati (1937: 29) observed that "nations are made of homes." For both these regimes, however, the nation is not merely made of homes; symbolically and discursively, it *is* home, a domain of selfless love and sibling solidarity, a realm of nonpolitics (Chatterjee 1989).

The language of the home acquired potency and validity for Indianism, precisely because it was imagined to be *not* the language of the colonized, Anglicized, public sphere. Untarnished by the West, it was the language of every Tamil speaker's heart, mind, and true self, and hence the means through which anticolonial resistance could be launched. The home, however, was also the abode of the mother, imagined as the true bearer of all that was noble and spiritual about Tamil (and Indian) culture. Just as crucially, the mother was also the vehicle through whom Tamil, the "mother tongue," would continue to be reproduced, even as in the outer, material world, away from the home, Tamil speakers, especially their menfolk, would perforce have to employ English. Not surprisingly, there was much agony among the devout over the alarming escalation in the use of English by women and girls, especially within the intimate and hitherto uncolonized space of the home. Why are we surprised, they asked, that there is no respect for Tamil when "even our women in their kitchens rejoice that they speak English" (Vasudeva Sharma 1928: 18)? An editorial in the nationalist daily *Cutēcamittiraṉ* (23 August 1917) similarly lamented that if this alarming trend were to continue, "we will be spoiled in every way."[11]

Although the construct of "mother tongue" frequently erupted in neo-Shaiva and classicist discourses, generating paradoxical formations such as "our divine mother tongue" or "our classical mother tongue," it was with Indianism from the turn of the century that the term assumed both popularity and political saliency. English, it was argued, would only turn Tamil speakers (and other Indians) into clerks and accountants; their "mother tongue," however, would transform them into patriots and citizens. As Kalyanasundaram declared in 1924, "The nation in which the mother tongue does not flourish will never achieve freedom. . . . The first step towards freedom is respect for the mother tongue" (Kalyanasundaranar 1935: 21).

Indianism was particularly concerned that such a "respect" for Indian languages was being denied by the colonial state's classification of these as "vernaculars"—"the language of the slaves." Thus S. Satyamurthy, a leading spokesman for the Congress Party, declared to the Madras Legislative Council in November 1928: "Vernacular means the tongue of slaves. I do not think we ought to insult our languages by calling them 'vernaculars' or tongues of slaves. Of course, the answer of the Englishman would be, 'My vernacular is English.' But he never uses the word 'vernacular' in connection with his mother tongue."[12]

Therefore, where classicism protested the categorization of Tamil as a "vernacular" by seeking recognition for its classicality, Indianism did so by insisting on its status as *tāymoḻi* (mother tongue)—as the language of the people, of their homes, and of their mothers. Consider the following statement from an essay entitled "Tāymoḻi," written by Kalyanasundaram, that appeared in his *Navacakti* in 1924:

> Every man reveres the woman who gives birth to him, the nation (*nāṭu*) where he was born, and the language he speaks, by referring to these as his "mother." As much as the love he has for the mother who carried him, ought to be his love for the nation that delivers him, and the language that rears him. A man who does not revere his nation and his language is like the sinner who does not reverence his own mother. Indeed, the language that one speaks is the very wellspring of the love for one's mother, and of devotion to one's motherland. A man who is not devoted to the mother tongue he speaks is a man who has reviled his own mother and his own nation.
> (Kalyanasundaranar 1935: 19)

So endemic does the identification of language with motherhood become with Indianist discourse that even when Tamiḻttāy herself was not specifically invoked, Tamil and mothers came to be spoken of in identical terms. In his memoirs Sivagnanam, an autodidact who remembers learning much of his Tamil at his mother's knee in her kitchen, writes, "As far as I am concerned, when I say Tamil is my 'mother tongue,' it is not rhetorical. It is really true. My knowledge of Tamil is my mother's gift. For that reason, Tamil *is* my mother tongue" (Sivagnanam 1974: 868). For its devotees, there was nothing more natural than referring to their language as "mother tongue" because it was literally something they acquired from their mothers. It was, as Sivagnanam reminds us, their mothers' gift.

INDIANISM AND HINDI

From early in the century, in the Madras Presidency as in other parts of the subcontinent, there were many who were concerned with the problem of developing a national language so as to overcome the dependence on English for interregional communication. Hindi was an early favorite candidate among many Tamil speakers, as it was in its own "home" in northern India (Dasgupta 1970). In 1906, in an article he published in *Intiyā,* Bharati endorsed the view that since Hindi was already spoken by eighty out of India's three hundred million, Tamil speakers, too, should embrace it. Yet, he lamented, no steps had been taken to promote it in the South (C. S. Subramaniam 1986: 443–44). Soon after, in a 1908 letter to the nationalist Tilak, Bharati wrote that he and his friends had started a small Hindi class in Madras city (Padmanabhan 1982: 48–49; see also Nuhman 1984: 55–61). In subsequent decades, other devotees of the Indianist persuasion backed the cause of Hindi and countered Dravidianism's demonization of the language by reminding their fellow speakers that supporting it did not necessarily amount to the "murder" of their mother, Tamil (Kalyanasundaranar 1935: 21; Sivagnanam 1974: 136–41). Convinced that the regional Congress Party was dedicated to the twin causes of promoting Tamil at the regional level and Hindi at the national level, devotees inclined to Indianism supported that party.

Yet the promotion of Hindi as key to national unity and integration posed many dilemmas for Indianism, caught as it was between devotion to "Tamil" and "India." Over the years and especially in the decade following independence, many an Indianist became increasingly suspicious of the Congress Party's aggressive Hindi policy, which was perceived as endangering Tamil, as Dravidianists had long maintained (Sivagnanam 1974: 138–41, 416–18, 505–7). They came to appreciate the realities of functioning in a multilingual polity in which, contrary to their conviction that all languages are equal "children" of Bhārata Mātā, one of them would be the privileged "imperial state language." Ramalinga Pillai captured their conflicting sentiments when he wrote that Tamil speakers were famed the world over for inviting other languages into their home and honoring these. However, he asked, to what extent should they let their own language and culture suffer in this process (Thaninayagam 1963: 12)? What would happen to Tamil and its glorious literature, others demanded, if state funds were redirected towards the support of Hindi? For, as Somasundara Bharati, professor of Tamil and a Congress supporter in his early years, insisted, "clothed with prestige and privileges peculiar to an imperial state language, Hindi is sure to become a dangerous rival to Tamil." Not surprisingly, he wondered if an old "evil," English, was being replaced by a new one, and whether Tamil would continue to suffer in this process (Somasundara Bharati 1937: 17).

Although opposed to compulsory Hindi education, many Indianist devotees like Kalyanasundaram and Sivagnanam continued to extend their allegiance to the Congress's policies into the 1940s, in reaction to the powerful anti-Hindi and anti-India demonology of Dravidianism, and in the face of the Dravidian movement's growing demand for retaining English as the common language. As colonial rule gave way to Congress rule, however, they became convinced that the cause of Tamil would be compromised by the larger cause of the (Hindi-dominated) Indian nation and its needs. Not surprisingly, by the late 1940s, Kalyanasundaram joined forces with the Dravidian movement to oppose Hindi (Kalyanasundaranar 1949). Similarly, in 1946, Sivagnanam formed an interest group called the Tamiḻ Aracu Kaḻakam, "Association for Tamil Autonomy" (henceforth Tamil Arasu Kazhagam), whose main agenda was to put pressure on the Congress to promote the increased use of Tamil in administration and education, to work towards the creation of an autonomous Tamil state out of a composite Madras Presidency, and to ease up on its pro-Hindi policy. As Sivagnanam wrote in April 1947 on the eve of Indian independence, "The Tamilian is prepared to be Indian. However, he is first and foremost a Tamilian. Only secondarily is he Indian" (Sivagnanam 1981: 105). By 1954, his organization was forced to part ways with the Congress, and in 1967, Sivagnanam even entered into an electoral alliance with the Dravidian movement—the same movement against which through much of the 1950s he had conducted so many campaigns (Sivagnanam 1974: 368–69, 535–55). Most indicative perhaps of Indianism's radical transformation through its dealings with the Hindi question is C. Rajagopalachari's changing stance. The chief promoter of Hindi who made its study mandatory in the late 1930s in the Madras Presidency, he began to insist "English ever, Hindi never" from the late 1950s, and even made electoral deals with his Dravidianist rivals by the 1960s (Rajagopalachari 1962).

THE CONGRESS AND INDIANIZED TAMIL

In 1967, the Congress, the party that prided itself on delivering India from colonialism and that had ruled Madras for the two decades since independence, suffered a stunning defeat at the polls and has never returned to power in the state since. For many a Tamil devotee, the Congress's defeat was its just deserts, for had it not shown, over the years, that it was the enemy of Tamil and Tamiḻttāy?[13] Supporters of the Congress have tried to counter such a charge. It was the Congress, more than the non-Brahman elite's Justice Party, that used Tamil from early in this century in party work and popular mobilization. It was under Congress rule that Tamil was extended as medium of instruction in high schools in 1938, and university education in 1960–61.[14] The Congress government also set up, in 1959, the Tamil Development and Research Council entrusted with producing Tamil school and college textbooks in the natural and human sciences, accounting, mathematics, and so on. It also helped finance a series of children's encyclopedias in Tamil, "lucid commentaries" on Caṅkam poetry, and an "authentic history of the Tamil people" in 1962–63.[15] And finally, in 1956, it was the Congress that passed the law instituting Tamil as the official language of the state

(Karthikeyan 1965–66; C. Subramaniam 1962). Yet, as its critics have been quick to point out, few of these measures seemed to have made any difference to life in the Tamil-speaking land. So, Mohan Kumaramangalam wrote in 1965:

> In practice, the ordinary man finds that the Tamil language is nowhere in the picture. . . . In Madras city, English dominates our life to an extraordinary extent. . . . Corporation property tax, electric consumption and water tax bills are only in the English language; all communications of the Collector are in English; in virtually all trade, including the smallest consumer goods, bills, receipts, etc. are made out in the English language. I think it will be no exaggeration to say that a person can live for years in Madras without learning a word of Tamil, except for some servant inconvenience!
>
> (Kumaramangalam 1965: 69–70).

As many of its supporters rightly point out, the Congress government's record on *tamil̲ppaṇi,* "service to Tamil," is not as terrible or as bleak as its critics portray it. Nevertheless, it pursued Tamil policies that were largely Indianist in complexion at a time when the growing Dravidianist discourse was very persuasively pointing to "India" as the source of many of the Tamil speaker's problems, and at a time when even Indianists within the devotional community were turning away from the Congress. Its Indianist predilections meant that the "improvement" of Tamil under Congress rule proceeded side by side with at least tacit support for the Indian state's Hindi policy. The Congress also resisted a number of devotional demands out of fear that these would open the "Pandora's box" of linguistic "balkanization": the renaming of Madras state as "Tamilnadu," the authorization of Tamil as primary liturgical language in temples, the use of pure Tamil instead of Sanskritized Tamil in school textbooks and administrative manuals, and so on. Above all, Congress policies, like orthodox Indianism's, were premised on the fundamental assumption that "Tamil" and "India" were intertwined, an assumption that it felt compelled to uphold if only to counter the separatist agenda of the Dravidian movement. It would be sacrilegious to think exclusively of Tamil as deserving the absolute allegiance of all its speakers. Thus the Congress, and even the Indianist regime, were never animated by the spirit of total and unconditional celebration of Tamil that characterized Dravidianism's attitude towards the language.[16] In the words of one devotee of Tamil whose own sentiments were contestatory classicist and Dravidianist, "None of the Congress Ministers of Tamil Nad was either a Tamil scholar or a Tamil-lover. The Congress leaders of Tamil Nad as betrayers of Tamil, cannot represent the State any more. Blind cannot lead the blind, much less the keen-sighted" (Devaneyan 1967: 25). In 1967, the Tamil electorate came to the same conclusion.

LANGUAGE OF THE NATION: DRAVIDIANIZING TAMIL

And so, finally, I turn to the Dravidianist regime that crystallized in the 1930s, gained momentum through the 1940s and 1950s, and peaked in the mid-1960s. Its primary terrain of activity was a series of anti-Hindi protests which dramatically drew together diverse elements of the devotional community in opposition to the regional and central governments that sponsored Hindi, itself caricatured as an evil and demonic force out to destroy pure and sweet Tamil (and its speakers). Contemporaries and participants alike marvelled that the common cause against Hindi threw together religious revivalists like Maraimalai Adigal with such avowed atheists as Ramasami; Gandhians like Kalyanasundaram with men like Annadurai who preached secession from India; university professors and elite antiquarians, such as Somasundara Bharati and Purnalingam Pillai, with populist street poets, pamphleteers, college students, and young men like Chinnasami who immolated themselves. Indeed, the poet Bharatidasan, the paradigmatic Dravidianist, had himself been a self-declared devotee of "India" up until the 1920s, and had published some passionate poems on Bhārata Mātā before his conversion to Dravidianism and anti-Hindi politics by the 1930s (Ilango 1982; Ilavarasu 1990). Other events of these decades—the creation of linguistic states out of the erstwhile Madras Presidency, the securing of appropriate borders with neighboring states, the struggle to rename Madras state Tamilnadu—also compelled devotees otherwise inclined, such as Sivagnanam, to turn to Dravidianism. Dravidianism is thus the crisis idiom of *tamiḻppaṟṟu,* the regime par excellence for mobilizing—albeit temporarily and sometimes reluctantly—diverse, even opposing, devotees under one umbrella, around events that were deemed to be threatening to the future of Tamil and Tamiḻttāy.

The most passionate and radical of all the regimes, Dravidianism routinely elicited from its adherents declarations of willingness to give up their wealth, their lives, and their souls for Tamil. It also produced some antagonistic, even violent, attitudes towards other languages and their speakers, as for instance in the following verse published by Bharatidasan, which is fairly typical: "Our first task is to finish off those who destroy [our] glorious Tamil! / Let flow a river of crimson blood!"[17] Its emphasis on fierce, public displays of devotion meant that images of battlefields, of blood, and of death proliferate in Dravidianist discourse. True Tamilians are those—like Chinnasami—who show their commitment to their mother/tongue by putting their very bodies on the line, and dying for it, if need be.

More so than the other devotional regimes, Dravidianism's driving imperative was a vision of the Tamil community as an autonomous racial and political entity (*iṉam*), even nation (*nāṭu*), whose sacral center is occupied solely by Tamil, from which all its members claim shared descent. So, where neo-Shaivism constituted Tamilian solidarity around the shared worship of Shiva and divine Tamil, and classicism emphasized a common ancient, literary past, Dravidianism focused on descent and kinship. Tropes of motherhood, siblingship, shared blood, the home, and the like mark its discursive style, as they do Indianism's. The significant difference between the two, of course, is that Dravidianism made a commitment to only one entity—namely, Tamil. As Tamiḻttāy herself insisted, sometime in the early 1960s: "Do not forget that you are all children who emerged from my womb. I *am* your mother. The learned call me Tamiḻttāy. You are called Tamilians (*tamiḻar*). You and I have been inextricably bound together for ever and ever through language. That language is what the good scholars call Tamil. . . . If we look closely, we have a home. That its name is Tamilnadu gives [me] great happiness" (Pancanathan n.d.: 9).

In this statement as elsewhere in Dravidianism, descent is reckoned solely from Tamil, which is not merely one among a "family" of languages *in* a putative Indian nation, as it is in Indianism, but is *the* language *of* the nation, imagined variously as "Tamilian" or "Dravidian." No doubt, by the 1970s Dravidianism became more accommodating on the question of India. But the fundamental imperative of this regime continued to be the establishment of the absolute rule of Tamil through the complete Tamilization of the political apparatus and its accompanying ideology, in a territorial space designated as Tamil or Dravidian, which at least into the early 1960s was seen as independent of, and indeed in opposition to, "India."

The political philosophy of Dravidianism was provided by a broad swathe of ideas associated with "the Dravidian movement" (*tirāviṭa iyakkam*). This movement made its impact on the Dravidianist regime when the elitist "non-Brahman" associational politics of the Vellala-dominated Justice Party (1916/17–44) was supplemented by the populist call for radical social reform by E. V. Ramasami and his Self-Respect League (founded in 1926) and the Tirāviṭar Kaḻakam, "Association of

Dravidians" (the DK, established in 1944). Although many Self-Respecters were concerned with Tamil (e.g., Velu and Selvaraji 1989), Ramasami himself was extremely critical of *tamiḻpparru,* especially of its valorization of the divinity, antiquity, and motherhood of Tamil. This did not stop Dravidianism from lionizing him and selectively appropriating his ideas of rationalist materialism, iconoclastic atheism, radical anti-Brahmanism, and Dravidian nationalism, for he provided the most polemical and sustained attacks on Indian nationalism, which this regime found useful. Ramasami's obvious dilemma was that Tamil devotion threatened his vision of a Dravidian nation that would incorporate all "Dravidians" of southern India, and not just Tamil speakers. Such a vision had to contend with the resistance of those putative "Dravidians" who were speakers of Telugu, Kannada, and Malayalam. In addition, it was compromised by Tamil speakers who did not necessarily want to participate in a multilingual polity, even if it was "Dravidian." And indeed, as the Dravidian movement itself split, when Annadurai parted company with Ramasami and his DK in 1949 to found his own party, the Tirāviṭa Muṉṉēṟṟak Kaḻakam or "Dravidian Progress Association" (DMK), the inherent tensions between the alternate conceptions of the "Dravidian" and "Tamil" nation came to the fore. By the late 1950s, as the DMK entered the domain of electoral politics, its agenda was primarily formulated in terms of a Tamil nation (albeit one often referred to as "Dravidian"), confined to the territorial space of a Tamil-speaking area, rather than coeval with the more ambitious nation that Ramasami envisaged comprising the speakers of all Dravidian languages.

Like the Dravidian movement, Dravidianism, too, had to contend with the tensions between an exclusive Tamil-speaking nation and a more inclusive Dravidian nation. It adopted various strategies to deal with this, such as suggestions that "Tamil" and "Dravidian" are the same; that since Tamil is the "mother" of all Dravidian languages, the latter are merely extensions of the former; and so on. So, like the other regimes, Dravidianism had its share of contradictions. Notwithstanding these, as a consequence of its discourse, Tamil comes to be firmly "Dravidianized," even as the "Dravidian" category, which had been gaining political and cultural visibility in the region since the 1880s, was unequivocally associated with Tamil.

In contrast to neo-Shaivism and classicism, Dravidianism advocated political radicalism and activism as the means to achieve the reign of Tamil: "We have talked enough. . . . [W]hen are you going to show your sacrifice to [Tamiḻttāy]? We are waiting every moment for the honor of being arrested."[18] Under the influence of Dravidianism, *tamil̲pparru* took to the streets, sometimes quite violently. Petition politics gave way to protest politics, increasingly radical and populist. Antiquarian and elite notions about Tamil and Tamil̲ttāy, hitherto confined to learned academies and scholastic journals, came to be invoked in street songs, polemical plays, and political speeches at populist anti-Hindi rallies; they were circulated in daily newspapers and street pamphlets, and plastered across billboards and wall posters. Dravidianism typically catered, like the Dravidian movement itself, to the Everyman, generically designated in its texts as *tamil̲an̲,* "Tamilian" (Barnett 1976: 114–15). It attracted its following from devotees who were predominantly from middle and lower castes, and from middle- or low-income families with limited or no formal education, like Chinnasami and his fellow self-immolators. At the same time, the DMK's support of literature and language also attracted numerous well-educated Tamil scholars and academics to Dravidianism. In turn, many DMK leaders have been devotees of Tamil. They have assumed titles—*ar̲iñar* (scholar) Annadurai, *kalaiñar* (the artist) Karunanidhi, *nāvalar* (the eloquent) Nedunceliyan—which display both their scholarly aspirations and the close links between populist ideology and high literature in the political culture of the region (Barnett 1976: 56–86). Dravidianism's paradigmatic exponents were undoubtedly well-known poets and politicians like Bharatidasan, Annadurai, "Pulavar" Kulanthai (1906–72), Perunchitran (1920–95), Mudiyarasan (b. 1920), Karunanidhi, and the early Kannadasan (1927–81). But encouraged by the Dravidian movement's populism and by Dravidianism's assertion that Tamil belonged to "the people," the Everyman, who remained anonymous or relatively unknown, took to writing and publishing poems, short stories, and essays on the language and on Tamil̲ttāy. Of all the regimes of *tamil̲ppar̲r̲u,* Dravidianism was thus the one that was truly populist, in spirit as well as constituency.

Dravidianism's fundamental agenda, of course, was to establish the absolute preeminence of Tamil in all spheres of life and being, and to ensure that devotion to the language (and its community) was not diluted by any other passions—for the Indian nation, for the gods of the Hindu pantheon, or even for the families and mothers of individual devotees. For Tamil is everything; it is the life (*uyir*), breath (*āvi*), and consciousness (*uṇarvu*) of every true Tamilian. In its purest form, there were no divided commitments in Dravidianism, no subordination of Tamil to Shiva, to literature and learning, or to India. Tamil was not a means through which to construct something else, be it an alternate religious or civilizational formation, or allegiance to India. In and of itself, it ought to be the very center of everything in the devoted Tamil speaker's life. Without it, there is nothing. So Bharatidasan wrote in a poem suggestively entitled "Living for Tamil Is the Only Life":

O Tamil! Homage to you!
. . . .
Your well-being is ours as well.
Your victories are ours as well.
We may as well be dead if we live for ourselves.
Living for Tamil is the only life![19]

For the Dravidianist devotee, Tamil was so much a part of the Tamilian's very essence that it would be impossible to separate the language from its speaker. So Bharatidasan insisted:

We can turn mountains into pits;
We can dry up the ocean bed;
We can fly speedily through the skies.
. . . .
We can even bring the dying back to life.

The Tamilian cannot be separated from Tamil
Even for a moment, by anyone.[20]

This conviction, that Tamil and its speaker-devotee had so blended into each other that it would be impossible to separate them, is echoed in other poems as well. Consider this verse by Kannadasan addressed to Tamiḻttāy:

Would I ever forget you? Would I cease to sing about you?
Even if they set me on fire,
In the burning flames of the fire,
The world will see only you, O dear mother of mine!
(Kannadasan 1968: 89)

Elsewhere, in 1954, in lines that eerily anticipate Chinnasami's immolation a decade later, the poet wrote, "even in death, Tamil should be on our lips. Our ashes should burn with the fragrance of Tamil. This is our undying desire" (Kannappan 1995: 22).

Given such sentiments, Dravidianism was particularly concerned with all alternate objects of passion that might draw its speakers away from Tamil, such as "India," their gods, and their families. It therefore focused as much energy to convince Tamil speakers of the illegitimacy of these other entities as to emphasize that it is Tamil that sustains their life and consciousness.

DRAVIDIANISM AND INDIA

While Indianism emphatically asserted that the liberation of Bhārata Mātā and Tamiḻttāy would have to proceed in tandem, Dravidianism, particularly in its early years, and most especially as expressed by its more radical exponents, saw in the very establishment of the Indian nation the downfall of Tamil. A poem that was published in the *Tirāviṭaṉ* on 31 August 1947, a fortnight after India was officially liberated from colonial rule, declared: "The foreign Bhārata Mātā (*aṉṉiyap pāratattāy*) has attained glory. / Our own dear Tamiḻttāy has been greatly disgraced."

Dravidianism, at its peak, portrayed the newly emergent Indian nation as an imperialist formation, as a tool in the hands of Brahmans and Banias (North Indian merchants), and as an instrument with which the material interests of Dravidians would continue to be subordinated to Aryan Indians (Annadurai 1974: 39–48, 1985: 22–23; Pancanathan n.d.; M. S. Ramasami 1947: 5–6, 19–20). Consider the following verse from a 1947 pamphlet revealingly entitled *Songs of Separation for the Dravidian Nation:*

> The Brahmans and Banias have united;
> We are all children of Bhārata Mātā, they lie to us[.]
> . . . .
> Our own Tirāviṭattāy [Mother Dravida] is our mother;
> Bhārata Mātā who belongs to the duplicitous, is a deceitful mother;
> If the Dravidians realize this, they will have no trouble.
> If we let down our guard, the Northerners will loot and plunder [us].
> (M. S. Ramasami 1947: 14)

Indianism, we have seen, offered Bhārata Mātā to Tamil speakers as a mother who would reproduce them as "Indians." In the logic of Dravidianism, however, she was clearly a false mother who sought to lure gullible Tamilians away from their true mother with promises of milk, nourishment, and even jobs. So, in 1958, Bharatidasan, who in his early years had waxed passionately on Bhārata Mātā and even declared her his true mother, published a poem in which he ridiculed the Tamilian who is confused about his "real" mother. The poem is addressed to Tamiḻttāy:

> "O glorious Tamilian! What is the name of your nation?"
> When I ask thus, he sheepishly says "India," O mother!
> How will this child ever improve if he confuses the evergreen
> Tamil nation with India, O mother!

Will he ever change, the one who does not recognize his mother as mother,
and declares the evil that destroys his motherland as mother, O mother!
Sitting in [his] mother's lap and nursing on the breast-milk of Tamil, how
can this child not know [his] mother's name, O mother!
Tamil *is* [his] mother tongue, and Tamilnadu is his motherland.
Does not the Tamilian realize this?[21]

So, while Indianism sought to naturalize "India" by presenting it in the familiar terms of the home and the mother, the Dravidianist logic lay in demonizing it as a "deceitful" or "evil" mother, and substituting Tami̱lttāy in its stead as the authentic, *sole* mother of all true Tamil speakers.

Dravidianism's antagonism towards India came to the fore in the numerous protests against Hindi, presented in its discourses as a bloodsucking demoness, lowly maid, seductive temptress, and false mother out to destroy the noble, righteous, but endangered Tami̱lttāy. Such Manichean images were deployed to create fear and hatred of Hindi, and to generate sentiments of love, loyalty, and filial piety for Tamil, which its loyal speakers were obliged to protect with life and limb. Just as crucially, the regional state government (in the control of the Congress) and the Indian nation were also rendered into objects that deserved the Tamilians' deepest opprobrium and the withdrawal of their support, emotional *and* electoral. Dravidianism thus seized upon the linguistic fact that Hindi was related to Sanskrit, and translated the assertions of radical neo-Shaivism and contestatory classicism against Aryan Brahmanism into political action against the Indian nation. For Dravidianism, the battle against Hindi was not only inevitable and natural, but necessary and morally legitimate; it was a "holy war" (*aṟappōr*) fought against evil and on behalf of the good and righteous (Ramaswamy, forthcoming). Although Hindi was in effect legislated out of Tamilnadu government schools in 1968 by the DMK, and although all kinds of accommodations with the North have been made since the 1960s, to this day the threat of Hindi has continued to be effectively used to reiterate the autonomy and uniqueness of a Tamil space within a larger Indian whole, to summon up the specter of non-Tamil elements entering the pure Tamil body politic, and to remind Tamil speakers of the dangers that await them if they cease supporting the Dravidian movement and its Tamil cause.

DRAVIDIANISM AND HINDUISM

In the years between the late 1920s and 1950s, when the influence of the iconoclastic and atheistic Ramasami was at its peak and before the

DMK actively entered the fray of electoral politics, Dravidianism also sought energetically to dissociate Tamil from all religious affiliations. Like radical neo-Shaivism, it castigated Hinduism as a Brahmanical, Sanskritic, and Aryan conspiracy hatched to destroy Tamil and Dravidian society. So, for Dravidianism, a true Tamilian/Dravidian is one who is emphatically *not* a Hindu. "A Hindu in the present concept may be a Dravidian, but the Dravidian in the real sense of the term cannot and shall not be a Hindu" (quoted in Harrison 1960: 127). Tamil speakers were therefore repeatedly called upon to destroy all (Hindu) irrationalisms and foolish beliefs, and to rescue themselves from *ārya māyai,* "Aryan illusion" (Annadurai 1969). Thus Bharatidasan, who in the 1920s had written passionate poems on Hindu deities and continued occasionally to publish religious verse into the 1930s, insisted in the 1950s that "there is no god" and told the Tamilian that his duty lay in weaning away his hapless fellow speakers from their false belief in divinities.[22]

And here is where Dravidianism parted company with neo-Shaivism: for in its attacks on religion, it did not spare either Shiva or the reformed "rational" version of Shaivism that Maraimalai Adigal and others were attempting to popularize (Sivathamby 1978: 30–31; Venkatachalapathy 1990). Neo-Shaivism may have insisted that Shaivism is the authentic Tamilian religion, radically different from Aryan Brahmanical Hinduism, but Dravidianism was not convinced about this. Nor was it ready to brook neo-Shaivite resistance to reforming and rationalizing the Tamil script, believed by many devout Shaivites to be Shiva's own handiwork (Sivathamby 1979: 71). Dravidianism was also not willing to define the Tamil/Dravidian community as Shaiva, for what would then happen to Tamilians/Dravidians who were nominally Vaishnavas, Christians, and Muslims? So Tamil is the life, the consciousness, and the soul of the Tamilian. It is indeed everything, but it certainly is not "divine Tamil," for to imagine it as such would entangle it with the irrationalisms, inequalities, and idiocies of Hinduism. Tamil speakers, too, consequently would be subordinated and demeaned in an inherently Brahmanical order of things, and they would lose all their "self-respect." In a revealing speech of 1944, Ramasami offered the following advice to his fellow Dravidians: "You may well ask, 'If we give up Hinduism, what religion can we profess to have?' Have courage and claim that religion which will not demean you as untouchable and lowly in society. If there is objection to this, you may always say you are Dravidian and that your religion is Dravidianism. If you have problems even with that, say that your religion is humanity" (Anaimuthu 1974: 446).

Contrary to Marguerite Barnett (1976: 274), who has suggested that "within the Dravidian ideology there was no coherent alternative to religion or Hinduism," I would argue that especially within the Dravidianist regime of *tamiḻpparru,* various efforts were made to create alternatives to both religion and Hinduism. Given the complex entanglements between Tamil devotion and Hinduism, however, such efforts were not entirely successful, nor were they as autonomous as Dravidianism would have desired. Minimally, those devotees of Tamil who turned to active electoral politics as members of the DMK distanced themselves from Ramasami's iconoclastic irreverence for Hindu scriptures, gods, and images. By the 1950s, both the DMK and Dravidianism generated a curious combination of agnosticism ("we do not ask whether there is god or not"), monism ("there is only one god and one community"), populism ("god lives in the smile of the poor"), and humanism ("we must develop that kind of outlook which treats all humanity as one"). This medley of diverse beliefs that Anita Diehl (1977: 29) has shrewdly characterized as "pragmatic, agnostic humanism" opened up a space for the steady incorporation of all kinds of elements from popular as well as the devotional religious practices of the region into the ideology of Dravidianism, such as the celebration of the harvest festival, Pongal; the worship of Murugan; and the apotheosis of Valluvar and his *Tirukkuṟaḷ* (Ramanujam 1971: 168, 175; Ryerson 1988: 108–93).

One other important strategy is followed by Dravidianism in filling up the space vacated by Hindu gods. Consider this 1959 poem by Bharatidasan, addressed to a *tampirāṉ,* "Shaiva monk-preceptor," in response to the opposition of the orthodox to the growing demand for use of Tamil as ritual language in temples:

> Is it religion (*camayam*) that is important, O *tampirāṉ*[?]
> It is fine Tamil that is indeed eminent, O foolish *tampirāṉ*[.]
> Why do you hate Tamil, O *tampirāṉ*[.]
> Why do you hate your mother, O *tampirāṉ*[?]
> Even if religion is destroyed, Tamilians will flourish[.]
> If good Tamil is destroyed, can there be a Tamil community[?]
> Do service to Tamil! O *tampirāṉ*[.]
> Tamil is the life of the Tamilian! O foolish *tampirāṉ*[.]
>
> Is it God who is great[?] O *tampirāṉ*[!]
> It is glorious Tamil that is indeed great[!] O foolish *tampirāṉ*[.]
> Even if God disappears, the Tamil community will flourish[.]
> If Tamil dies, its community, too, will die, O *tampirāṉ*[.]
> Do you intend to destroy the Tamil creed (*tamiḻneṟi*) by invoking Shaivism (*caivaneṟi*), O foolish *tampirāṉ?*

Service to Shaivism is not great, O *tampirāṉ*[.]
It is auspicious service to Tamil that is eminent, O *tampirāṉ*[.]
. . . .
Only one thing is greater than [our] mother(s)! O *tampirāṉ!*
Is that not Tamil, O foolish *tampirāṉ?*[23]

There are few clearer statements than this of Dravidianism's attempt to displace conventional gods and the religious beliefs associated with them, and to substitute Tamil in their stead. Indeed, Dravidianism sacralized Tamil, even while refusing to participate, at least overtly and consciously, in its divinization. Dravidianism's ambivalence towards religiosity and Hinduism notwithstanding, Tamil was offered to its speakers as an iconic object that deserves all the adulation, adherence, and service they had hitherto reserved for their gods. In this process, even within Dravidianism, Tamil was imagined as desired by the gods, and was every now and then deified. So, in his controversial 1945 poem, *Tamiḻiyakkam* (The resurgence of Tamil), Bharatidasan asked whether Tamil, "which is life itself," is not dear to the gods (Bharatidasan 1969: 27). On a more personal note, in his autobiography the poet Mudiyarasan, who identifies himself as an ardent follower of Ramasami and Annadurai, asks, "I consider Tamil as god (*kaṭavuḷ*). How can I be an atheist (*nāttikaṉ*)?" (Mudiyarasan n.d.: 86–87). A similar sentiment undergirds the DMK government's institution of the homage to Tamiḻttāy as the state song in 1970. The government may have announced that it was doing this because the song had no "religious or sectarian associations," an assertion it was able to make because it carefully edited out Sundaram Pillai's original title, *Tamiḻt teyva vaṇakkam,* "Homage to *Goddess* Tamil." Nonetheless, in its official statement (in English), Tamiḻttāy herself is referred to as "goddess of Tamil," and the hymn is characterized as "prayer song."[24]

DRAVIDIANISM AND THE TAMIL FAMILY

Dravidianism did not just have to de-legitimize the "other mother," Bhārata Mātā; it also had to ensure that flesh-and-blood Tamil-speaking mothers themselves did not pose a threat to the absolute devotion and loyalty owed to the sacralized language. This was a very complicated task, for motherhood was the ground on which both Indianism and Dravidianism constituted *tamiḻppaṟṟu*. Indeed, Dravidianism was not content with merely establishing similitude between language and one's mother; more strikingly, it insisted that language *is* that mother:

> When I was a child, you snuggled me and placed me on your lap;
> You placed flowers in my hair, and adorned me, and admired my beauty;
> You are the sweet mother who protected me, in the shade and in the heat;
> O my ancient Tamil! May you live long!
>
> (Ulakanathan 1969: 4)

Similarly, the well-known DMK rhetorician R. Nedunceliyan, who later became a key member of the government, insisted in 1960 that there was no difference between one's mother and Tamil:

> There is *no distinction at all* between our mother who bore us for ten months, gave birth to us, watched over us, sang lullabies to us, and fed us milk and guarded us, and our Tamil language which taught us about good conduct and tradition, and granted us good values and knowledge, and which is the very reason that we live well and in prosperity. We have the same attachment to our language as we have for our mother; we have the same devotion to our language as we have for our mother; we have the same love for our language as we have for our mother. He who disregards his language . . . is like he who disregards his mother and forsakes her.[25]

Dravidianism may have invited speakers of Tamil to imagine it as their mother. At its most dramatic, however, it elevated Tamil to a position of absolute preeminence, even transcending the status and authority of one's birth mother. For instance, the poet Pulavar Kulanthai declared passionately:

> I will never refuse to obey my [own] mother's words;
> But if harm befalls my precious Tami<u>l</u>ttāy,
> I will not fear to set aside my own mother's words.
> I will chop off the head of [Tami<u>l</u>ttāy's] enemy,
> Even if [my] mother prevents me.
>
> (Pulavar Kulanthai 1972: 21)

By extension, this kind of loyalty extended to fellow Tamil speakers as well, as is apparent from Bharatidasan's much-cited declaration: "I will not leave alone the man who scorns the greatness of Tamilians / *Even if [my] mother prevents me*" (Bharatidasan 1958: 5, emphasis mine).

Indeed, Dravidianism even insisted that service to Tamil and to Tami<u>l</u>ttāy should take priority over the Tamilian's family—over spouses, children, and parents. So Perunchitran demanded as late as 1975: "Are the troubles of your own mother more important than the terrible suffering of our glorious Tami<u>l</u>ttāy? / . . . / Are the words of your own mother sweeter than our Tamil language, which is like ambrosia?" (Perunchitranar 1979: 109).

Yet in thus subordinating the family to Tamil, Dravidianism only overtly and consciously articulated a sentiment that was widespread in the devotional community as a whole. As we will see later, in the life stories of individual devotees as these are narrated in memoirs and biographies, their families are typically superseded in favor of devotion to the Tamil cause. The family, which is a primary site for cultivating devotion to the language, is ultimately transcended within the regimes of *tamiḻppaṟṟu*. Such a transcendence is deemed necessary, for not even the family can—or can be allowed to—intervene between the devotee and his language.

THE DMK AND DRAVIDIANIZED TAMIL

Deriving considerable political capital from its self-appointed role as the guardian of Tamil and from demonizing the Congress as an agent of "evil" North Indian interests during the prolonged anti-Hindi protests of the 1950s and 1960s which it spearheaded, the DMK swept the state polls in 1967. Two days after the party's victory was assured, its leading newspaper, *Nam Nāṭu,* carried the headline, "Tamiḻttāy's Desire of Many Years Fulfilled." The *Muracoli*'s front-page cartoon showed Tamiḻttāy, a smile on her face, placing a crown on Annadurai, her "chief son."[26] And it was declared that Tamiḻttāy's victory was the fruit of penances undergone by her followers for Tamil's sake: "In order that Tamiḻttāy be enthroned, in order that Tamiḻttāy should abide with honor, so that Tamiḻttāy may be crowned . . . so many became prey to gunfire, so many drowned in an ocean of red blood, so many martyrs set themselves on fire, so many great ones passed away. This we know. Today, we see Tamil blooming everywhere. You must all go to the Legislative Assembly. You will hear good Tamil there."[27]

The DMK takes great pride that so many of its leaders—Annadurai, Nedunceliyan, and Karunanidhi, among others—have been hailed as great scholars of Tamil and of literature in their own right. So, for many Dravidianists, the DMK's victory finally fulfilled Bharatidasan's dream, voiced years earlier in 1945, that "only the Tamilian who knows Tamil should rule as the chief minister of Tamilnadu" (Bharatidasan 1969: 19).

Regardless of what its opponents may say or statistics may reveal, the DMK has promoted itself as selflessly dedicated to the Tamil cause. Party literature as well as government publications provided details of the measures that it undertook to promote the language: the increasing use of "chaste" and "good" Tamil in administrative and public facilities; the publication of Tamil encyclopedias, scientific manuals, and textbooks; the increasing support of Tamil scholars and Tamil studies both within and outside Tamilnadu; and so on—programs pursued by the Congress government as well to varying degrees. In addition, under the DMK, Hindi was in effect legislated out of state schools in 1968; steps were taken, although not successfully, to introduce Tamil as the exclusive language of higher education and as medium of worship in high Hindu temples; and the state itself was renamed Tamilnadu, "land of Tamil." DMK cultural policy also focused on creating a new literary and historical canon, by drawing upon the findings of *tamiḻppaṟṟu*, especially upon contestatory classicism and Dravidianism. Not surprisingly, the poems of the Caṅkam corpus occupy a hallowed place in this canon, Karunanidhi himself offering a new interpretation in 1987 (Karunanidhi 1987a). Similarly, the *Tirukkuṟaḷ*, the new "scripture" of Dravidianism, is valorized, as is the *Cilappatikāram*, as exemplars of the "secular," "egalitarian," and "chaste" essence of true and pure Tamil culture, free from the influences of Sanskritic Aryan Brahmans with their priestly ways.

Correspondingly, a new pantheon of secular icons surrounding the presiding deity, Tamiḻttāy, has sprung up. It includes Tiruvalluvar, the author of the *Tirukkuṟaḷ*; Kattabomman, who died a martyr's death during the late-eighteenth-century British expansion into South India, and who is considered a paradigmatic symbol of Tamil heroism (Ramaswamy 1994); and Kannagi, the heroine of the *Cilappatikāram*, who is imagined as the ideal Tamil woman, renowned for her chastity and wifely fidelity (J. Pandian 1982). Similarly, Ramasami and Annadurai were lionized for giving Tamil speakers their "self-respect," and many DMK narratives contain laudatory poems on their achievements. And it was under DMK rule that Chinnasami and his fellow devotees who burned themselves alive were immortalized. New mythologies and praise poems on all these figures were written and circulated. Their life stories were narrated and offered as paradigms for Tamil speakers to emulate. Commemorative memorials were set up, and festivals conducted in their honor. In 1968, the government used an academic gathering in Madras, the Second International Conference of Tamil Studies, to treat the populace to a spectacular celebration of Tamil, featuring giant floats of Tamiḻttāy, Tiruvalluvar, and other Tamil icons. The party's leaders must believe that such acts carry symbolic as well as political capital, for as recently as 1984, its election manifesto chose to present its achievements to the electorate in the following terms:

> In order that Tamiḻttāy's jeweled crown should shine,
> We built the historic temple to Valluvar whose fame reaches the very skies;
> And the world-famous new town of Poompukar with its *Cilappatikāram* museum, seven stories high!
> And a fort in the memory of Virapandya Kattabomman at Panjalamkurichi.
> We enabled all these, not just one, not just two, but plenty! plenty!

And yet, as critics as well as supporters of the DMK are quick to ask, have such gestures really helped the cause of Tamil? I quote Sivagnanam, who, despite his recent rapprochement with the DMK, lamented thus:

> A museum commemorating the *Cilappatikāram* and a memorial celebrating Kattabomman have been built. The names of ministers and homes have been changed. Street names have been changed, and so have the names of towns. But Tamil's fortunes have not changed. Formerly, Tamiḻttāy was worshipped three times a day. Today, she is worshipped six times a day. She is worshipped with great pomp and splendor. But the chains that fetter her arms and legs have not been destroyed. . . . Tamil will not grow by changing the names of streets, towns, and gardens.
>
> (Sivagnanam 1978: 269)

DRAVIDIANISM AND ITS DISCONTENTS

And this is a lament that we continue to hear to this day, even after about a century of Tamil devotional activity. Sivagnanam's statement points to a fundamental problem with which the Tamilnadu state has had to contend, especially in the past three decades or so, when it has been under the rule of political parties which are ostensibly dedicated to the Tamil cause. In addition to confronting the crucial issue of which Tamil to promote—"classical" Tamil, "pure" Tamil, the "people's" Tamil, and so on—there has been growing awareness that the socioeconomic and political realities of Tamil's status as a regional language within the linguistic economy of a multilingual nation-state, itself embedded within a larger global environment in which English dominates as the world language, preclude the active implementation of public policies that will ensure the supremacy of Tamil in all spheres at all times, the ideal of Dravidianism (on this, see Tamilkudimagan 1990). Strapped by financial and political constraints, it has been easier for the state to indulge in symbolic activities, such as changing street names and instituting official anthems, rather than to ensure high-quality education in Tamil studies, or to create job opportunities that would convince Tamil speakers that the study of Tamil is a viable end in itself. Tamil's devotees undoubtedly recognize the value of the symbolic act, but Sivagnanam's lament also reminds us that Tamil devotionalism demands much more, especially from a party that claims to be ruling on behalf of Tamiḻttāy. From the start, Dravidianism, like Indianism, placed its hopes in the political process. The establishment of a Tamil state and the Tamilization of the political apparatus, it was proclaimed, would ensure the triumph of Tamil, everywhere and in everything. And yet, this has not happened. This is a tragedy that casts its long shadow not just on Dravidianism, but on the rest of the Tamil devotional community as well.

This has not been the only cross that Dravidianism has had to bear. The Congress's policies caused the increasing disenchantment of devotees of Indianist sentiment and compelled several to embrace Dravidianism. Similarly, the empowerment of the DMK has accompanied the progressive Indianization of the message of Dravidianism, as its radical separatist vision and its credo that Tamil is everything have been progressively diluted in favor of the Tamil community's coexistence with India. Numerous compromises made by the DMK government on linguistic and cultural policies may be cited to support this claim, but perhaps the most illuminating here is the sanitized version of Sundaram Pillai's 1891 hymn that was instituted as the state "prayer song" in 1970.

Of course, the state song is still loyal to Dravidianism's "secular" recasting of Tamiḻtteyvam, "Goddess Tamil," as Tamiḻttāy, "Mother Tamil." The lines from the 1891 hymn that likened Tamiḻttāy to the primordial lord Shiva—which neo-Shaivism kept alive through the next century—are excised, on the grounds that an appropriate prayer song for a modern Tamil community should have no religious or sectarian associations. This significant erasure is not surprising given radical Dravidianism's antagonism to the divinization of Tamil and to Hinduism. And yet, the government order explicitly refers to Tamiḻttāy as the "goddess of Tamil," a slippage that is not accidental. For it indexes the progressive accommodation with religiosity that characterizes DMK cultural policy through the 1950s and 1960s. It also reminds us that within Dravidianism itself, Tamil increasingly took on the mantle of conventional Hindu deities, even as it displaced them.

Next, the recast anthem comes close to compensatory, rather than contestatory, classicism's stance on Tamil, for the government also deliberately excised the much-quoted lines of the original hymn that had referred to Sanskrit as a "dead" language and had declared the superiority of the ever-enduring Tamil (*kaṉṉittamiḻ*). In his reminiscences, Chief Minister Karunanidhi maintains that these lines were not incorporated into the state prayer song because "it is not appropriate to disparage or ridicule other languages, and to use inauspicious words such as 'ruined' or 'dead' in a hymn in praise of Tamiḻttāy to be recited at government functions" (Karunanidhi 1987: 233). Yet, as we have seen, both contestatory classicism and Dravidianism built their arguments on the assumption that Sanskrit was a "dead" language whose very presence had sucked the life out of Tamil.

Finally, Sundaram Pillai's hymn was selected over numerous others precisely because it simultaneously acknowledges the legitimacy of both *tirāviṭa nāṭu* (Dravidian nation) and *paratak kaṇṭam* (Indian nation). Indeed, the government insisted that the state's prayer song would in no way supplant the Indian national anthem: while the former would be sung at the commencement of official functions, the latter—and no other—would be recited at their conclusion. Thus the modern Tamil community—as envisioned by the DMK government in this hymn—has been symbolically framed in terms of its dual "Dravidian" and "Indian" heritages, a position that clearly conforms more closely to the Indianist, rather than to the radical Dravidianist, imagining of Tamil. In what ought to have been Dravidianism's paradigmatic moment of triumph—the institution of a daily celebration of Tamil and Tamiḻttāy by the DMK—it appears as if it is Indianism, and its vision of Tamil as part of the Indian whole, that wins out.

THE MANY FACES OF TAMIL

This chapter has taken its cue from a number of recent studies which claim allegiance to a new area of scholarly inquiry called "language ideology." As the anthropologists Kathryn Woolard and Bambi Schieffelin note, language ideology provides a "much-needed bridge between linguistic and social theory, because it relates the micro-culture of communicative action to political economic considerations of power and social inequality" (Woolard and Schieffelin 1994: 72). My own analysis here has allied itself with one subset of concerns in this burgeoning field in its focus on "ideologies of language," those networks of representations and significations about language which emerge within particular literary, social, political, and religious formations. However natural and timeless they might appear, conceptions about a language among its interested speakers are rarely neutral or innocent; they are produced at specific historical moments, they are generally linked to efforts to create or retain power and control, and they change through time. Such conceptions are "partial, contestable, and contested, and interest-laden": disguising their historicity, they present themselves as eternally true; hiding their cultural specificity, they masquerade as universally valid and commonsensical (Woolard and Schieffelin 1994: 58; see also Joseph and Talbot 1990).

I have suggested that the endowing of Tamil with various extraordinary attributes—divinity (*teyvattaṉmai*), classicality (*uyarttaṉicemmai*), purity (*tūymai*), antiquity (*toṉmai*), motherhood (*tāymai*), and so on—has to be located within larger social and political projects conducted by its numerous devotees. Other languages in other places—Afrikaans, Arabic, English, Hebrew, to name a random few—have been similarly empowered. But few have been studied in any historical depth to reveal the extent of ideological work necessary to transfer them into sites of privilege, potency, and power (for examples of this, see Alter 1994; Ferguson 1968; R. Jones 1953; Roberge 1992). My analysis of such work done on Tamil suggests that although consensus eventually emerges around such certain key contentions, this is a process that is riddled with contradiction and contrariety. The very importance of Tamil for its adherents has meant that there is much at stake in the manner in which it is constituted, and hence its imaginings are subject to many negotiations within the community united in devotion to it. *Tamiḻppaṟṟu* is neither a wholly homogenous nor an entirely consensual activity, because the principal entity at its center is itself not conceived in a singular manner. Instead, Tamil's devotees bring their own varying visions and shifting agendas to bear on their imaginings about their language and its role in their lives. As a consequence, Tamil devotion flourishes as a multifaceted enterprise, fissured by countervailing purposes and contrary passions, as we have seen.

But important questions remain. If the language has been subjected to all these alternate imaginings, as I have suggested, how are its devotees able to mobilize so many of their fellow speakers to rally around it? What is it that led many of them to claim as they did that they lived for its sake, and would die for it? Indeed, what is it that compelled them to speak and write with so much passion and fervor about its state of being—its past glory, its present ignominy, and its future fate? To answer such questions, I turn to the figure of Tamiḻttāy.

Figure 1. "Tamilttāy." Color poster, 1981. Courtesy Professor A. Alagappan, Annamalai University, Chidambaram.

Figure 2. “Tamilttāy.” Color poster, c. 1941. Courtesy Kamban Kazhagam, Karaikkudi.

Figure 3. Tamiḻttāy. Cover of the literary journal *Tamiḻ Vaṭṭam*, 1967. Courtesy Maraimalai Adigal Library, Madras.

हिमालयं समारभ्य यावदिन्दुसरोवरम् ।
तं देवनिर्मितं देशं हिन्दुस्थानं प्रचक्षते ।।
बार्हस्पत्य शास्त्रम्

Figure 4. "Bhārata Mātā." Contemporary picture postcard. Rashtriya Swamsevak Sangh, Karnatak.

Figure 5. "Rajagopalachari Hurls the Knife of Hindi at Tamilttāy." Cartoon, *Viṭutalai,* 18 May 1938. Courtesy Periyar Library, Madras.

Figure 6. "Rajagopalachari's Bravado: The Dishonoring of Tamilttāy." Cartoon, *Kuṭi Aracu,* 19 December 1937. Courtesy Periyar Library, Madras.

Figure 7. Tami<u>l</u>ttāy sheds tears over Chinnasami, Sivalingam, and Aranganathan. Cover of *Muttāram,* 15 March 1966. Courtesy Anna Arivalayam Library, Madras.

Figure 8. Poem on Tamil with drawing of female figure, presumably Tami<u>l</u>ttāy, 1971. Souvenir of second conference of Ulakat Tami<u>l</u>k Ka<u>l</u>akam (World Tamil Association), 1971. Courtesy Professor R. Ilavarasu.

Figure 9. "Tamil̲an̲n̲ai." Official government of Tamilnadu poster, 1987. Tamil Arasu Press, Madras.

Figure 10. Tamiḻttāy in tears. Cartoon, *Muracoli,* 19 January 1965. Courtesy Anna Arivalayam Library, Madras.

Figure 11. Tamiḻttāy. Statue in her temple in Karaikkudi, 1993. Courtesy Kamban Kazhagam, Karaikkudi.

Figure 12. Tami<u>l</u>ttāy's temple, Karaikkudi. Photograph, 1993. Courtesy Kamban Kazhagam, Karaikkudi.

CHAPTER THREE

Feminizing Language

Tamil as Goddess, Mother, Maiden

Tamil's devotees do not merely relate to it as their language. They are able to breathe so much life and inject so much passion into practicing *tamil̠ppar̠r̠u* because Tamil to them is more than an intangible abstraction. Instead, embodied in the figure of Tamil̠ttāy, it is a near and dear being—their personal goddess, their devoted mother, even their beloved lover—who commands their veneration and adulation, and deserves their love and loyalty. Yet, like the language she embodies, Tamil̠ttāy appears differently to different devotees at different moments in their lives, and is thus variously represented as *teyvam,* "goddess"; *tāy,* "mother"; and *kan̠n̠i,* "virgin maiden." Consequently, she does not have a singular persona. Indeed, this is how Tamil devotion, fundamentally a network of patriarchal discourses conducted largely by men, solves the "problem" of having a female figure enshrined at the very heart of its enterprise. She is first isolated and abstracted from the "real" world in which Tamil-speaking women of all shades have been disempowered through much of this century; she is then endowed with a plenitude of powers and possibilities which transform her into a strikingly exceptional Woman, not readily confused with the flesh-and-blood women on whom she is also obviously modelled. Though she may be thus empowered, her potential to exceed the control of her (male) creators is contained through her fragmentation. The plethora of multiple personae that she is endowed with works to prevent her consolidation as a threatening, all-powerful being, even as it simultaneously opens up the possibility that her various selves may be deployed in contradictory ways for the different projects of her devotees.[1] Tamiḻttāy thus is yet another classic example of the objectification of woman as a thing "to be appropriated, possessed, and exchanged in the social relations of cooperation and competition among men" (Uberoi 1990: 41). Although we will see later that some Tamil-speaking women have their own way with her, Tamiḻttāy, like other exemplary female icons, is far from cutting a feminist figure in her guise as tame goddess, benevolent mother, and pure virgin. Visible and valorized she may be, but she is very much a figment of the patriarchal imaginations of modernity in colonial and post-colonial India.

THE POETICS AND POLITICS OF PRAISE

The founding narrative which popularized the habit of imagining Tamil as goddess, mother, and maiden is P. Sundaram Pillai's 1891 hymn, "Tamiḻt teyva vaṇakkam," "Homage to Goddess Tamil." Sundaram Pillai, of course, occupies a hallowed niche in the pantheon of *tamiḻppaṟṟu* as a truly loyal son of Tamiḻttāy. As his fellow devotees exclaim, was it not remarkable that although he lived all his life in Kerala, a non-Tamil-speaking region, he confessed to Tamiḻttāy, "I may reside in [the land of] Malayalam, but I think of [only] you as my mother" (Sundaram Pillai 1922: 23)? Born in 1855 in Allepey into a middle-income Vellala family of traders, Sundaram Pillai had a master's degree in philosophy. Aside from a brief bureaucratic stint as commissioner of separate revenues for Travancore (1882–85), he taught history and philosophy at the Maharaja's College in Trivandrum until his death in 1897. His historical researches on Tamil literature secured for him membership in the Royal Asiatic Society and the coveted title of Rao Bahadur from the colonial state (Pillai et al. 1957).

In writing his hymn on Tamiḻttāy, Sundaram Pillai took great care in locating it within a prior Shaiva tradition of deifying Tamil (Sundaram Pillai 1922: 9; Kailasapathy 1970: 102–9). Like his seventeenth-century predecessor, Karunaiprakasar, he refers to Tamil as deity and even boldly establishes a parity between the mighty Shiva and his Tamiḻtteyvam, both of whom are deemed "primordial," "everlasting," and "boundless." Nonetheless, Sundaram Pillai was indeed inaugurating a new sensibility when he explicitly feminized Tamil as goddess, mother, and maiden. Aside from a few verses, the feminization of the language was quite underdeveloped prior to his hymn, but since then it has gained an immense following. Furthermore, large numbers of subsequent poets, especially those influenced by the Dravidian movement, have abandoned the conventional practice of beginning their works by calling upon the traditional Hindu deities to shower their benedictions on them. Instead, they more typically appeal to Tamiḻttāy as their sole muse and guardian deity (Kailasapathy 1970). In doing so, they broadcast their allegiance to the Tamil cause and secure membership for themselves in the Tamil devotional community, even as they elevate the language to a status commensurate with that of the gods.

Equally striking, since Sundaram Pillai's time many devotees have not just been content with short invocatory verses on Tamiḻttāy; instead they have also produced long and elaborate praise poems on her, many of which have been—and continue to be—published in literary journals and popular newspapers, or printed in anthologies (e.g., Nagarajan 1980; Somasundara Pulavar n.d.; Velayutam Pillai 1971). Indeed, praise poetry is one of the principal technologies through which devotion to Tamiḻttāy is produced and circulated. For while there are a number of devout prose writings in which Tamiḻttāy figures, it is praise poetry written in Tamil that is her favored niche.

Praise poetry has a long history in the literary cultures of the region, and it may be traced back through the devotional verses of the second millennium to the royal panegyrics of the ancient Caṅkam corpus. Most such praise poems focused on deities, sovereigns, and spiritual notables, although occasionally other subjects of praise, like Tamil itself, materialized (Krishnan 1984; Ramaswamy 1996). As literary practice, praise poems enabled poets to articulate sentiments of love and adulation for their chosen subjects, to recount the salvific powers and glorious actions of the deity or the sovereign, to dwell lovingly upon his or her beautiful form and appearance, and the like. Many conventional genres of praise—such as the *tirupaḷḷiyeḻucci,* the *tirutacāṅkam,* the *piḷḷaittamiḻ,* the *tūtu,* and so on—have been extremely productive over the centuries, offering standardized templates that a poet could readily deploy in the praise of a chosen subject or patron (Zvelebil 1974: 193–219).

Remarkably, such genres, which were predominantly reserved for deities or sovereigns in the premodern praise literature, are used from the early decades of this century to laud Tamil. Thus, there are many examples of *Tamiḻttāy paḷḷiyeḻucci,* "the awakening of Tamiḻttāy from sleep"; *Tamiḻttāy tirutacāṅkam,* "the ten constituents of [the kingdom of] Tamiḻttāy"; and of *Tamiḻttāyppiḷḷaitamiḻ,* "Tamiḻttāy as extraordinary child." There are innumerable versions of *Tamiḻttāymālai,* "garland of Tamiḻttāy"; at least two poems written in the ancient *āṟṟuppaṭai,*

"guide," genre in which poets direct their fellow speakers to the presence of a glorious and bountiful Tamiḻttāy whom they had forgotten;
and two poems featuring Tamil as messenger, *tūtu* (Amirtham Pillai
1906; Arangasami [1977]; Parantama Mudaliar 1926; Somasundara
Pulavar n.d.: 8–10, 35–43; Sundara Shanmugan 1951; Velayutam Pillai
1971: 56–61, 83–84; Pekan 1986). Additionally, popular and folk
genres such as the *kuṟavañci* and the *villuppāṭṭu* have also been appropriated in narratives such as the *Tamiḻaracikkuṟavañci* (The fortune-
teller song on Queen Tamil) and *Tamiḻ Vaḻarnta Katai* (The story of
Tamil's growth) (Navanitakrishnan 1952; Varadananjaiya Pillai
[1938]). At the very least, all this suggests the energy with which modern devotees of Tamil have colonized high as well as popular forms,
so that a space may be cleared for their chosen one among the more
conventional objects of adulation in the Tamil life-world. Through the
deployment of such poetic genres and praise strategies, they have endowed their language with the powers and charisma that have gathered
around gods, sovereigns, and notables over the centuries—the right to
command allegiance, demand loyalty, and mobilize followers. In turn,
her devotees are encouraged to relate to Tamiḻttāy as they have inter-
acted with these figures—with a mixture of adulation, reverence, and
deep love.

Praise, Arjun Appadurai suggests, is a "regulated, improvisatory
practice" that creates a "community of sentiment involving the emotional participation of the praiser, the one who is praised, and the audience of that act of praise" (A. Appadurai 1990: 94). The praise poem
on Tamiḻttāy personalizes the language, presenting it to its devotee as a
tangible being who is familiar, even intimate—a personal god, patron-
sovereign, guardian muse, object of desire, and increasingly, mother
figure. The praise poem also knits together the language and its devotees
into a community of adulation and worship, each act of praise allowing
them an opportunity to dwell lovingly upon the wonders and powers
of their beloved Tamil. Finally, the praise poem allows its authors to
renew their faith in themselves and in each other as devotees of Tamiḻttāy. The praise of Tamiḻttāy through poetry thus is more than just a
literary or political gesture, signifying one's adherence to Tamil; it is,
also, crucially, a *ritual* act through which *tamiḻppaṟṟu* is continually
renewed and reaffirmed. It is therefore not surprising that many such
praise poems, particularly by hallowed devotees such as Sundaram Pillai, Subramania Bharati, or Bharatidasan, are recited over and over

again in devotional circles, especially at times that call for a heightened demonstration of piety and loyalty.

All this is not to say that poetry is the only form of expression in Tamil devotion. Certainly, its devotees wrote a great deal about Tamil in prose, especially on matters relating to language and cultural policy, on the promotion of Tamil in education, government, and public activities, and so on. In such prose narratives, however, especially when they were written in English, it is comparatively rare to find Tami<u>l</u>ttāy. Instead, Tamil generally appears in prose as a nonpersonified language—not as an animate being, as it frequently does in its poetry. This in itself is perhaps not surprising, for prose narratives on Tamil were often produced for the consumption of the state, in the process of petitioning the government for various favors. In contrast, poetry on Tami<u>l</u>ttāy is typically generated for the consumption of its speakers. Indeed, especially in the colonial period, the state appears to have been remarkably disinterested in this whole sphere of activity that was so prolific and widespread among Tamil's devout. So the striking dependence on poetic discourse in Tamil devotional circles was more than just a literary habit, dictated by the norms of a culture in which poetry, rather than prose, was until fairly recently the privileged mode of literary expression. Rather, the recourse to Tamil poetry was also a strategic practice through which its devotees expressed and constituted their devotion to their language through a medium (Tamil) that is considered their very "own," through a form (poetry) that is deemed authentically and deeply "Tamil," and through forums (such as community-based literary and revivalist activities) that were outside the interests of the state. Poetry made possible intimate, even veiled, discourse about the language, allowing participation only to those who were familiar with its imagery, meters, rhetorical nuances, and so on. Thus poetry enabled Tamil's devout to practice what I would characterize as "intimate politics" in which affect and passion were deployed to establish the boundaries of a community united in devotion to the language.

And yet, although poetry had been the preferred mode of precolonial literary work, with the onset of modernity and its privileging of prose as rational, objective, and scientific, poets were increasingly pushed to the margins of social prestige and economic well-being in many parts of colonial India, and certainly in the Tamil-speaking region. Paradoxically, this itself may account for poetry's popularity as a discursive form among Tamil's devotees. Because prose, especially prose in English, was so closely associated with the existing power structures, poetry, I suggest, emerged as the favored form for the disenfranchised and the disempowered. Concomitantly, poetry also presents itself as a form of expression for those who want to oppose the existing system and the dominant ideology. In her marvellous ethnography on the ideology of poetry in Bedouin society, Lila Abu-Lughod suggests as much and notes that among the Bedouins, "poetry is, in so many ways, the discourse of opposition to the system[,] . . . [a] symbol of defiance" (1986: 233–59). I appropriate her suggestion, applying it as well to the production of poetry by *tamiḻpparṟu,* which has clearly been a discourse of opposition conducted around sentiments of decline, loss, and disempowerment. On the one hand, poetry is widely believed to encapsulate the best of Tamil's literary tradition; it is associated with the Tamil past, especially the past of the ancient Caṅkam age when poets, we are repeatedly told, commanded even kings. Poetry, it is nostalgically believed, is a deeply and authentically Tamil form. On the other hand, at least in the past century or so, its very subordination to prose within the regimes of colonial modernity meant that it emerged not just as a means but as a site of resistance to dominant ideologies, as well as to the new literary and linguistic forms that threatened what was perceived as authentically Tamil. For all these reasons, when Tamil's devotees want to write most passionately, intimately, and fiercely about their language, they turn to poetry.

In the praise poetry on Tamil and Tamiḻttāy since the time of Sundaram Pillai, there is no singular conception of *paṟṟu,* "devotion," that reigns. Instead, like the language and like Tamiḻttāy, devotion, too, is multifaceted, and here I examine three of its modalities. In what I wish to call its "pietistic" mode, it is Tamiḻttāy's persona as *teyvam,* "goddess," that is foregrounded, and the devotee casts himself as a pious worshipper. The predominant sentiment of this modality is reverence for a divine being, the relationship between the language and its *pious* devotee modelled on the ritual relationship between an omniscient goddess and her subordinate worshipper. I characterize the second of the modalities as the "somatics of devotion." Here, the emphasis is on Tamiḻttāy's persona as *tāy,* the "mother" of her devotees, who correspondingly cast themselves as her "children." In this modality, the relationship between the language and its *filial* devotee is biological and corporeal, modelled on the genealogical and familial bonds that tie a mother to her child. Here, devotion takes on a distinctly filial flavor, predominantly expressed in the domestic idiom of the family and the home. And then, there is a third modality that I characterize as the "erotics of devotion." Here, it is Tami̱ttāy's persona as woman that is highlighted, the devotee casting himself as a desiring man. In this modality, the relationship between the language and its *desiring* devotee is charged with eroticism, although Tami̱ttāy's status as *kaṉṉi,* "virgin maiden," obviously complicates an already ambivalent situation. I have analytically distinguished these modalities of devotion (pietistics, somatics, and erotics), these three aspects of the devotee (pious, filial, and desiring), and these three personae of Tami̱ttāy (goddess, mother, and maiden). But in much of the discourse of *tamiḻppaṟṟu,* they are all quite intertwined, making Tamil devotion a very fraught and complicated affair indeed.

TAMIL AS DEITY: PIETISTICS OF TAMIL DEVOTION

In Sundaram Pillai's founding hymn, Tami̱ttāy figures prominently as a goddess, variously invoked as *teyvam, aṇaṅku,* and *tāy.*[2] Poems featuring Tami̱ttāy as deity are generally more frequent in the religious and Indianist regimes of *tamiḻppaṟṟu* (Bharati 1988: 117; Ramalinga Pillai 1988: 19, 474; Velayutam Pillai 1971), although many a Dravidianist poet who vigorously challenged the divinization of the language also occasionally slipped into this imagery. Consider a poem by Mudiyarasan entitled "Tamiḻ Eṉ Teyvam" (Tamil is my deity). A dedicated Dravidianist, the poet consciously distances himself from religiosity in his personal reminiscences, but he did not hesitate to write about Tamil thus:

> Residing in my heart that is your temple (*kōvil*), offer me grace;
> Adorned in your garland of poetry, offer me protection;
> Resting on my tongue, grant me good sense;
> In verse and word, I will be strong.
> . . . .
> I worship you every day and talk about your fame everywhere;
> The world deems me a mad fellow (*pittaṉ*), a fanatic (*veṟiyaṉ*);
> Don't you see?
>
> (Mudiyarasan 1976: 27–28)

There are clear resonances here with the rhetorical modes and vocabulary of (Hindu) religiosity, so that even in a poem produced under the ideological mantle of the Dravidian movement, the relation between the language and its devotee is one of divine piety and reverence.

In this modality, Tamiḻttāy may be a goddess, but she is not imagined as a transcendent remote divine being. Instead, true to the spirit of the devotional, *bhakti* Hinduism of the region, she is an immanent figure who is intimately and personally connected with the lives of her devotees. Indeed, one of the most striking features of the pietistics of *tamiḻppaṟṟu* is the immediacy of bonds between the goddess and her worshippers; the truly devout can not only feel her presence, they can also see her, even touch her. Further, as in *bhakti* Hinduism, she is not only god to her pious devotee, but she is also his parent, guide, sovereign, friend, lover, and child. At different moments in his life as her pious worshipper, she may manifest herself to him in these various roles. As such a worshipper, Navaliyur Somasundara Pulavar (1878?–1953), a Tamil teacher at the Vattukottai school in Jaffna, Sri Lanka, declared:

> Like [our] mother, she gives us food;
> Like [our] father, she gives us learning;
> Like our wife, she creates pleasure at home;
> Like our child, she gives sweet words pleasant to our ears.
> (Velayutam Pillai 1971: 86)

This multiplicity in her persona as *teyvam* notwithstanding, Tamiḻttāy is above all a personal god, and the pious devotee relates to her on those terms. When he contemplates her, he does so oblivious to the presence of any other deity or being. Many praise poems are replete with references to actions (*vaṇaṅkutal, parāvutal, pōṟṟutal*) that are typically used in the reverencing of Hindu divinities: "so that we may attain well-being, let us place on our head the flowerlike feet of our youthful goddess Tamil (*paintamiḻtēvi*)," or "let us bow at the feet of our ancient goddess Tamil" (Velayutam Pillai 1971: 34–35). Tantalizing as these utterances may be in indexing an attitude of worshipfulness, it is not clear if the pious devotee actually offered *pūja*, that paradigmatic Hindu act of divine worship, to his goddess Tamil, thus casting into doubt whether Tamiḻttāy, even in her overtly divine manifestation, is ever treated unambiguously as a Hindu divinity within *tamiḻppaṟṟu*.

Crucial to the pietistics of devotion is the deliberate adoption of strategies of archaization and "subterfuges of antiquity" (Kaviraj 1993: 13). Although there are certainly ancient precedents to her present incarnation, Tamiḻttāy is clearly a modern creation, not older than a century or so. But this is not what her pious devotee maintains. He claims that like the language she embodies, Tamiḻttāy is a primeval deity. And the poems about her only support such a claim, so striking a throwback are they to ancient literary forms of veneration and adoration in the baroque motifs they use, their aesthetic structure, and their rhetorics. Through such strategies of archaization, her pious follower certainly establishes his own literary reputation as a skilled, learned poet; but just as crucially, he bestows a halo of venerable and formidable antiquity upon Tamiḻttāy herself. And in a culture where the aura of primordiality carries with it a power that is as immense as it is intangible, this itself contributes towards the power of the goddess.

TAMIḺTTEYVAM: PORTRAIT OF A GODDESS

So what are the various ways in which Tamiḻttāy has been constituted as primeval deity, the beloved of the gods, and the most bountiful of all beings?

"You were there, even before the mighty Himalayas emerged, and Kumari Nadu submerged!" A fundamental strategy for establishing the antiquity of Tamiḻttāy is by placing her in the company of the gods, as their companion, confidante, and friend. For some of her pious following, she, like the gods themselves, has no beginning. Sundaram Pillai hinted at this by comparing her with the primordial Shiva. Somasundara Bharati, too, referred to her as *mutalilaḷōr,* "one who has no beginning," and *mūppumilaḷ,* "she who is ageless" (Velayutam Pillai 1971: 23). Abstracted from the vagaries and contingencies of secular time, Tamiḻttāy thus lives in cosmic time. Yet, being a modern himself and very much aware of the power of historical memories, the pious devotee also links her to ancient historical personages of the Tamil-speaking countryside. So he fashions for her a biography assembled from stories and legends of the Shaiva canon and from the newly emerging "facts" of ancient Tamil history. Tamiḻttāy was created by Shiva (sometimes with the aid of the goddess Earth, but at other times single-handedly), and delivered to the world (through the intervention of that paradigmatic Tamil god, Murugan, in some versions) by the mythical sage Agastya. From his abode in the Potiyam mountains (in the Western Ghats), Agastya adorned her with her very first "jewel," the legendary grammar called *Akattiyam.* Subsequently, she matured as a child in the antediluvian academies of the Pandyan kingdom, which flourished under the benevolent patronage of Shiva himself. She slowly moved out of cosmic time into history as she came of age in the last of the academies in Madurai, proudly fostered by the "triumvirate" (*mūvēntar*), the famed

Pandya, Chera, and Chola kings celebrated in the Caṅkam poems. From then on, as an ever-virginal maiden, she enjoyed the patronage of various Tamil rulers. During this time, she was gifted with some more spectacular "ornaments" which adorn her body—the five great epic poems (*pañcakāviyam*), the *Tirukkuṟaḷ*, the *Tiruvācakam*, and so on. This is, of course, a biography with no end, for, being a deity, she has no end.

"There is no one like you! This is indeed the truth" Not only is Tamiḻttāy the most ancient and primordial of all beings, she is also incomparable. "O goddess Tamil! There is no other deity like you," declared Somasundara Pulavar (Velayutam Pillai 1971: 87). Incomparable she may be, but the pious devotee does invoke her likeness to the five elements (fire, water, earth, air, and ether), to the everlasting *karpaka* tree, to the sun and the moon, and so on. He also compares her to tasty fruits, beautiful flowers, and flavorful foods. So, Tamiḻttāy is hailed as "the sea of ambrosia," as "the golden creeper, ripe with sweetness," as one "who shames the sweet sugarcane." In early medieval religious poetry where gods are routinely praised thus, it has been suggested that such visual and taste-oriented metaphors exemplify the devotee's intimate sensory experience of the divine presence (Cutler 1987: 199). This may also be true for Tamil's pious devotee, who yearns to capture Tamiḻttāy's wondrous qualities and present these to his fellow speakers in terms both familiar and desirable. But more often than not, he declares helplessly that words are inadequate to capture her greatness, her fame, and her beauty. "O mother, who will find it easy to talk about all your excellent virtues?" asked A. Venkatachalam Pillai (1888?–1953), chief poet of the Karanthai Tamil Sangam and first editor of its *Tamiḻp Poḻil*. And Thudisaikizhar Chidambaram (1883–1954), who worked for a while in the colonial police service, a job he gave up to dedicate himself to Shaiva revivalism, wondered plaintively, "Is it even possible for someone like me to sing your greatness?" (Velayutam Pillai 1971: 11, 66).

"She encircles the resounding world" Flourishing as she has from remote antiquity, Tamiḻttāy is also sovereign of the world, and of all the peoples who live in it, and of all the languages they speak. For had she not preceded all of them, and indeed, was she not responsible for their creation? So, the eight cardinal directions echo to the sound of her victorious drums and the songs of her fame (Velayutam Pillai 1971: 78–

80). In picture posters produced by organizations like Kampan̲ Kaḻakam in Karaikkudi (henceforth Kamban Kazhagam) and by notables in Annamalainagar, as well as on the covers of magazines like *Tamiḻ Vaṭṭam* (1967), Tamiḻttāy thus appears seated on a globe, her "throne" (figs. 1–3). From early in the century, *tamiḻppaṟṟu* had claimed that since Tamiḻttāy had formerly ruled the world, there was little doubt that she would reign supreme, once again, in the future. For her devotees seeking to mobilize their fellow speakers around the cause of Tamiḻttāy, such an imagining of Tamil as an ecumenical language of the world served to keep alive the aura of its ancient sovereignty in an age of disenchantment and decline.

"You are sovereign of the fine Tamil world" In the spirit of divine and kingly cultures of the region in which gods are kinglike, and sovereigns are godlike, Tamiḻtteyvam is also imagined as Tamiḻ Araci, the queen of the fine Tamil world (*naṟtamiḻulakam*), the empress of the entire Dravidian land (Vedanayakam Pillai 1879: 285). Poems composed in the *tirutacāṅkam* (the auspicious ten limbs) genre enumerate the ten "royal limbs" of her kingdom—her sovereign title, land, capital city, river, mountain, vehicle, army, drum, garland, and banner. Tamiḻttāy's "army" is the might of her poetry; her "royal mount," the tongue(s) of her glorious poet(s). The three branches of Tamil—literature (*iyal*), music (*icai*), and drama (*nāṭakam*)—make up her "royal drum"; she wears Tamil poems around her neck as her victorious "garland"; her "royal banner," appropriately enough, is the flag of knowledge made up of all the goodness of the incomparable Tamil; and so on (Velayutam Pillai 1971: 83–84). Yet Tamiḻttāy is clearly conceived by her admirers to be more than a goddess of learning and knowledge. The Herderian notion circulated through colonial knowledges, that language provides the legitimate foundation for distinctive nation-states, is enrolled into her constitution as a goddess of polity as well, as a queen who rules over the Tamil land and community. Most typically, Tamiḻttāy's "kingdom" extends from the Venkatam (Tirupati) hills in the north, to Cape Kumari in the south, and from coast to coast, the traditional *tamiḻakam* (Tamil home) of the ancient Caṅkam poems. Some devotees, especially of contestatory classicist inclination, were more ambitious and maintained that she was queen of all of India. Thus in the Kamban Kazhagam poster (fig. 2) as well as in the frontispiece of the 1947 edition of Velayutam Pillai's anthology, *Moḻiyaraci* (Queen of languages), Tamiḻttāy is seated on a map of (prepartition) India. In such visuals, she clearly

challenges the authority of Bhārata Mātā, who is generically shown standing on a map of India with her arms stretched out to encompass the east and the west, her head in the Himalayas, her feet resting in the South (fig. 4). For contestatory regimes of *tamiḻppaṟṟu,* it is Tamiḻttāy, however, who should legitimately occupy the land now appropriated for Bhārata Mātā.

At the same time, her pious devotee also takes care to establish Tamiḻttāy's intimate connections with the Tamil-speaking landscape. So, rivers like the Tamaraparani and the Kaveri are imagined as ornaments that snake their way across her body; the two mountain ranges (Western and Eastern Ghats) are visualized as her arms; the cool and fragrant southern breeze (*teṉṟal*) is likened to her sweet breath; and so on. A sacred geography thus emerges around her persona: Potiyam, the mountain home of the sage, Agastya, is hallowed as her "birth" place; Madurai, that seat of Tamil learning, is where she reigned as queen; the Vaigai River is where she performed many of her miracles that demonstrated her supernatural powers; and so on. Like Tamil itself, the land where it is spoken and over which Tamiḻttāy rules is sacred as well (Velayutam Pillai 1971: 73–98).

"You are knowledge itself" Her pious devotee also insists that Tamiḻttāy's "kingdom" is not just the earthly spread of the Tamil land (or India, or the whole wide world). Instead, she is queen of something even more superior, the kingdom of knowledge. In the words of R. Raghava Aiyangar, a leading member of the Madurai Tamil Sangam and the first editor of its journal, *Centamiḻ:*

> O sweet Tamiḻttāy! May you flourish forever here and offer grace to your devotees!
> You produced the poetry of Kapilar and other poets of the good academy in the southern land.
> You fed the world with the *Kuṟaḷ* of Valluvar.
> You destroyed darkness with mighty Kamban.
> . . . .
> You stand as source of all learning.
> . . . .
> You caused learning to grow among women.
> . . . .
> You created scholars to nourish our minds.
> . . . .
> O fine Tamiḻttāy! Look at all you have accomplished!
>
> (Velayutam Pillai 1971: 41–42)

The world's best knowledge, of course, is in Tamil; its poets are the finest, and so is its literature. The more contestatory devotee insists that Tami<u>l</u>ttāy's learned productions are far superior to anything that other languages, especially Sanskrit, can offer. Sundaram Pillai himself set the tone in his paradigmatic 1891 hymn when he asked polemically why should the (Sanskritic) *Manusmṛti,* which advocated a different norm for each caste, be forced upon Tamil speakers when they have their own *Tirukkuṟaḷ?* Why do we need the *Veda* when we have the *Tiruvācakam,* which melts the stoniest of hearts (Sundaram Pillai 1922: 22–23)? Since his time, of course, others have continued to declare that their Tamiḻttāy's auspicious words are more glorious than the words of the *Veda,* the *Vedānta,* the *Bhagavad Gītā,* and other such hallowed texts of Sanskritic Hinduism.

For the less contestatory devotee, however, Tamiḻttāy appears to have been a Saraswati-like figure. Indeed, that paradigmatic Sanskritic goddess of learning and wisdom is sometimes portrayed as Tamiḻttāy's friend, who commands poets to sing to her in Tamil so that she, too, may enjoy that wondrous language (Velayutam Pillai 1971: 89). At other times, Tamiḻttāy is herself referred to as *kalaimakaḷ* (= Saraswati), and in many a visual and iconographic representation, the similarity between the two goddesses is quite striking. Given the antagonism towards Sanskritic Hinduism that characterizes so many of the regimes of *tamiḻppaṟṟu,* Tamiḻttāy thus appears to displace Saraswati in the affections of many a pious devotee. As such, she, and not Saraswati, was the fount of all learning, the mother of all languages, and the inspiring muse for scholar and devotee alike.

"She is the goddess who commands the gods who guard us" Nothing more clearly suggests the desire of her pious devotee to move Tamiḻttāy into the space occupied by his traditional gods than the many verses in which she is credited with performing various miraculous deeds conventionally attributed to Shiva, Vishnu, and other deities of the Hindu pantheon. So Chidambaram declared that Tamiḻttāy, too, performed the three cosmic deeds of creation, maintenance, and destruction for which Shiva is famed (Velayutam Pillai 1971: 66). C. Venkatarama Chettiyar (b. 1913), who taught Tamil at Annamalai University, wrote that the three branches of Tamil embodied "this precious world which was formerly spanned by the three steps of that lofty Lord of Lakshmi [Vishnu]" (Velayutam Pillai 1971: 44). That her pious devotee could go

to great lengths to make such claims is clear from a long poem in which Chidambaram addresses Tamiḻttāy:

> You dispatched the Lord of all devotees as messenger!
> . . . .
> Is there anything more to be said of your greatness?
> . . . .
> You transformed poison into ambrosia!
> You made the rock thrown into the ocean to float as a raft!
> You coaxed the murderous elephant to bow down to that great devotee!
> You transformed a mere pile of bones into a woman!
> . . . .
> You caused palm-leaf manuscripts to float on the floodwaters! you protected
>   them from being scorched by the worst of fires!
> . . . .
> You opened the doors [of the temple] of Tirumaraikadu!
> You cured the hunched back of the great Pandyan!
> You taught the heretical Jains to learn the wonders of the great Shiva!
> . . . .
> My! My! What greatness! What wonder!
>
> (Velayutam Pillai 1971: 66–67)

These lines may sound arcane and esoteric, but they remind us, once again, that the power of Tamiḻttāy in this modality is constituted by deliberately archaizing her, by placing her in another time, in a world of mysterious but wondrous acts and beings. They also confirm what every pious devotee would like to hear, that his goddess would do anything for those who were devoted to her—quench the anger of a murderous elephant who was threatening to kill one of her adorers, cure the chronic fever of another, even play the role of a lowly messenger so that the love life of one of her worshippers would thrive. Indeed, this is a fundamental aspect of the structure of piety that is constituted around the divine Tamiḻttāy: in return for services rendered to her by her devotees, she would protect them, grant them miraculous favors, and shower wealth and grace on them. In short, she would do anything for those who were truly her adoring dependents.

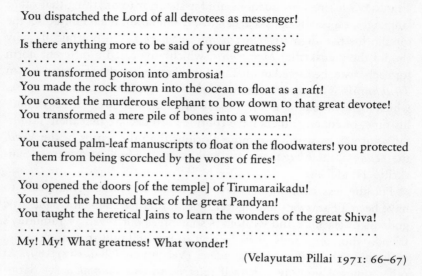

But most crucially, these lines recall incidents from the life stories of famous devotees of Shiva in which the latter tests the devotion of his followers to punish those who were cruel to them, to reveal to them his compassion, and to grant eternal bliss to his truly devout (Peterson 1989). And yet, these same incidents are invoked in the modern discourses of *tamiḻpparru* with a significant, even cosmic, difference. For here, Tami<u>l</u>ttāy is the inspiring force behind Shiva's activities, the true author of these wondrous deeds, and the paradigmatic savior of the world.

"The supreme one who has no beginning and no end, ardently desires you" Although her pious devout, especially orthodox Shaivites, are careful to not let Tami<u>l</u>ttāy's powers overtly challenge Shiva's, some of them do not hesitate to point out that not only Shiva but also Vishnu and the other gods are at her bidding, enthralled as they are by her beauty, virtue, and learning. They declared that "in order to see [her], the lord Vishnu himself, with the northern *Veda*s in tow, followed [her]," and they reminded each other that Shiva's cosmic weariness flees when Tamil sounds fill his divine ears with pleasure. Shiva may be Tami<u>l</u>ttāy's father-creator, but that great lord may also desire her. So filled was he with longing to hear her words that he left his celestial abode and came down to earth to preside over the Tamil academy of Madurai. So eager was he to have her near him that he ordered the recital of Tamil hymns every day, not finding comfort in the Sanskrit *Veda*s (Velayutam Pillai 1971: 4–6, 66–68, 108–15).

Because she is the beloved of the gods, her pious devotee calls upon the more established divinities to protect her, or prays to them to grant grace so that he himself could serve her better. Thus the opening invocatory verse to the *Mo<u>l</u>iyaraci* anthology declares, "I pray to Murugan who dwells in the grove, so that I may be born in the Tamil land where words flourish." The pietistics of *tami<u>l</u>ppa<u>rr</u>u* thus appears to have a curious contradiction. On the one hand, her pious adorer imagines Tami<u>l</u>ttāy as a supreme, omniscient being who is not just the beloved of the gods, but even commands them and inspires them to perform their various godly deeds. On the other hand, because many who participated in this modality were also for the most part quite religious themselves, they never do totally abandon their faith in the established gods of the Hindu pantheon. Instead, they continue to pray to them so that their own personal goddess, Tami<u>l</u>ttāy, may also benefit from the good will of those great beings.

"I am your devotee; you are my refuge" For the pious devotee for whom she is his personal deity, Tami<u>l</u>ttāy is the source of everything in this world—of knowledge and happiness, of wealth and prosperity, of bliss and light, indeed of life itself. She is the destroyer of darkness and

of false illusions. She cures her followers of anger and jealousy, and grants them true vision. She cures them of afflictions and weeds out their troubles. At her feet, even the worst sinners find salvation. By her very presence, she destroys the sins of her devotees. She is indeed their ultimate refuge. A. Kantasami Pillai (1885–1969), a professor of Tamil, declared:

> O Tamiḻttāy, may you flourish blissfully as a sovereign queen!
> You gave birth to us, and embracing us, fed us nectar from your beautiful breasts;
> You taught us to speak as infants, and also the full meaning of numerous words;
> You caused our evil habits to flee, and firmly established in their stead good conduct that is dearer than life and fame. . . .
> You taught us to respect ourselves, and teaching us about the experiences of the past and the present,
> You have shown us the road to eternal release!
>
> (Velayutam Pillai 1971: 4)

Similarly, R. Raghava Aiyangar wrote eloquently that "with the help of [your] divine ladder of priceless books, we can climb straight up to the heavens" (Velayutam Pillai 1971: 41). Even more dramatically, for Somasundara Pulavar there was only one cure for the endless disease that is life, and it lay at the feet of his noble Tamiḻttāy (Velayutam Pillai 1971: 93). The pious devotee is indeed convinced that Tamiḻttāy may be the most omniscient of gods, and the most powerful of sovereigns, but she has the compassion and the tenderness of one's own mother. She therefore never forsakes even the most humble and most lowly of her adherents. She is infinitely forgiving—even overlooking the faults of those who turned their backs on her, so benevolent and compassionate a being is she (Velayutam Pillai 1971: 12). There is little doubt, therefore, as A. Varadananjaiya Pillai (1877–1956), a member of the Karanthai Tamil Sangam and author of several praise works on Tamiḻttāy, insisted, that it was she who was going to abide with them for ever and ever, even accompanying them to the world beyond the present one (Velayutam Pillai 1971: 26–28).

Tamiḻttāy is thus both the means to their salvation and salvation itself. By constituting her in such terms, these pious devotees were only expressing in religious terms the foundational message of *tamiḻppaṟṟu* that Tamil is everything to its speakers—their body, their life, their spirit, and, ultimately, their soul itself.

PROFILING THE PIOUS DEVOTEE

So, who are the true adorers of Tamil? For this modality, they are those who think of Tami̲ttāy as their *teyvam* and have faith and confidence in her divinity, her compassion, and her supreme abilities. The pious devotee chastises his fellow speakers for failing to reverence Tami̲ttāy, or for ridiculing and scorning her. "There are base people who do not know about the depth of your excellence! Grant me grace, so that I do not become one of them." Because her detractors' minds were filled with confusion, they say harsh things about her. "What indeed is the worth of their knowledge?" her adorers demanded (Velayutam Pillai 1971: 61–62).

Since her pious devotee believes that Tami̲ttāy is an omniscient being, the source of his life and wisdom, and his ultimate refuge, he is also convinced that his salvation, and that of his fellow Tamilians, lies in securing her grace (*aruḷ*). Her *aruḷ* would cure Tamil speakers of laziness and sloth, and grant them manliness and courage; it would destroy all illusions and rid them of all sins, past and present; and it would release them from the cycle of births. So her devotee beseeches her to open her eyes and grant him grace. Indeed, one of his favorite poetic genres is the *tirupaḷḷiye̲lucci* (the awakening [of the lord] from sleep), for he is convinced that ignored by her followers, Tami̲ttāy has gone to sleep, and thus no longer offers them grace. As Diana Eck notes, "In the Hindu view, not only must the gods keep their eyes open, but so must we, in order to make contact with them, to reap their blessings" (1985: 1). Thus, crucial to the structure of piety that develops around Tami̲ttāy is the belief that both she and her speakers must "awaken" and "open their eyes"; it is only then that she would be able to grant grace, and they could receive it. All would then be well with the (Tamil-speaking) world.

Just as he longs to receive her *aruḷ*, the pious devotee also yearns to experience her, with his mind, heart, and all his senses. So he imagines her as residing on his tongue. He longs to "immerse" himself in her and blend with her very being (Velayutam Pillai 1971: 61–62). There is an erotic subtext to the piety of the devout in *tami̲lppar̲r̲u,* as there is in so much of devotional Hinduism. Indeed, some of her adorers are so overcome when they contemplate her beautiful and splendid form that, they confess, "[Our] bodies brim with ecstasy; our hair quivers in excitement; [our] tongues stammer with love; and [our] bones melt" (Velayutam Pillai 1971: 68; see also Sivalinga Nayanar 1940). In Varadananjaiya Pillai's words:

> Our hands in prostration, our minds throbbing with joyousness,
> the hair on our bodies quivering in excitement,
> Brimming with ecstasy, we offer you our prayer!
> May you live long, O Tamil̠ttāy! O mother of ours!
> May you flourish for ever and ever and ever.
>
> (Velayutam Pillai 1971: 82)

This kind of ecstatic piety supplements the more overt but secular sexual economy of the erotic modality of Tamil devotion, as we will see. Increasingly, as the imagining of Tamil as a familial mother figure came to dominate *tamil̠ppar̠r̠u,* desire for Tamil̠ttāy could only exist in the interstices. But within the modality of pietistics, erotic sensibilities were granted some latitude, for divine sexuality continued to have a kind of currency that was not so readily conceded to maternal sexuality within the new bourgeois codes of morality that were put in place in colonial South India.

THE IDEOLOGY OF PIOUS DEVOTION

At its heart, the structure of piety produced by this modality turns around a dyadic relationship between the language, imagined as a benevolent, bountiful, and omniscient goddess, and its devotees, who cast themselves in the role of pious, submissive, and helpless worshippers, totally dependent on her for succor, inspiration, and salvation. She is the protector, and they are the protected; she is the muse who inspires, and they are the poets who breathlessly yearn to be inspired. Imagined thus as an omniscient perfect being, the language she embodies is correspondingly omniscient and perfect as well. This modality is therefore particularly favored by the religious regime of *tamil̠ppar̠r̠u* that treats Tamil as a perfect, complete language of plenitude which had unfortunately fallen on hard times, because of the evil ways of other languages, because of being ignored by its own speakers, and so on. The principal agenda of this regime, as of classicism, is the restoration of all of Tamil's "wealth" (*celvam*) that had been tainted or lost over time. There is less concern here with renovation, as there is in Indianism and Dravidianism, for how could one improve something that was already so perfect?[3]

Perhaps the most striking feature of this modality is the passion and fervor with which her pious devotees appear to believe that in their Tamiḻttāy, they are faced with a divine presence so perfect and so powerful that they themselves could do nothing but sing her praises and spread her word. It is she who has to give them grace and lead them to salvation; it is she who is the agent, the active principle. Tamil's devotees, I have repeatedly emphasized, are clearly moderns, living in a century when they have been exposed, in varying degrees, to all kinds of modern technologies, knowledges, and ways of being. Yet, when writing about their language in this mode, they consciously deny to themselves the most modern and secular of all attitudes, that of placing themselves as the center of their cosmos. Instead, they choose to insert their divinized language into that spot, throw themselves at her mercy, and await her grace.

TAMIL AS MOTHER: SOMATICS OF TAMIL DEVOTION

"Is there anything comparable to the mother's love?" So asks Sivagnanam in his reminiscences (1974: 30). Not really, as far as Tamil's devout were concerned, and in their imaginings, the incomparable Tamil was increasingly likened to their incomparable mothers. The representation of Tamil as mother, variously invoked as *tāy, ammā, mātā,* and *aṉṉai,* was particularly acute in the modality of somatics which gained ground as the Indianist and Dravidianist regimes gathered momentum from the 1920s on. Although Tamiḻtteyvam is also hailed as *ammā* and *tāy* (not surprisingly, considering that goddesses and mothers are symbolically and emotionally intertwined in the Hindu life-world), the mother who figures in the modality of somatics is essentially a familial, domestic, and secular being. Rhetorically and aesthetically as well, the modality of somatics was populist rather than archaizing, relying on the imagery of the quotidian and the vocabulary of the spoken language rather than on the high literary Tamil typically used by the pious devotee.

Within the discourses of *tamiḻpparṟu,* the confluence of "language" and "motherhood" may be traced back to the late nineteenth century. So, in 1879, S. Vedanayakam Pillai (1826–89), author of the first Tamil novel, unambiguously declared, "Tamil gave birth to us; Tamil raised us; Tamil sang lullabies to us and put us to sleep" (Vedanayakam Pillai 1879: 285). A few years later, in the 1887 foreword to his edition of the Caṅkam anthology, the *Kalittokai,* Damodaram Pillai pleaded with his readers to financially help him salvage ancient manuscripts, asking of them, "Is not Lady Tamil (*tamiḻ mātu*) your mother?" (Damodaram

Pillai 1971: 69). In 1891, Sundaram Pillai dedicated his play, *Maṉōṉmaṇīyam,* with its well-known invocatory hymn on Tamiḻttāy, to his *tamilmātā,* "Mother Tamil" (Sundaram Pillai 1922: 12). A year later, T. Lakshmana Pillai wondered if those who considered Tamil as their *mātā* and *tāy* (mother) would come forward to honor her, and Suryanarayana Sastri insisted that his Tamil could not be compared to a barren mother (*malaṭi tāyār*) (Lakshmana Pillai 1892–93: 154, 185–86; Suryanarayana Sastri n.d.: 59). As the next century advances, this occasional practice of referring to Tamil as "mother" coalesces into a well-entrenched linguistic and cultural habit. Increasingly, the *analogy* between language and motherhood is displaced by the *convergence* of the two domains, so that Tamil *is* the mother of the filial devotee. In essay after essay, poem after poem, devotees speak and write about their beloved Tamil as they would about their mothers, and vice versa (Maraimalai Adigal 1967b; Purnalingam Pillai 1930: 56–58; see also Ramaswamy 1992a).[4]

In the modality of somatics, the language and its devotee are held together not so much through the supernatural powers of a divine being as through the emotional powers invested in the maternal body. Where the pious devotee praises her miraculous abilities and awe-inspiring deeds to elicit the devotion of the Tamil speaker, the modality of somatics relies instead on various parts and substances of Tamiḻttāy's body: her fertile womb, her nurturing milk, her pitiful tears, her scarred face, and her fettered limbs. In contrast to the modality of pietistics, where the bond between the language and its devotee is registered in intangibles such as the granting of *aruḷ* (grace), the filial devotee emphasizes the sharing of corporeal substances like milk and blood. Thus he insists that since Tamiḻttāy's womb had given birth to speakers of Tamil, and her milk had raised them, in return her "children" ought to serve her by putting their own bodies at her disposal. In turn, those bodily parts and substances that foreground such bonds of birth are the most frequently invoked. While the pious devotee expresses his devotion on a religious terrain, the filial devotee registers it in uterine terms. Speakers of Tamil are Tamilians not necessarily because they worship Tamiḻttāy, but because they have been borne by Tamil, and nurtured and raised on it. They are all thus "siblings," because they have shared the womb and milk of Tamil. Occasionally, Tamiḻttāy appears as *cevilittāy,* "foster mother." But more often than not, she is explicitly identified as the birth mother, *īṉṟatāy.* So the intimacy between the language and its speakers in this modality is constituted by bringing Tamiḻttāy right into their homes, as their mother who gave birth to them and raised them to be loyal and devoted Tamil speakers.

In maternalizing Tamiḻttāy thus, her filial devotee drew upon the model of the "new mother" produced in bourgeois imaginations in so many regions of colonial India. She is a domestic paragon, furnished with a modern education but still retaining a modicum of religiosity and presiding over her neat and disciplined home, and her by now largely nuclear family (Chatterjee 1989; R. Kumar 1993: 32–52; Ramaswamy 1992a). In pre-colonial Tamil literature as well as in modern folklore, mothers are benign as well as threatening, nourishing as well as destructive, compassionate as well as fierce and malevolent (Shulman 1980: 223–67; Trawick 1990). In the discourses of *tamiḻpparru*, however, Tamiḻttāy is unambiguously compassionate, nourishing, pacific, and benign. This may seem surprising because she is always represented as a virgin, and the virginal or single mother/goddess, it has been suggested, frequently displays vengeful, punitive behaviors (Erndl 1993: 153–58). For both Indianism and Dravidianism, however, with their agendas of transforming Tamil speakers into a productive, enlightened, and educated community imagined as a harmonious and united family, an uncontrollable, threatening, and violent mother figure was not only embarrassing but counterproductive as well. Great care was therefore taken not to cast Tamiḻttāy in the image of the many fierce mother-goddesses that her filial devotee was undoubtedly familiar with from both high and popular Hindu religious practice. Instead, she was modelled on the "new" mother who they hoped would eventually come to reign in Tamil-speaking homes—disciplined but compassionate, educated but modest and feminine, and respectable and virtuous.

All the same, the empowering of Tamil by appropriating the figure of the mother has had its advantages and its disadvantages for *tamiḻpparṟu*. On the one hand, Tamil's filial devotee is only too pleased to tap into the enormous reservoir of affective powers associated with motherhood in this region, especially since that reservoir had been significantly replenished in a colonial culture where mothers were constituted as the custodians of the authentic, pure, and uncolonized community. On the other hand, the devotee also had to be careful that his beloved language, in thus benefitting from its association with the mother, would not be entirely consumed by that very crucial figure of the life-world of its speakers. Increasingly, as the century wears on, the filial devotee was inclined to declare the superiority of Tamiḻttāy's motherhood over that of his human mother. *Tāyiṉum ciṟantat Tamiḻ*, "Tamil that is superior to [our] mother," is a sentiment frequently encountered in devotional discourses from the 1930s on, especially in the Dravidianist idiom. As Margaret Trawick (1990: 156) rightly notes, "Many children in Tamilnadu grow up with more than one 'mother' and experience more than one household as home." The filial devotee, however, had to ensure that Tamilttāy and her "home" were never just one among many for his fellow Tamil speakers, but the most important of them all.

TAMIḺTTĀY: PORTRAIT OF A MOTHER

Filial anxiety and concern lace the sentiments of affection, love, and admiration for Tamiḻttāy in the modality of somatics. Typically, she is featured as a once-glorious but now-endangered mother—frail, pitiful, and in desperate need of help from her sons: "O young Tamilians! What is the condition of our Tamiḻttāy today? She stands without jewels and gems; she has lost her radiance; her crown has vanished; her fragrance is gone; she stands dejected and in tears; she grieves in sorrow; she is emaciated" (S. Subramanian 1939: 1).

Both Indianism, in its struggle against English and British colonialism, and Dravidianism, in its battle against Hindi and North Indian imperialism, circulated various images of Tamiḻttāy as abandoned and desolate, the pitiful state of her body calling attention to the endangered state of Tamil. Consider the following poem by Bharatidasan, published in 1960:

> O Tamiḻttāy, you struggle for life in an ocean of grief
> Grasping at the smallest stick, seizing it as if a giant raft!
> O Tamiḻttāy, buffeted around by fierce storms,
> you clutch at worms in the soil, as if at roots!
> O Tamiḻttāy, writhing in the scorching heat,
> You hurry to the stagnant pool as if to a waterfall.[5]

Such images of a suffering Tamiḻttāy are also supplemented by allusions to her decaying, diseased body. Sivagnanam exhorted his listeners at an anti-Hindi rally held in Madras in 1948: "It is Tamiḻttāy who gave birth to us. When we were infants, it is in Tamil that we would have called out to our mothers, *ammā, ammā*. If such a loving mother's face is scarred by pox marks, and if we have the strength to prevent this, do we stand by doing nothing?"[6] Years earlier, in a public talk he gave to the Karanthai Tamil Sangam in 1927, Maraimalai Adigal, too, pleaded, "Do not allow the pox marks of Sanskrit to scar Tamiḻttāy's fine body."[7] His plea was greeted with loud claps and cheers of "Long live Tamil! Long live pure Tamil! Long live Tamiḻttāy! Long live Maraimalai Adigal!" (M. Tirunavukarasu 1959: 527). The modality of somatics thus thrives on the patriarchal imagining of the woman as passive victim, dependent on her male kin to protect, honor, and save her.

THE VIOLATED BODY OF TAMIḺTTĀY

Most potently, aiming to provoke the filial passions of Tamil speakers, her devotees circulated stunning images of Tamiḻttāy being violated. She is incarcerated in dark dungeons; her golden body is trapped in iron manacles; her enemies suck up her blood; they hurl spears at her breast; they threaten to decapitate her, and so on. In the late 1940s, for instance, as the tensions over the creation of linguistic states out of Madras Presidency escalated with the impending loss of chunks of Tamil-speaking border areas to neighboring states, Sivagnanam ended his editorial in his journal *Tamiḻ Muracu* on 15 April 1947: "O Tamilians! P. N. Rao's plan hangs like a sword over our Tamiḻaṉṉai's [Tamiḻttāy's] head. The Malayalees with their craving for land are waiting to chop off her feet. If we do not hasten, Tamiḻaṉṉai will certainly be murdered. After we lose Venkatam and Kumari, our Tamil land will look like a mother with both her head and feet amputated" (Sivagnanam 1981: 112).

Being moderns, of course, her filial devotees are very much aware of the power of mass media and the visual image. Numerous cartoons published in Dravidian movement newspapers during the anti-Hindi protests of midcentury presented the reading public with striking visual enactments of various acts of violation of Tamiḻttāy's body. One such cartoon, printed in several key Dravidian movement newspapers and magazines, showed the premier of the Presidency, Rajagopalachari, the archsupporter of the Hindi cause in the 1930s, attacking with a dagger a bejeweled Tamiḻttāy, who stands undefended, carrying in her hands the ancient literary texts, the *Tirukkuṟaḷ* and the *Tolkāppiyam* (fig. 5).[8] Another, published in the 1950s in the DMK paper *Aṟappōr,* depicts a man personifying "North Indian Hegemony" cutting off a weeping Tamiḻttāy's tongue with a sickle. Yet others showed Tamiḻttāy locked up in prison, or shedding tears over the bodies of her children shot down by the police during anti-Hindi demonstrations.[9]

Perhaps the most dramatic of these cartoons was published in *Kuṭi Aracu* in 1937 on the eve of the first major anti-Hindi protests (fig. 6).[10]

Entitled "Āccāriyār Sākasam: Tamiḻaṉṉai Māṉapaṅkam," "Rajagopalachari's Bravado: The Dishonoring of Tamiḻttāy," it depicts a woman of obvious distinction, wearing a crown and a halo, and carrying a scepter. She stands with tears flowing down her face, surrounded by a group of men, one of whom, clearly identifiable as the premier, Rajagopalachari, is attempting to disrobe her. The accompanying text tells the reader that although many of her venerable sons in the Madras Legislative Assembly watched with growing anger as Tamiḻttāy was being thus treated, they were too cowardly to do anything about it and stood by with their heads hanging in shame. The text ends on an appeal: "O true Tamilians! What are you going to do now?" The cartoon revived, of course, the well-known incident recounted in the ancient Sanskrit epic, the *Mahābhārata,* of the disrobing of Draupadi by her Kaurava cousins as her Pandava husbands look on helplessly. A few years earlier, Subramania Bharati, in his poem *Pāñcāli Capatam* (Draupadi's oath; 1912–24), had drawn upon the story to allegorize the dishonoring of the nation/mother (Bharati 1987: 193–309).[11] Given the antipathy to Sanskritic Hinduism within the Dravidian movement which spearheaded the anti-Hindi protests, the plot here follows a different course: rather than the lord Krishna coming to Tamiḻttāy's rescue, as he does with Draupadi, it is the vastness of her own learning and the respect of her people that ultimately save her honor in the cartoon.

Of the many messages packed into this cartoon, the most striking is the act of *māṉapaṅkam,* "dishonoring," carried out through the disrobing of Tamiḻttāy in a public space as hallowed as the state's legislature. This is not the singular instance of the use of this theme in *tamiḻpparṟu,* although it is unique in the explicitness with which it singles out a man, and a very identifiable public figure at that, as perpetrating the crime. A year after the publication of the cartoon, at the Velur Women's Conference held on 26 December 1938, Narayani Ammal, a Tamil scholar who would be incarcerated for participating in the anti-Hindi protests two months later, reminded the assembled women that like Draupadi of yore, Tamiḻttāy was in danger of losing her honor to Dushasana (Sanskrit and Hindi). "I hope her screams reach your ears," she concluded.[12] More unusually, in a poem by Vanidasan (1915–74), a disciple of Bharatidasan, Hindi is identified as a *vēci,* "(female) prostitute," and charged with the offense of "snatching away the mother's garment."[13] In general, however, her devotees leave ambiguous the gender or the identity of the entity which disrobes Tamiḻttāy. Consider this excerpt from the proscribed text *Iṉpat Tirāviṭam* (Sweet Dravidian land), particularly striking because its author, Annadurai, did not generally employ the gendered vocabulary typically used by many of his fellow Dravidianists. Addressing the disloyal son who has turned his back on his "dishonored" mother (here signifying the Tamil land rather than language), Annadurai wrote: "How can you stand by and watch [our] enemy turn your motherland (*tāyakam*) into a *veḷḷāṭṭi* [maid/concubine]? Does not your blood boil when you see [him] uncoiling her braid, rubbing off the vermilion on her forehead, peeling off her clothing, and kicking her with [his] feet?" (Annadurai 1989: 91).

These lines are particularly dramatic for the care with which they systematically specify the manner in which the mother's body is violated and dishonored, stopping just short of suggesting actual rape. Indeed, it is important—but heartening—to emphasize that in none of the narratives I have collected on Tamiḻttāy is there any explicit description of her rape.[14] Although one could argue that the very possibility of rape that such vivid imagery suggests is just as threatening, its explicit absence contrasts with the reality of rape that has haunted women's lives in colonial and post-colonial India, as well as with allusions to the "rape" of a feminized land or nation in other parts of the world (Kolodny 1975; R. Kumar 1993: 127–42; Montrose 1992). Given the enormous emphasis that her devotees place on their Tamiḻttāy being a virgin, and given the ritual and symbolic power accorded to the sexual purity of the woman, the rape of Tamiḻttāy would have been both inappropriate and unproductive, for it would render the figure unavailable, even useless, for continual deployment within the sexual and patriarchal economies of *tamiḻppaṟṟu*. Instead, even while hinting at the potential for rape that lurks behind the disrobing of Tamiḻttāy, her devout followers deploy the sentiments of shame and outrage associated with the violation of the mother's body. The image of disrobing is particularly effective in a culture where such a high premium is placed on honor, and where women's sexual purity and virtue underwrite the honor of their male kin in particular. The dishonor associated with public disrobing is especially heightened in this case because it involves the hallowed figure of the mother. The mother's public disrobing suggested not just the dishonor inflicted upon her individual self but, more damagingly, the dishonor visited upon all those who shared her flesh and blood—namely, her Tamilian "children," most especially her sons. So, the poet Vanidasan wrote in 1948, "The mother's honor is the Tamilian's honor. Think of saving yourself!"[15] It is telling that in all such instances, as has been noted by Radha Kumar in another context, the violation of the female body is not specifically presented as an act of violence against women (R. Kumar 1993: 37). It is instead, very quickly, translated into the violation of the community and its honor.

THE FERTILE WOMB OF TAMIḺTTĀY

Because the modality of somatics constructs its structure of devotion on the terrain of uterine bonds, the womb of Tamiḻttāy is of particular importance to the filial devotee. So wrote a poet named Tamilkkovan in a poem entitled "My Life Is Yours":

> O beautiful Tamiḻttāy! The other day, I was born from your womb!
> . . . .
> I am your son who brings you victory!
> O mother, if someone scorns you
> Of what use is my birth and life?[16]

Her womb, of course, produced not just Tamilkkovan but all other speakers of Tamil as well, who are therefore transformed into each other's "siblings" by virtue of this somatic fact. It is her womb that unites them all as members of one "family." So Suddhananda Bharati (1938: 104) reminded his fellow speakers that wherever they may be and in whatever state, they ought to remember that "they are children of one mother's womb (*vayiṟu*)." Tamiḻttāy's womb thus functioned as a mnemonic device, reminding all speakers of Tamil of the bonds of birth that tied them to their language which had laboriously and patiently borne them all. As Tamiḻttāy herself reminded them, "Do not forget that you are all children who emerged from *my* womb (*maṭi*). I am *your* mother. . . . You are all called Tamilians" (Pancanathan n.d.: 9). In turn, one of her devotees, Viracolan, reiterated, "O mother, in embryonic form conceived, in fetal form enlivened, we were firmly planted in your womb (*vayiṟu*). Then we were delivered to the world."[17] So, her womb in this discourse serves somatically to confirm the facticity of birth as speakers of Tamil and as constituent members of the Tamil "family."

Her womb is also deployed by her devout to eliminate other mothers—such as Bhārata Mātā or Āṅkilattāy (Mother English) or Hindi—who may offer nourishment to Tamilians, raise them up, or secure them jobs. Nevertheless, the fact that their wombs had not given birth to Tamil speakers meant that their motherhood was, at worst, false and, at best, inferior to that represented by Tamiḻttāy.[18] For Indianism, obviously, Bhārata Mātā's womb mattered just as Tamiḻttāy's. As Bharati insisted in his 1907 poem "Vantē Mātaram" (Homage to Mother [India]): "Those who are born from the same mother's womb / Are they not brothers though they may squabble with each other?" (Bharati 1987: 51).[19]

Years later, Ramalinga Pillai reminded his fellow speakers:

> This venerable Intiyattēvi [Bhārata Mātā] gave birth to three hundred and thirty million children!
>
> . . . .
>
> For how many days did she carry us?
> How many troubles did she face for us?
> We forgot all her difficulties; she endured all our faults!
> Millions and millions of foreigners came here to plunder;
> She put up with millions of them, and took care of her children!
>
> . . . .
>
> Such a noble lady we forgot.
>
> . . . .
>
> Will not her womb that gave birth to us burn?
> Will not her tender heart grieve?
> When her own children to whom she gave birth forsake her, how can a woman endure that?
>
> (Ramalinga Pillai 1988: 309–10)

In the logic of Indianism, Bhārata Mātā's womb enables Tamil speakers to be reborn as "Indians." In that capacity, they owed her filial duty and love. To forget this meant the "betrayal of the mother's womb," causing it to "burn" and allowing it to be "violated" (Ramalinga Pillai 1988: 303–16). The maternal womb becomes the ground on which contrary allegiances thus come to be negotiated, with Dravidianism making a commitment to only Tamiḻttāy's and Indianism to Bhārata Mātā's as well (see also Lakshmii 1990).

Tamiḻttāy (as indeed Bhārata Mātā) may be a virgin, but her womb was immensely fertile and fruitful. In the imaginations of some of her more ambitious devotees, her womb had given birth to not just Tamilians but to other languages and their speakers as well. Perhaps the earliest use of this notion was Sundaram Pillai's famous hymn, which declared that Tamiḻtteyvam's *utaram*, "womb," had given birth to the four other Dravidian languages: Kannada, Telugu, Malayalam, and Tulu (Sundaram Pillai 1922: 22). By 1891, when Sundaram Pillai published this hymn, many of Tamil's devotees were familiar with Robert Caldwell's assertions that Tamil was the oldest and most cultivated member of the Dravidian "family" of languages. Yet Caldwell also insisted that Tamil was one "dialect" among the many Dravidian dialects, and not "the original speech" from which they had all descended. It certainly was not, in his reckoning, the "mother" of the Dravidian family (Caldwell 1856: 26, 52, 61). Sundaram Pillai, however, not only so declared it but even used that most maternal of somatic parts, the womb, to secure this claim. Since his time, of course, the notion that Tamil's womb generated all Dravidian languages has acquired an enormous materiality, especially in Dravidianism, whose more ambitious exponents stake a claim on the bodies of all Dravidians (and not just Tamil speakers) on the ground that they are after all Tamiḻttāy's children and owe loyalty to her (e.g., E. V. Ramasami 1948: 30).

THE NOURISHING MILK OF TAMIḺTTĀY

For her filial devotee, Tamiḻttāy's milk (*pāl*) is just as significant as her womb. As early as 1879, Vedanayakam Pillai described Tamil as "the language which our mothers and fathers fed us along with milk" (Vedanayakam Pillai 1879: 285). In 1891, Sundaram Pillai's *Maṉōṉmaṇīyam* featured a dramatic monologue in which the hero, Jeevakan, declared that it is through mother's milk that pride in one's language and one's land is imbibed. By the turn of this century, the assumption that Tamil was mother's milk had become so naturalized that in 1913, when the senate of Madras University proclaimed that the "vernaculars" would no longer be compulsory for students, the *Ñāṉapāṉu* protested by comparing this resolution with one that would dictate that it was no longer mandatory for mothers to raise their children on their own milk.[20] And in 1914, V. V. Subramania Aiyar, an Indianist devotee of Tamil, insisted that it would be impossible for anyone to produce great works of literature in a language that had not been taken in with the mother's milk (Subramania Aiyar 1981: 20). Over and again during this century, Tamil has been invoked by its devotees as "the milk of our youth," the "fine milk," "the glorious mother's milk," and the like (Ramaswamy 1992a: 49–51). The 1931 *Census* even lent the blessings of the colonial state to such an imagining by defining the "mother tongue" as "the language which [one] had taken in with mother's milk" (Government of India 1932: 287).

Sometimes, Tamil is imbibed through the human mother's milk, a suggestion that has had important, even conservative, implications for Tamil women's identity (Ramaswamy 1992a; see also Lakshmi 1990). But more often than not, her filial devotee insists that it is Tamiḻttāy herself who raises her children on her nourishing milk. Thus, borne by Tami̱ttāy's womb, and having shared her milk, Tamil speakers are rendered "siblings," members of the same "family." By midcentury, so entrenched were such assumptions that Ramasami's rationalist attack on the feminization of Tamil was launched under the title *Tāyppāl Paittiyam* (The madness over mother's milk) (E. V. Ramasami 1962: 7–17). This powerful attack, however, has not detracted either its devotees or others from continuing to compare Tamil to mother's milk, a hit song from the recent film *Aṇṇāmalai* (1992) being a case in point.

If Tamil is mother's milk, then foreign languages, like English, are likened to "bottled milk," even "tonics." Their virtues are infinitely inferior to those of mother's milk/Tamil, which they may supplement but never replace. So, in 1956, during the debate in the Madras Legislative Assembly on replacing English as the official language of the state with Tamil, one of the members passionately declared: "Today our mother tongue reclines royally on the throne of government. For a child, its mother's milk is far more necessary than bottled milk. Even if the children who grow up on bottled milk survive, there are excellent substances (*cattu*) in their mother's milk. Children who drink their mother's milk have fine dispositions as well."[21]

It is interesting that the legislator, P. G. Karuthiruman, used the Tamil word *cattu* to refer to the substances contained in mother's milk, for some of the meanings of that word are truth, virtue, goodness, and moral excellence. These are precisely the fine qualities that every true speaker who was reared on Tamil is supposed to imbibe. Accordingly, the filial devotee insists that it is Tami̱ttāy's milk that cultivates in the Tamil speaker *mo̱lippa̱ṟru* (devotion to language), *nāṭṭuppa̱ṟru* (devotion to nation), *āṇmai* (manliness or courage), and *ta̱nmā̱nam* (self-respect) (Iyarkaiselvan 1959: 8).[22] Not surprisingly, Tamil's enemies (like Sanskrit or Hindi) were characterized, especially in Dravidianism, as languages that poison the purity of Tami̱ttāy's milk (Bharatidasan 1948: 4; Perunchitranar 1979: 57).[23]

In premodern Tamil literary culture, mother's milk was typically associated with purity, coolness, and creativity (Shulman 1980: 93–104). In her ethnography of contemporary Tamil family life, Margaret Trawick (1990: 93–94) has suggested that the importance of mother's milk derives from the belief that it is the substantial repository of mother's love (*a̱npu*). These are all characteristics that her filial devotee would readily associate with Tami̱ttāy's milk. But there are also ideological uses to which the mother's milk has been put in the discourses of Tamil's modern adherents. For one, imagining Tamil as mother's milk enables the language to be symbolically incorporated into the bodies of its individual speakers to become part of their very essence. As such, it would be impossible to separate the language from its true and loyal speaker, as Bharatidasan declared on many occasions. Equally important, the inscription of Tamil as mother's milk allows the filial devotee to remind his fellow Tamilian of the duty (*kaṭamai*) he owed Tamiḻttāy, as in the following call issued during the 1938 anti-Hindi protests by C. Velsami: "When one sees Tamiḻttāy suffering, can any heroic Tamilian who has been born in Tamilnadu, and raised here, and has joyously drunk her sweet milk—can he have the heart to watch her suffering?"[24]

Like the mother's womb, the mother's milk, too, serves simultaneously as a mnemonic device that somatically reminds all Tamil speakers of the facticity of birth into the Tamil community and as a mobilizing device—*aṉṉaiyiṉ pāl kaṭamai,* "obligation to mother's milk"—that seeks to arouse them into taking action out of recognition of this "fact."[25]

THE PITIFUL TEARS OF TAMIḺTTĀY

Finally, I turn to the tears of Tamiḻttāy, which, of all her bodily parts and substances, most clearly indexed her current state of utter distress. Especially from around the 1930s on, discourses of *tamiḻppaṟṟu* abounded with allusions to the weeping Tamiḻttāy, to the tearful Tamiḻttāy appealing to her children to help her, to Tamiḻttāy sitting in a corner, wailing away, and so on. Soon after the self-immolation of Chinnasami, Aranganathan, and Sivalingam in 1964–65, a DMK newsmagazine, *Muttāram,* carried a striking cover with the faces of these youths in the foreground. The backdrop is the close-up of the face of a woman—most likely, Tamiḻttāy—with large drops of blood-red tears flowing down her cheeks (fig. 7).[26] That Tamiḻttāy's tears are meant to not just create affect, but also to incite and mobilize is clear from the following passage from Karunanidhi's memoirs in which he describes the first large-scale political protest spearheaded by the DMK against the Congress and its Hindi policy. In 1953, the DMK called upon the Congress government to change the name of a town called Dalmiapuram in Tiruchi district (named after a North Indian cement magnate) to its Tamil original, Kallakudi. So, on 15 July, Karunanidhi and a group of his DMK followers reached the railway station of Dalmiapuram, erased the Hindi name on the station board, and painted the Tamil name of Kallakudi in its stead.

They then proceeded to lie down on the railway tracks; in the resulting altercation between the police and the protesters, two men lost their lives, and many were severely wounded. Consider how Karunanidhi represents this event to his readers:

> We have reached the battlefield. We have reached the place where our glorious Tamilttāy stands insulted. We have reached the place where our once-magnificent mother now stands, shedding tears. Our wonderful mother who nurtured and raised us on glorious Tamil . . . huddles wearily, her limbs fettered in the enemy's chains. They have put up a railing of guns around her shackles which we came to destroy. Our mother stands shaking and weeping! "Look at her from afar. Do not touch her. Savor her suffering form," so says the government.
>
> (Karunanidhi 1989: 196)

Having set the stage thus, Karunanidhi turns to describe the death of the first young man, Natarajan:

> O mother! O Tamilttāy! Look at your son Natarajan to whom you gave birth. You used to be adorned with gold and jewels once upon a time! Today, you are adorned by the corpses of your martyred sons. Is this fair? Look at his corpse which soaks your lap with blood. You gave birth to millions of children. Now you have the fate of lighting their young bodies on their funeral pyres. . . . O mother! Weep! Cry out! It is only if you cry, it is only if you shed your tears that we can gather together an army that will bring down the reign of cowards. . . . Weep, mother, weep. O glorious Tamilttāy, you once upon a time wore a smile; now you shed tears of blood. . . . But your tears will not be in vain.
>
> (Karunanidhi 1989: 204–5)

"Your tears will not be in vain": in the logic of Tamil devotion, especially Dravidianism, on reading (or hearing) statements like these which were circulated through street poetry and political speeches at anti-Hindi rallies, her "children" would rush to the rescue of their mother, wipe away her tears, and restore her, and the language she embodied, to well-being. The tears of Tamilttāy came to somatically index the sad state of the body politic in Tamil devotion. Indeed, in neighboring Sri Lanka, where Tamil nationalism has been driven by a rather different set of imperatives, a 1977 pamphlet on the suffering of Tamil speakers on the island under Sinhala domination is entitled *The Tears of Tamilttāy* (*Tamilttāyin Kaṇṇīr*). Nowhere does the work mention Tamilttāy, yet it is clear that for its author, her tears were enough to recall for his readers the state of utter desolation of Tamil speakers in Sri Lanka (Puttoli 1977).

PROFILING THE FILIAL DEVOTEE

More than the modality of pietistics, the modality of somatics has a conscious mobilizing agenda—not surprisingly, since it was the mode most favored by Dravidianism with its militant stance on *tamiḻppaṟṟu*. So, images of the distressed, diseased, and violated mother were circulated not just for rhetorical effect but also to incite her "children" to take up arms and come to her rescue. Tamiḻttāy herself implored thus in 1965:

> O Tamilian, my dear son to whom I gave birth!
>
> . . . .
>
> Where have you gone, leaving to suffer your mother who bathed you, fed you, sang lullabies, nurtured you, showered you with love?
>
> . . . .
>
> Your mother has been cast into prison!
> Will you not rescue her from there?
> Your mother has been shackled!
> Will you not break her chains?
> Did I not feed you fine food?
> Was not the milk that you drank heroic milk?
>
> O son who has forsaken me! O Tamil son who has gone off to sleep!
>
> . . . .
>
> Your mother is calling out to you! Can you not hear her whimpers and see her tears?
>
> Are your ears deaf? Are your eyes blind?
> Where are you, my son! Where are you?[27]

Those Tamil speakers who refused to respond to such an impassioned plea laid themselves open to charges of betraying their own mother, even matricide (E. M. Subramania Pillai 1951–52: 161–63). During the anti-Hindi protests of 1938, Suddhananda Bharati declared: "The Tamilian who rejects Tamil rejects his own mother. The Tamilian who does not reverence Tamil has forgotten his own mother. Can you ever forget the mother who gave birth to you? Our ancient mother stands in dishonor among the languages of the world, and sheds tears. Will not her sons come forth and wipe away their mother's tears?" (Suddhananda Bharati 1938: 110). Equally dramatically, the poet Pulavar Kulanthai insisted that "the murder of Tamil is like the murder of one's mother" (Pulavar Kulanthai 1972: 35). In this modality, it was not enough for Tamil speakers to put their literary and scholarly talents at Tamiḻttāy's disposal; they had to be prepared to surrender their bodies as well. In its economy of devotion, along with the sharing of the mother's womb and milk, the shedding of the son's blood has a great deal of currency. So, Perunchitran was willing to declare in 1965 in a poem he wrote in a Kadalur prison:

> When they tell me
> This body, and all the blood and sinews and feelings that it contains, belongs to Tamilttāy and to the Tamil people,
> I lose all my fatigue!
>
> (Perunchitranar 1979: 66)

Similarly, an essay published in the *Āṉantapōtiṉi,* a literary journal that was largely Indianist in sentiment, asked, "O youthful Tamilian! Does not your mother's Tamil blood run in your heart? Do you not love your mother? . . . Wake up. . . . Let your Tamil blood boil over and rouse you" (Mutthu 1938: 336).

Such statements, of which there are innumerable examples, graphically illustrate the extent to which the somatics of devotion operated, discursively and symbolically, at a gut level. Seeing Tamilttāy in tears, the Tamil son is reminded of the mother whose womb had borne him, whose milk had nourished him, and whose blood runs in his veins. This memory leads him to shed his own blood to prove his *tamilpparru:*

> I will push back the hostility of other languages beyond the oceans;
> "May the Tamilians stand loftily! Long live Tamil!"
> I will thus beat my drum.
> . . . .
> Even as I am being cut down, and as the blood spurts out from my fierce wounds,
> I will fall down on my Tamil soil, crying out "Tamil!" "Tamil!"
>
> (Pulavar Kulanthai 1972: 11–12)

Her impassioned devotee is of course ready to shed not just his own blood but also that of the numerous enemies of his Tamilttāy. So declared a twenty-three-year-old youth at an anti-Hindi rally in Madras city in 1938: "If the Tamilians have any heroism, the blood of several thousands of members of the Aryan race must be shed. The blood of the Aryans must be shed and a river of blood should flow in this country. The leaders may not have faith in violence, but we have faith in violence. . . . [T]housands of youths will arise for planting our red flag, and giving up their lives for the sake of Tamil."[28]

Tamil devotion has certainly contributed to literary and linguistic efflorescence in Tamilnadu and undoubtedly helped the political empowerment of the disenfranchised and the colonized. All the same, it has also underwritten an economy of violence and death, an economy in which dying for Tamil and Tamiḻttāy is superior to living without her. That such an economy did not exist merely in the discursive spaces of devotional narratives but actually came to touch the lives of Tamilians, especially in the 1960s, is apparent from the stories of Chinnasami and numerous others who sacrificed themselves in the battle for Tamil. Further, in its somatic mode, *tamiḻppaṟṟu* relied heavily on regimes of violence directed against the female body in order to elicit the allegiance and loyalty of the Tamil speaker to Tamiḻttāy. Indeed, Tamil devotion in this mode appears to need such images of the violated female body for the particular strategies of persuasion and incitement that it employed to whip up the passions of the "sleeping" Tamilian. Figures of the violated mother are deployed again and again, not so much to draw attention to acts of violence against women as to highlight the plight of the language and the dishonor wreaked upon the community of its speakers.

THE IDEOLOGY OF SOMATIC DEVOTION

In contrast to the pietistics of *tamiḻppaṟṟu,* in which Tamiḻttāy reigns as an all-powerful sovereign goddess holding in thrall her worshippers, in the modality of somatics she is a diseased and *powerless* personage, helplessly dependent on her children for restoring her to her former state of health and glory. She is no longer the protector and the patron of her devotees; instead, it is they who have to come to her aid. This difference in the manner Tamiḻttāy is imagined in the two modalities captures in turn the difference in the way the language and its devotees related to each other in the religious and classicist regimes, as opposed to the Indianist and Dravidianist imaginaries. The latter two were essentially populist and pragmatic, concerned with improving the language, revamping it with new vocabularies and new genres, and closing the gap between its literary and spoken forms. In spite of their inherent faith in Tamil, devotees who participated in these regimes were aware that much had to be done to transform Tamil to make it a suitable language for politics, education, and modern communication; and they were particularly anxious that invocations of its ancient greatness and wonders often detracted their fellow speakers from this all-important task. They were also painfully aware that rather than just relying on the talents of literary pandits and great Tamil scholars, Tamil would only improve if every Tamil speaker in every Tamil-speaking home joined the cause. For all these reasons, for devotees who were of Indianist or Dravidianist persuasion, the image of Tamil as an endangered, emaciated, and powerless mother was much more appropriate than that of Tami̱ttāy as a glorious, perfect, and all-powerful goddess-queen.

Moreover, the pious devotee cast Tami̱ttāy as an all-powerful goddess who is the primeval generator of thought, of the arts and the sciences, and of civilization itself. In contrast, in the somatics of devotion, such a Tami̱ttāy is replaced by a mother figure, celebrated for her reproductive and domestic role in the idealized Tamil family. Consider the following from an essay on Tamil published in 1938 during the first wave of anti-Hindi protests:

> Who is the woman who comforted you with her sweet words when you were young and tired? Who is the glorious woman who assuaged your hunger with milk when you were infants? Who is the fine woman who rocked you to sleep in your cradles with her sweet words? Who is the woman who taught you to speak your first words so that your parents and kinsmen rejoice? Who is the woman who guided you and helped you when you played happily in the streets?. . . . She is indeed the fine and incomparable Tami̱ Aṉṉai [Tami̱ttāy].
>
> (Sivananda Adigal 1937–38: 601)

Here, in contrast to the pietistics of *tami̱ppaṟṟu*, the language is celebrated for its biologically *reproductive* role as collective mother of Tamil speakers—for parenting, rearing, and nourishing them—rather than for its culturally *productive* role as the fount of literature and high civilization. Thus goddesses and queens, who provided the dominant models for imaging the language in the elite religious and classicist regimes (and in the modality of pietistics), were displaced by the Tamil woman, celebrated as an ever-youthful, fertile mother who confirmed that all Tamil speakers were each other's "siblings" and members of the same "family" because they had shared the same womb and drunk the same milk.

Indeed, the somatics of *tami̱ppaṟṟu* reminds us that identity claims in modernity do not rest merely on abstract formulations or on symbolic statements of fraternity, solidarity, and unity. They also crucially rely upon sensory symbols and visceral entities that call attention to the bonds of birth, to the sharing of substances, to the very commonalties that emerge from belonging to what Benedict Anderson has so persuasively characterized as the "imagined" community. In Anderson's formulation, the nation is one such imagined community "because the members of even the smallest nation will never know most of their fellow-members, meet them, or even hear of them, yet in the minds of each lives the very image of their communion" (Anderson 1983: 15). Extending Anderson, I would propose that bodily images of shared womb and milk, of the blood and tears of the members of the community, and indeed of the mother figure herself are devices that are deployed to enable this act of communion that so critically and intimately binds together all members of the imagined community as one "family." Even as such bodily metaphors, images, and substances determine membership *in* the community, they also serve as boundary maintaining devices by identifying those who are *not* in the community. So, it is clear that for Tamil's devotees, those who did not recognize that they were born from Tamiḻttāy's womb and raised on her milk, and those who were not moved to come to her aid when they saw her shackled body or her tears of sorrow, were emphatically *not* Tamilian. They were discursively written out of the Tamil community and symbolically cast out.

TAMIL AS MAIDEN: EROTICS OF TAMIL DEVOTION

Like so many other love stories, Tamil devotion, too, has its triangle of desire constituted by three protagonists: Tamiḻttāy, imagined as a beautiful, desirable, but emphatically virginal mother; the male devotee, typically portrayed as young, heterosexual, virile, and desiring; and the female devotee, young and heterosexual like her male counterpart, beautiful and desirable like her mother/language, but destined to be a married mother entrusted with the task of reproducing the language and its community. By virtue of being constituted as a hallowed mother figure to whom absolute devotion and loyalty is owed, Tamiḻttāy obviously does not enter the field as an equal player, and she frequently interrupts the sexual and familial bonding of her human devotees. Nevertheless, the devotional triangle is not just disruptive but productive as well, which is not least of the reasons that it flourishes. For the circulation of desire among the three protagonists, however complicated and conflictual it may seem on the surface, only ensures that the language and its devotees are indelibly interlocked in structures of pleasure and service which further increases their longing for each other. The work of the modality of erotics reminds us that Tamil devotion is not just about loss, pain, suffering, and death, but also about enjoyment and pleasure. Passions of the tongue may be pious and filial, but they are erotic as well.

At the core of the structure of sentiment that is constituted by the modality of erotics is the desiring male devotee's undiluted pleasure in Tamil and in Tamiḻttāy, rather than his awed reverence or filial anxiety. The Tamil word that is generally used for expressing this pleasure is *iṉpam* (and its cognate, *iṉimai*). This polysemic word means joy, delight, sweetness, and bliss, but in a large number of contexts, it signifies sensual pleasure and romantic love. So, the numerous verses and essays entitled *iṉpattamiḻ,* "sweet Tamil," or *tamiḻiṉpam,* "pleasures of Tamil," are certainly replete with images of Tamil's innocent beauty and delights, the pleasures of hearing its mellifluous sounds, the joy of speaking the language and reading its literature, and so on (Bharatidasan 1986: 87–89, 94; Sethu Pillai 1968). But consider the following 1938 verse by Bharatidasan, recited during the anti-Hindi protest marches of that year:

> Our bodies, our wealth, our very breath,
> We will surrender to our sweet Tamil (*iṉpattamiḻ*)!
> Even the pleasures woman alone gives do not compare to our great Tamil!
> We will declare!
>
> (Bharatidasan 1948: 9)

This explicit comparison by the poet of the pleasures (*cukam*) offered by a woman and by Tamil is not fortuitous, as evidenced in several poems written by male poets with titles such as "Tamiḻ eṉ Kātali" (Tamil is my beloved) and "Tamiḻ Eṉ Maṉaivi" (Tamil is my wife) (Mudiyarasan 1976: 34–39; Nagarajan 1980: 26–34). Thus, in "Tamil is my beloved," Mudiyarasan, one of the better-known poets of the Dravidian movement, declared passionately:

> In order to acquire you, I wander all around;
> If you reject me, how can I endure this life?
> Is it not your sweet passion that drives me to frenzy?
> O delicious language of mine! Gather me up and embrace me!
>
> (Mudiyarasan 1976: 35)

Or consider this verse in which there is a striking slippage from Tamil as "mother" to Tamil as "wife":

> [You] are the mother who fed us milk;
> You are the food that sates our hunger;
> You are the song that gives so much delight (*iṉimai*);
> You are the light we bring into our Tamil homes with the bond of marriage (*tāli*);
> O Mother/Goddess Tamil (*tamiḻaṇaṅkē*)![29]

So, just as Tamiḻttāy comes to occupy a space inhabited by their conventional gods and human mothers, she also competes, as a woman, with their human spouses and lovers in the imagination of many a male devotee. The desiring devotee dwells on her physical attributes as a beautiful, sensuous woman, praising her "glorious, golden body," "abundant breasts," "lustrous lips," and so on. He rejoices that her "dark spear-shaped eyes" beckon him, that her "glowing face" rivals the luster of the moon, that her "narrow waist puts lightning to shame," and the like. He pronounces ecstatically that "his heart surges with the nectar of pleasure" when he beholds her, and that the pleasure (cukam) she gave him when she embraced him in the moonlight caused him to tremble (Mudiyarasan 1976: 34–36; Velayutam Pillai 1971: 84–89). Many such statements are highly stylized, of course, and follow the conventions of erotic Tamil literature. However, occasionally we also get more personalized glimpses of the devotee's desire for his beloved Tamiḻttāy. T. K. Chidambaranatha Mudaliar (1882–1954), a well-known Tamil scholar and expert on the medieval poet Kamban, recalls that as a young boy studying in high school in the 1890s, he heard a public lecture by Swaminatha Aiyar at a local college in Tiruchirapalli. The lecture was on the glories and greatness of Tamil. Chidambaranathan remembered it well in 1935:

> The reverend Aiyar listed the beautiful jewels worn by our Lady Tamil (tamiḻmakaḷ):
>
>> The Cūḷāmaṇi adorns her head;
>> The Cintāmaṇi is on her breast;
>> The Kuṇṭalakēci hangs from her ears;
>> The Vaḷaiyāpati encircles her arms;
>> Her waist wears the Maṇimēkalai;
>> And her ankles are adorned with the Cilappatikāram.
>
> As soon as he recited this, I became completely entranced (mayaṅkip pōyviṭṭēṉ). That night, all I could do was dream about this—that Lady Tamil (tamiḻaṉaṅku) was approaching me, and bewitching me with her every step and turn with the beauty of her jewels.[30]

Yet Chidambaranathan and his fellow male devotees could only dream of Tamiḻttāy as such, for their desire for her, however passionate, could never be consummated, lurking as it had to in the interstices of the two dominant structures of imagining their beloved: she was their mother, and she was a perpetual virgin. Indeed, one of the most frequent ways in which Tamiḻttāy is described in Tamil devotional discourses from its very inception is as *kaṉṉittāy*, "virgin mother,"[31] a deliberate contradiction which only emphasized her extraordinary exceptionalism (K. Appadurai 1944: 28–29, 33; Kathiresan Chettiar 1959–60: 170; Pancanathan n.d.: 25; Sharif 1990: 8–9; S. Subramanian 1939: 36–37). Tamiḻttāy's bodily intactness underscored the inviolability of the language she embodied, its purity and autonomy as well as its self-sufficiency, even its divine wholeness. Immensely fruitful though her womb may be, the insistence that she is a virgin meant that her sexual purity (*tūymai*) is not compromised by her fertility and productiveness (*vaḷamai*). As one devotee proudly noted, "Our Tamiḻaṉṉai [Tamiḻttāy] flourishes as a virgin, as queen of chastity (*kaṟpu*)" (Tamilmallan 1984: 62). Cast as an asexual figure confined to perpetual virginity and hallowed motherhood, Tamiḻttāy is rendered sexually "safe," an object of filial longing at best, of unconsummated desire at worst. The dilemma this poses for the desiring devotee is best expressed by Ramalinga Pillai in a poem suggestively entitled "Kaṉṉit Tamiḻ," "Virgin Tamil":

> She came towards me, adorned with blossoms,
> Filling me with such delight (*iṉpam*);
> Transported to the world of gods, I rejoiced;
> O, how can I describe my bliss!
>
> Gold and gems she may not have;
> Even so, she was filled with beauty;
> With her sweet gentle smile,
> she filled my mind with pleasure (*iṉpam*).
>
> . . . .
>
> Enchanted by her virginal beauty,
> I reached forward to tightly embrace her!
> Seeing then that she was my mother, I shrunk back, and fell at her feet, my body doubled up in shame!
> "Filled with alien thoughts, I totally forgot the mother who gave birth to me.
> Alas! I lost my mind."
> So I grieved in distress.[32]

Underlying the medley of ambivalences here—of shame and guilt, of desire and revulsion, of grief and joy—is the (sexual) unavailability of Tamiḻttāy, however desirable she may be. Her state of perpetual virginity transforms Tamiḻttāy into a passive, undesiring female herself, erasing all traces of active sexuality from her being, but it also meant that the male devotee's desire for her went unrequited. It remained as fantasy, never to be consummated. In Tamil devotion therefore, as indeed in so many ideologies, female virginity proves to be both disempowering and empowering: disempowering because it marks the female body as undesiring; empowering because it suggests impenetrability, self-sufficiency, and unavailability.

The emptying of active sexuality from Tamiḻttāy's being is critical to the work of the devotional triangle of desire, for this is what allows the Tamil-speaking woman to enter the male devotee's regimes of pleasure. As the flesh-and-blood embodiment of Tamiḻttāy, she acts as her surrogate but without the imperative to maintain a virginal status. In fact, the very reproduction of Tamil required the woman to abandon her virginity through a chaste monogamous marriage to the male Tamilian (Ramaswamy 1992a). All the same, because the male Tamilian is also devoted to Tamil in these narratives, there is a concern that the primary commitment to Tamiḻttāy should not be compromised by the necessary sexual bonding with these human surrogates. So, in a long poem published as recently as January 1993 in a daily newspaper, the hero declares to his beloved that only after he had destroyed Hindi, which was threatening to enslave and wipe out Tamil, would he even "think about [her] beautiful breasts, and caress and enjoy [her]!"[33] Similarly, years earlier, during a December 1956 debate in the Madras Legislative Assembly on instituting Tamil as the official language of the state, one of the members burst into a story about two lovers, in which the woman waits impatiently for the arrival of her beloved only to find out that he had been delayed on his way over to meet her. The hero tells her: "I was hurrying along thinking about you. At that time, I heard someone making a speech in sweet Tamil (*iṉpattamiḻ*); hearing that, I forgot myself and stayed on."[34] The legislator, V. Balakrishnan, goes on to tell his (predominantly male) audience that this is why we have been told that *iṉpattamiḻ,* "sweet Tamil," has more *kātal,* "(romantic) love," to offer us than even our *kātali,* "female lover." The explicitness of the analogy here between the woman and Tamil as *kātali* is all the more remarkable because it is made in the state's legislative chambers and in the context of promoting the cause of Tamil as official language.

Caught between his language/mother and his wife/lover, the male devotee looks for ways in which he could have them both. One solution for accomplishing this, which Bharatidasan offers in one of his poems, is for the male devotee to work together with his beloved in serving Tamil. So the hero tells his lover:

> I have been born for you, truly, my beloved!
> You have been born for me, O cuckoo bird, my shining beam!
> . . . .

I gave myself to you. . . .
You gave yourself to me. . . .
. . . .
[My] mother hailed me. . . .
She hailed you. . . .
Our mother's land, our Tamil
We have to rescue from ruin!
This is *iṉpam!* This is *iṉpam!*
What else do we desire but this?[35]

Thus the male devotee calls upon his beloved to give up their mutual pleasure in each other for the sake of Tamiḻttāy. Here, we see that the devotional triangle works not so much to disrupt the dyadic relationship between the male and female devotee as to rewrite the very meanings of "pleasure" and "desire" themselves: the poem begins with a celebration of the sexual union of the male devotee with his beloved and ends with a call to jointly sublimate that pleasure in each other in service of the language. Through such an act of sublimation, the language and its devotees, male and female, come to be ever more tightly bound to each other through bonds of pleasure and desire—fueled, denied, and rekindled.

This is of course not the only way out. The male devotee also confesses that if he indeed had to abandon himself to a sexual relationship with a human lover, it could be with none other than a Tamil-speaking woman, imagined as the very living embodiment of Tamil—a surrogate Tamiḻttāy cast in her image, but without the ambivalent burdens of virgin motherhood. Many poems suggest this, some even maintaining that it would be an act of betrayal and disloyalty for the Tamilian male to marry anyone other than a "true" and "pure" Tamilian woman, but there is one text I want to focus upon here, entitled *Kātalikku* (For my beloved). Published in 1961, the work is cast in the form of a series of letters written by an ardent male adorer of Tamiḻttāy to his human beloved, who appears to be severely vexed over his intense attachment to the language/mother which frequently takes him away from her side. The purpose of the letters appears to have been not only to convince her of the worthiness of his work for *tamiḻppaṟṟu* but also to convert her to its cause, because only then, it is clear to him, could he consummate his relationship with his beloved. So, in the penultimate letter he declares in response to her question, "Do you want me? do you want Tamil?": "Dearest! I need you; I need Tamil as well; I need both you and Tamil. I need you as one who has herself blended with Tamil. . . .

Dearest! For me, you are sweet Tamil (*iṉpattamiḻ*)." He then goes on to compare different parts of his beloved's being and body to the different aspects of Tamil and its literature, writing, "In your youth—your beauty—your dark eyes—your fine brow—your eyelids—your black hair— . . . in the very movement of your limbs, I see only precious Tamil. . . . [Y]ou are living Tamil. I want you. I want only you as the very embodiment of Tamil (*tamiḻ kalanta nī tāṉ vēṇṭum*)" (Arulsami 1966: 80–86).

In this narrative as well, the work of the devotional triangle is productive. The hero is an ardent devotee who, passionately dedicated as he was to the cause of Tamil, is drawn to the Tamil-speaking woman precisely because in her, he sees the flesh-and-blood embodiment of his dear Tamiḻttāy. The narrative also works to successfully constitute him as an object of desire of the female Tamil speaker: she starts out as a reluctant lover, not entirely enchanted with either him or *tamiḻppaṟṟu*. By the end of the narrative, in the final letter of this exchange, his narration of his work for Tamil wins her over to him and to its cause (Arulsami 1966: 87–88).

These fascinating instances clearly suggest that Tamil devotion cannot be confined to its more obvious pious and filial manifestations alone. The modality of erotics, however, exists only in the interstices of *tamiḻppaṟṟu*, erupting every now and then, tantalizingly, in the writings of Tamiḻttāy's desiring devotee(s). This may seem surprising in light of the vigorous traditions of pre-colonial erotic poetry in the Tamil-speaking region as indeed in other parts of India. But these traditions did not fare particularly well with the introduction of new Victorian and bourgeois norms of sexual morality which took deep root in colonial India, under the scathing missionary, Orientalist, and colonial scrutiny of "Hindu" sexuality (Metcalf 1994: 92–105; Sinha 1995). This colonial scrutiny was itself reflective of a major realignment in notions of respectability and "correct" sexuality within ideologies of nationalism from the early decades of the nineteenth century in modern Europe (Mosse 1985). For twentieth-century South India, the conflicts between older forms of sexual expression and its newer, more "respectable" bourgeois manifestations have scarcely been documented. But it does appear that the colonial critique only heightened puritanical norms and sexual ethics that the upper castes of the region routinely supported in pre-colonial times. The Dravidian movement, in its own attacks on Brahmanism, celebrates what it identifies as the authentic Tamil form of premarital love and sexual union, *kaḷavu,* which is held up as the desirable alternative to the "arranged" intra-caste marriage dictated by Brahmanical norms. At a rhetorical level, the movement certainly promotes freer expressions of love and sexuality. Nevertheless, it too practices its own politics of virtue in which the chastity, modesty, and sexual fidelity of the Tamil woman underwrite not just the honor of the Tamil man but also the purity and honor of Tamil culture, land, and language (Lakshmi 1990; M. S. S. Pandian, Anandhi, and Venkatachalapathy 1991). So M. Rajamanikkam declares, "As we safeguard the purity of women, we ought to guard the purity of [our] language" (quoted in Tirumaran 1992: 159). Caught between the new norms of bourgeois respectability and older, deeper conventions of female chastity and sexual virtue, the modality of erotics has a troubled and shadowy presence in the discourses of Tamil's devotees. Consequently, the erotic and sensuous persona of Tamiḻttāy is displaced by the compassionate and nurturing image of de-sexualized and spiritualized motherhood.

ON THE FEMINIZATION OF LANGUAGE

Its devotees may empower their language by drawing upon three different models of femininity—an all-powerful goddess, a compassionate but endangered mother, and a desirable but unattainable maiden. But eventually and hegemonically, it is the maternal image that came to dominate devotional imaginations, overwriting the divine and the erotic. Why? And why feminize the language at all? In the pre-colonial poetic traditions to which Tamil's modern devotees are indebted in myriad ways, the feminization of Tamil was largely underdeveloped, although not entirely absent. And the language was not associated with motherhood. In the rare instances when it was personified, its gender was either unspecified or even male.[36] Yet, from the late nineteenth century on, the personification of Tamil relied extensively on the female form, and especially on the female form clothed in maternal garb. Such a feminization of the language, however, was neither idiosyncratic nor exceptional, but symptomatic of a fundamental regendering of culture and community under colonial rule and modernity. Two complex imaginaries converged to provide the terrain on which this took place: a dominant colonial identification of all things Indian as feminine (or effeminate); and bourgeois nationalist discourses of modernity conducted around the hallowed figure of the mother.

Their many contrary impulses notwithstanding, colonial discourses fundamentally contrasted the natural "masculinity" of British imperial culture with the inherent "femininity" of (Hindu) India, the former being preordained to rule and command, the latter to obey and follow. This in turn was the gendered expression of the Orientalist imaginary that undergirded colonial rule, in which the natural and inherent superiority of the rational, secular, industrious, progressive (masculine) West prevails over the irrational, spiritual, passive, and unchanging (feminine) East (Metcalf 1994: 92–112; Said 1978; Sinha 1995). It was not only India that was feminized thus. At least since the time of James Mill, the Indian woman, too, metonymically came to represent "Indian" culture and civilization, just as, in another context, the (white) European woman was a sign of her culture and civilization. Identified as it was in colonial discourses as the site of the authentic India, the female domain assumed a new significance in anticolonial and countercolonial discourses which mounted their resistance on the same terrain. When imagined as the repository of all that was uncolonized, Indian women became the embodiment of all that is truly and purely Indian. Correspondingly, all that is deemed authentic, true, and pure is by definition feminine, domestic, and private, for the male, public world was tainted by its association with colonialism (Chatterjee 1989).

The language of that public world was of course English, whose very dominance had consigned India's languages to the inner, private domain of the home and the family—the domain of the woman. Inhabiting the same domain as the woman, India's languages, too, were perforce feminized in the discourses of the colonized. Like the woman with whom they now shared space, they became embodiments of all that was imagined to be authentically Indian. Sivagnanam best captured this transformation, although he confined his remarks to Tamil, in a speech he gave to an anti-Hindi conference in Madras in 1948, soon after Indian independence: "Formerly, when the British empire sought to destroy Tamil by introducing English, men took to its study for jobs and status. At that time when Tamil was neglected and relegated to the kitchen, it was Tamil women who guarded it with their own arms. Now that English rule has come to an end, our women who have hitherto been protecting Tamil are now returning Tami<u>l</u>ttāy back to us."[37] The easy slippage in the last sentence from "Tamil" to "Tami<u>l</u>ttāy," from Tamil-as-language to Tamil-as-woman, is possible because in Sivagnanam's imagination, as in that of numerous other Indians like him, it is women who are the "custodians" of India's languages, watching over them until they could be reclaimed and restored to their former glory (by men).

And yet Indian women themselves—as indeed women in so many other parts of the world—had been radically reconfigured by bourgeois discourses of modernity, for if woman was idealized as the repository of all that was glorious and wonderful in one's culture, she was also firmly put into her place, in the home and amid her family as "mother" (Mosse 1985: 90–91). Many studies have demonstrated that the consolidation of nationalist ideologies in different regions of the world was accompanied by an "extravagant celebration of motherhood" (Margolis 1984: 28). This was especially true in western Europe, which provided the model for so many ideologies that crystallized in colonial India. There, bourgeois nationalist discourses were marked by the discursive and symbolic separation of the "home" from "work," and of the "nation" from the "world." The home and the nation were hallowed as noncompetitive, depoliticized arenas, and as sacral repositories of moral values and virtue. The reproduction of these arenas, as such, was ensured by insisting that women are "by nature" self-sacrificing, virtuous, unambitious, and nonpolitical beings, destined to be child bearers and nurturers. As George Mosse notes (1985: 97), "Women as national symbols exemplified order and restfulness. Woman was the embodiment of respectability; even as defender and protector of her people, she was assimilated to her traditional role as woman and mother, the custodian of tradition, who kept nostalgia alive in the active world of men." Such a representation was only further consolidated within nationalist ideologies seeking to put the nation on a pedestal as an iconic object of platonic affection and unconditional devotion, for how much more successfully could this be done than by recasting the nation itself as a selfless, compassionate, and de-sexualized Mother, disaggregated from the public realms of politics, self-interest, and sexual competition (Badinter 1981; Davin 1978; Margolis 1984; Poovey 1988: 1–23)?

In colonial India as well, at different times in the nineteenth century, the "woman's question" loomed large in the writings of newly westernized and middle-class (Hindu) elites. Mostly centered in the urban hubs of Calcutta, Bombay, and Madras, they sought to counter the colonial censure of Indian culture and tradition by "reforming" their women and transforming them into virtuous, educated "companions." By the turn of this century, this reforming zeal yielded to a "new" nationalist patriarchy, as the nation came to be valorized as a "home" and "family" whose health could be guaranteed by ensuring the re-signification of largely middle-class women as the educated mothers of its future citizens (Chatterjee 1989; R. Kumar 1993; Lakshmi 1990).[38] The woman-as-wife or sexual being was subordinated to the woman-as-mother or reproductive being, for as one Swami Jagadiswarananda insisted in 1933, "motherhood is the fulfillment of wifehood" (quoted in Visweswaran 1990: 67). As Visweswaran rightly notes, motherhood emerged as "a strategy of containment" that was both oppositional and hegemonic: "Oppositional because it resisted the British 'sexing' of all Indian women as potential 'wives,' opting for a spiritual, de-sexualized woman, 'the mother.' Hegemonic because the other side of the British equation of the sexual Indian woman, was the asexual, spiritual Victorian woman" (Visweswaran 1990: 66).

Thus, in Indian nationalist discourses, while the home is presided over by the woman-as-mother, the nation-as-home is presided over by her archetype, Bhārata Mātā, a nationalist icon like Britannia or Marianne, but one who also embodies the difference of Indian spirituality and tradition. For nationalist thought in Tamilnadu, Subramania Bharati's statement in his essay "The Place of Woman" marks this convergence of the woman in her guise as mother and India as Bhārata Mātā:

> Nor is it without significance that the country of spiritual liberation, India, should, at this hour of her mighty awakening, have adopted as her most potent spell, the words "Vande Mataram," i.e., "I salute the Mother." That means that the first work of a regenerated India will be to place the Mother, i.e., womankind, on the pedestal of spiritual superiority. Others speak of their Fatherlands. To us, the Nation is represented by the word "Mata" [mother].
>
> (Bharati 1937: 27)

In projects like *tamiḻppaṟṟu,* which were conducted in the outlying regions of the emergent nation, this nationalist valorization of India as mother was supplemented by the celebration of language as mother, itself at odds with Bhārata Mātā in the Dravidianist imagination, as we have seen. Given the cultural politics of Tamilnadu, where a large number of Tamil's devout asserted that they were victimized not just by British colonialism but by North Indian "imperialism" as well, the Tamil-speaking home and its mother—and their language—were doubly burdened. They not only had to define authentic Tamil subjectivity against the colonial West; in addition, and even more urgently in the decades following Indian independence, they were enrolled into the project of guarding the purity and fidelity of Tamil speakers from what in many accounts was considered a more enduring enemy, the Aryan Sanskritic Brahmanic North.

So, the representation of the language as Tamiḻttāy; as *tāymoḻi*, "mother tongue"; *tāyppāl*, "mother's milk"; or simply *tāy*, "mother" surfaced in a late colonial situation in which motherhood came to be privileged, not only as the *sine qua non* of women's identity but also as the foundational site on which pure and true subjectivities and communities could be imagined and reproduced. In the fractured colonial context in which the (Tamil) male was increasingly tainted by his association with the outer, non-Tamil-speaking colonized public domain, the home-family-domestic nexus was imagined as the site where an essential "Tamil" unity, spirituality, and wholeness continued to be maintained. As the woman in her incarnation as "mother" came to be marked as the very human embodiment of this wholeness, spirituality, and unity, the (Tamil) language she spoke (= "mother tongue") correspondingly also found itself reconstituted in her image, taking on her persona of femininity, spirituality, and de-sexualized motherhood. Of course, given the powerful anti-Hindu and even antireligious sentiments of many of her devotees, great care was taken—although not with unconditional success, as we may recall—not just to de-sexualize Tamiḻttāy but to de-spiritualize her as well. So the image of Tamiḻttāy as deity and desirable maiden is progressively overshadowed by her reincarnation as a familial and secular *tāy*, "mother."

Its devotees themselves offer two kinds of explanations for why they have imagined Tamil as mother. It is customary, they tell us, to think of one's language as one's mother; it is "ancient Tamil tradition" (Government of Tamilnadu 1990: 49; Purnalingam Pillai 1930: 56–58). As we have seen, however, this "tradition" was neither ancient nor customary. The devotees also insist that their language, like their mothers, gives birth to Tamil speakers, and nourishes and raises them. Like their mothers, their language, too, abides with them for ever and ever. In a world where there was nothing more assured than the love of a mother for her child, K. Appadurai asked what could one say about "the love of the mother of all of Tamilnadu who bore not only our bodies, but also bore the mothers who bore us, and bore the mothers of the mothers who bore us?" (1944: 20). For Tamil's devotees, it was natural to valorize the one bedrock of their existence as a community, that is, their language, by assimilating it to that foundational figure which they claimed guaranteed their existence as individuals, namely, their mother.

The new ideologies of motherhood that confirmed motherly love as foundational were thus enrolled in reinforcing the new ideologies of modernity in which language was seen as foundational to community and nation. In the discourses of *tamiḻpparru*, there are multiple roles played by this foundational metaphor of the nourishing and compassionate mother. It *familiarizes* and *familializes* the relationship between Tamil speakers and their language by couching it in the comfortable everyday terms of the home and the family. The metaphor also *naturalizes* this relationship by constituting a sense of originary and selfless love that Tamilians, as her "children," necessarily and naturally owe to their language/mother. It *de-historicizes* the bonds between the language and its speakers by presenting them as timeless, essential, and beyond the vagaries of history. Above all, it *depoliticizes* the relationship by enabling the abstraction of the community of speakers of Tamil from politics, and by re-signifying it as a "family" whose members were united as harmonious siblings bonded together through sharing Tamiḻttāy's womb and milk.

VISUALIZING TAMIḺTTĀY

The struggle over the multiple linguistic imaginings and the many conceptions of femininity that have gone into the constitution of Tamiḻttāy came to the fore when the devout attempted to fashion for her a consistent and credible iconographic presence. In January 1981, almost a century after her first appearance in the poetry of her admirers, a statue of Tamiḻttāy was officially installed in Madurai, on the occasion of the Fifth International Tamil Conference, by the Tamilnadu chief minister, M. G. Ramachandran. One critic scoffed at the government's attempt to pass off an archaic female figurine as Tamiḻttāy (Ilantiraiyan 1981: 67–68). Another wrote:

> It is a matter of great sorrow that they have made a statue, called it Tamiḻttāy, and have even conducted an inauguration ceremony around it. There cannot be anything more foolish than this. In these days when we say that we should not have any statues of even our gods, *they have turned what is merely imagination into solid form.* They have sown the seeds of great danger for future generations who will come to believe that all this is true. This is foolishness of the highest degree. Formerly, during the nationalist movement, this is how the Congress wove its lies around figures such as Cutantira Tēvi [Goddess Freedom], Bhārata Mātā, and so on, by creating statues for them and painting their pictures. *There is nothing wrong in imagining that Tamil, or our nation, is our mother, and in praising them as such.* But to then turn around and create statues for them is not very rational.
>
> (quoted in Ilantiraiyan 1981: 67, emphases mine)

This critic objected not so much to the feminization of the language as mother as to the transformation of "mere imagination" into concrete reality. That such an objection should have emerged is perhaps not surprising, for it is hard to miss the irony of an overtly material form of Tamiḻttāy receiving the blessings of a government that was putatively dedicated to implementing the ideology of the Dravidian movement. At least since the 1920s, that movement had attacked the rationality and sensibility of a Hindu culture that generated multilimbed, multiheaded material manifestations of what ought to be a singular, formless godhead (Annadurai 1969: 42–43; Ryerson 1988). Thus Ramasami asked every true Dravidian to solemnly pledge, "I will not worship images anymore; I will not go to temples where images of divine forms are placed" (Anaimuthu 1974: 317). And Bharatidasan declared, "God has neither figure nor name. . . . It is not a Tamil principle to worship stone or copper" (quoted in Ryerson 1988: 82–83). Yet, and the irony continues, some of the earliest material and visual manifestations of Tamiḻttāy appeared during the anti-Hindi protests of the late 1930s that were spearheaded by Ramasami and his Self-Respect movement. In 1938, Dravidian movement newspapers carried visuals of Tamiḻttāy being assaulted by C. Rajagopalachari (figs. 5, 6).[39] And when Ramasami himself was arrested in 1938, thousands of his followers protested by carrying in a procession a giant statue of Tamiḻttāy in a posture of mourning through the streets of Madras (Visswanathan 1983: 236).

Indeed, it was not until the 1930s that the verbal habit of imagining Tamil as Tamiḻttāy was supplemented by visual practice. By that time, visual and material representations of Bhārata Mātā were fairly common, even in Tamilnadu (Baskaran 1981). Occasionally, drawings of Tamiḻttāy began to appear in literary magazines, often accompanying poems or essays on her; on mastheads of Tamil devotional journals; and sometimes in advertisements for shops or publishing houses that carried her name (fig. 8). Consumption of these visuals, as of the journals that they appeared in, would have been by a largely urban, scholarly elite, interested primarily in Tamil literature and poetry and hence by no means a popular audience. More recently, she has also been featured on covers of books on language issues and on Tamil poetry (Bharatidasan 1992; Govindarajan 1988; Nagarajan 1980; Sivagnanam 1978). And, over the years, many Tamil revivalist and literary organizations as well as individual devotees—the Kamban Kazhagam in Karaikkudi; a group of notables headed by Professor A. Alagappan of Annamalai University;

and, more recently, the Tamilnadu state—have printed and circulated large color posters, very much like the posters of Hindu goddesses and popular personalities that one frequently encounters in modern homes and public spaces everywhere in India (figs. 1, 2, 9) (Guha-Thakurta 1991). Statues of Tamiḻttāy are less frequent. Giant floats carrying Tamiḻttāy's statue were part of the grand state-sponsored public processionals of the Tamil conferences held in Madras in 1968 and Madurai in 1981.[40] A statue in wood adorns the entrance foyer of the library of the Tamil University in Tanjavur. Large stone statues of Tamiḻttāy may be found in Madurai and Karaikkudi. Significantly, there are no statues of Tamiḻttāy in Madras, the political capital of the region. This in itself is a sign not just of the state's ambivalence towards religious and female iconography, but also of its very different attitude towards language and Tamil devotion, as we will see later.

These statues and pictures show clearly that Tamiḻttāy's iconography as generated by *tamiḻppaṟṟu* is a melange of traditional and nouveau forms, of conflicted dependence on religious and secular imagery, and of an ambivalent reliance on old esthetic devices to iconize what is after all a brand-new personage. Their best efforts to the contrary, her devotees have found it often difficult to escape the vise of Hindu religious as well as Indian nationalist imagery. For one thing, unless she is clearly identified as "Tamiḻttāy," it is very easy to confuse her visually with the hundreds of other goddesses and female divinities that are popular in this region. For another, in the cartoons in which she was featured in the 1960s, she could easily be mistaken for—or deliberately be read as—an everyday Tamil woman (fig. 10). While in quite a number of the visuals that are printed in magazines and journals she is left unnamed, leaving it to the reader to figure out from context who she is, in a large majority of cases she is named specifically as Tamiḻttāy. The fact that her devotees have to regularly resort to identifying Tamiḻttāy through inscribing her name suggests, at the very least, that no iconographic canon has as yet crystallized around her, as it has around well-known deities such as, say, Lakshmi or Ganesha who arguably do not need to be identified as such. At the same time, given the low literacy rates in the region, the use of writing to identify her visuals has obvious implications for who has, and who does not have, ready access to Tamiḻttāy.

Naming is not the only strategy that her devotees have used to identify their Tamiḻttāy visually. They have also tried, with mixed success, to generate a repertoire of distinctive iconographic features that would give her a visual presence that cannot be readily confused with other well-known goddesses. First and most clearly, an important feature of Tamiḻttāy's iconography is that she is almost invariably shown carrying a sheaf of cadjan leaves in her left hand. Ironically, given the important role played by print capitalism in disseminating the assertions of Tamil devotion, there are very few visuals which show her with a printed book. The use of cadjan leaves instead of the printed book underscores the archaizing strategies in devotional poetry, conveying to the viewer the impression that she is an ancient and hoary figure. At the same time, when the leaves are left unnamed, as they are in a large number of cases, Tamiḻttāy could be easily mistaken for Saraswati, whose iconographic tradition also has her holding such palm-leaf manuscripts. In a number of cases, however, the leaves in Tamiḻttāy's hand are identified specifically as the *Tirukkuṟaḷ*. Additionally, the Annamalainagar poster of Tamiḻttāy (fig. 1), as well as pictures of her published in journals like *Tamiḻt Teṉṟal* (1 July 1948) and *Nakkīraṉ* (15 January 1960), visually translate the poetic notion that the many "gems" of Tamil literature are jewels that adorn Tamiḻttāy's body. In particular—and here one may note the clever play on the titles of these various texts—the *Cilappatikāram* jingles on her feet as anklets, the *Maṇimēkalai* encircles her waist as a jeweled belt, the *Kuṇṭalakēci* hangs from her ears as gold rings, the *Vaḷaiyāpati* adorns her arms as bracelets, and the *Cīvaka Cintāmaṇi* crowns her head as a diadem.

Other iconographic features drawn from Tamil literary and historical traditions serve to bestow upon Tamiḻttāy a visual presence that distinguishes her from that "other" mother, Bhārata Mātā. In the Annamalainagar poster, Tamiḻttāy sits on a throne inscribed with the symbols of the fish, the bow, and the tiger, which are claimed to represent the ancient Pandya, Chera, and Chola kingdoms, the oldest in the recorded history of the region (fig. 1). The same symbols may be seen in the official Tamilnadu government statue and in the poster released by the state (fig. 9). The Annamalainagar poster, as well as the Kamban Kazhagam's, also links her visually with the three "branches" of Tamil, *iyal* (literature), *icai* (music), and *nāṭakam* (drama), by incorporating images of a literary manuscript, a lute, and drums (figs. 1, 2). In many visual and material manifestations, Tamiḻttāy holds a musical instrument in her hand; once again, the similarity here with Saraswati, the Sanskritic goddess of music, is unmistakable. Yet her followers insist that Tamiḻttāy's musical instrument is not Saraswati's *vīṇā* but the much more ancient *yāḻ* mentioned in Caṅkam poems.

In general, there is unusual unanimity in presenting Tami<u>l</u>ttāy visually as a young woman, albeit one who often appears rather matronly. This is in keeping of course with her dominant image as a *ka<u>n</u><u>n</u>i* (maiden), and with the assertion that Tamil is an evergreen, ageless, undying language (*ka<u>n</u><u>n</u>ittami<u>l</u>*). So far, I have only found two exceptions to this general pattern. First, in a cartoon that appeared in a DK journal, *Pōrvāḷ,* during the anti-Hindi protests of 1948, Tamil is cast as an old woman who contemptuously looks at the newborn babe, Hindi, with which the Indian state was planning to displace her. The cartoon resorts to the image of the old woman to juxtapose the venerable antiquity of Tamil with the upstart immaturity of the "infant" Hindi.[41] And second, in illustrations accompanying a set of poems written in the *pilḷaittami<u>l</u>* (extraordinary child) genre and published in 1981, Tami<u>l</u>ttāy is featured, in keeping with the requirements of that genre, as a little infant and young girl, albeit one who has the face of a grown woman.[42] These exceptions aside, in the majority of cases in which she appears as a young woman, Tami<u>l</u>ttāy is generally depicted sedately seated and chastely clothed, which suggests, if we follow George Mosse's comparable discussion of Marianne of France, the imperative to associate her with stability and bourgeois respectability (1985: 91). In quite a few cases, Tami<u>l</u>ttāy wears a sari and blouse in the modest style that comes to be associated with the middle-class woman. But equally strikingly, in a large number of instances, including the official state poster, she appears in garments truer to a more archaic iconographic tradition—tight-fitting short upper bodice, no top cloth, and figure-hugging clothing from the waist down (figs. 9, 11). This is typically how the devotional assertion that Tamil is an ancient "classical" language has been visualized; the body of Tami<u>l</u>ttāy is archaized by clothing her in the (imagined) garbs of an ancient Hindu goddess or literary heroine. Here, parenthetically, one may note Mosse's observations about the comparable archaizing of the clothing and accoutrements of European icons of the nation, such as Germania and Britannia. "Like all symbols," he comments, "the female embodiments of the nation stood for eternal forces. They looked backward in their ancient armor and medieval dress [suggesting] innocence and chastity, a kind of moral rigor directed against modernity—the pastoral and the eternal" (Mosse 1985: 98).

Despite the ambivalently developed but nevertheless manifest eroticization of the Tami<u>l</u>ttāy figure, I have not come across a single visual representation of her as an object of (sexual) desire, with one potential exception: the 1967 cover of the literary journal *Tami<u>l</u> Vaṭṭam,* which features a sensuous, beautifully adorned Tamiḻttāy seated rather seductively on a globe (fig. 3). In all her other visual appearances, Tamiḻttāy is a remarkably de-sexualized figure with little indication of her poetic persona as a desirable woman. The female allegorical figure, Madelyn Gutwirth suggests, "operates to reify female untouchability." The "mute remoteness" and "emptiness of expression" worn by many a statue of Tamiḻttāy, their voluptuousness notwithstanding, hardly make them suitable objects of desire (Gutwirth 1992: 256–57). The absence of visuals of a sensuous Tamiḻttāy only underscores the precarious life of the modality of erotics within the world of Tamil devotion.

The alternate conceptions of the language generated by the religious and classicist imaginations on the one hand, and Indianism and Dravidianism on the other, visually manifest themselves in the contrary images of Tamiḻttāy as a glorious, bejeweled woman in some of her pictures, and as a disheveled woman in a state of disarray in others. In general, the latter is restricted to the various cartoons generated during the anti-Hindi protests of the midcentury in contexts that were clearly populist. These cartoons thus show Tamiḻttāy in various stages of distress—as weeping behind bars, bending over the bodies of her dead children, cowering in a corner with tears running down her face, and so on (figs. 7, 10).[43] One striking visual which was published in February 1965 even has a weeping Tamiḻttāy holding the charred body of Aranganathan in her arms.[44] At the end of the Hindi struggle in 1967 with the coming of the DMK to power, Tamiḻttāy recovers her beatific stance, once again, as she is portrayed happy, smiling, and back on her throne.[45]

Another important area of visual contestation is over Tamiḻttāy's representation as a queen on the one hand, and as an everyday Tamil mother/woman on the other. In the former, her limbs are adorned with jewels; she wears a crown, or is being adorned with one; and she carries a scepter: she is clearly the sovereign of her putative kingdom.[46] But during the 1950s and 1960s, Tamiḻttāy was more often than not featured as an everyday woman, clad in a sari and blouse (fig. 10). Some of these visuals mark her distinctiveness by bestowing a halo around her or placing a small crown on her head. Nevertheless, she could quite readily be mistaken for a generic Tamil-speaking woman, especially when the pictures do not name her. So cartoons of Tamiḻttāy crying over the bodies of her children fade into newspaper pictures of women shedding tears over the death of their near and dear ones.[47] The feminization of the language is so pervasive that texts and essays on Tamil, or on "our mother tongue," routinely begin to carry the figure of a woman either playing with her children or reading to them.[48] Such images only visually reinforce the notion that the Tamil-speaking woman, especially in her guise as mother, is after all a surrogate Tamiḻttāy.

But undoubtedly the biggest area of contestation in the visual politics around Tamiḻttāy, as in the written and spoken discourses on her, surrounds her representation as "goddess." The reliance on the canons and materials of Hindu iconography has meant that the over-riding impression imparted by the various statues and some of the posters of Tamiḻttāy is that she could well be a goddess: she wears the crown that many Hindu divinities typically wear; she holds her right hand in the typical gesture of offering grace to her devotees; she sits on a large lotus, or her feet rest on it, as is typical of many goddesses; and her face often carries the same look of remoteness and transcendence that marks the countenance of many a deity. The real distinctive marker, however, of whether a particular picture or statue intends to present Tamiḻttāy as a goddess lies in the number of arms she is endowed with. As is well known, the supernatural quality and the power of Hindu deities find iconographic representation in the multiple arms they bear. Typically, deities with great power are shown with four arms, while minor deities, female consorts, and godlings have two. The mother-goddess is generally portrayed with four arms, sometimes more.

In general, the large majority of these pictures and statues, especially those produced under the mantle of the Dravidian movement and Dravidianism, show Tamiḻttāy with two arms. She is not a supernatural, superhuman figure participating in all the irrationalities of Hindu religiosity; instead she is a near and dear mother. The seductive maiden on the cover of the 1967 issue of the *Tamiḻ Vaṭṭam* is four-armed, however, and so is the Tamiḻttāy of the poster issued by the Kamban Kazhagam (figs. 2, 3). The statue of Tamiḻttāy that the latter sponsored is also four-armed, the four arms signifying, I was told, the three branches of Tamil learning (*iyal, icai,* and *nāṭakam*) and grace (*aruḷ*) (fig. 11). This very same statue was recast again in 1981 as the official, government-sponsored figure of Tamiḻttāy installed in Madurai. But the state's statue shows Tamiḻttāy with only two arms; in all other respects, it is identical to the four-armed statue of the Kamban Kazhagam. The two additional arms were left out on specific orders from the highest levels of the government—even from the chief minister himself, I was told (compare figs. 9 and 11). This concession to Dravidianist iconoclasm aside, it is telling that the state's visual representation of Tamiḻttāy is in all other respects truer to her religious persona as goddess than to her secular incarnation as mother. For the state would very much like to capitalize on the enormous attention that Hindu divinities continue to command among the populace, in its own effort to pass itself off as a devotee of Tamiḻttāy, albeit a reluctant one.

Today, the Kamban Kazhagam's four-armed statue of the goddess sits in a "temple" to her that has been built in the southern town of Karaikkudi (fig. 12). The foundation for the temple was laid in April 1975 with the blessings of the DMK government of M. Karunanidhi, which also sanctioned the hefty sum of five lakh rupees for the project. The temple was finally opened to the public in April 1993. Its central sanctum houses, in addition to Tamiḻttāy, the images of her two most ancient "sons," the grammarians Agastya and Tolkappiyar. Three subsidiary sanctums carry the images of Ilango, Tiruvalluvar, and Kamban, three of Tamil's most famous poets. The temple itself is shaped in the form of a triangle, the three angles signifying the three most ancient kings—the Chera, the Chola, and the Pandya, Tamiḻttāy's oldest patron-sons; alternatively, they also represent the three branches of Tamil, *iyal* (literature), *icai* (music), and *nāṭakam* (drama). Although the structure is referred to as a *kōvil,* the sponsors are very clear that it is not a "temple" in the religious sense; the image of Tamiḻttāy is not an object of worship, nor are Hindu religious rituals performed. This is a temple that commemorates, in their vision, the language that belongs to the entire world; accordingly it is open to all who revere Tamil. Indeed, during the dedication of the temple in 1993, it was clear that everybody assembled there was careful to distance themselves from all overt signs of religiosity. In his speech, Karunanidhi, who officially opened the temple to the public, even pointed out there should be no mistake about his extending his approval to an image that had four arms. Rather than signifying irrational divinity, the four arms represented the four languages that Tamil had given birth to: Kannada, Malayalam, Telugu, and Tulu. Tamiḻttāy was not a goddess to be worshipped but a guardian who will guide us, he insisted. For his part, Kunrakudi Adigal (1925–95), the controversial head of the Shaiva *maṭam* (monastery) at Kunrakudi, also concurred, making clear his hopes that Tamil speakers visiting the temple would renew themselves as Tamilians and resolve to write, speak, and think in Tamil, always.[49]

All the effort invested in creating for her a distinctive iconographic presence notwithstanding, there is no single, standardized image of Tamiḻttāy that reigns today. Even as it underscores the many quandaries inherent in translating into visual and material media what is after all an abstraction, the absence of a singular pictorial representation provides a powerful visual reminder of the multiplicity of conceptions about the language, and the many models of the feminine, that have gone into the imagining of Tamiḻttāy within the poetic and prosaic productions of her devotees. And as with the verbal discourses on Tamiḻttāy, in iconographic practice as well the struggle has been waged on several fronts, producing a range of variations in her visual persona. That out of all this a single standardized hegemonic image has not emerged is not necessarily a sign of failure; on the contrary, the existence of this multiplicity and fluidity—what Paul de Man has characterized as a "surplus of meaning" (Gutwirth 1992: 255)—ensures the iconographic availability of Tamiḻttāy, as goddess, queen, mother, and maiden all rolled into one, that future devotees can continue to cash in on.

CHAPTER FOUR

Laboring for Language

The State of Tamil Devotion

From its inception, Tamil devotion meant that speakers of Tamil had to be at the service of the language, to labor in its name and on its behalf. Glossed in devotional narratives as *tami<u>l</u>ppaṇi,* "Tamil work," or *tami<u>l</u>t-toṇṭu,* "Tamil service," this labor is presented as honorable, virtuous, and meritorious. It is mandatory for all those who claim to be Tamilians for it is an obligation (*kaṭamai*), even a debt (*kaṭa<u>n</u>*), that they owe, by virtue of being speakers of Tamil, to their language. Sundaram Pillai set the tone for this when he presented his 1891 play, *Ma<u>n</u>ō<u>n</u>maṇīyam,* with its invocatory hymn to the goddess Tamil, as "tribute" (*kaṭamai*) to his *tami<u>l</u>mātā,* "Tamil mother," and called upon his fellow Tamil speakers to fulfill their debt (*kaṭa<u>n</u>*) to her by rescuing from obscurity ancient Tamil works and creating new literatures (Sundaram Pillai 1922: 9–12). Since then, again and again devotees have represented their work on behalf of the language as *a<u>r</u>appaṇi,* "meritorious work," or *tiruttoṇṭu,* "auspicious service." Indeed, in 1959, Bharatidasan even explicitly declared that it was not service to God that was important, but service to Tamil (*tami<u>l</u>ttirutoṇṭu*).[1]

While there was general consensus among its devotees that talk about Tamil had to be translated into work, and that *tami<u>l</u>ppa<u>rr</u>u* in and of itself was incomplete without *tami<u>l</u>ppaṇi,* there was much less agreement, as can be expected, on what constitutes appropriate labor, on what kind of Tamil one should serve, and on who ought to be involved in this. In the logic of neo-Shaivism and classicism, laboring for Tamil meant the establishment of learned literary academies, as well as the publication and circulation of ancient religious texts and literature. Indianism and Dravidianism, on the other hand, proposed that it was through seizing political power that Tamil's fortunes would turn. For devotees like Maraimalai Adigal, the cleansing of Sanskrit from the speech of the elites would by itself lead to the revival of the language, whereas for a Bharati or a Bharatidasan, it was the people's speech that ought to be the basis for a rejuvenated Tamil. Moreover, there was much disagreement over identifying the putative enemies of Tamil against whom its devotees had to labor. Was it Sanskrit, English, or Hindi? Was it the Brahman or the colonial? Was it the scholastic Tamil pandit or the uneducated Tamil mother? If these were all threatening Tamil, what was the best way to prioritize the tasks ahead? Should the work of Tamil improvement precede the Tamilization of the political apparatus, or should it be the other way around? The questions were many, the problems manifold.

Laboring for Tamil also meant that its devotees had to contend with the state. Should *tamiḻppaṇi* be conducted by individual devotees and their associations, or should the state be the principal agency? Although they did occasionally interact with some of its institutions in the pursuit of their agendas, both neo-Shaivism and classicism largely steered clear of the state. Indianism and Dravidianism, on the other hand, were directly concerned with changing the nature of power relations and the structure of political authority. They aimed to get rid of the British and Brahmans, respectively, and to place in their stead loyal and pure Tamil speakers in positions of power and authority. The state, in turn, has vacillated in its relationship to *tamiḻppaṟṟu*. During the late colonial period, prior to the accession of the Justice Party to power in 1920, the state basically stayed aloof from devotional activities or, at most, played a mediating role between various conflicting interest groups and agendas. In the 1920s and 1930s, however, with the Justice Party and the Congress at the helm, the state began to accommodate, although not without resistance, various devotional demands, especially in the domain of education (e.g., demands for the institution of Tamil as medium of instruction and as subject of study in schools and colleges, the establishment of a Tamil University, and other such measures that Nambi Arooran [1980: 70–139] has analyzed). In the years following 1947, when several of Tamil's devotees were elected to political office and even became chief ministers, not only did this imperative to accommodate accelerate but the state was compelled to progressively "Tamilize" itself, sometimes through conscious involvement in devotional efforts, at other times through actively implementing distinctively pro-Tamil policies in various public, governmental, and educational arenas. And yet, in its Tamilization the state has been reluctant at best, and even recalcitrant at times. Indeed, the state has often assumed the role of a follower rather than a leader, and it frequently appears to be succumbing to pressures from the devotional community, rather than staking out its own autonomous trajectory.

There are obviously many reasons why the state's work for Tamil has been riddled with reluctance, contradiction, and failure, and why it has rarely met the high expectations of the devotees of the language. The most compelling of these reasons are their very different conceptions about language. The everyday, administrative functioning of the modern state demands the adoption of what we may characterize as a "rationalist-bureaucratic" imagination in which language is treated as an *object:* as an "instrument" of communication and education, a "tool" for governance, and a "vehicle" for the transmission of ideas, thought, and knowledge. On the other hand, the emotional and cultural life of its devout was underwritten by a passionate attachment to Tamil, imagined as the very life, spirit, and soul of every Tamilian. For its followers, Tamil was not just an inanimate object but a near and dear *person* whose well-being is likened, again and again, as we have seen, to the well-being of one's own mother. This is not to say that the state, particularly in its post-colonial manifestation, was unaffected by this symbolic investment in Tamil̲ttāy: it makes several gestures in this direction, as we have seen. Nor does it mean that the devotional community did not have its own share of the rationalist, instrumentalist conception of language. Nevertheless, the state's attitudes and intentions towards Tamil are quite different from its devotees', and this difference manifested itself repeatedly in the realm of policy making. Certainly, language and cultural policies in Tamilnadu have been highly contested because of the multiple, contrary meanings with which Tamil has been invested over the decades by its devout. But these policies are also riddled with contradictions because of the different conceptions about the language that drove the state, in contrast to those that reigned in the community of its devotees.

WORSHIPPING WITH TAMIL: LANGUAGE AND LITURGY

In the 1950s and 1960s, more than half a century after *tamil̲ppar̲r̲u* reared its head, the state took up for legislation an issue that was dear to neo-Shaivism from at least the 1920s on. This issue, glossed as *tamil̲ aruccan̲ai* (Tamil worship), turned around the use of Tamil and its religious texts in temples in Tamilnadu where Sanskrit was still the dominant liturgical language.[2] Neo-Shaivism insisted that in ancient Shaiva religion, it was Tamil, rather than Sanskrit, that was used as language of worship. But then "[Brahmans] introduced the words of their northern language in which one can see very little trace of any kind of divinity, empowered them, and denigrated our great and glorious Tamil scriptures, the *Tēvāram* and the *Tiruvācakam,* as 'songs of the Shudras' " (Maraimalai Adigal 1967a: 150).

Moreover, Brahmans were not just content with empowering Sanskrit in this way; they also ensured that it was only after they had chanted the *Veda*s, had received the deities' blessings, and were out of earshot that Tamil hymns were even recited. They had thus displaced the divine Tamil from its own temples with the upstart Sanskrit (Kandiah Pillai 1947; K. Subramania Pillai 1940: 97–106; Swaminatha Upatiyayan 1921: 22–24).[3] The language of liturgy therefore emerged within the practice of *tamil̲ppar̲r̲u* as a key site on which was waged the battle between Brahmanical Hinduism and Tamil Shaivism, between Sanskrit and Tamil scriptures, and above all, between Brahman and "non-Brahman" as ritual specialists and social elites.

Although the relative importance of Tamil and Sanskrit in temple worship has varied from sect to sect, the two languages have been an integral part of the region's institutionalized scriptural Hinduism from the late first millennium C.E. (Cutler 1987:187–94; Peterson 1989: 54–56). Over the centuries, periodic doctrinal and sectarian conflict had erupted around the question of language and liturgy (A. Appadurai 1981: 77–82), but beginning in the 1920s, with neo-Shaivism taking on an increasingly radical stance, the call came for completely excising Sanskrit and its scriptures from Tamilnadu temples and replacing these with Tamil and its scriptures. Along with this also came the demand, as was voiced in 1943 by the Tamil̲ Uṇarcci Mānāṭu, the "Tamil Consciousness Conference," for de-Sanskritizing the names of deities, temples, and temple towns and replacing them with their original or former Tamil names (Ilankumaran 1991: 175).[4] One enthusiast even urged that throughout Tamilnadu, all temples ought to follow only one uniform Tamil liturgical text and priests should be taught to remember that they are Tamilians, should be assured that conducting worship in Tamil would bring in more remuneration, and should be granted honors if they perform good *aruccan̲ai* in Tamil.[5] For the loyal devotee of Tamil, devotion to the (Hindu) gods could not, and should not, be allowed to compromise devotion to Tamil.

By the 1940s and 1950s, populist organizations like K. A. P. Viswanatham's Tamiḻar Kaḻakam (Society of Tamilians) and Sivagnanam's Tamil Arasu Kazhagam had extended their support to the neo-Shaiva demand for Tamil *aruccaṉai* (Sivagnanam 1960: 53–54, 1974: 448).[6] Paradoxically, political parties, like the DK and the DMK, also stepped into this arena of ritual and liturgical politics by the 1950s. As we have seen, the Dravidian movement and the Dravidianist idiom of *tamiḻp-paṟṟu* poured rationalist scorn on Brahmanic Hinduism and neo-Shaivism alike. All the same, by the 1940s Dravidianism began to support the demand for *tamiḻ aruccaṉai* (Sundara Shanmugan 1948: 12, 30; Velu and Selvaraji 1989: 78).[7] As the poet Bharatidasan eloquently observed in 1945, every day in temples across Tamilnadu, the Tamilian relinquished "Tamil honor" by acquiescing to the use of Sanskrit hymns in worship (1969: 27). For the DK and the DMK in the 1950s, *tamiḻ aruccaṉai* assumed saliency as another issue with which to contest both Brahmanical power and the Congress government. Thus at a public meeting in 1957, S. Gurusami, the editor of the DK newspaper *Viṭutalai,* declared that Brahmans had used Tamilian labor to build their huge temples and carve their sculptures, and had then prevented Tamilians from offering worship there. Instead of the richness of Tamil, the "filth" of Sanskrit filled these temples, and E. V. Ramasami, Tamilians were told, would soon lead a protest to help Tamil, the language of *aruccaṉai.*[8]

The iconoclastic Ramasami himself, as we will see, spared no words in denouncing neo-Shaivism's divinization of Tamil. Yet, as early as 1926 he demanded, "Why should we worship our deities in an alien language?"; and in his usual irrepressible fashion, he asked in 1972, on the eve of his death, "What business has a god in Tamilnadu if he does not want Tamil?" (quoted in Diehl 1977: 71). His atheistic agenda for completely ridding all traces of religiosity from Dravidian consciousness notwithstanding, through the 1950s and 1960s Ramasami promoted the cause of Tamil as liturgical language as a means through which Tamil speakers would regain their self-respect. He argued that it would free them from servitude to Aryan Brahmanism and Sanskrit (Anaimuthu 1974: 1043–44). Indeed, for Ramasami and the DK, *tamiḻ aruccaṉai* was only one of several fronts on which to conduct their war against Brahmanical Sanskritic Hinduism, which included the breaking of Brahman monopoly on priesthood, the opening of the *sanctum sanctorum* in temples to all castes, and the public burning of Sanskrit scriptures.

Neo-Shaivism and Dravidianism, contrary ideologies though they may be, thus came together to support *tamiḻ aruccaṉai,* united by their common cause against Brahmans and Sanskrit. Ironically, however, the neo-Shaiva agenda for instituting Tamil as liturgical language was realized in practice not by insisting upon its divinity, but by invoking its status as "mother tongue" and hence a language intelligible to its speakers.[9] This is the argument that was used, for instance, by Kunrakudi Adigal, one of the key spokesmen on this issue. For him, Tamil *aruccaṉai* was a weapon with which to counter not just Sanskritic Brahmanism's hegemony but the Dravidian movement's atheism as well. In 1953, at a time when Ramasami's campaigns against religion and Hinduism were gaining momentum, he argued that it was Sanskrit's "unintelligibility" that rendered it incomprehensible to the Tamil populace and that, not surprisingly, promoted irreligiosity among them. "If the *pujari*s [priests] were to cast off their superiority complex and to conduct *archanai*s [worship] in a language understandable to the average devotee, there would be no anti-god demonstration in the street" (quoted in Presler 1987: 115–16). As if to prove this point, in 1971, when Karunanidhi was chief minister, he declared that following a nearby temple's 1953 switch to Tamil *aruccaṉai,* the number of its patrons as well as the temple's revenues had dramatically escalated.[10]

Karunanidhi made this statement in Coimbatore, in support of the DMK government's attempts in 1970 and 1971 to authorize the use of Tamil as primary language of worship, at a time when many temples across Tamilnadu were actually already doing so, under various guises. Although it is his government that is most closely associated with the *tamiḻ aruccaṉai* issue, this had been a matter of concern for the state for the past couple of decades. At least since the late nineteenth century, its avowed policy of religious neutrality notwithstanding, the colonial state had steadily increased its jurisdiction over temples. But its predominant concern continued to be regulation of temple administration and finances, and the language question did not invite legislation (A. Appadurai 1981; Mudaliar 1974). During the 1950s and 1960s, however, the Congress-led state could no longer ignore demands for Tamil *aruccaṉai,* and the Hindu Religious and Charitable Endowments Department (HRCE) "quietly promoted," as Franklin Presler notes, the increasing use of Tamil hymns in temples. Yet during these years, there was no attempt to substitute Tamil for Sanskrit, only to "strengthen

Tamil's place alongside Sanskrit rituals" (Presler 1987: 115). This did not save the Congress government from being pressured to do away entirely with Sanskrit, replacing it with worship solely in Tamil.[11] Responding to such demands, M. Bhaktavatsalam, the minister for the HRCE—and not a Brahman—declared in 1959 that when he listened to the *aruccaṉai* being offered in Tamil, he was not inspired, did not understand it, and found it "boring."[12] Another Congress member in the Assembly, P. S. Krishnaswami Ayyangar, a Sri Vaishnavite Brahman, insisted that if Tamil were instituted as the liturgical language, non-Tamil devotees who came to temples would find it difficult to comprehend their gods' worship—the assumption here, of course, being that Sanskrit could be understood by one and all.[13] The government's position was that since religious "tradition" (*campratāyam*) should not be interfered with by the state, and since it did not matter which language was used to offer worship, "traditional" (i.e., Sanskritic) forms of worship ought not be abolished. So, Bhaktavatsalam declared in the Legislative Council: "Worship has to be offered according to tradition and custom. It is not proper to change that order. There is no point in raising the issue of Sanskrit or Tamil in worship. The demand for bringing in Tamil to do *aruccaṉai* is a meaningless agitation. *Aruccaṉai* means the recitation of names of the deity. What difference does it make [whether the name is in Sanskrit or Tamil]? . . . This is a meaningless agitation."[14]

Yet, the government's position to the contrary, the protest against the use of Sanskrit in temples had been launched in the first place precisely because "tradition" had been radically reinterpreted over the past few decades; because it made all the difference whether something was named in Sanskrit or Tamil; and because religion and language could not be dissociated from each other, as neo-Shaivism had repeatedly insisted from the turn of the century.

The Congress government no doubt resisted the demand for *tamiḻ aruccaṉai,* partly because of its reluctance to oppose Sanskritic Hinduism,[15] but also partly because in this, as in other matters concerning Tamil in the 1950s and 1960s, it tried to counter the growth of "linguism" and regionalism (as sponsored by the Dravidian movement) that were perceived as threats to Indian nationalism (the basis for its own power). As the Congress was compelled to take a stand on Tamil in variance with large sectors of the Tamil devotional community, the language of liturgy became one of the key issues on which the party was rendered vulnerable to demonization as an enemy of Tamil.

The "quiet encouragement" of the Congress government in strengthening the place of Tamil alongside Sanskrit in temples gave way to its active promotion with the coming to power of the DMK in 1967. In mid-1971, the government formalized its informal support by issuing a series of orders which declared that "the Tamil Nadu people desire that in all temples *archanai*s should be performed in Tamil" (quoted in Presler 1987: 116). In August 1971, Sanskrit was demoted from its status as the normative liturgical language and was declared optional. Its place was now taken by Tamil.[16] In spite of resistance mounted against such orders by many Brahman priests as well as by organizations such as the Madras Temple Worship Protection Society, there were numerous well-publicized performances of Tamil *aruccaṉai* in many temples, conducted in the presence of members of the DMK government (Presler 1987: 116).[17] Though the government nowhere overtly banned the use of Sanskrit or compelled the sole use of Tamil, at least one deputy commissioner interpreted its order in such terms. This sparked off a major uproar, resulting in the eventual staying of all Tamil *aruccaṉai* orders by the Supreme Court in August 1974.[18] The *Centamiḻc Celvi,* which for decades had been publishing essays promoting the use of Tamil in temples, had the following comment:

> In Tamilnadu, there is resistance to Tamil music; there is resistance to Tamil as official language; there is resistance to Tamil as medium of instruction in colleges; there is resistance to reconverting the names of places and towns to pure Tamil; there was resistance to naming Madras state as Tamilnadu; there is resistance to the conduct of domestic rituals in Tamil; there is resistance to pure Tamil. When we have resistance like this everywhere, it is no surprise that there is so much opposition to worship in Tamil.[19]

What are some of the implications of the controversy over Tamil *aruccaṉai* for the public practice of Tamil devotion? First, neo-Shaivite claims about the illegitimacy of Sanskrit for religious practices in the Tamil-speaking region received the sanction, albeit ambiguously and fruitlessly, of the Tamilnadu state. Chief Minister Karunanidhi defended his actions thus: "If the right to perform the *archanai* in Tamil is denied, Sanskrit considered as Devabhasha [language of God], and along with that God and religion also, will be driven out from Tamil Nadu to north India. . . . If the gods in south India cannot tolerate Tamil *archanai*s, let the gods move to north India" (quoted in Presler 1987: 130). Similarly, the minister in charge of implementing the *aruccaṉai* policy declared, as neo-Shaivism had from the beginning of this century, that "it was wrong to say that God could follow only Sanskrit" (quoted in Presler 1987: 116).

Furthermore, neo-Shaivite assertions of the divinity of Tamil also received the blessings of an ostensibly "secular" state that was in the control of a party, the DMK, which at various times had vociferously declared its opposition to religious beliefs of any kind. In Karunanidhi's words, "A section of the people claim that Tamil language has no divinity and hence there is nothing sacred about it. *It is only to controvert this view,* the Tamil Nadu Deviga Peravai and the HRCE Department have introduced Tamil *archanai*s. The Tamil *archanai* only move is born more out of our love and attachment to Tamil than ill will or hatred towards any other language" (quoted in Presler 1987: 118, emphasis mine). Its detractors claimed that the DMK's actions followed from the fact that it was a antireligious party "with no faith in God"—God and religion being identified here, of course, with Sanskrit and the Sanskritic tradition. Yet the DMK's support of *tamil̲ aruccan̲ai* was clearly part of its overall policy of Tamilizing the public sphere. Indeed, contrary to its detractors' claim, it was also in line with the many accommodations that that party had made since at least the 1960s with various aspects of high Hinduism through a corresponding Tamilization of that religion, as I noted earlier.

Moreover, in many religious systems, including scriptural Hinduism, the magical power of a sacred language is predicated on its unintelligibility to the lay worshipper. Quotidian, "profane" languages that are readily comprehensible are believed to not have the same ritual efficacy (Tambiah 1985: 22–30). Indeed, Dakshinamoorthy Bhattar, a priest who challenged the government's orders, argued that the efficacy of ritual depended on the particular sounds of Sanskrit and that there would be "disaster" if he "dared to perform the *archanai* in Tamil" (Presler 1987: 117; see also Harrison 1960: 130). And much to the dismay of many a Tamil devotee, it was not only a Brahman priest who argued thus, but also Gnanaprakasar Tecikar, a respected "non-Brahman" Tamil scholar.[20] But the state's argument was not couched in the vocabulary of ritual efficacy. For regardless of the doctrinal and metaphysical premises on which neo-Shaivism asserted the divine potency and ritual powers of Tamil, the state's *aruccan̲ai* orders derived their eventual legitimacy from the democratic logic that the language of worship ought to be understandable and intelligible to the people, that it ought to be the "mother tongue."[21] Sanskrit's legitimacy was undermined not by questioning its divine status (as neo-Shaivism did), but by declaring its "unintelligibility" among the people. By the same token, Tamil was ordered in its place not just because it was divine, but because it had the "love and attachment" of the people and was their "mother tongue." Here, the Tamil *aruccaṉai* issue appears to provide another illustration of the "demoticization" of liturgical languages—such as Hebrew or Latin or Arabic—that has inevitably accompanied the nationalization and democratization of political and social systems with modernity (Anderson 1983: 68–69). Yet Sanskrit was not threatened by an ordinary "demotic" tongue but by another "sacred" language that had also been recently empowered as "mother tongue." This is what makes the demand for Tamil liturgy unusual.

Finally, the Tamil *aruccaṉai* controversy gave the lie to the state's assertion that "language is not the essence of religion" (quoted in Mudaliar 1974: 223). The Congress government had resisted the demands to replace Sanskrit with Tamil in the 1950s on this basis. It is "meaningless," Bhaktavatsalam had insisted, to raise the language issue in matters of worship. Interestingly, in 1974 the Madras High Court defended the DMK-led state's legislation by invoking the same principle (Mudaliar 1974: 223): "It cannot be taken that unless religious matters are expressed in a particular language they cease to be religious" (quoted in Presler 1987: 117). Yet, as neo-Shaivism had asserted again and again, was it even possible to contemplate god without divine Tamil? Even the DMK minister in charge of the state's religious policy declared in the Legislative Assembly in 1971 that it was god himself, filled with "Tamil consciousness," who had enabled the institution of Tamil *aruccaṉai.*[22] From the point of view of many a devoted Tamilian, god and Tamil could not be separated at will or through state legislation.

CLEANSING TAMIL: LANGUAGE AND PURITY

One evening, when she was barely thirteen, Nilambikai was taking a stroll in their garden with her famed father, Maraimalai Adigal (who at that time still went by his Sanskritic name, Swami Vedachalam). He began to sing a verse from Ramalinga Adigal's famous *Tiruvaruṭpā;* but when he came to the second line of the verse, Vedachalam stopped and said to his daughter: "Is it not wonderful that Ramalinga Adigal has sung this song so beautifully in pure Tamil (*tūyattamiḻ*)? But, instead of using the Sanskrit word *tēkam* in the second line, would it not have been better if he had used the pure Tamil (*taṉittamiḻ*) word, *yākkai?* Because Sanskrit words have been allowed in Tamil, it has lost its beauty and Tamil words have gone out of use." Father and daughter resolved, from that day on, to speak and write only in *taṉittamiḻ* (lit., "exclusively Tamil," but more generally glossed as "pure Tamil") (Nilambikai 1960: iii).

This incident is cited as the originary moment of what comes to be called *taṉittamiḻ iyakkam,* the "pure Tamil" movement, and is dated by most scholars to 1916, though the roots of Maraimalai Adigal's own personal predilections in this regard may be traced back to the late 1890s. The movement has invited considerable criticism and resistance, even within the devotional community. Nonetheless, it still continues to have its share of enthusiasts who publish books and journals advocating its virtues, and who seek, with varying degrees of success, to make *taṉittamiḻ* into an everyday habit in contemporary Tamilnadu. For the ardent purist, there is no difference between "Tamil" and *taṉittamiḻ;* good Tamil is always already *taṉittamiḻ,* the only language in the world that is capable of flourishing without the aid of other languages (Nilambikai 1960: 40–51). This has meant that for purists, even their fellow devotees who do not follow the ideals of *taṉittamiḻ* are, by definition, enemies of Tamil; they are not the true "sons" of their language/mother (Ilankumaran 1991: 130–36, 168–69). "Those who oppose *taṉittamiḻ* are murderers of Tamil," the purists declare unequivocally (quoted in M. Tirunavukarasu 1959: 520).

Soon after the incident in the garden, Vedachalam Tamilized his name (and those of his children), and from then on referred to himself, at least in his Tamil publications, as Maraimalai Adigal. Vedachalam was not the first to do this.[23] A few years earlier, in 1899, another Tamil enthusiast, V. G. Suryanarayana Sastri, had published a collection of sonnets in which his name appeared in its Tamil form as "Paritimāl Kalaiñar." Although this was the only occasion in which Suryanarayana Sastri used his *taṉittamiḻ* name, his act is much cited in purist circles, not just because of his fame as a Tamil scholar but also because he was Brahman (Tirumaran 1992: 118–23). Since that time, many of Tamil's adherents have Tamilized their given Sanskritic names and have bestowed *taṉittamiḻ* names on their children (Kailasapathy 1986: 30). The pure Tamil movement, however, advocates more than just symbolic acts such as the Tamilizing of personal names and, by extension, the names of towns, streets, deities, temples, and so on. It is equally concerned with transformations in written and spoken Tamil, with the conscious refusal, in both public and domestic contexts, to rely on words that are deemed non-Tamil.[24] As early as 1906, the Tamil scholar and

Murugan devotee Pamban Swami (1851–1929) published a book of verses called *Cēntaṉ Centamiḻ,* in which care was taken not to allow even one Sanskrit word to appear (Tirumaran 1992: 123–26). And with the more concerted efforts of Maraimalai Adigal and his followers, this trend picked up momentum from the 1920s—with varying degrees of success, of course (Maraimalai Adigal 1930a: xxv–xxvi, 1934: 11–12). It has been estimated that even at the height of Maraimalai Adigal's enthusiasm for *taṉittamiḻ* in the 1930s, at least 5 percent of the words in his texts continued to be Sanskritic (Nambi Arooran 1976: 345–46). Nevertheless, even impressionistically speaking, the marked decline in the use of foreign words, especially of Sanskritic origin, in Tamil literary, scholarly, and even bureaucratic circles over the past half century is quite striking. The *taṉittamiḻ* movement, however, has paid less attention to excising foreign syntactic patterns and Sanskritic rules of compounding and suffixes, Sanskritic phraseology, and so on, all of which have arguably had a more enduring impact on Tamil literary and speech styles (Annamalai 1979: 48; Kailasapathy 1986: 30–31).

Even the most ardent of purists would readily admit that it has been impossible to totally cleanse Tamil, not least because no real criteria have been developed to determine what constitutes a "pure" Tamil word. Purists castigate the continued use of non-Tamil words in short stories, novels, newspapers, and cinema, and they lament that the earlier enslavement to Sanskrit has now been supplemented by dependence on English, especially in popular speech and culture. Such laments remind us that language purification efforts, not just in Tamilnadu but elsewhere in the world, are elite literary enterprises. Typically, they appear as an imposition of a norm from above, rather than as a manifestation of a need or sentiment from below. Purists like Maraimalai Adigal even insisted that it is indolence and lack of discipline among its speakers that was responsible for Tamil's "corruption," and that it was the duty of disciplined, alert literati to rectify this "problem." "Defiling one's speech by mixing up with it extraneous elements simply indicates laxity of discipline, looseness of character, and lack of serious purpose in life," he scolded (Maraimalai Adigal 1980: 32). Not surprisingly, when couched in such terms, language purification efforts have certainly not caught the popular or populist political imagination, and they are frequently chastised for going against the flow, for trying to set the clock back, and for reviving archaisms (Jernudd and Shapiro 1989; G. Thomas 1991). As one critic declaimed in the *Madras Mail* in 1927:

> A shortsighted nationalism compels such folk to strive to keep all immigrant words out. . . . Fortunately such purists do not control the growth of a language. That is the work of the common people. The purists may frown at slang, they may grumble that the language is being debased by slipshod and lazy talkers and writers, but fifty per cent of what they condemn eventually finds its way into the language, to be defended by a later generation of purists as violently as the earlier fought for its exclusion. Language cannot be successfully cribbed, cabined and confined.
>
> (quoted in Nambi Arooran 1976: 341–42)

All the same, these movements have emerged with such frequency all over the modern world because they are rarely concerned with language alone. Instead, they are crucially intertwined with questions of identity, of definitions of self and other. Maraimalai Adigal, for instance, deplored the habit of "imitation" among his fellow speakers, especially those belonging to urban upper castes. This habit had led them to use Sanskrit words instead of their Tamil equivalents. Such imitation was only a linguistic reflection of the social and religious enslavement of Tamilians to Sanskritic Brahmanism. Carrying this logic further, *ta̱nittamiḻ* adherents who follow in Maraimalai Adigal's footsteps, such as Nilambikai, Devaneyan, Ilakuvan, and Perunchitran, proposed that Brahman power in Tamilnadu would be subverted if Tamilians stopped using Sanskrit words in Tamil writing and speech.

Yet efforts to cleanse Tamil have not always been directed just against Sanskrit; nor have attempts to use pure Tamil necessarily been motivated by hostility towards other languages (Varadarajan 1966: 99–130). Indeed, the range of opinions offered by Tamil's devotees about the feasibility, the desirability, and the necessity of *ta̱nittamiḻ* captures quite effectively the multiple imaginations about the language that prevailed among them. The *ta̱nittamiḻ* movement associated with Maraimalai Adigal and his followers was largely an expression of contestatory classicism and radical neo-Shaivism. Their efforts to cleanse Tamil were propelled by hostility towards Brahmanism and its literary and ritual vehicle, Sanskrit. Even among them, however, numerous differences prevailed (Ilankumaran 1991: 129–37, 189–90; Tirumaran 1992: 153–208). For instance, the neo-Shaiva support for pure Tamil was linked to a religious project of Tamilizing Shaivism and of a return to pre-Sanskritic rituals and worship (Nilambikai 1960; Swaminatha Upatiyayan 1921). On the other hand, contestatory classicism's secular concern with purifying Tamil emerged from its agenda of restoring literary Tamil to its imagined state of pure classicality. Indeed, for contestatory classicism, the medieval religious texts which are the foundational scriptures for neo-Shaiva revivalism were themselves responsible for the flood of Sanskrit words that inundated Tamil literature after the pristine Tamil of the Caṅkam poems (Devaneyan 1972; Tirumaran 1992: 189–204).

Dravidianism, too, lent its support to the contestatory classicist project, motivated principally by the political imperative of countering (Sanskritic) Indian nationalism. However, given its own populist agenda, it was cautious about unilaterally embracing purification efforts with their inherently classicizing, archaizing, and prescriptive consequences. Thus Dravidianist prose eliminates Sanskrit words wherever possible, but not at the cost of distancing Tamil from the everyday language of the people. Indeed, among many in the Dravidian movement, like Ramasami and Annadurai, there was even hostility to pure Tamil advocates and their attempts to impose scholastic, high caste linguistic norms on the populace (Sivathamby 1979: 71–73).

But this is the not only reason that Maraimalai Adigal's *taṉittamiḻ* movement has not been greeted with cheering enthusiasm by many Tamil scholars and adherents. For some proponents of compensatory classicism, attempts to cleanse Tamil of Sanskrit words was not just unnecessary but even undesirable (Swaminatha Aiyar 1991d: 52–53; Vaiyapuri Pillai 1989: 4–6; see also Tirumaran 1992: 274–77). And here, one may recall an interesting 1941 essay in which U. V. Swaminatha Aiyar defended the use of Sanskritic terms for food, such as *pōjaṉam* and *nivētaṉam,* instead of their Tamil equivalent, *cōṟu,* on the grounds that the former constituted the true "Tamil tradition" (*tamiḻ marapu*). Swaminatha Aiyar's argument certainly betrays an overtly classist and paternalistic stance, for he proposed that while it was all right to use the Tamil word, *cōṟu,* with a poor servant, it was not appropriate to do so with a notable (Swaminatha Aiyar 1991a). Not surprisingly, this essay elicited an angry response from at least one fellow devotee, K. A. P. Viswanatham, who was clearly anguished that the venerable Tamil scholar appeared to be more devoted to Sanskrit than to Tamil (Viswanatham 1941: 360). At one level, Swaminatha Aiyar's essay is clearly in line with compensatory classicism's agenda of presenting Tamil and Sanskrit as twin contributors to an Indic literary civilization. At another level, this exchange also shows that purists had to struggle against both upper-caste (Brahman and high "non-Brahman") and upper- and middle-class linguistic dependence on Sanskritized Tamil.

Absence of explicit hostility towards Sanskrit also marked Indianism's efforts to cleanse Tamil (Ramalinga Pillai 1953; Sivagnanam 1960). Between July and November 1915, a little prior to Maraimalai Adigal's explicit "conversion" to the pure Tamil cause, Subramania Sivam, Chidambaram Pillai, and others whose *tamilpparru* found its expression in imagining an Indianized Tamil advocated the need for a *tanittamil* style that would be free of foreign words, including Sanskrit and English; they even announced a prize (of five rupees) for anyone who would submit essays in pure Tamil. One of their statements specifically targeted Sanskrit as the "first enemy" of Tamil. Ironically—and showing the Sanskritic inflection of Indianist prose—their appeals continued to use the Sanskrit word for language, *pāṣā,* rather than the pure Tamil *moli* and were replete with other Sanskritic words.[25] These appeals by Sivam (and other Brahmans) have been interpreted by some apologists as proof that devotees who were nominally Brahman were not necessarily enamored with Sanskrit to the detriment of Tamil (Sivagnanam 1970: 91–93). All the same, Indianism's attempts to overcome the marked dependence on Sanskrit words was motivated less by religious, antiquarian, or political imperatives, as was the case with neo-Shaivism, contestatory classicism, and Dravidianism, than by its populist concern with supporting the "language of the people" (Sivathamby 1979: 48–67). But the Tamil of most Tamil speakers for much of this century has been shot through with Sanskrit (and words from other languages). So, since Indianism also sought to ensure, like Dravidianism, that the "natural," "living" language of the people prevailed, it did not fetishize the elimination of Sanskritic words, confining itself instead to the discontinuation of arcane literary terms, both Sanskrit *and* Tamil, favored by orthodox pandits and scholars.

Further, in contrast to Maraimalai Adigal's *tanittamil* movement, Indianism's call for cleansing Tamil was clearly anticolonial rather than anti-Brahman. Its predominant concern was with ridding English words from Tamil, and the expunging of Sanskrit was put on hold, for the time being at least. Indeed, responding to a criticism by a "Son of India" published in the nationalist daily *Cutēcamittiran,* and realizing that essays submitted to his prize competition were unable to disentangle themselves from Sanskrit, in November 1915 Subramania Sivam went back on his earlier declaration of July 1915:

> We have only insisted that we should write in a Tamil that is free of English. We have never said that we should have a *tanittamil* that is free of Sanskrit. . . . There is little doubt however that Tamil is a unique language (*tanipāṣai*).

> Nevertheless, because of the interactions between Tamilians and Aryans for a long time, Tamilians have become habituated to innumerable Sanskrit words. If we thought it was possible to easily write essays these days in a *taṉittamiḻ* that is free of Sanskrit, would we announce that we would reward someone for this?[26]

Thus, for Indianism the elimination of colonialism and its language, English, took precedence over the task of de-Sanskritizing Tamil. In direct contrast, Maraimalai Adigal explicitly declared in 1927 at a presentation to the Karanthai Tamil Sangam that liberation from Aryanism and its language, Sanskrit, constituted the first "*cuyarājyam*" ("independence") for Tamilians (M. Tirunavukarasu 1959: 528). Years later, Devaneyan Pavanar also insisted that Tamilnadu did not win its freedom with the withdrawal of the British. Only the withdrawal of Sanskrit would constitute true independence for Tamilians (Devaneyan 1972: 339). Contrary to what their critics may claim, however, these purists did not support the intrusion of English words into Tamil. Nonetheless, for them, unlike the Indianists, Sanskrit was the more enduring foe.

All these conflicting agendas for cleansing Tamil of "foreign" words came to a head in the 1930s, when its devout started to seek state patronage for the creation of appropriate vocabularies and glossaries for pedagogical purposes, and especially for instruction in the sciences (Nambi Arooran 1976: 339–40). As early as 1916, several devotees in Salem town had organized themselves into a Tamil Scientific Terms Society, and the first issue of its journal, edited by C. Rajagopalachari, confessed: "The greatest difficulty that confronts those who wish to produce books in the languages of the country . . . is, we believe, the absence of adequate and precise terms for scientific ideas and the chaotic state in which attempts to build up such terms are left to remain" (quoted in Irschick 1969: 303–4). Faced with this "difficulty" and "chaos," many turned, to the dismay of purists, to Sanskrit as the source for new scientific vocabularies. So, in 1932, the state-sponsored glossary of scientific terms (*kalaiccol*) for pedagogical use was highly derivative from Sanskrit and also relied heavily on English. This only confirmed the purists' suspicion that the state was in the clutches of Brahmanical elements who were enemies of Tamil (Ilankumaran 1991: 191–93; Tirumaran 1992: 244–46).

The release of this glossary galvanized many purists to organize, and in 1934, under the auspices of the Ceṉṉai Mākāṇat Tamiḻc Caṅkam (Madras Presidency Tamil Sangam), based in Tirunelveli, they formed a collective called the Kalaiccolākkak Kaḻakam (the Committee for Scientific Terms). They organized several conferences, ran a short-lived journal called *Tamiḻttāy*, and in 1938 published a glossary with around ten thousand technical terms in physics, chemistry, mathematics, geography, and other subjects. Along with coining *taṉittamiḻ* terms, the glossary also eliminated the special *grantha* letters that had been incorporated into the premodern Tamil script to register Sanskritic phonology. Although the 1938 text was a real triumph for the *taṉittamiḻ* cause, the state's glossaries and vocabularies for the next two decades continued to be dependent on Sanskrit and English (Ilankumaran 1991: 194–97, 202–6; E. M. Subramania Pillai 1951–52).[27] Not surprisingly, into the 1950s purists lamented that "even though *taṉittamiḻ* has the approval of the common people, it has not secured a place in government" (Tirumaran 1992: 167). Some DMK legislators even suggested that under cover of creating new administrative terms, the (Congress) government had given a new lease to Sanskrit words and erased authentic Tamil words from the people's life.[28] Struggling under the sheer weight of centuries of administrative routines, the state's lukewarm response to *taṉittamiḻ* efforts was undoubtedly motivated by its primary concern with ensuring bureaucratic efficiency and convenience of usage. At the same time, the party in power, the Congress, favored an Indianized Tamil and was especially hostile towards any anti-Sanskrit purification attempts.

This became particularly clear during the debates in the later half of the 1950s and the early 1960s over the Tamilization of the language of administration. Allapichai, a Congress legislator in the council, warned the government to keep out of state committees on administrative and pedagogical terminology "linguistic fanatics," who would only create vocabularies which might please ancient grammarians and purists, but would be incomprehensible to "the people."[29] C. Subramaniam, the Congress minister for education, indeed put the ball back into the court of the purists by declaring in 1956: "The Tamil language has power (*cakti*). Those who allege that exposure to the words of other languages will lead to its destruction, will block its development, and will tarnish its excellence must have no faith in the power of our Tamil language."[30] Devotee-cum-legislator Muthukannappan responded, "We cannot forcibly bring in words from another language. . . . [I]f we do so, Tamiḻttāy is powerful. She will destroy these words, or she will subdue those other words. Everybody should recognize her power."[31] Nonetheless, through the 1950s the Congress-led state put up a good deal of resistance to demands for ushering in the reign of (*taṉi*)Tamil. These included the replacement of the Sanskritic term *ākāśvāṇi* for radio by the pure Tamil term, *vāṉoli,* and the Tamilizing of personal honorific terms, *śrī* and *śrīmati,* as *tiru* and *tirumati.*[32]

It was not until the DMK came to power in 1967 that such demands were fulfilled, and the pure Tamil cause received a boost, although purification efforts are not particularly high on the agenda of either the Dravidian movement or the Dravidianist idiom of *tamiḻppaṟṟu.* Among the DMK government's first actions was to put up a giant sign, appropriately illuminated with neon lights, on the ramparts of the secretariat building in Madras, which read, in pure Tamil, *tamiḻaka aracu talaimaic ceyalakam,* "head offices of the government of the Tamil land." The state motto in Sanskrit, *satyemeva jayate,* was translated—although not replaced—as the (*taṉi*) Tamil *vāymaiyē vellum,* "truth always triumphs" (Ramanujam 1971: 26). Sanskritic designations for various government officials, members of the state legislature, state departments, and so on were all replaced with pure Tamil equivalents, and today, in public functions conducted by the government as well as in official publications of all kinds, it is rare to encounter obviously Sanskritic or English words (although they are not entirely absent). Since 1967, the Tamil that one hears on the radio, as well as on television, is comparatively free of non-Tamil words. State committees appointed by the DMK government for creating pedagogical and administrative terminologies, as well as for producing textbooks, have been dominated by purists, thus ensuring that pedagogical Tamil and bureaucratic Tamil are as pure as they can be (Annamalai 1979: 50). And indeed, the 1971 glossary of administrative terms released by the state seemed at last to be taking the right step in the direction of fulfilling the purist's dream that in the streets of Tamilnadu, it is (*taṉi*)Tamil that ought to reign.

What are some of the implications of the *taṉittamiḻ* movement for the pursuit of *tamiḻppaṟṟu?* Most immediately, it offers another striking example of how discourse about Tamil in the devotional community has translated itself into practice, and how this process has been plagued by so many problems, not least because of the multiple notions about the language that concurrently prevail. Tamil's devotees who have participated in the movement attempt to cleanse their own speech and writing styles; they use Tamil instead of Arabic numerals, and they follow a putative Tamil dating system that commences with the birth date of Tiruvalluvar, fixed by Maraimalai Adigal at 31 B.C.E. Over the past few decades, many have conducted public campaigns among merchants and shopkeepers in cities like Madurai and Coimbatore to Tamilize the names of commercial establishments (Tirumaran 1992: 255–56). In 1987, the state joined in this campaign by issuing similar orders (see Tamilkudimagan 1990 for the public response to this). Critics wonder if such efforts to Tamilize life and culture in Tamilnadu is akin to fighting a battle that has already been lost—first to Sanskritization, but these days more enduringly to Anglicization and westernization. They parody the neologisms of *taṉittamiḻ* and criticize them for getting in the way of the "real" tasks of modernizing education, restructuring the economy, erasing social inequities, and so on. And they question its tyrannical and homogenizing tendencies that spell death for the creative and "natural" flow of language and literary culture (Tirumaran 1992: 273–320).

Yet, such criticisms notwithstanding, the pure Tamil movement has succeeded in *disabling* all those who had claimed that Tamil was incapable of expressing thoughts that could only be expressed in Sanskrit or English, and who maintained that Tamil cannot flourish without the aid of other languages; conversely, it has *enabled* those who wanted to use Tamil words but had been unable to do so because of the domination of words of other languages. From the 1930s on, *taṉittamiḻ* adherents have published dictionaries and glossaries of "pure" Tamil words (including both neologisms as well as rehabilitated ancient ones) for use in public as well as domestic contexts. They have also provided Tamil speakers with lists of pure Tamil personal names as well as names for their houses, suggestions on how to write letters and publish invitations for special occasions without resorting to non-Tamil words, and so on (Nilambikai 1952).[33]

All this does not minimize the reality that Tamil speakers of all class, caste, and professional backgrounds by and large continue to depend on words borrowed from other languages—Sanskrit, Telugu, Persian, Arabic, Hindustani, and English—for the myriad tasks of modernity. This only foregrounds the tragedy of not just the pure Tamil movement but of language purification efforts everywhere in the world. In seeking to cleanse languages, such movements attempt to resist and undo the reality of hybridity that characterize the societies in which they emerge (Vaiyapuri Pillai 1989: 4–12). Not surprisingly, it is this attempt to homogenize and singularize the language to conform to some imaginary pure originary moment that has invited the displeasure of critics. So, V. Ramaswamy, the well-known essayist and founder-editor of the literary journal *Maṇikkoṭi,* asked: "What is Tamil? *paccaittamiḻ* [unrefined

Tamil] is Tamil, so too is vulgar (*koccai*) Tamil. Marketplace Tamil is Tamil as well. A child's youthful prattle, too, is Tamil. Even the mixed *maṇipravāḷa* [Sanskritized] Tamil is Tamil" (quoted in Tirumaran 1992: 280).

But for the *taṉittamiḻ* devotee, such a suggestion would be sacrilegious, as would be the corollary to this statement: the speakers of all these various forms of the language have the right to call themselves "Tamilians." Indeed, the *taṉittamiḻ* movement attempts to transform Tamil speakers not just into subjects of Tamil but into subjects of a particular kind of Tamil—*taṉittamiḻ*—that is deemed to be its only right and possible form. If Tamil devotionalism aims to ineluctably connect the subjectivity of Tamil speakers to the language, *taṉittamiḻ* goes further and links this subjectivity to a particularly narrow and rigid definition of Tamil. The *taṉittamiḻ* project is thus concerned not merely with cleansing the language but also with singularizing and homogenizing the subjectivity of its speakers, for ultimately, it is only the speaker of pure Tamil who is worthy of being called a Tamilian.

"WHAT'S IN A NAME?": RECHRISTENING MADRAS STATE

From the earliest days of *tamiḻppaṟṟu,* the territorial space in which Tamil was spoken was referred to as either *tamiḻakam,* "home of Tamil," or *tamiḻnāṭu,* "land/nation of Tamil," an area that in the colonial period was named "Madras." Since neither had an overtly political agenda, neo-Shaivism and classicism were not particularly concerned about conducting their devotional activities in a territorial space which both was ruled by a foreign power and was signified by a foreign word. But for Indianism and Dravidianism, with their obvious interest in ensuring the rule of Tamil in all spheres, it was sacrilegious that the very land in which the language was spoken did not officially bear its true Tamil name. Quoting from a primary school textbook, S. B. Adithan (1905–81) wrote indignantly in 1958: " 'The nation we inhabit is called India. In it, we inhabit the southern portion that is South India, called Madras State. . . . ' Here, we do not even see the term 'Tamil Nadu.' What is wrong in teaching that the land we inhabit is called 'Tamil Nadu'? Do they fear that if they use the term 'Tamil Nadu,' our impressionable Tamil children will develop attachment to Tamil Nadu?" (Adithanar 1965: 5).

To many a devotee of Tamil, this incongruity became especially inexcusable after 1956 when the multilingual Madras Presidency was dismantled, leaving only the Tamil-speaking region to continue on as Madras state. Prior to this date, adherents of Indianist inclination had been willing to wait till the Indian state had honored the demand for linguistic states, which were created only after a protracted struggle from the late 1930s through the mid-1950s. In turn, in 1938 the Dravidian movement had launched its battle cry, "Tamilnadu for Tamilians," a cry that by the early 1940s transmuted itself into "Dravidanadu [Dravidian nation] for Dravidians." For the next decade or so, until they had sorted out the many differences over whether they were fighting for the autonomy of Dravidians of the putative Dravidanadu, or just for the Dravidians of Tamilnadu, the DK and the DMK used both terms, Dravidanadu and Tamilnadu, interchangeably. After the States Reorganization Act of 1956, the dream of a multilingual Dravidanadu was abandoned, and followers of the Dravidian movement joined proponents of Indianism in their demand for renaming the state—with one major difference, of course (Karunanidhi 1989: 316–17, 519–21). For Dravidianism, at least until the early 1960s, the state renaming was linked to a separatist project for creating an independent Tamil nation. The Indianist regime, on the other hand, always steadfastly maintained that the renaming of the state as Tamilnadu was not contrary to the spirit of Indian nationalism. Indeed, it was a celebration of India's multilingual plurality.

These differences did not deter devotees of rival factions from coming together, with the common cause of ensuring that the state be renamed. In the late 1950s, the two political parties most enthusiastically concerned with this issue were the Nām Tami̱ḻar (We Tamils) and Sivagnanam's Tamil Arasu Kazhagam. The We Tamils party was founded in 1958 by a wealthy London-trained barrister, S. B. Adithan, the publisher of the popular Tamil daily *Ti̱natanti*. The party's principal agenda was the founding of a sovereign Tamilnadu.[34] The many ideological differences he had with Adithan and his own ambivalences over *tami̱ḻp-pa̱ṟru* notwithstanding, Ramasami lent his considerable influence to the We Tamils, his vision of a sovereign Dravidanadu having been rendered unfeasible (Anaimuthu 1974: 1878–79; E. V. Ramasami 1961). In 1960, the We Tamils conducted statewide protests for the secession of Madras and the establishment of a sovereign Tamilnadu. The protests were marked by the burning of maps of India (with Tamilnadu left out), and they led to the arrests of Adithan, Ramasami, and numerous others (Sundararajan 1986: 32–35).[35] Soon after, in early 1961, Sivagnanam, an Indianist devotee of Tamil who was ideologically opposed to men like Adithan and Ramasami on many fronts, spearheaded the protests launched by his party, Tamil Arasu Kazhagam, outside government offices and the legislature in Madras, as well as in several other cities all over the state, leading to the arrest of hundreds (Sivagnanam 1974: 851–65).[36]

These protests and arrests themselves followed the tragic death in Virudhunagar of a sixty-year-old Gandhian and lifelong social reformer, Shankaralinga Nadar (1895–1956), on 13 October 1956, after a prolonged fast of seventy-seven days. Foremost among his list of demands was the renaming of Madras state (Sundararajan 1986: 68–76). The Congress government ignored Shankaralingam's demands, and even the DMK later formally distanced itself from his act.[37] But his sacrifice did not go unnoticed among Tamil's devout (Karunanidhi 1989: 282, 711; Pancanathan n.d.: 29–31; Sivagnanam 1974: 809–10).[38] Indeed, a decade later when Madras was formally renamed Tamilnadu, Annadurai reminded his fellow members in the Legislative Assembly of Shankaralingam's martyrdom for the Tamil cause, and in 1970, when Karunanidhi became chief minister, a monthly pension was granted to the dead man's wife (Karunanidhi 1987b: 225).[39]

Shankaralingam's death, prior to the 1957 general elections, did not visibly alarm the Congress party, but the protests of 1960–61 led by the We Tamils and the Tamil Arasu Kazhagam did elicit a response, highlighting as they did the growing threat of the Dravidian movement on the very eve of the 1962 elections.[40] In early 1961, the government partially relented and, after a lengthy debate in the legislature, agreed that within Tamilnadu, when communications were conducted in Tamil, the name "Tamil Nad" would henceforth designate Madras state. For communications with other states, the central government, and the rest of the world, especially as these were conducted in English, the state would continue to be referred to as Madras.[41] In consigning the English name, "Madras," to use in the world outside the Tamil-speaking region, which would henceforth be designated by the Tamil name, "Tamilnadu" (albeit misspelled "Tamil Nad"), the state's legislation at least conceded the devotional community's demand that in the intimate sphere of the home and the family, it is Tamil that should reign.

But the respite purchased with this gesture was only temporary, for many of the devout and the rival political parties that backed them continued to keep the pressure on the government. In 1963, the matter was debated at length in the Indian Parliament where, following the submission of a nonofficial bill, Annadurai offered an impassioned defense for unilaterally adopting the name "Tamilnadu" on all fronts.[42]

The bill was turned down, on the grounds that the request had to be made officially by the state government. However, in 1964 the Congress government of M. Bhaktavatsalam, already pushed to the wall by the rising wave of anti-Hindi sentiment in the state, once again rejected renewed demands.[43] It was not until the DMK came to power that things changed. One of its very first acts was to pass a resolution in July 1967 confirming the change of name, and on 14 January 1969, Madras state was officially rechristened Tamilnadu.[44] So, after more than a decade of petitioning and debating, and after many centuries of having been a literary and cultural reality, "Tamilnadu" became a political reality as well. When Annadurai "raised his voice to say 'Hail, Tamil Nadu,' every member, including Congressmen followed suit. How could any Tamilian remain unmoved?" (Ramanujam 1971: 26)

Through the maze of petitions and protests, it is clear that the Congress—the "nationalist" party that under colonial rule took pride in contesting English, and that fostered linguistic consciousness in the Madras Presidency as a counter to British power—increasingly pushed itself, and was in turn thrust, into a corner from which it vigorously defended the legitimacy of the colonial inheritance. Its spokesmen insisted that they were in favor of retaining the old colonial name as a matter of expediency; in no way should this be mistaken as an absence of "love" for Tamil on the Congress's part. "We have foreign monuments and roads and streets named after foreign persons. . . . We have indeed so much else of the hangover of the past that we cannot take a big broom and sweep them away."[45] There were several grounds on which this paradoxical defense of the colonial "hangover" was mounted. First, the Congress insisted that in contrast to "Madras," the name under which "we have lived for centuries," the name "Tamil Nadu" had no foundation in the literature and history of the region.[46] The Congress persisted in this argument over the years. So, in May 1963, T. S. Pattabhiraman declared in the Rayja Sabha:

> There has been Bengal and there must be Kerala historically. But there has been no Tamil Nad historically. It is only the creation of politicians, of political parties of a recent date. There was nothing in existence as a unified Tamil Nad till about five hundred years ago. It was "Pandya Nad" or "Chera Nad" or "Chola Nad." There has never been historically a "Tamil Nad." And why do you want to create a new one, when historically it is not justified? It is not justified politically. It is not justified democratically.[47]

Not surprisingly, this argument about the alleged illegitimacy of "Tamil Nadu" and the implicit historical legitimacy of "Madras" provoked angry responses. The most notable of these were Annadurai's documentation of the deep historicity and antiquity of the term during the parliamentary debate in 1963 and Sivagnanam's similar effort in the Madras legislature in 1967. "The name Tamilnadu did not appear yesterday or today. We hear of the name from the time of Tolkappiyar 2,500 years ago," skeptics were told.[48] As its detractors did not fail to point out, the absurdity of the government's position was apparent from the fact that the ruling party's regional wing had renamed itself *Tamilnadu* Congress in the 1920s. Indeed, throughout the debates in both Madras and New Delhi, all parties concerned, including the Congress, liberally used the term "Tamilnadu" when they referred to Madras state. As one critic of the government remarked astutely, "Their very speeches nail down this point. What [we] seek to do is to give *de jure* recognition to a *de facto* fact that is there."[49]

Second, the Congress insisted that the word *nāṭu* in the compound "Tamilnadu" was inherently dangerous, for it suggested that Tamil speakers might want a separate nation (*nāṭu*) of their own and did not want to be a part of *pārata nāṭu,* "India." Bharati may have referred to the Tamil space as *centamiḻnāṭu,* "glorious Tamilnadu." But "that might have been appropriate in song, and for arousing devotion towards one's *nāṭu.* Today, however, we are independent and rule ourselves under a parliamentary system. . . . Is Tamilnadu our *nāṭu* or is it India that is our *nāṭu?* How can we say that this is our *nāṭu* and that too is our *nāṭu?*"[50]

Here, Chief Minister Bhaktavatsalam was deliberately playing upon the multiple meanings that have historically coalesced around the word *nāṭu,* the most recent of which, of course, was the modern sense of "nation" that Bharati, Kalyanasundaram, and others had popularized from the turn of the century. This was a strategic move on Bhaktavatsalam's part, for it was bound to remind everyone that the parties demanding the renaming had been only a few years ago also demanding secession from India in the name of a sovereign Tamilnadu. Given that Madras was in the throes, in the early 1960s, of the most violent of anti-Hindi protests, renaming the state Tamilnadu would be tantamount to surrendering to "antinationalist" forces, in the view of the government. Further, such a renaming would also alienate the many non-Tamil-speaking peoples who still lived in the state and considered it their home. Would this mean that they would have to leave the state? "The 'We Tamil' Party will say that only Tamilians should reside in Tamil

Nad and all others should get out. This will be opening the Pandora's box."[51]

Third, and most consistently and steadfastly, the government repeatedly asserted that much was invested in the name "Madras," for it was the name by which everybody in the world knew the state. "When our eminent people go to America, to Germany, and to France, they are recognized only if they say they are from Madras." What would happen to the reputation and fame of the state if Tamilians gave up its familiar name and adopted a new name such as "Tamilnadu"? supporters of "Madras" asked repeatedly.[52] Another Congress member pointed out—most injudiciously, under the circumstances—"Just because 42 per cent of the people in India speak Hindi, we do not call it Hindi Nad."[53] More astutely, in 1964 Bhaktavatsalam reminded everyone that by retaining the colonial word, the government was not declaring its devotion to the English language; instead, it was staking a claim on the very name "Madras," at a time when there was such danger of losing the city that bore that name to neighboring Andhra Pradesh. It is our way of saying to the Andhras that Madras is "ours," not "yours," he declared.[54] Indeed, it is telling that until the very end, even when the renaming resolution was submitted by the DMK in 1967 and every other party supported it unanimously, the Congress representative, Karuthiruman, suggested that perhaps members should consider the hyphenated term "Tamilnadu-Madras state," which in his view conveyed a desirable union of the English and Tamil names.[55] In effect, the Congress, this most "anticolonial" of political parties in the state, was implicitly declaring that modern Tamil speakers as a political and territorial community could only have a presence in the world by allowing themselves to be mediated through a colonial category.

There are good political reasons why the Congress doggedly refused to accede to the demand for renaming, even though prior to 1947, it had just as vigorously sponsored the cultivation of linguistic consciousness and regional pride to neutralize colonial power. "I do not see any reason why, when we [Indians] are in power, we should not give effect to what had been done when we were not in power," one of its critics wondered.[56] But the reasons would have been apparent to everyone, as the demand for renaming was most enthusiastically voiced by parties which were clearly in opposition to the Congress, and whose strength was on the rise in the various regions of the nation. That itself was a sign that linguistic and regional pride (as sponsored by these oppositional parties) would challenge the nation (and the Congress party). The establishment of linguistic states, the internecine struggles between them over borders and resources, the switch to regional languages for their administration, and the resistance from various quarters to Hindi all pointed towards the fragmentation that threatened the union of India, as well as Congress power. As one Congress member put it, "It will be opening the Pandora's Box, once you begin to give recognition for a language as the basis for renaming a state."[57] Pushed against the wall by the upsurge of linguistic sentiments, the Congress was repeatedly forced to take a stand that went against its own reputation as a defender of linguistic consciousness in the colonial period. So the same party that had vigorously upheld de-Anglicization and vernacularization, and that had renamed the Parliament "Lok Sabha" and India "Bharat," now held out against the demand for renaming Madras: "they want the names to be changed after the language; *just because* it was named by the British people, they want to change it."[58] The (mock) incredulity in this member's tone betrays the Congress's realization that the "Pandora's box" of linguistic pride that it had helped open, as an anticolonial strategy, had to be now tightly reclosed if the union (and Congress power) were to be maintained, even if this led it to mount a defense of English and the colonial inheritance.

Thus the Congress was compelled to make its case on pragmatic grounds: everybody in the world knows us as Madras; why should we risk losing our reputation by changing our name? When there were "so many problems of importance concerning the daily life of the people with which we are trying to grapple," the demand for renaming was not just inconsequential but even distracting:

> It is perhaps necessary to remind ourselves that in this House we are trying to tackle fundamentals. Once we find proper solutions to basic questions affecting our life, the life of the society, its economics, its goals, political and social, the rest will take care of themselves. When we solve our economic problems, when we solve our cultural problems, these changes in names of places and of roads and of persons will adjust themselves to the changing conditions.[59]

The Congress's materialist pragmatism sharply contrasts with the devotees' "sentimental" attachment to the name "Tamilnadu." The government may well have asked, "What is in a name?"; but for Tamil's devotees, and various other supporters of the renaming, this particular name was everything, for it was the one "named after our language." When asked "What do you gain by renaming [Madras] as Tamil

Nadu?" Annadurai replied: "We gain satisfaction sentimentally; we gain the satisfaction that an ancient name is inculcated in the hearts of millions and scores of millions of people. Is that not enough compensation for the small trouble of changing the name?" By renaming Madras as Tamilnadu, "something is changed in our thinking, in our soul, in our fiber," he concluded.[60] Similarly, a few years later, Sivagnanam declared, "Nobody has a right to refer to me by someone else's name. . . . I should be referred to by the name of my language, my ethnicity, and my land."[61] For its devotees, the very "fundamentals" of life and livelihood were invested in Tamil. The honor shown their language by renaming their state after it was far from an incidental matter that would follow after the "basic questions affecting life" had been tended to. For Tamil, as they had repeatedly asserted, was life itself.

ENTHRONEMENT OF TAMIL: DILEMMAS OF RULE

In December 1956, on the very eve of the 1957 general elections, the Madras legislature passed a bill instituting Tamil as the official language of the state (*āṭci moḻi;* lit., "language of rule"). The implications of the bill were potentially momentous for the course of *tamiḻppaṟṟu,* for it was declared that progressively over the next few years, all the official proceedings of the Madras government, so far dominated by English, would be entirely conducted in Tamil. Certain important caveats notwithstanding (such as the continued use of English in courts, especially at the higher levels), the bill seemed to fulfill a long-cherished dream of the entire devotional community: namely, Tamil ought to reign, once again, in its own land. As one member, R. Krishnaswami Naidu, enthusiastically declared in the Legislative Assembly, "All our troubles have now ceased as Tamiḻttāy reclines in royal style on her auspicious throne." Another member echoed this sentiment, proclaiming that "from now on, we will progress and advance."[62]

Embedded in these as well as in many other declarations made in the legislature in the 1950s and 1960s was the implicit recognition that until the state intervened in Tamil improvement activities that had hitherto been conducted largely by the devotional community, the language and its speakers would not really prosper. As Gajapathy Nayakar, a Tamil scholar who was also a member of the Legislative Council, declared, resorting to the logic of gender endemic to *tamiḻppaṟṟu:* "It is only when a man marries a woman that family life can be conducted. In the same manner, we should think of the state as man, and the language as woman. It is only out of their union that proper rule will ensue."[63]

And yet, over the next few years the state itself repeatedly admitted its inability to ensure the rule of Tamil in its own land and in the community of its speakers. Only a few years after he presented the Tamil as Official Language Bill with such enthusiasm in 1956, C. Subramaniam was compelled to confess: "As a first task, we restored her rightful throne back to Tamiḻttāy. We did this believing that if our Tamiḻttāy were enthroned, we would be filled with happiness, and that happiness would give us the enthusiasm to attend to our other tasks. However, even though we have now installed Tamil as our lofty language of rule, we have been unable to implement it" (C. Subramaniam 1962: 24). What accounts for the state's helplessness in Tamilizing itself, and what does this state of helplessness imply about the cause of *tamiḻppaṟṟu?*

Here, it is instructive to consider the debate on the bill in the legislature in December 1956, for this itself anticipated many of the problems the state faced over the next few decades in implementing its provisions. First, this was one of the rare occasions in which the figure of Tamiḻttāy entered arenas of government and found a presence in official discourse.[64] It is telling that Subramaniam, the education minister, offered the bill as a ritual tribute to Tamiḻttāy, declaring that members should set aside their political differences and join in her "enthronement ceremony" (*muṭicūṭṭuviḻā*).[65] He was not alone in invoking her name, and the speeches made by other members were liberally sprinkled with references to the "liberation" of Tamiḻttāy and her "enthronement." Both metaphors clearly suggested that Tamiḻttāy, the former queen of the Tamil kingdom who had been displaced from her throne by rival languages and had been reduced to the status of a lowly maid (*paṇippeṇ*), had now been restored to her rightful place in the hierarchy of power and command. In enabling her reinstatement, not only did the legislators fulfill their own "debt" (*kaṭaṉ*) as her subjects/children, but they also signaled their intention to ensure that despite the continued presence of other languages (English and Hindi, most notably) in the Tamil home/kingdom, Tamil would reign supreme. It would rule as the language of power, while the others would merely be languages of communication with the rest of India and the world.

The Official Language Act might well be the fruit of the decades of hard work put in towards Tamil's liberation by its devotees, as Subramaniam graciously acknowledged in his opening remarks.[66] All the same, the act would be the instrument with which the importance of

Tamil would be impressed upon recalcitrant sections of the society, through the agency of the state. Ironically, therefore, at what ought to have been a moment of great triumph for its devotees, the act clearly represented the realization that love or passion for Tamil would not ensure that it prosper as much as would material and pragmatic considerations. Jobs and the exercise of power were now dependent on knowing and using the language: "If Tamil comes in as language of rule, and if we insist that it is the language everyone has to learn in colleges, how many will want to read Shakespeare and Milton? . . . Desire for the Caṅkam poems will bloom. Tamil, too, will flourish."[67] Political power and material needs perhaps would secure for Tamil what love and passion had so far not accomplished.

Second, from the start, the state openly acknowledged that for the time being, the enthronement of Tamil was more symbolic than real. It was all well and good to "love" Tamil, but logistically, the rule of Tamil would take time, enthusiasm, and resources to implement. "If we decide suddenly that everything has to be in Tamil, that will only give rise to confusion," Subramaniam informed legislators in December 1956.[68] L. Raghava Mudaliar warned his fellow legislators that devotion to the language (*moḻippaṟṟu*) should not lead them to a hasty implementation of an *āṭci moḻi,* "official language," that would be incomprehensible to the very people for whose benefit it was being created.[69] It was therefore decided that the official language policy would at first be implemented, starting in 1958–59, in eight departments of government. By 1962, this was abandoned in favor of implementation in four phases (Kumaramangalam 1965: 68–73). It was acknowledged that it would be easiest to switch to Tamil as *āṭci moḻi* at the lowest rungs of the district administration where English had hardly penetrated. It would be most difficult to ensure the use of Tamil at the highest levels of government, in the state secretariat at Madras, and this was scheduled for only the fourth phase. It is telling that no time limit was explicitly stipulated for the unilateral use of Tamil in all spheres.[70]

Indeed, the state's troubles over the next few years show clearly that it took the plunge before it was ready. Subramaniam himself compared his government's dilemma to that of someone who did not know how to swim but realized that he could only learn by throwing himself into the water.[71] This analogy is quite revealing, for the list of tasks to be accomplished before Tamil could actually become *āṭci moḻi* was formidable, ranging from the technological to the ideological. For instance, Tamil could not really be used for bureaucratic communication until government offices were stocked with Tamil typewriters.[72] This in turn depended on the standardization of the keyboard, on which there was much disagreement from the start. Further, typists had to learn to use these Tamil keyboards, and a network of training institutes, as well as economic incentives for those who underwent the training, had to be set up. The absence of skills in Tamil shorthand was also a glaring problem.

Another key requirement, of course, was the creation of a glossary of Tamil administrative terms. Here, in addition to the ongoing debate between purists and nonpurists on the relative "Tamilness" of these terms, there was the more demanding task of overcoming years of bureaucratic dependence on English, especially in higher circles of the government, and instilling in its place the new habit of using Tamil. Further, once the glossary was created, various laws and statutes had to be translated into Tamil. In certain areas, such as legal procedures, there was doubt from the very beginning whether Tamil was even capable of expressing "with precision" the language of the courts.[73] Finally, all these measures depended on the existence of a pool of government officers and clerical staff who were equipped to use Tamil in administrative contexts. Many legislators pointed out the obvious paradox of bringing in Tamil as language of rule, even before institutionalizing its use in school and college education.[74] But here, as late as 1963, Chief Minister Bhaktavatsalam dismissed demands for Tamil as principal medium of instruction in colleges as "not a practical proposition, . . . not . . . in the interests of national integration, not in the interests of higher education, and not in the interests of the students themselves" (quoted in Kumaramangalam 1965: 62–63). Even a casual survey of government records in the 1950s and 1960s shows that this brief treatment only touches upon the surface of the numerous dilemmas faced by the state in implementing the bill that was passed so confidently in December 1956.

So, why did the state take the plunge well before it was remotely ready to govern in Tamil? One obvious reason is that it gave in to the continual demand for bringing in such legislation, voiced since at least the 1920s not just by Tamil's devotees but also by Congress nationalists. In 1948, two districts had been selected for a trial run; the relative lack of success of this experiment did not deter supporters of Tamil from continuing to push their cause.[75] Up until 1956, the reality of Madras's multilinguality prevented any easy abandonment of English. Indeed, over the years from the 1920s, there had been repeated demands from various legislators that the "regional language" (which invariably meant Tamil) ought to be the language of the legislature, since a growing number of members of that august body did not know English (Sundaresan 1986). A. Ramalingam declared in March 1939, "I do not understand [anything] if English is spoken in this Assembly. I only understand Tamil. Our land is Tamilnadu. We ought to speak in Tamil."[76] Such a demand, not to mention the continual overwriting of "Madras Presidency" as "Tamilnadu," only caused anxiety and hostility among non-Tamil-speaking legislators, which in turn mirrored the confusion that would prevail if Tamil indeed became the language of rule in a multilingual province.[77] By late 1956, however, after the linguistic states became a political reality, the Congress government in Madras was hard-pressed to defend itself successfully from the criticisms increasingly leveled against it by opposition parties for being soft on Tamil issues. Although the government resisted this accusation, there were many who pointed out that the Congress rushed through the legislation on Tamil as official language as a preelection gesture. I would also suggest that whenever the state had passed such a bill, it would have faced similar problems. For there was growing consensus that mandating the use of Tamil through legislation was the only way to ensure the Tamilization of the administration and bureaucracy. The limits of *tami̲lppar̲r̲u* as well as of community-spurred improvement activities are clearly revealed in this realization.

Third, the state's 1956 legislation also showed up the category of "mother tongue" for what it was: a metaphorical construct. The demand for Tamil as the language of rule drew its power from Indianist and Dravidianist assertions that the language of the people—of their homes and their mothers—ought to be the language of government. Yet there was dawning awareness that just because a language had been imbibed through one's mother's milk, or learned at her knee, one did not necessarily "know" the language sufficiently to administer a modern state with it. Indeed, the technologies and complexities of modern government inevitably inserted a gap between the *āṭci mo̲li*, "official language," and the *tāymo̲li*, "the mother tongue," although they might both be named "Tamil." So, for much of the decade following 1956, legislators and planners argued the pros and cons of ensuring that the *āṭci mo̲li* stay as close as possible to the *tāymo̲li*. There were purists among the legislators (many of whom, like V. V. Ramasami and Muthukannappan, were Tamil scholars and devotees) who demanded the complete erasure of all Sanskritic and English words from the language of rule, insisting that there was little reason to ponder at length over the creation of new administrative terms, for these had existed from time immemorial since the days of the *Tirukkuṟaḷ* and the *Cilappatikāram.*[78] Those who countered this demand maintained that an *āṭci moḻi* based on old Tamil would be totally incomprehensible to the people. An insistence on "pure" Tamil words was not an expression of *tamiḻppaṟṟu* but of *tamiḻveṟi,* "Tamil fanaticism," one legislator insisted.[79]

The Congress government itself adopted an anti-English and pro-Sanskrit stance. Only the elimination of English words was set up as part of the government's strategy for creating the *āṭci moḻi,* on the grounds that Sanskritic words were comprehensible to the people, and hence were "Tamil," after all. And even in this respect, the government was quite flexible, appropriating as "Tamil" all those English words (such as "revenue" or "police") that had become naturalized in popular parlance.[80] Here, the government's position was similar to that of liberals who maintained that English words like "collector" or "radio" were so much part of the vocabulary of the Tamil speaker that these, too, were Tamil, and ought not to be eliminated in favor of some unfamiliar and panditic neologism. One cannot legislate into existence a totally new language, it was asserted.[81] In contrast to Tamil's devotees, who insisted that their language was their life and soul, some legislators like Allapichai declared (in English): "Language is only a vehicle of expression that we speak in. . . . [I]t is only a vehicle of thought to express oneself better. Such being the case, there is no meaning whatsoever in insisting upon people to speak only in Tamil."[82] Insisting that it was unfair to dismiss those who wished to speak English or Sanskritized Tamil or English-inflected Tamil as disloyal Tamilians, some legislators reiterated that the institution of Tamil as official language did not necessarily mean the elimination of other tongues from Tamilnadu. On the contrary, Tamil would benefit by drawing upon all languages to enrich itself (C. Subramaniam 1962: 19–20).

Thus in the debate on the *āṭcimoḻi,* there was an important reversal of the relationship between the language and its speaker. The devotional community had defined a Tamilian as one whose "mother tongue" was Tamil. Language defined the speaker, as the latter was rendered a subject of Tamil through *tamiḻppaṟṟu.* In contrast, when the state stepped in to institute the "mother tongue" as language of rule, it became clear that the speaker defined the language: "Tamil" was whatever the Tamilian spoke, be it shot through with English, Sanskrit, or any other language. Language was thus defined by the speaker: "The Tamil that the people understand is good Tamil," in Subramaniam's words.[83] The subjection of the speaker to the language in the discourses of Tamil devotion was thus unsettled by the work of the state.

Finally, the debate on the institution of Tamil as official language and the subsequent attempts to implement it show that in spite of having been grandly (re)installed as "queen" of the Tamil state in 1956, Tamiḻttāy was not really sovereign in her own kingdom. As late as 1970, the government was compelled to confess that "in no department is business conducted 100 percent in Tamil,"[84] and its devotees insist that this is true even today. Most immediately, it is the continued dependence by the state on English that limits Tamil's sovereignty. The devotional community, including adherents of Indianism, the most anti-English of its regimes, conceded that English was necessary for the development of the sciences, for keeping up with the rest of India, and for the continued participation of the Tamilian in an international world. For its devotees, however, Tamil ought to reign supreme within the Tamil home and homeland. But the government repeatedly confessed in the 1950s and 1960s that even within the Tamil homeland, the "use of English will be unavoidable" and "that we are not able to give up English."[85] Ironically, the speeches made by numerous legislators in December 1956, when the "Tamil as Official Language Bill" was offered as a "ritual tribute" to Tamiḻttāy, were replete with Sanskritized Tamil and English words. Over the next few years as well, Tamil speeches delivered in the legislature continued to be dominated by Sanskrit and English, and several Tamil scholars-cum-legislators periodically submitted resolutions calling attention to the fact that in the state's highest governing body, Tamil still did not reign. As one of them lamented, expressing his dismay in gendered terms, "Tamil is the mother, English is the companion (*tōḻi*). The mother needs the help of the companion. But the companion has displaced the mother and even become the lover [of the Tamilian], with whom she romps around, hand in hand."[86] And in the years following 1956, English continued to rule the roost, drawing strength from arguments that Tamil was not precise enough, that it was not neat and clear enough to be used for writing government notes, that complicated scientific and technical terminology could just not possibly be expressed through it, and so on.

But it is not English alone that troubles Tamil. As long as Tamilnadu is part of the Indian union, Hindi also continues to erode Tamil's absolute sovereignty. As the official language of the nation, Hindi vies with Tamil even within its own homeland on money order and telegraph forms, on postage stamps and currency notes, as well as in military, railway, and other central government institutions that are based in the land of Tamil. Hindi has continued to be taught in schools affiliated to the central government's education board and in schools run by minorities even after 1968 when the state government legislated out the language from its schools; and it has taken up the lion's share of nationalized television broadcasts until recently. Further, it is knowledge of Hindi (and/or English), rather than of Tamil, that provides access to lucrative central government employment. Indeed, critics like Mohan Kumaramangalam argued in 1965 that "instead of the regional language becoming *more* and *more* dominant, the tendency in the non-Hindi areas [like Tamilnadu] was already beginning to slip back towards English, almost as if it were in defence against the advance of Hindi" (Kumaramangalam 1965: 51). In Kumaramangalam's reckoning, a fundamental inequity had been written into the constitutional position of Indian languages through the privileging of Hindi. In the triangular battle between Hindi, English, and Tamil, it is the latter that has suffered the gravest injuries and is facing a slow death.

Kumaramangalam's critique did not raise the possibility that Tamil might never be sovereign as long as Tamil speakers participated in the Indian union. But other critics did openly make this argument. Adithan, the founder of the We Tamils movement, wrote in his *Tamiḻp Pēraracu* (The Tamil empire) that not until Tamilnadu overthrew the "imperialism" of Delhi and Hindi could Tamil truly become a sovereign language of rule (Adithanar 1965: 26–30). And the parties of the Dravidian movement used such an argument through much of the 1950s and 1960s both to empower themselves and eventually to rise to power in 1967 by battling the "demoness Hindi."

BATTLING THE DEMONESS HINDI

On 23 January 1968, the Madras government decreed that the central government's three-language formula would no longer be in effect in schools under its jurisdiction; henceforth, students were not required to study Hindi. As of that date, Hindi, the putative official language of India, was deprived of pedagogical and political privilege in the state. This legislation followed the resumption of anti-Hindi protests in December 1967 that involved considerable loss of lives and property. These protests were launched in response to the Official Languages Amendment Bill passed by the Indian Parliament on 16 December, which strengthened the position of Hindi relative to English and overturned an earlier resolution specifically stating that a compulsory knowledge of Hindi was not mandatory for central government employment. Perceiving a direct threat to their fortunes and futures, college students in Tamilnadu mounted fierce anti-Hindi demonstrations all over the state, the more radical among them demanding immediate secession from the nation. These protests were not just directed at the central government but also threatened the very stability of the newly elected DMK government in the state. The DMK may have promised to protect Tamil from Hindi and risen to power on the strength of its anti-Hindi leadership. Nonetheless, if the protests had not been so ferocious, it might not have been compelled to legislate against Hindi in Tamilnadu (Barnett 1976: 240–49; Ramanujam 1971: 28–40).

In successfully passing the anti-Hindi legislation, the DMK did reinforce its image as Tamil's guardian. All the same, the circumstances under which Hindi was legislated against suggest that the state had, once again, succumbed reluctantly to Tamilizing itself. Indeed, even earlier, from the 1930s through the 1950s, the Congress-led state government had often been compelled by local pressures to take a position in opposition to the dictates of the party's high command in New Delhi. Soon after independence, when the central government urged all states to promote the compulsory study of Hindi in preparation for its installation as the sole official language of the union in 1965, a vigorous series of protests in 1948–49 led the Madras government to make it an optional subject. Through the 1950s, the Madras government kept the pressure on the central government to retain English alongside Hindi as official language, its education minister P. Subbarayan even appending a lengthy dissenting note to the report of the Official Language Commission in 1956 (Subbarayan 1956). Caught between the central government's demands and pressures at home, the Madras state's Hindi policy from the 1930s through 1968 was dogged by contradictions, retractions, and ultimately failure.

The 1968 anti-Hindi legislation followed a half century of intense opposition to the language. The specific occasion which sparked off the first wave of protests was an April 1938 order by the Congress government of C. Rajagopalachari ordering the compulsory study of Hindi in 125 secondary schools in the Madras Presidency.[87] The government justified its action thus:

> The attainment by our Province of its rightful place in the national life of India requires that our educated youth should possess a working knowledge

> of the most widely spoken language in India. Government have therefore decided upon the introduction of Hindustani in the secondary school curriculum of our province. Government desire to make it clear that Hindi is not to be introduced in any elementary school whatsoever, the mother tongue being the only language taught in such schools. Hindi is to be introduced only in secondary schools and there too only in the 1st, 2nd and 3rd forms, that is to say in the 6th, 7th and 8th years of school life. It will not therefore interfere in any way with the teaching of the mother tongue in the secondary schools. . . . Hindi will be compulsory only in the sense that attendance in such classes will be compulsory and pupils cannot take Hindi as a substitute for Tamil, Telugu, Malayalam or Kannada, but must learn Hindi only in addition to one of these languages.[88]

Despite the government's insistence that the "mother tongue" was in no way endangered by the Hindi policy, this is exactly how it was interpreted by many devotees of Tamil. Between late 1937 and early 1940, they spearheaded numerous anti-Hindi demonstrations which led to the incarceration of close to 1,200 and to the death of two young men. Although this particular order was withdrawn in February 1940, the Congress continued to promote Hindi in Madras schools into the 1950s, even in the face of mounting resistance. Throughout this period, the anti-Hindi cause was clearly linked to the DK and DMK's separatist demand for a sovereign Dravidian or Tamil nation. No longer content with protest marches and making speeches, protesters tarred Hindi names on official name boards, picketed stores run by North Indians, burned facsimiles of the Indian map and the Constitution (itself characterized as the material manifestation of Hindi imperialism), obstructed train services, and so on. Following the 1963 constitutional amendment that banned political parties with separatist agendas, overt demands for secession were muted in Madras, although not entirely absent. Instead, the focus was on reversing the provisions of the Constitution which decreed that on 26 January 1965, English would be replaced by Hindi as the *sole* official language of India. In the most dramatic phase of the anti-Hindi movement, launched in 1963, hundreds were arrested; schools and colleges were closed as thousands of students all over the state took to protest marches; several hundred students went on hunger fasts; and the effigy of the "demoness" Hindi, as well as Hindi books, was burned. There was extensive damage to government and private property; and many lives were lost.[89] Not least, it was at this time that *tamiḻppaṟṟu* acquired its most celebrated martyrs with the self-immolation of Chinnasami and others.

In numerous respects, these waves of anti-Hindi protests have critically shaped the contours of party politics in modern Tamilnadu, arguably more so than the anticolonial agitations against the British. A steady stream of anti-Hindi demonology from the 1930s clearly identified and vilified the putative enemies of Tamil. These included Hindi-speaking North Indians/Aryans, Tamil Brahmans, and the state government in the clutches of these Brahmans. But above all, this demonology discredited the Tamilnadu Congress party, despite numerous differences within its own ranks on the Hindi issue. Over the decades, the party found it difficult to shake loose the reputation it acquired as the "enemy" and "slayer" of Tami̲ttāy, as a front for Brahman and Bania (North Indian merchant) interests, and as a stooge in the hands of "Hindi imperialists" of the North. Caught between coping with the dictates of its high command in New Delhi and stemming the growing popularity of the Dravidian movement in Madras, the Tamilnadu Congress became a victim of its attempts to broker Tamil interests in the national arena. By the same token, all of the party's rivals—the Justice Party, the DK, the DMK, the Tamil Arasu Kazhagam, the We Tamils, and others—were able to promote themselves as protectors of Tamil and as true representatives of Tamil interests, precisely by opposing the Congress's Hindi policy. These parties spearheaded the Hindi protests in the state, providing popular and organizational ballast to *tami̲ppar̲r̲u*'s arguments against the language even as they reaped rich political rewards in the process. To this day, one of the surest ways to gain political and electoral support in Tamilnadu is to raise the anti-Hindi standard, and it is telling that since 1967, the Congress has never returned to power in the state.

All the same, growing numbers of Tamil speakers have in recent years taken to studying the language, and Hindi propagation societies are doing a thriving business in Tamilnadu today.[90] Indeed, except for a brief few months when the angry sentiments against the language spilled over into antagonism towards Hindi movies and songs, the latter have a popularity in Tamilnadu quite incommensurate with Hindi's pedagogical and political status in the state. It would be a mistake, therefore, to assume there has been no popular support for Hindi in Tamilnadu. Well before the state took up its cause in the late 1930s, various civic organizations began promoting Hindi in the Presidency. While the need for a common language other than English was voiced in Madras newspapers by the turn of this century, with both Hindi/Hindustani and Sanskrit being proffered as early candidates, concerted efforts to spread Hindi date to the founding of the Dakshin Bharat Hindi Prachar Sabha (Institution for the Propagation of Hindi in South

India) in 1918 by Gandhi. The Sabha ran schools, trained teachers, conducted examinations, and awarded numerous diplomas of proficiency, though well into the 1930s the Tamil-speaking area lagged behind others in the Presidency in its enthusiasm for Hindi (Nambi Arooran 1980: 186–91). The Sabha's endeavors received a boost when the Indian National Congress decreed in 1925 that all its proceedings, hitherto carried out in English, "shall be conducted as far as possible in Hindustani" and provided funds for the promotion of the language (Nayar 1969: 59–60). Through the 1920s and 1930s, the Sabha, as well as other organizations such as the Hindustani Seva Dal and the Hindustani Hitashi Mandal, petitioned the state to join in the promotion of Hindi in the Presidency and succeeded in convincing many Congress-led local governments to introduce the compulsory study of Hindi in schools in the 1930s (Irschick 1986: 212–14; Nambi Arooran 1980: 188–94). So Rajagopalachari's decision to make the study of Hindi mandatory was not a total innovation. Nevertheless, the extension of state patronage to what had hitherto largely been a civic and Congress party activity completely changed the stakes in the Hindi game, especially in the face of complaints of Tamil's devotees that the state was not doing much to promote the study of Tamil.

All the same, it would also be a mistake to argue, as the Congress did, that popular hostility towards Hindi was an illusion. For example, Rajagopalachari declared in 1938 that the opposition to Hindi did not stem from devotion to Tamil but was mounted by those "cursed with the prejudices of anti-Aryanism" and "with the hatred of Congress" (Nambi Arooran 1980: 195). Through the 1950s and early 1960s, other Congress leaders continued to insist that the DK and the DMK had duped the hapless Tamil masses by stirring up anti-Hindi sentiments in order to garner power for themselves. Yet, ironically, if there is one effort that succeeded—more so than any other undertaken by Tamil's devotees and pro-Tamil politicians—in making *tami̲ḻpparṟu* visible among a general populace, it was the Hindi policy of the central and state governments. As I have already noted, the anti-Hindi movement took Tamil devotional ideas out of the narrow elite and literary circles in which they had hitherto circulated. For the first time in the 1930s, the idea that Tamil might be endangered caught on among those who were not necessarily its ardent devotees; consequently, the hitherto scholarly, elite male ranks of Tamil's devotees swelled over the years with the addition of the street poet, the petty shopkeeper, the small-time pamphleteer, the college-going student, and the woman. By the

1960s, even the English-speaking middle class, which had hitherto stayed out of both Tamil devotional activities and the anti-Hindi movement, was galvanized (Barnett 1976; Rocher 1963).

Equally ironically, it is the battle against Hindi, rather than any sustained activity on behalf of Tamil, which spurred the devotional community to unite in harmony, setting aside differences and dissensions. Regardless of their disagreements over the meaning of Tamil, proponents of neo-Shaivism, contestatory classicism, and Dravidianism came together in response to the threat posed by Hindi by the late 1930s. Devotees of Indianist persuasion still kept their distance from this emerging consensus, but this was to change by the late 1940s, as is apparent from the attendance at a large anti-Hindi conference held in Madras city in July 1948. Convened under the aegis of the Dravidian movement, the conference featured devotees like Bharatidasan, Annadurai, Maraimalai Adigal, Kalyanasundaram, and Sivagnanam, all speaking on the same platform against Hindi.[91] The presence of Bharatidasan, Annadurai, and Maraimalai Adigal was not unusual, since they had been writing and speaking passionately against the government's Hindi policy for more than a decade. But Kalyanasundaram and Sivagnanam had built their literary and political reputations as Congress nationalists in the 1920s and 1930s, during which time they had both supported the cause of Hindi. Sivagnanam (1974: 268) recalls attending Hindi classes when he was in prison in the 1940s, although he confesses that he never did become proficient in the language. Similarly, in 1925 so concerned was Kalyanasundaram with the slow progress of Hindi in the Presidency that he called upon Tamil youth to join the Hindustani Seva Dal and help in its dissemination (Nambi Arooran 1980: 189). A native of Tiruvarur, Kalyanasundaram grew up in a poor family in Madras city where, after finishing the tenth grade, he clerked for a while and taught Tamil in local schools from 1910. At great cost to his own material welfare, he became involved in nationalist politics beginning in 1917, and he was a member of the Tamilnadu Congress as well as the Madras Presidency Association, the party formed by "non-Brahman" nationalists to counter the Justice Party. A devout Gandhian and reformed Shaivite, Kalyanasundaram was the editor of key nationalist newspapers like *Tēcapaktaṉ* (1917–20) and *Navacakti* (1920–40) through which he popularized a style of writing Tamil, especially for use in politics, that was simple but refined; it was free of foreign words, both English and Sanskrit. Kalyanasundaram's *tamiḻppaṟṟu* in those early decades was clearly Indianist; although he was a close friend of both Maraimalai Adigal and E. V. Ramasami, his devotion to Tamil did not lead him into antagonism towards Sanskrit or Hindi. Neither was he anti-Brahman nor a supporter of the Dravidianist separatist agenda. Yet by the 1940s, Kalyanasundaram was certainly marching to a different tune. To the delight of many a Dravidianist, he came out publicly in support of the Dravidian movement and its demand for a separate Tamilnadu, declaring that in this lay the hope for a truly socialist community (Kalyanasundaranar 1949).[92] By the 1930s, Kalyanasundaram had already become disillusioned with the Congress and its promotion of upper-caste, upper-class interests. This led him to increasing involvement in the labor movement, a cause he had adopted as early as 1918 (Kalyanasundaranar 1982). The Congress's aggressive pursuit of the Hindi policy only convinced him that not only was that party inimical to Tamil interests but so too was the language that it promoted with such enthusiasm. Thus in 1948, the same Kalyanasundaram who had worked to popularize Hindi in the 1920s dismissed it now as a language that was impoverished and that promoted the subservience of women and "Shudras." "Tamil," he declared, "has the capacity to change a monkey into a man; Hindi, on the other hand, can make monkeys out of men."[93]

While the battle against Hindi diluted the Indianist passions of devotees like Kalyanasundaram, Sivagnanam, Suddhananda Bharati, and others, it also drew into the fray Tamil schoolteachers and scholars who, for the first time, took to the streets, courted arrest, and served prison sentences. Prior to the 1930s, few Tamil scholars had been driven to political activism by their passion for Tamil. The anti-Hindi movement changed this, however. Although Maraimalai Adigal himself did not go to prison, two of his daughters-in-law and his son, Tirunavukarasu, joined the picket lines in Madras and served prison sentences in 1938–39.[94] Not surprisingly, when scholars and teachers like Somasundara Bharati, K. Appadurai, Mudiyarasan, and Ilakuvan took part in protest meetings, or courted arrest or were sent off to prison, they received much publicity in the opposition press, for this clearly disproved the government's claim that the anti-Hindi movement was the mischief wrought by politicians and their uneducated "rabble" followers.

The anti-Hindi movement also made Muslim participation in Tamil devotional activities more visible (Abdul Karim 1982: 250–61; More 1993). From the turn of this century, devotees who were Muslims by faith wrote eulogistic essays and verses on Tamil, an early example being Abdul Kadir Rowther's long poem in praise of the various Tamil academies of Madurai (Rowther 1907). Rowther himself was one of three Muslim poets who were members of the Madurai Tamil Sangam in its first years, and he won the admiration of his fellow devout for "his deep devotion to Tamil, his unbounded sympathy for every thing Tamil" (Rowther 1907: 1). P. Dawood Sha, another Tamil enthusiast, who received a gold medal from the Madurai Tamil Sangam, was editor in the 1920s of the journal *Dar-ul-Islam,* which promoted pure Tamil and criticized Muslim theologians for their poor command of the language (More 1993: 88). Also of particular interest is an essay published in the nationalist journal *Āṉantapōtiṉi* by A. Mohamed Ibrahim of Papanasam, in which the author praised Tamil and Tamiḻttāy by invoking the various premodern Shaiva hymns on the language (Ibrahim 1920). Later in the century, the poet K. M. Sharif (1914–94) received much praise for many of his verses on Tamil, and for his passionate editorials in the 1940s and 1950s in journals like *Tamiḻ Muḻakkam* and *Cāṭṭai.* In these editorials, Sharif, a member for a while of Sivagnanam's Tamil Arasu Kazhagam, promoted many of the latter's causes: the use of Tamil in schools and government, the creation of a Tamilnadu whose borders conformed to those described in the ancient Caṅkam poems, the glories of ancient Tamil culture, and so on (Sharif 1990, 1992).

In a recent essay, J. B. P. More traces the growing collaboration during the 1920s and 1930s between the Tamil-speaking Muslim leadership of the Madras Presidency and Ramasami's Self-Respect movement. This collaboration was based on the latter's rejection of Hinduism and Brahmanism, its support of lower-caste conversion to Islam, and its vision of a Dravidian society which would honor Muslims. In turn, the Tamil Muslim leadership drew upon the support of the Dravidian movement in its own efforts to counter the domination of a Urdu-speaking Muslim elite in the Presidency. Whereas many among the latter supported Hindustani on the grounds that "the language is one [although] the scripts are two," Tamil-speaking Muslim leaders joined forces with the Dravidian movement in opposing Hindi. So one of them, Khalifullah, declared in the Legislative Assembly: "I may at once say that I am a Rowther myself; my mother tongue is Tamil and not Urdu. I am not ashamed of it; I am proud of it" (quoted in More 1993: 98). More documents the extensive participation of Tamil-speaking Muslims in various anti-Hindi protests and rallies in different cities and towns of the Presidency, and he rightly notes that it was "the language agitation which finally led Tamil Muslims to affirm their distinct Tamil identity," even at the cost of parting ways with their putative coreligionists who nonetheless spoke a different tongue, Urdu (1993: 102). Instead, they chose to join forces with Tamil-speaking "non-Brahmans" and "fellow" Dravidians. Clearly, in this case language bonds and ethnic ties triumphed over religious affinity.

Further, it was in the context of these anti-Hindi protests that various new technologies for demonstrating and disseminating *tamiḻppaṟṟu* were deployed, beyond the elite literary journal and the scholarly publication. These included subversive acts, such as writing on Hindi exams slogans like "Down with Hindi" and "Long Live Tamil" (Nayar 1969: 199); the public and dramatic burning of facsimiles of the Constitution or the map of India; the tarring over of Hindi names and the Devanagari script on official billboards; and the self-immolations and suicides of young men. In the early years, as the Congress itself took delight in reminding everyone, the protesters appropriated many of the strategies that Indian nationalists had developed in their anticolonial struggles against the British: the peaceful picketing of schools where Hindi was taught and of government buildings and official residences, black flag demonstrations, and public processions and meetings. The Gandhian strategy of fasting was also appropriated, although with not much success or support, as we will see. In big cities and small towns alike, hundreds of anti-Hindi protest meetings were held, frequently attracting thousands. Such meetings often opened and closed with the singing of a pro-Tamil song or hymn and concluded with the staging of plays that propagated the message(s) of Tamil devotion and the Dravidian movement.

As popular as public meetings were protest marches, sometimes drawing thousands, marked by the reciting of slogans and the singing of pro-Tamil and anti-Hindi songs and ditties. Protesters walked through city streets carrying the Tamil banner (which bore the symbols of the fish, the bow, and the tiger for the ancient Tamil dynasties of the Chera, the Pandya, and the Chola); they would also carry colorful placards emblazoned with anti-Hindi and pro-Tamil slogans; and they distributed handbills publicizing the evils of Hindi and the wonders of Tamil. The most spectacular of these protest marches was the one undertaken by the *tamiḻar paṭai,* the "Tamilian Brigade," in August–September 1938. Jointly organized by the Self-Respect movement and the Muslim League, the brigade of a hundred or so young men set out from Tiruchirapalli on 1 August, under the stewardship of Kumaraswami Pillai and Ramamirtham Ammal. During the next forty-two days, members of the brigade walked through 234 villages and 60 towns; and they addressed eighty-seven public meetings attended by at least half a million. Opposition newspapers carried daily news of the brigade's progress and noted the "rousing reception" it received in various towns and villages of the Presidency on its six-hundred-mile trek. In September 1938 it finally reached Madras, where many of its members joined the picketing activities in the city and were arrested. Not the least of the consequences of the march of the anti-Hindi brigade (which, contemporaries did not fail to note, resembled Gandhi's famous march to Dandi, and Rajagopalachari's to Vedaranyam in 1930) was the formation in smaller towns and villages of similar brigades, which took up the cause of spreading the anti-Hindi and pro-Tamil message (Ilanceliyan 1986: 114–23; Visswanathan 1983: 211–13).

The battle against Hindi also spurred the proliferation of numerous populist organizations devoted to protect Tamil from the new threat. So, at the organizational level as well, *tamil̲ppar̲r̲u* came to be transformed during these years, as populist associations such as Tamil̲ Vaḷar Nilayam (Academy for Tamil Development), Tamil̲ar Kal̲akam (Society of Tamilians), and Tamil̲ar Nalvāl̲vu Kal̲akam (Society for Tamilian Welfare) joined the ranks of more elite literary societies such as the Madurai Tamil Sangam, Karanthai Tamil Sangam, and the like. The founding charters of many of these organizations declared the need to cherish Tamil̲ttāy and the mother tongue, to protect the Tamil people, and to oppose Hindi. The Tamil̲p Pātukāppuk Kal̲akam (Society for the Protection of Tamil), founded in Tirunelveli in 1937 by devotees associated with both the Shaiva Siddhanta Kazhagam and the Karanthai Tamil Sangam, issued a circular asking Tamil speakers to Tamilize their personal names and the names of their homes and workplaces, of streets and towns, of eating places, and so on. The circular ended with the words, "Do service to Tamil and secure freedom" (Visswanathan 1983: 197–99).[95] Furthermore, in many towns and even in the occasional village, anti-Hindi leagues and Tamil societies and student associations sprung up. Although such organizations were invariably short-lived, their very existence reminds us that the anti-Hindi movement promoted the percolation of Tamil devotional ideas down to the grassroots level. Because Tamil's devotees had made clear that it was the Tamilian who was going to save their language from Hindi, the Everyman began to be integrated into the devotional community and its activities in a manner not done before. The Tamilian—the ordinary Tamil speaker—became the heart and soul of Tamil devotion at last, in the context of the movement against Hindi. Indeed, opposition to Hindi came to ultimately define the loyal Tamilian, for the Tamil subject is not just anyone who is devoted to Tamil but is one who is convinced that Hindi threatens the mother/language and is prepared to take to the streets to demonstrate this conviction.

Like many an oppositional practice, the anti-Hindi movement of Tamil's devotees has had many consequences—some paradoxical, some tragic. How may we assess its success? from whose viewpoint? Their protests may have allowed Tamil's devotees to set aside various crucial differences, if only temporarily, and heal the fissures among them; they may have aroused the interest of even the disinterested in *tamiḻppaṟṟu*, compelled the state to take a more sustained interest in the promotion of Tamil, and put a brake on Hindi domination. But all this has not come without its costs, the most obvious of which, of course, is that speakers of Tamil who grow up in Tamilnadu, and depend on state-sponsored education, do not have the ready opportunity to learn the putative official language of India and avail themselves of the potential benefits this brings. Just as crucially, the anti-Hindi movement has re-signified the very meaning of *tamiḻppaṟṟu*. Increasingly in the discourse(s) of many devotees, resistance to Hindi (*inti etirppu*) has received more emphasis than laboring for Tamil (*tamiḻppaṇi*). Correspondingly, the paradigmatic Tamil devotee is not necessarily the one who has worked all her life to improve Tamil but rather the one who gave up his life in the battle against Hindi. Indeed, even those who disavow *tamiḻppaṟṟu* are admitted into the ranks of Tamil's devotees because of their opposition to Hindi. Paradoxically, therefore, like all identities that are defined in opposition, the Tamilian self is (re)cast in terms of resistance to Hindi: "true" Tamilians are those who may or may not speak good Tamil or even care for it; but they are certainly those who gave up their bodies, lives, and souls in the battle against Hindi.

CHAPTER FIVE

To Die For

Living for Language

It was the year 1887 in Madras city. After more than six years of laboring over the palm-leaf manuscript of the ancient epic poem *Cīvaka Cintāmaṇi,* Swaminatha Aiyar had just handed over the final sections of the text to his printer. For the past few years, his entire life had been wrapped up in the *Cintāmaṇi:* he woke up thinking about it and stayed up late into the night, deciphering and transcribing archaic words. His fingers were sore from turning over the brittle leaves of the manuscript, and his eyes ached from going over proofs by the dim light of oil lamps. He had spent most of his summer and winter vacations, and all other days he could steal from his teaching responsibilities, travelling back and forth between the printer's workshop, in Madras city, and his college and home, far south in Kumbakonam. There had been moments of great anxiety when he had been convulsed with fear he would run out of money, that the press would burn down, or that malcontents would tamper with his proofs. But all that was now in the past. He had seen the work through to its final printed form. It was only then, after all those years of laboring day and night, that he allowed himself the luxury of succumbing to his tiredness. He was still at the printer's. He laid himself down, right there and then on the floor, and slept deeply and happily. When he woke up, he saw a man standing before him. "Here, sir, is the *Pattuppāṭṭu,*" the man said, and handed over to Swaminathan another palm-leaf manuscript. He thought, "Tamiḻaṉṉai [Tamiḻttāy] herself has sent [this man], commanding me to go on with my service to Tamil," and he addressed her: "O mother! You have (re)adorned yourself with the

Cintāmaṇi that I, your poor devotee, gave back to you. Continue to offer me grace, so that I, your servant, can go on with my work of recovering all your other jewels." So saying, he reverenced Tamiḻttāy with all his heart, and continued, he tells us, for the rest of his life trying to fulfill her wishes (Swaminatha Aiyar 1982: 612–13).

As this incident illustrates so well, the heart and soul of the practice of Tamil devotion are the deeply personal bonds of reverence, affection, and passion that tie the devout to the language, bonds that are only further reaffirmed in the stories that its devotees tell about themselves and each other. Indeed, if praise poems are one of the means through which a community of sentiment tying its devotees to Tamil is constituted, then stories that recount the hardships they faced, the resistances they encountered, and their success in overcoming these difficulties to triumph in their *tamiḻppaṟṟu* are another. In many such stories, her devotees speak directly to their Tamiḻttāy, complain about the numerous woes that beset them, and beseech her to grant them grace. She, too, talks with them, recalls the many afflictions that trouble her, and pleads with them to meliorate her condition. In all such accounts, the language is not an impersonal, abstract, distant entity. Instead, it is imagined as a concerned, deeply involved participant in the lives of its speakers, an intimate member of their families. So in 1942, on the eve of the Japanese invasion of Singapore, S. B. Adithan, who had a flourishing law practice there, was torn between staying on or returning to Tamilnadu. He wrote down the words "Stay on in Singapore" and "Return to Tamilnadu" on two chits, folded these up, and then picked out the one which commanded him to return home. "Adithan[ar] should return to his motherland, and serve Tamilnadu, the Tamil people, and Tamil: this was Tamiḻttāy's will," his biographer concludes (Kuppusami 1969: 11). Tamiḻttāy could also exercise her will to bring her straying "children" back to the fold. In the 1930s, K. Appadurai, a comparatively late convert to *tamiḻppaṟṟu,* was involved in an activity that amounted to cardinal sin in the eyes of most devotees of Tamil: the teaching of Hindi. During these years, he also lost his father and his (first) wife, as well as fracturing his leg and spending months in the hospital. "This was the punishment that Tamiḻttāy herself gave [Appadurai] for laboring for Hindi," his fellow devotees concluded. After this, he dedicated himself totally to Tamil, we are told (Mamani 1992: 49).[1]

It is a measure of the intimacy between the language and its devotees that their births are imagined as Tamiḻttāy's gift and blessing; their deaths, her loss. Many recall that it is their *tamilpparru* that carried them through critical periods of their life, helping them overcome hunger and poverty, humiliation and rejection, illness and suffering. The poet Mudiyarasan spent most of his life as a poorly paid Tamil schoolteacher. Yet he notes with pride, "As long as I have Tamil in my heart, I am not poor" (Mudiyarasan n.d.: 101). Similarly, Sivagnanam writes that plagued by a terrible stomach ulcer, he carried on his daily life in a state of acute pain. Indeed, he even thought of committing suicide. "What prevented me from doing so was the deep devotion I had for Tamil, and the great desire I had for realizing a new Tamil land" (Sivagnanam 1974: 774–75). In all such stories, Tamil's devotees refer to each other by titles which remind one and all of the intimate bonds with their beloved language. Thus Maraimalai Adigal is *tamilk kaṭal,* "ocean of Tamil," or *tamilmalai,* "mountain of Tamil"; Viswanatham is *muttamilk kāvalar,* "guardian of the three Tamil(s)"; Kalyanasundaram is *tamilt tenral,* "southern Tamil breeze"; and Umamakeswaram (1883–1941) is *tamilavēḷ,* "great Tamil hero," to name just a few. Even as such epithets bestowed a mantle of honor generally reserved for sovereigns, deities, and other notables on Tamil's devout, they also suggest that these individuals attained meaning only in relation to Tamil.

This is also suggested by many devotees' desire to confer upon themselves and their children names that invoke Tamil and its literature. Sivagnanam named his daughter Kannagi, because she was born after he had immersed himself in the study of the *Cilappatikāram.* "After the Tamil language, I have the deepest devotion to my daughter Kannagi," he writes. If we do not even have Tamil names for ourselves, how will we make Tamil proud? he demands of his readers (Sivagnanam 1974: 775–76). Similarly, Ilakuvan, who Tamilized his given Sanskritic name, states: "They may ask what's in a name. One's name is everything. Tamilians should only bear Tamil names. Those who refuse this cannot be devotees of Tamil" (Ilakuvanar 1971: 4). Today, of course, many Tamil speakers, and not just those overtly devoted to the language, bear personal names containing the word "Tamil," such as Tamilcelvi, "daughter of Tamil"; Tamilanban, "lover of Tamil"; Tamilarasi, "Queen Tamil"; even Tamilpitthan, "mad about Tamil."

The stories that circulate in the devotional community also dwell on the numerous small but by no means insignificant ways in which devotees lived out, on an everyday basis, their love for their language. In the

1930s, Sivagnanam, who hailed from a very poor family and whose formal education ended in the primary school, collected all the Tamil books that he could lay his hands on and ran a Tamiḻttāy Library in Madras city, so that even the working-class community in which he lived could have access to the wealth of Tamil (Sivagnanam 1974: 116–17). In the late 1930s and early 1940s, when the demand for an independent Tamilnadu surfaced, the poet Pulavar Kulanthai printed the words "Tamilnadu for Tamilians" on the borders of saris and towels, and distributed these all over the Presidency (Pulavar Kulanthai 1971: 58). Somasundara Bharati named his newly built house (in his home town of Ettaiyapuram) Tamiḻakam, "Abode of Tamil" (Sambasivanar and Ilankumaran 1960: 84). Although not particularly affluent herself, Dharmambal, who played a leading role in the anti-Hindi protests of the 1930s, donated her family home to the Karanthai Tamil Sangam (K. Tirunavukarasu 1991: 208). Umamakeswaram Pillai, for many years the president of Karanthai Tamil Sangam, at his own expense printed and distributed among the general populace copies of Sundaram Pillai's signature hymn on Tamiḻttāy (Sambasivanar 1974: 35). And V. V. Ramasami, who was editor of the literary magazine *Teṉṟal* and a member of the Madras Legislative Council in the 1950s, began all his letters with the phrase *tamiḻ velka!,* "may Tamil be victorious."[2]

These are just a few incidents from the many stories that Tamil's devotees tell about each other. These narratives undoubtedly labor under the weight of despair that its enthusiasts experienced on behalf of their ailing language/mother. In the interstices of this rhetoric of decline and dismay, however, lurks the absolute joy or wonder that fills its devotees when they chanced upon the sweet sounds of Tamil, in song or word; when they had the good fortune of meeting a fellow devout; when they saw some sign, however small, that their beloved language was flourishing. Indeed, it is telling that in these stories, Tamil's triumphs are experienced as personal victories, just as its defeats are narrated as personal failures. Such stories obviously reaffirm the intimacy of the bonds with Tamil that manifests itself in every sphere of its devotees' lives. They also simultaneously keep alive the memory of Tamil's devotees in their community; for had not Bharatidasan insisted passionately, again and again, that there is no death for the true follower of Tamil (Bharatidasan 1958: 22)?[3] But above all, such stories transform, through various narrative strategies, certain individuals into paragons of Tamil devotion and paradigmatic Tamilians whose lives are worthy of emulation by all good and loyal speakers of the language. These stories are therefore the sites for the production of what I characterize as the *devotional subject,* whose self merges into the imagined self of Tamil, whose life experiences are subordinated to the superior cause of the language, and whose story is the story of Tamil.

There are many models of devotional subjectivity that are produced by these stories. Because the unmarked Tamil devotee is always a male who is not Brahman, and who claims Tamil as his "mother tongue," I begin by exploring the stories of those who do not fall into this category: the stories therefore of the Tamil enthusiast who is woman, who is European missionary, and who is Brahman. I then turn to the stories of the model devotee who is poet and scholar, the devotee who is publicist and patron, the warrior devotee, and the devotee who becomes martyr to the Tamil cause. I close with the story of a man who all his life resisted being drawn into the devotional community, but nevertheless is enshrined, through the inexorable logic of *tamiḻppaṟṟu,* as a paradigmatic *tamiḻaṉpar,* "Tamil devotee."

THE WOMAN DEVOTEE

From the time of Vedanayakam Pillai's 1879 novel *Piratāpa Mutaliyār Carittiram* through Bharatidasan's numerous plays in the 1940s and 1950s, to Mudiyarasan's 1964 epic poem *Pūṅkoṭi,* the Tamil reading public has been offered the image of the ideal Tamil woman as an enthusiastic devotee of Tamil. It is Vedanayakam's spirited heroine, Gnanambal, rather than the hero of his novel, who mounts a fiery attack on the infatuation with English among lawyers of her time, producing in that process one of the earliest passionate eulogies of Tamil in devotional discourses (Vedanayakam Pillai 1879: 279–90). In a radical departure, Mudiyarasan's heroine Poonkodi even rejects marriage and motherhood, dedicating her entire life to the service of Tamil. Mudiyarasan yearned to see a woman who gave herself up to the Tamil cause, like Manimekhalai, the nun who dedicated her life to Buddhism in the ancient epic poem *Maṇimēkalai* (Mudiyarasan n.d.: 94–95). Like Manimekhalai, Poonkodi, too, spurns a life of pleasure and comfort, refuses to marry her ardent suitor Komagan, immerses herself in a passionate pursuit of Tamil learning, and even goes to prison to save her beloved language from its enemies. On her deathbed in prison, Tamiḻttāy appears to her in a vision, praises her for her services, and offers her blessings to her selfless daughter (Mudiyarasan 1964).

Mudiyarasan's image of the woman devotee who is not wife and mother is comparatively rare in (male) devotional discourses. In general, as custodians of Tamil, women are celebrated less for their achievements in their own right as poets, authors, or thinkers, and more for their role as the heroic mothers (*vīrattāy*) of Tamiḻttāy's children, especially her sons (Ramaswamy 1992a; see also Anandhi 1991b; Lakshmi 1990). In the writings of Tamil's devotees, the Tamil-speaking woman is recast as a surrogate Tamiḻttāy. So M. Kathiresan Chettiar (1881–1953), professor of Tamil at Annamalai University, introduced Tamiḻttāy to his readers thus: "Who is Tamiḻ Aṉṉai [Tamiḻttāy]? Our mothers, too, are Tamiḻ Aṉṉai. All mothers who speak Tamil are Tamiḻ Aṉṉai . . . [at the same time], the Mother who instructs all the mothers of the world in speech and is the very embodiment of the sweetness that we call 'Tamil'—she is the person we call Tamiḻ Aṉṉai" (Kathiresan Chettiar 1959–60: 169).

Here, as in numerous other instances, the Tamil woman perforce came to be figured as the visible and substantial presence of intangible abstractions—the language, and the community imagined around it. As the living embodiment of Tamil, she is charged with the responsibility of reproducing (literally, as well as metaphorically) Tamil society and culture, most especially the language. Modelled on the "new woman" who emerged in middle-class imaginations everywhere in colonial India, she is appropriately educated to run a neat, disciplined, and efficient home where she nourishes her children on her pure Tamil milk, raising them to be heroic sons who would willingly go into the world to work for Tamil's welfare and fertile daughters who would become good, educated mothers themselves. Devotional writings spur women on to embrace this vision by dredging up images of the heroic mother of the Caṅkam poems, who rejoices on the day she learned that the son whom her womb had given birth to, and her milk had nourished, now lay dead on the battlefield, having fought honorably for lord and land—and by extension, of course, for his language (Bharati 1988: 318–20; Nilambikai 1960: 82–91; M. Raghava Aiyangar 1986; C. S. Subramaniam 1986: 397–99).[4]

Its female devotees did not reject either the motherhood of Tamil or their own in their writings. On the contrary, rather than seeing motherhood as "a strategy of containment," as some feminist scholars are wont to do today (Visweswaran 1990: 66; see also Lakshmi 1990), Tamiḻttāy's daughters saw it as an opportunity for self-empowerment. They pursued this opportunity through appropriating the figure of Tamiḻttāy, even though such an appropriation necessarily took place in the crevices of the patriarchal structures that were relegitimized by *tamilpparru* itself. Almost without exception, its female devotees maintained that because Tamil is woman and mother, they, as women and mothers, have a better understanding of Tamilttāy's plight and needs. They insisted that women ought not to just passively participate in Tamil devotional activities initiated by men, but ought to lead and march ahead of them (Ramaswamy 1992a: 46–48). Although such an empowerment was necessarily premised on the essentializing of the woman as mother, in this deployment of Tamilttāy her female devotees replaced the docile mothers of male devotional discourses, who are followers, with mothers who are leaders.

In a recent essay, Janaki Nair rightly notes: "the question of female agency in history, whether that agency takes the form of consent, transgression, or subversion, can neither be wholly contained within a delineation of structures of oppression nor exhausted by accounts of female presence in history, but must be posed within specific contexts and placed along a continuum where various forms of agency may coexist" (Nair 1994: 83). And indeed, in the stories of women devotees that are circulated within the devotional community, there is a continuum which ranges from Nilambikai's conservative advocacy of women's responsibility in educating their children to Thamaraikanni's spirited call for militant warriors to battle for the Tamil cause. And in the stories of those women who during the anti-Hindi protests of the 1930s and 1940s took to the streets, organized protest marches and conferences, and even went to prison, the radical female devotee resembles the male, as she transgresses the function of the domestic paragon that has been assigned to her. These stories, even when we hear them through male voices, remind us that these women contested and subverted the patriarchal demands of *tamilpparru,* while simultaneously appearing to give their consent to the confinement to marriage and motherhood that it demanded (Ramaswamy 1992a).

Nilambikai has been described in the biography written by her brother as a woman who came into this world solely for the purpose of serving Tamil: "she embodies *tamilpparru;* her life is the life of Tamil; she cannot be pried apart from Tamil" (M. Tirunavukarasu 1945: 50). Born in 1903, Nilambikai's life and future as a Tamil devotee was overdetermined. The favorite daughter of Maraimalai Adigal, she was raised on the shoulders and laps of other well-known devotees such as Arasan Shanmugan (1868–1915) and Pandithurai Thevar (1867–1911), who were her father's friends and patrons. Her father appears to have taken great pride in her love for Tamil, even making her memorize, when she was thirteen, one of his essays on the duties of motherhood, which she publicly recited at a scholarly meeting in Madras. So impressed was he with his young daughter, her brother tells us, that Maraimalai Adigal declared passionately one day, "Nila's face resembles that of Shelley and Shakespeare and other great savants" (M. Tirunavukarasu 1945: 8–12).

In the devotional community, Nilambikai occupies a special niche for her role in spurring her famous father into launching his pure Tamil movement in 1916. Her brother recalls that Nilambikai bestowed pure Tamil names upon her siblings, and would use only those; she would speak and write as far as possible in pure Tamil; and she would correct anyone who used a foreign word when speaking in Tamil (M. Tirunavukarasu 1945: 14–15). Soon after, in 1918, when she turned sixteen, Nilambikai met the twenty-eight-year-old Tiruvarangam Pillai (1890–1944), who a few years later was to set up the famous Shaiva Siddhanta Kazhagam. Her brother remembers that his entire family had come to see Tiruvarangam as a godlike figure, their father's savior and patron. It is perhaps not surprising that young Nilambikai fell in love with him, although she was not allowed to marry him for almost ten years (M. Tirunavukarasu 1945: 21–35).

Intertwined though her life may have been with those of these famous devotees, Nilambikai nevertheless strived to serve Tamil on her own as well. By the time she was in her early twenties, she had published numerous essays on the virtues of *taṉittamiḻ* in the face of considerable opposition to the pure Tamil movement (Nilambikai 1960).[5] She followed this up in 1937 with a dictionary, the first of its kind, which demonstrated the existence of pure Tamil equivalents for seven thousand Sanskrit words that had swamped Tamil (Nilambikai 1952). She also taught Tamil in girls' schools; spoke at various Shaiva conferences; and wrote extensively on the revival of Tamil, the spread of Shaivism, and the improvement of women. By all accounts, she was alarmed by what she saw as an absence of interest in Tamil among its female speakers, a concern that she voiced especially strongly in her inaugural address to the Tamilnadu Women's Conference summoned in November 1938 to register Tamil women's protest against Hindi.[6] Of course, Nilambikai's vision for how women should help their language fell within the parameters of middle-class motherhood. They should establish *taṉittamiḻ* women's colleges and bookstores, encourage widow education, and become Tamil teachers. But such public services should never compromise their primary function as educated homemakers who raised their children to be well-read, disciplined, and pure Tamil speakers (Nilambikai n.d.). She wrote and spoke ardently on such matters in spite of poor health, and in spite of having to take care of her own eight children. At least by her brother's account, she took great pride in her own motherhood, raising her children to be devout Shaivites and Tamil speakers (M. Tirunavukarasu 1945: 38–43). But it is hard to deny that the birth of eleven children over a period of about fifteen years must have taken its toll on her health, and she was only forty-three when she died in 1945, a year after her beloved husband and fellow devotee had passed on.

At the 1938 Tamilnadu Women's Conference which Nilambikai addressed, another woman spoke with great passion about the need for Tamil women to "rise up in anger" and step forth to help their ailing mother, Tamiḻttāy. Her name was V. P. Thamaraikanni (1911–71). Named Jalajatchi at birth, she was raised in a family of musicians and patrons of Tamil, and later Tamilized her given (Sanskritic) name. An author of many essays and novels, she did not get actively involved in politics, because both her father and husband were government employees (Lakshmi 1984: 77–78; Rajagopalan 1989: 5–7). By the late 1930s, however, she aligned herself with Ramasami's Self-Respect movement and was a key speaker at many anti-Hindi conferences organized in Madras, Salem, Velur, Nagapattinam, and elsewhere. In 1938, she also published a short story called "Punitavati Allatu Tamiḻar Viṭutalaip Pōr" (Punithavathi, or the Tamilian fight for freedom), which features a heroine, Punithavathi, who forsook her husband and her young daughter to help Tamiḻttāy, and was arrested in this process (Ramaswamy 1992a: 53–56). Thamaraikanni's spirited heroine asks, "What is the use of wealth, of freedom, and of human relationships, when I can be in the front ranks of those who serve Tamiḻttāy?" (Thamaraikanni 1938: 21).

Thamaraikanni herself did not go to prison on behalf of her beloved language. But many other women did, following her impassioned speech at the November conference. This was the first time women—anywhere in the world, by some reckoning—had ever taken to the streets to battle on behalf of their "mother tongue," it is proudly claimed. By February 1939, the battle against Hindi had intensified, and official figures show that thirty-six women, nine of them described as "ladies with children," were arrested and sentenced to six months' imprisonment; these figures almost doubled over the next few months (Ramaswamy 1992a: 56–57). Prison records show that many of the women had distinctly Tamil names; their ages ranged from eighteen to seventy; they were mostly illiterate and unemployed, and hailed from different parts of the Presidency. Devotional stories collapse their individuality into a larger narrative of Tamil devotion. Many of them are identified as daughters, wives, or daughters-in-law of well-known (male) anti-Hindi activists; as mothers, many of whom went to prison with their infant children; and as women who took pride in informing their sentencing judges that they were protesting against Hindi for the sake of their language and for the future of their children (Ilanceliyan 1986: 143–48).[7]

Two of these women stand out. One of them is "Doctor" Dharmambal (1890–1959), who was honored in 1951 with the title *vīrat tamil̲an̲n̲ai,* "heroic Tamil mother," for her various services to Tamil and to women's causes. Born in the small town of Karuntattankudi near Tanjavur, Dharmambal learned Tamil from Tamil scholars like Panditai Narayani Ammal when she moved to Madras. Prior to her involvement in the anti-Hindi movement, she had already made a reputation for herself as an activist concerned with women's issues, especially education, and as a practitioner of *siddha* medicine (hence her title "doctor"). In addition to leading the anti-Hindi women's protests in Madras in November 1938, she was also actively involved in the demands for better remuneration for Tamil teachers, and she spearheaded the Māṇavar Man̲r̲am (Student's Association) which cultivated *tamil̲ppar̲r̲u* among the city's Tamil-speaking youth. Along with Dharmambal, two of her daughters-in-law, Saraswati and Sita, were arrested for participating in the protests against Hindi (K. Tirunavukarasu 1991: 200–213).

And then there was Ramamirtham (1883–1962), a native of the small village of Moovalur near Tanjavur, who was raised in a *devadasi* (temple dancer) family. With no formal education, much of Ramamirtham's life, prior to her involvement in the anti-Hindi cause, had been devoted to the abolition of the *devadasi* system. In 1921, she joined the Congress and allied herself with its radical faction headed by Ramasami. When the latter quit the Congress in 1925–26, she followed him, became a member of his Self-Respect movement, and continued her struggle for various women's causes, encouraged by Ramasami's own radical ideas on the subject (Anandhi 1991a: 741–42). Although there is little to indicate that she joined the anti-Hindi movement because she was a devotee of Tamil, she certainly threw herself into it with great enthusiasm, even though she was in her fifties. She played a key role in organizing the Tamilian Brigade, which marched on foot from Tiruchirapalli to Madras in August–September 1938, and was in charge of providing food for the protesters on their six-hundred-mile journey. On their reaching Madras, she joined in the picketing of the Hindu Theological School along with Dharmambal and others, and she was thrown into prison for six months beginning in November 1938 (K. Tirunavukarasu 1991: 168–78). Ten years later, she spoke out against Hindi again, at the 1948 anti-Hindi conference organized in Madras. While not asking them to reject their responsibility as educated mothers, she nevertheless called upon the women gathered there to take to the streets and, like their menfolk, march against Hindi. Unlike men, she suggested shrewdly, women would be treated much more benevolently by the government, and hence could be more effective in the campaign to save Tamil. Women, she claimed, have the capacity to create as well as destroy. Therefore, Tamil women should now rise up and destroy the scourge of Hindi. Her commitment to Dravidianism notwithstanding, Ramamirtham invoked the mythical epochs of Sanskritic Hinduism as well as its archetypical heroines, declaring that Sita had destroyed the *trēta* epoch and Draupadi had brought an end to the *dwāpara* age; today, Tamil women would rise and destroy the *kali* epoch created by Hindi, she asserted.[8]

THE MISSIONARY DEVOTEE

Along the beachfront in Madras city called the Marina are a series of statues that dot the mile-long esplanade, commemorating various personalities from the Tamil past, distant and recent: the sage Tiruvalluvar, the author of the *Tirukkuṟaḷ;* Kannagi, the heroine of the epic poem *Cilappatikāram;* the seer-poetess, Auvaiyar, who wrote numerous didactic verses; Kamban, the author of the *Irāmāvatāram;* the poets Bharati and Bharatidasan; and the nationalist V. O. Chidambaram. Interspersed among these statues are three others whose plaques identify them as the "Italian savant" Veeramamunivar [Beschi] and the "English scholars," Robert Caldwell and George Pope. It is perhaps not surprising that in 1968, when the DMK government set up these statues to commemorate the Second International Tamil Conference, these three Europeans should have joined the ranks of poets and scholars who are revered within the devotional community as among the noblest of Tamiḻttāy's numerous gifted sons and daughters. For a special aura surrounds those Westerners who, over the centuries, came to Tamil's home, learned the language, and spread its glories in distant lands. They have been integrated into Tamiḻttāy's family as her "noble sons"; they have been made honorary Tamilians. In his memoirs, after a discussion of his correspondence in 1891 with the French scholar Jules Vinson over some missing texts, Swaminatha Aiyar proudly notes that while Tamiḻttāy was being cast into fire and floods in Tamilnadu, her jewels were well preserved in a distant city like Paris (Swaminatha Aiyar 1982: 688–89). Elsewhere, he rejoices that Tamil had crossed the seas and found such love abroad (Swaminatha Aiyar 1991c: 4). Similarly, a long prose poem called *Tamiḻ Vaḷarnta Katai* (The story of Tamil's growth) flags the contributions made to Tamil through the ages by such hallowed figures as Kumarakuruparar, Sivagnana Munivar, Meenakshisundaram Pillai, Arumuga Navalar, and Sundaram Pillai, and then notes:

> And then came the scholars from foreign lands;
> With his lofty *Tēmpāvaṇi*, the eminent Veeramamunivar raised [Tamil] to new heights;
> The noble Caldwell joyously bestowed upon Tamil a comparative grammar;
> The incomparable G. U. Pope gifted [to it] his translation of the Tamil *Veda*, the *Vācakam;*
> He prided himself as a student of Tamil;
> Scholar Winslow created its dictionary, and supported Tamil and praised it.
> (Navanitakrishnan 1952: 22–23)

The text then laments, "Our Tamilians do not have the *tamiḻppaṟṟu* that these [men] had. Alas ! Alas! O Tamilnadu!"

Indeed, a virtual hagiography has emerged around these figures whose "missionary" presence in the region is glossed over in favor of their role as "Christian devotees" of Tamiḻttāy. Adulation of these European missionaries within devotional discourses contrasts curiously with the powerful critique of missionary linguistics in Western academic circles in recent years. For rather than innocently recovering dying languages and lost literatures, missionaries colluded with colonial power structures in reconfiguring "native" vocabularies, restructuring "indigenous" grammars in accordance with Western categories, superimposing alien ways of conceptualizing languages over conventional notions, and so on (Cohn 1985; Fabian 1986; Rafael 1988). However, Tamil's enthusiasts, and even academics in Tamilnadu today, rarely allege that these missionaries violated Tamil, though they so accuse other "foreigners," such as Brahmans and Aryans from North India. And yet some missionaries themselves acknowledged that they had been responsible for creating a new kind of Tamil. Thus George Pope wrote in 1900 in the preface to his much-lauded translation of the *Tiruvācakam:*

> There exists now much of what is called Christian Tamil, a dialect created by the Danish missionaries of Tranquebar, enriched by generations of Tanjore, German and other missionaries; modified, purified and *refrigerated* by the Swiss Rhenius and the very composite Tinnevelly school; expanded and harmonized by Englishmen, amongst whom Bower (a Eurasian) was foremost in his day; and finally, waiting now for the touch of some heaven-born genius among the Tamil community to make it as sweet and effective as any language on earth, living or dead.
>
> (Pope 1979: xii)

Occasional antagonistic statements about these missionary devotees did surface within Tamil devotional discourses, in Indianism in particular as part of its attack on colonialism and English. Subramania Bharati complained in 1906 that while the colonial government was only too happy to extend its patronage to ("white") missionaries like Pope and to their scholarship, it did not help out Tamil scholars like Swaminatha Aiyar who had for years slaved over ancient manuscripts (C. S. Subramaniam 1986: 362).[9] Years later, Sivagnanam carefully noted the "great service" done by Caldwell, Pope, and others, which deserves "immense praise." Nevertheless, they also sowed the seeds of separatism among Tamilians and widened the gap between Sanskrit and Tamil, he writes. Furthermore, they did not contest colonial rule nor oppose the oppression of Tamilians by the British. "Christian missionaries came to the Tamil land not to help Tamil grow but to spread Christianity," he concludes (Sivagnanam 1970: 51).

All the same, Sivagnanam also notes that "from its early past, Tamil has never been the sole possession of the people following a particular religion. From the beginning of history it has been the people's language, transcending religious differences" (Sivagnanam 1970: 48). And indeed, this statement accounts for the remarkable absence of animosity towards the European missionary among a large majority of the devout. They assert, in terms that we have now come to identify as Orientalist, that the missionary interest in Tamil only proved that even the West was mesmerized by its beauty. Moreover, these missionaries only demonstrated that devotion to Tamil transcends religious boundaries, for Hindus, Muslims, and Christians are all children of Tamiḻttāy and members of the same Tamil family. Love for Tamil is a superior form of love, precisely because it does not recognize sectarian and religious differences. Christian devotees of Tamil are living proof that Tamil is a truly ecumenical language. Not surprisingly, these missionaries are appropriated by the devotional community, "converted" into honorary Tamilians, and enshrined as adopted "sons" of Tamiḻttāy.

Ranking high among these adopted sons is Constantius Beschi (1680–1746/7), who was honored with the name Veeramahamunivar, "heroic great sage," by fellow Tamil scholars for his demonstrated mastery of their language. A native of Castiglione in Italy, Beschi joined the Society of Jesus in 1698, and came to Tirunelveli around 1711. Over the next few years, he served in various adjoining parishes before he moved to the general region of Tiruchirapalli where he spent most of the rest of his life (Caldwell 1881: 240–43). Tamil's adherents take delight in noting that Beschi cast off his European clothes, adopted the ochre robes and life-style of a mendicant, learned Tamil, and "Tamilized" his Christian name as Dairiyanathan. Beschi is best-known for his pioneering work in grammar and lexicography, but his crowning achievement was the narration of the life of St. Joseph in Tamil in his poem *Tēmpāvaṇi*, probably completed around 1729. Within the devotional community, Beschi's works are represented as "adding to Tamiḻttāy's beauty"; the *Tēmpāvaṇi* in particular is "the gift to Tamiḻttāy on behalf of the Christian religion" (Sivagnanam 1970: 48). Beschi died in 1747 in Ambalakadu and is buried there, but in the words of a fellow devotee, his *Tēmpāvaṇi* adorns Tamiḻttāy as an "unfading garland" (Sethu Pillai 1964: 10).

It is with equal affection, if not more, that the services of Reverend Robert Caldwell are celebrated. Caldwell published a number of works on the history and religious practices of southern India, many of which contain several disparaging statements on its cultural practices (Dirks 1995), but he is most remembered as the author of *A Comparative Grammar of Dravidian or South-Indian Family of Languages* (1856). Although Caldwell's assertions have not gone unchallenged in the devotional community, there is general consensus that he laid the groundwork for the tremendous groundswell of pride in Tamil in the century following his work. In the words of a fellow devotee, Devaneyan Pavanar, "Tamil's antiquity was spread all over the world by that worthy man, Caldwell; the seeds for *taṇittamiḻ* [pure Tamil] were sown by [Suryanarayana Sastri]; the revered Maraimalai Adigal raised it into a plant; I am cultivating it into a tree" (quoted in Tirumaran 1992: 109). Thus Caldwell has been not only incorporated into the family of Tamil's devotees but given pride of place at its head, by one of their own.

Robert Caldwell, born in Ireland in 1814, arrived in Madras in 1838 as a missionary for the London Missionary Society. He spent most of his life in the small town of Idayankudi near Tirunelveli with the Society for the Propagation of the Gospel, and in 1877 he became bishop of Tinnevelly. A fellow devotee, R. P. Sethu Pillai, writes with affection that in the fifty-odd years he worked in Tamilnadu, Caldwell went home on furlough only three times. When he went back to England the third time, his friends there begged him to stay. But he refused. "I have lived all these years for Indians. As long I am alive, I will toil for them. I will give up my life in their land." And so he did, and when he died in 1891, he was buried in Idayankudi on the grounds of the church that he had himself built. "Caldwell Aiyar worked selflessly for fifty-three years for Tamilnadu. Is he not one of Tamiḻttāy's true sons?" concludes Sethu Pillai (1964: 32).

And there was George Pope (1820–1908), beloved among Tamil's enthusiasts for translating into English their most revered texts, the *Tirukkuṟaḷ* and the *Tiruvācakam*. Late in his life, Pope recalled a conversation he had with a "native friend in South India." He reportedly said to him: " 'I am going to live for Tamil. It shall be my great study; your people shall be my people; and I hope that my God will be theirs.' The friend replied: 'Sir, that is very delightful; but it means for you contempt and poverty.' "[10] Tamil's devout mention with delight that although he himself had declared that "Tamil scholarship is the direct road to poverty," Pope dedicated his entire life to the "service of Tamil" (Sethu Pillai 1964: 11).

Born in Nova Scotia in 1820, Pope and his family emigrated to England, where at fourteen he resolved to become a missionary. He set sail for India in 1838, reportedly studying Tamil for the first time on his eight-month voyage over. He became so good at it that he preached his first sermon in Tamil upon landing in Madras. Attached at first to the Wesleyan Missionary Society, he later joined the Society for the Propagation of the Gospel. His base of operations was Sawyerpuram in Tirunelveli district, where he founded a seminary. Around 1850, now married, Pope moved to Tanjavur; there, under the tutelage of the Tamil poet and fellow Christian Vedanayaka Sastri (1774–1864), he immersed himself in the study of ancient Tamil literature. This was also the most productive of his years in India, when he wrote a number of Tamil handbooks, textbooks, and dictionaries. After stints in Ootacumand and Bangalore, he returned to England in 1880 and joined Oxford University in 1884, where he taught Tamil and Telugu. It is then that he published his translations of the *Tirukkuṟaḷ* (1886), the *Nālaṭi-*

yār (1893), a partial translation of the *Maṇimēkalai* (1900), and, most important, the *Tiruvācakam* (1900). With great enthusiasm, an admirer, Saravana Pillai, greeted Pope's translation of the *Tiruvācakam:*

> Who is that great scholar who rendered into faultless English our divine Tamil *Veda*'s truths in such a manner that even those who do not know the glorious Tamil may understand?
> Born as jewel of the English land,
> He has with affection embraced our precious Tamiḻttāy as his foster mother.
> He is a worthy Christian preceptor.
> He is the notable who bears the name Pope
>
> (quoted in Sethu Pillai 1964: 18)

Although Pope did not die in the Tamil country nor is he buried there, Tamil enthusiasts mention with satisfaction that he had insisted that his epitaph should bear the phrase *tamiḻ māṇavaṉ,* "student of Tamil."[11]

THE BRAHMAN DEVOTEE

For most sections of the devotional community, and indeed for the bulk of the Tamil-speaking populace today, the very category "Brahman devotee of Tamil" would be a contradiction in terms. Yet, in the early decades of *tamiḻpparṟu,* many who were nominally Brahman wrote and spoke enthusiastically about the glories and wonders of Tamil, about the need to improve it, and so on. In contrast to his comparatively high visibility in those early years, the Brahman devotee becomes a rare presence by the 1930s, especially as radical neo-Shaivism, contestatory classicism, and Dravidianism consolidated their explicitly anti-Brahman agendas. The Brahman adherent indeed offers a curious counterpoint to the missionary devotee; where the latter's demonstrated love for Tamil allows him to erase the stigma of foreignness and his association with the colonial power structure, the former is not able (or allowed) to transcend his primordial identity as Brahman. His putative Brahmanness makes his devotion suspect, his love for Tamil spurious.

While defense of Tamil-speaking Brahmans continues well into the century, especially within Indianism and compensatory classicism, and while they were progressively rehabilitated by the 1950s into the Tamilian community in official DMK rhetoric, a question that was repeatedly raised in the discourses of many of Tamil's devotees from the turn of the century is "Are Brahmans Tamilian?" The answer, increasingly, was an emphatic "No." Brahmans are exclusionist and caste conscious; they identify themselves with the North, with Aryan culture, and with Sanskrit. Above all, and most sacrilegiously from the radical enthusiast's point of view, they disparage Tamil, treating its high literature and culture as derivative of Sanskrit. So in 1926, Ramasami—not particularly devoted to the language himself, as we will see—insisted that Brahmans had sold out "Tami̲ttāy's chastity" to traitors of Tamil by introducing Sanskrit words into it (E. V. Ramasami 1985: 84). And in *Tami̲lttāy Pulampal* (The lamentations of Tami̲lttāy), Tami̲lttāy herself lamented that the Brahman had been borne by her womb, and had been nourished on her milk; yet he had rejected her and her other children. "Will he even call himself a son of Tamil?" she asks (Arunagirinathar 1937: 12). The message was increasingly unambiguous: Brahmans were not supporters of Tamil; they were ashamed to accept, or refused to admit, that they were Tamil speakers. As Ramasami thundered in *Viṭutalai* in 1960, "Where can we see a Brahman who is ready to declare that Tamil is his mother tongue?" (Anaimuthu 1974: 998–99). With the gathering Hindi threat, the Brahman became an even more menacing figure, colluding with North Indians to destroy Tami̲lttāy (Bharatidasan 1948: 17). In August 1938, at an anti-Hindi gathering in Madras, the lead speaker, Pavalar Balasundaram, asked his audience, "What is to be done with the Brahman community which is killing our [Tami̲lttāy]?" [12]

The response to this question varied over the years; it included the progressive dislodging of Brahmans from positions of bureaucratic and political power from the 1920s with the ascendancy of the Justice Party, as well as the more radical, albeit unsuccessful, calls for Brahmanicide by Ramasami and some of his followers in the 1950s. Not surprisingly, that anomalous figure, the Brahman who did profess his love for Tamil and dedicated his life to its cause, is tainted by association with the community of which he is recognized as a nominal member. He was further tainted because his love for Tamil was generally compensatory classicist and Indianist in complexion. This meant that he was not overtly anti-Sanskritic, anti-Aryan, or anti-India, even when he expressed his passionate desire for Tamil. Instead, he insisted on seeing Tamil as coexisting with Sanskrit and Sanskritic culture; and, not surprisingly, he is increasingly peripheralized within the devotional community. Consider the fate of M. Raghava Aiyangar, a leading member of the Madurai Tamil Sangam, who between 1905 and 1910 helped edit its famed journal, *Centami̲l*. In 1913, Raghava Aiyangar was appointed as the chief Tamil pandit in the committee set up to produce the multivolume *Tamil Lexicon,* and he received the prestigious title of

Rao Sahib in 1936 for his efforts. In addition, he wrote several historical and literary theses in a compensatory classicist vein, many critical commentaries, and a study of the ancient grammar, *Tolkāppiyam* (Zvelebil 1992: 203–5). The latter in particular was severely attacked within the devotional community, by contestatory classicists as well as Dravidianists, for its portrayal of the sexual morality of ancient Tamilians (Maraimalai Adigal 1936b; Pulavar Kulanthai 1958: 22–23). In August 1938, at an anti-Hindi rally held in Madras, Pavalar Balasundaram fumed:

> Raghava Ayyangar has written a commentary on Tolkappiyam. . . . I shall read to you what he has written. . . . "Tamilian women of those days were flirting with whomsoever they came across; the Aryans taught and gave them education to be chaste. . . ." How dare he write like this? Today, it is the Brahman who plays the part of pimps. . . . [W]ith whom have our women flirted? Can a Tamilian who keeps quiet after this claim to be a human being? . . . Who can put up with such an insult? . . . Are not the Tamilian women our mother [*sic*]? [13]

A little earlier, in 1936, Panditai Gnanambal wrote a searing essay defending the fidelity of Tamil women and questioning the sexual morality of Brahman women and their Aryan gods. She called upon the government to confiscate Raghava Aiyangar's "traitorous text" that set out to dishonor Tamilians, especially the woman. Otherwise, she concluded, Tamilians would be compelled to rise up in anger all over Tamilnadu to protect their tarnished honor (Gnanambal 1936).

Another enthusiast whose devotion became suspect was V. V. Subramania Aiyar, editor briefly of the nationalist newspaper, the *Tēcapaktaṉ* (1920–21). In 1922, with the help of funds from the Congress and private patrons, Subramanian established a residential Tamil school (*tamiḻk kurukulam*) first at Kallidaikurichi and then at Sheramadevi (in Tirunelveli) for the purpose of teaching students in Tamil, following the principles of the national education scheme. His intention, he explained in a 1924 editorial in the journal *Pāla Pārati* that he launched from the school, was "to restore Tamil to its natural state of unrivalled preeminence." [14] He planned to do this by teaching students not only ancient arts and sciences but modern ones as well, and by imparting to them the spirit of social service. Subramanian himself resigned from the management of the school in 1925 after a scandal erupted when it was learned that Brahman students were fed separately. Soon after, he died in an accident while trying to save his young daughter from drowning (Visswanathan 1983: 45–55).

Subramanian did not start out as a Tamil devotee; on the contrary, he first made a name for himself as a nationalist who advocated violence as the principal means to secure freedom from colonial rule. Born in a small village near Tiruchirapalli in 1881, he went on to get a B.A. in history, economics, and Latin from Madras University. He worked for a few years as a lawyer in Tiruchirapalli and in Rangoon before going to London in 1907 to study for a law degree. There, he linked up with V. D. Savarkar and, over the next three years, got drawn into the circle of militant nationalists around him. On his return to India in 1910, he went to Pondicherry, where he met Subramania Bharati and became part of the poet's circle. Subramanian's devotional activities included an English translation of the *Tirukkuṟaḷ* in 1915 and the establishment of a Tamil publishing house in 1916 (Mani 1993). In a number of essays on Tamil he published beginning in 1914, he took an Indianist stance on the language; in 1924, he even insisted (to the ire of many fellow devotees) that for its replenishment and modernization, Tamil should turn to Sanskrit, "the great treasure house." He pointed out that hostility towards Sanskrit was misplaced when even the earliest works of Tamil literature had so many words of Sanskritic origin (Subramania Aiyar 1981; Mani 1993: 116).[15] His own Tamil was highly Sanskritic, and drew criticism even from someone like Kalyanasundaram, a fellow Indianist. Another of its devotees sarcastically asked how Subramania Aiyar could claim to restore Tamil to its "natural state of unrivalled preeminence" if his own speech was so inflected with Sanskrit (Mani 1993: 187–88).

The 1925 scandal over the Sheramadevi Tamil school, which led to Subramania Aiyar's earlier record as a "militant nationalist" being overshadowed by his putative Brahmanness, was soon followed by attacks on other Brahman adherents of Tamil. In 1926, Ramasami published an essay in his *Kuṭi Aracu* in which he ridiculed his fellow "non-Brahmans" who had established the prestigious Madurai Tamil Sangam only to have that association hijacked by Brahmans and their Sanskritized Tamil (E. V. Ramasami 1985: 82–83). Soon after, in 1933, a group of Tamil enthusiasts, several among them Brahmans, organized the Tamiḻaṉpar Makānāṭu (Tamil Devotees Conference) in Madras to discuss publication of Tamil books in the sciences, the creation of new words to express modern thought, the dissemination of ancient Tamil literature among the populace, the reform of the Tamil script, and the removal of books which promoted caste consciousness from school curricula. But the conference was bitterly attacked in both the Dravidian movement press and in journals like *Centamiḻc Celvi,* whose spirit was neo-Shaivite and contestatory classicist. It was seen as a means through which, among other things, Brahmans tried to pass themselves off as "devotees of Tamil," to corner the publishing market, and to introduce more Sanskrit words into Tamil in the name of "improvement." Is it not revealing, critics asked, that these Brahman enthusiasts called the conference by the Sanskritic word *makānāṭu* instead of the pure Tamil *mānāṭu?* These "lovers of Tamil" (*tamiḻ aṉpar*) were actually "deceitful lovers," it was declared. In a decade marked by the rise of the Self-Respect movement and by efforts of pure Tamil advocates to create *taṉittamiḻ* scientific vocabularies, it is not surprising that the proceedings of the conference were disrupted. In 1934, members of the rival *taṉittamiḻ* faction convened their own conference, the Ceṉṉai Mākāṇat Tamiḻar Mānāṭu (Madras Presidency Tamilians Conference), which released proposals challenging those of the Tamil Devotees Conference (E. M. Subramania Pillai 1951–52: 141–43; Velu and Selvaraji 1989: 17–78).[16]

All this antagonism towards Brahmans came to a head in the late 1930s during the anti-Hindi protests, not least because the author of the government's compulsory Hindi policy was a Brahman: the much-maligned Rajagopalachari, the premier of the Presidency from July 1937 to October 1939. A native of Salem district and a lawyer by profession, Rajagopalachari, like many other Brahman adherents of Tamil, started his devotional career as an Indianist. More than any of his fellow devotees, he was involved in local Congress politics from very early on, serving as a member, then as chairman, of the Salem Municipal Council from 1911 to 1919. His interest in Tamil-related activities dated to the 1910s, when he demanded the adoption of Tamil as medium of instruction in schools (Rajagopalachari 1956) and, along with some friends, in 1916 instituted the Tamil Scientific Terms Society. The early few issues of its short-lived journal published various scientific terms relating to botany, chemistry, physics, astronomy, and mathematics (Irschick 1969: 303–5; Kailasapathy 1986: 32). Rajagopalachari's interest in creating scientific vocabularies in Tamil continued in subsequent years as well when he published books such as *Tamiḻil Muṭiyumā?* (Can it be done in Tamil?; 1937) and *Tiṇṇai Racāyaṉam* (Chemistry on the front porch; 1946). For example, the former, a translation of an English-language physics textbook, set out to demonstrate that physics (*pautika cāttiram*) could be studied in Tamil. In its preface, Rajagopalachari apologized for the preliminary quality of his efforts and called upon Tamil scholars, with more courage, time, and love for Tamil than he had been able to summon up, to continue this work (Rajagopalachari 1937). The book had a mixed reception in the Tamil devotional community, not least because of its reliance on Sanskrit roots to coin new Tamil words. This reliance was not surprising, for from the start, Rajagopalachari was a great admirer of Sanskrit and its literature, an admiration which he did not see as being at cross-purposes with his attachment to Tamil (Rajagopalachari 1962: 66–67).

His obvious involvement in Tamil "improvement" activities notwithstanding, during the anti-Hindi protests Rajagopalachari was repeatedly identified as an "enemy" of Tamiḻttāy and her "destroyer."[17] Dravidian movement newspapers circulated inflammatory cartoons showing him hurling a dagger at Tamiḻttāy and disrobing her (figs. 5 and 6). The antagonism against him mounted not least because Rajagopalachari persisted in publicly disparaging the struggle against Hindi in the most elitist (and Brahmanical) terms possible, even casually dismissing the death of a young protester in 1938 when asked about it in the Legislative Assembly. "While Tamilians shed tears of blood that their hero had died, the Aryan members [of the assembly] laughed and clapped their hands," one critic declared indignantly (Ilanceliyan 1986: 173). In the 1940s, Rajagopalachari extended his support to the Tamil music movement and, by the 1960s, lent his considerable influence to the anti-Hindi protests of that decade, but all this helped little in overcoming his predominant image as the Brahman who had tried to "snuff out the life of our ancient Tamiḻttāy."[18]

Of course, not all Brahmans fared this way, and there are at least three devotees whose Brahmanness is pondered over, debated, and then set aside in favor of their incorporation into the devotional community. Thus Swaminatha Aiyar, the much-revered *tamiḻ tātā,* "grandfather Tamil," did attract some ire for his defense of Sanskritic Tamil. Nevertheless, he is praised widely for his painstaking efforts to recover and publish the ancient manuscripts of the Caṅkam corpus, although a suggestion was aired in the 1950s in *Kuyil,* a journal edited by Bharatidasan, that he may have tampered with these.[19] Similarly, V. G. Suryanarayana Sastri, a novelist and essayist who in 1902 was the first devotee to vehemently demand recognition of Tamil's "classical" status, is much praised. Brahman he may nominally have been, but in his *Tamiḻmoḻiyiṉ Varalāṟu* (1903), Suryanarayana Sastri offered a spirited defense of the autonomy, originality, and uniqueness of Tamil, refusing to subordinate the language to Sanskrit in any realm. Suryanarayanan was born into an orthodox Smarta Brahman family of Vilacceri near Madurai in 1870. His father was a scholar of Sanskrit, and Suryanarayanan formally studied the language from his early youth. It was not until he went to high school, however, that his love for Tamil was really kindled, and by the time he was twenty, he was learned enough to start writing literary pieces. In 1890, he moved to Madras for his college education, and he graduated with top honors. Although he could have had any job for the asking, as a true devotee of Tamil he chose to become a Tamil pandit, low salary and all, at Madras Christian College. Over the next decade, he became renowned not just for his mastery of literary Tamil but also for his attempts to introduce innovative ideas, from English literature, into Tamil prose, plays, and poetry. Yet he never let his admiration for English compromise his love for Tamil: indeed, his fellow devout recall with delight that as a student, when challenged by one of his English professors, he had declared that Kamban's verse from centuries before was superior to Tennyson's. Not surprisingly, for all his work he won the admiration of the famed scholar and fellow devotee Damodaram Pillai, who bestowed upon him the title *tirāviṭa cāstiri,* "Dravidian Brahman scholar," a title which even in those days already appeared oxymoronic (N. Subramanian 1950). And he became a close associate of another Tamil litterateur and fellow devotee, M. S. Purnalingam Pillai, whose journal, *Ñāṉapōtiṉi,* he helped co-edit and who declared, when Suryanarayanan died young at thirty-three in 1903, that he had become a "martyr to Tamil" (Purnalingam Pillai 1985: 347).

Suryanarayanan's reputation as Tamil adherent also rests on a singular act that has elicited much admiration from successive generations of the devout. In 1899, in an anthology in which he attempted to introduce the sonnet into Tamil poetry for the first time, he adopted the pen name "Paritimāl Kalaiñar," the pure Tamil rendering of his own given (Sanskritic) name. In his preface to the text, he was clear about why he did this; he was worried about his innovation and was keen on getting his fellow scholars' frank criticisms of his attempt. The work went on to elicit much enthusiasm, and its second edition was published with its author's Sanskritic name (N. Subramanian 1950: 81–84). Although he was hailed as a founder of the *taṉittamiḻ* movement by some later devotees, his critics fault him for using his pure Tamil name only once; they also point out that his plays and novels featured characters bearing Sanskritic names, and his own Tamil was inflected with Sanskrit (Tirumaran 1992: 118–23).[20]

And then, finally, there is the most famous of them all, Subramania

Bharati. One can do little justice to Bharati in the space of a few pages, but my concern here is with considering whether his Brahmanness factors into the ambivalence with which he has been treated for a good part of this century, his hallowed status today notwithstanding. So, speaking in 1960, Ramasami demanded that if Bharati was such a great devotee of Tamil as they all say he is, how is it that in his poetry, Tamilttāy herself declares that she is a companion of Sanskrit. How is it that he does not proclaim her autonomy from Sanskrit (E. V. Ramasami 1960: 9–10)? A few years earlier, a short piece in the Dravidianist journal *Tīcuṭar* declared,

> They say Bharati is an immortal poet. . . . [E]ven if a rat dies in an *akrakāram* [Brahman settlement], they would declare it to be immortal. . . . All of Tamilnadu praises him. Why should this be so? Supposedly because he sang fulsome praises of Tamil and Tamilnadu. What else could he sing? His own mother tongue, Sanskrit, has been dead for years. What other language did he know? He cannot sing in Sanskrit. . . . [He says Tamilnadu] is the land of Aryas.[21]

Similarly, another fellow devotee, the Dravidianist poet Pulavar Kulanthai, wrote in the 1950s that "in the name of 'nationalism,' Bharati inserted Sanskrit into Tamil, caused Tamilians to lose pride in their own community, and enslaved them to Northerners" (Pulavar Kulanthai 1958: 22).

Thus the charges against Bharati are similar to those brought against other Brahman devotees; even in claiming devotion to Tamil, he repeatedly sacrificed Tamilttāy at the altar of Sanskrit and Aryanism. Bharati's vision of Tamil is vulnerable to such attacks, for it falls well within the parameters—indeed, it provides the defining moments—of the Indianist imagination. Yet, as Bharati's many admirers also do not fail to point out, the poet was clearly ambivalent about his Brahman status; he cut off his hair-tuft and sacred thread characteristic of many orthodox Brahmans of his times, and sported a mustache; he wrote essays and poems over the years in which he was clearly critical of Brahmanical privilege (Bharati 1987: 51–52, 1988: 264–67); and intimate accounts by friends and family suggest that he hardly led a conventional Brahmanical lifestyle, thereby inviting the wrath of many in his putative community. Indeed, by the 1940s when he had been confirmed as modern Tamilnadu's greatest poet, albeit not without considerable controversy (Sivathamby and Marx 1984), many an ardent Dravidianist, like Annadurai, glossed over the issue of his Brahmanness, preferring to focus on his roles as the "people's poet" and as revolutionary social reformer (Annadurai 1948). And even an acerbic anti-Brahman critic like Bharatidasan, who was to become the poetic muse of the Dravidian movement, did not hesitate to call himself the "slave" (*tāsaṉ*) of Bharati, the latter's Brahmanness notwithstanding.

All the attention he has received after his death might have come as quite a surprise to Bharati, for during his own lifetime, although he had an ardent coterie of friends and admirers, his genius went largely unrecognized. In fact, towards the very end of his life, when he tried to raise money from the public to have his manuscripts published, he received hardly a response. He died in 1921, broken and dejected, and a man very much in debt (Padmanabhan 1982b: 153–59). Bharati's life—as indeed the life of many a Tamil devotee—clearly underscores one of the principal claims of Tamil devotion: namely, that even in the putative "kingdom" of Tamiḻttāy, it was impossible to make ends meet as a Tamil poet or writer or journalist. It was because of this fear that his father, as Bharati tells us in autobiographical verses published in 1897 and in 1910, had compelled his son to learn that "foreign" language English, when Bharati himself would have preferred to have studied the "sweet" Tamil which Shiva favored with his grace. But, he adds, there were few who cared for such a glorious language (Bharati 1987: 1–3, 173–90). Following his father's injunction, the young Subramanian did study English; but in his spare moments in his native Ettaiyapuram, he stole off with his childhood friend and fellow devotee, Somasundara Bharati, to a nearby temple to surreptitiously read Tamil literature away from the eyes of watchful adults.

Subramanian's poetic abilities received early acclaim when he was just eleven, and he secured the title "Bharati" (the learned) from the landlord of Ettaiyapuram (Padmanabhan 1982b: 4–12). His poems did not begin to be published regularly until 1905. By then, he had graduated from high school and gotten married (1897), spent a few years in Benaras studying Sanskrit and Hindi (1898–1902), and taught Tamil in the high school attached to the Madurai Tamil Sangam for a few months (1904). A friend who knew him in his Benaras days later recalled that he had had no idea then that Bharati was interested in Tamil literature, for he could be seen wandering around the city with a copy of Shelley's poetry.[22] In fact, soon after he returned to Ettaiyapuram in 1902, he formed a local Shelley literary guild and even wrote a few essays under the pen name Shelleydasan, "follower of Shelley" (Padmanabhan 1982b: 16).

In late 1904, he moved to Madras to work for the nationalist daily *Cutēcamittiraṉ,* where his job involved translating into Tamil news received in English. The pay was poor and the work difficult, but it provided the foundation for Bharati's lifelong passion for transforming Tamil into an easy language of modern communication and politics. Under him, the *Cutēcamittiraṉ* began to rid itself of its reliance on English (but not Sanskritic) words, for which it had become notorious in Tamil devotional circles. Around this time, Bharati also got involved in nationalist politics; attended the annual meetings of the Congress; and published fiery essays and poems in *Cakravarttiṉi,* the women's magazine that he edited in 1905–06, and in *Intiyā,* the newspaper of which he was editor from 1906. From the start, Bharati's nationalism was heavily inflected with religious fervor, and of course, some of his most famous, and much-recited, poems were on Bhārata Mātā. In 1908, fearing that he, too, would be caught in a general crackdown on "seditious" writers initiated by the Madras government, he fled to Pondicherry, then a French colony, and was in exile there until 1918. These were also his most productive years as poet, essayist, and journalist, and much of what we now have of his oeuvre today, including some of his most passionate statements on Tamil, belongs to this period. In 1918, he returned to British India and was thrown into prison for a brief while. At the time of his early death in 1921, he was in Madras where he had been working, once again, on the editorial board of *Cutēcamittiraṉ.*

Much of his later life was marked by poverty, even destitution; poor health; the burdens of taking care of his family; and the attempts to find patrons who would publish his work. Yet the stories that circulate about Bharati today emphasize that he did not let any of these stand in the way of expressing and pursuing his primary passions—devotion to India and to Tamil. Sprinkled through his personal letters to friends and relatives, which recount his many financial and health problems, are his injunctions to them to not abandon Tamil. So, in a 1918 letter to his brother that shows him clearly troubled about his many financial problems, he takes the time to insist, "Do not write me letters in English any more. However colloquial your Tamil may be, I am eager to read it. If you cannot even write in colloquial Tamil (*koccaittamiḻ*), write to me in Sanskrit" (quoted in Padmanabhan 1982b: 134). And in another much-cited letter to his close friend Nellaiyappar, which ends with his numerous personal problems, he writes, "Tamil! Tamil! Tamil!—think ceaselessly that it is your duty to make it prosper!" He goes on, "Oh! what can I do. I suffer when I see languages other than Tamil prosper. I will not accept that men who are not Tamilian are forging ahead, in knowledge and strength. My heart grieves when I see women who are not Tamilian look so much more beautiful" (quoted in Padmanabhan 1982b: 130). Is it any surprise that latter-day devotees rejoice over sentiments like this, and embrace Bharati as one of their own, his Brahmanness notwithstanding?

THE POET DEVOTEE

Poetry, I have suggested, is the paradigmatic mode of practicing intimate Tamil devotion. The poet, correspondingly, is a particularly heroic figure within the regimes of *tamiḻppaṟṟu,* however marginalized he may be within the economies of modernity. While in the early years of Tamil devotion Bharati was the poet devotee par excellence, his putative Brahmanness set aside in favor of the passionate poetry he produced, in the later years it is his self-proclaimed disciple, Bharatidasan, who is the model poet devotee. Reverenced by his fellow devotees as *pāvēntaṉ,* "king of verse," and as *puraṭcikkaviñar,* "revolutionary poet," Bharatidasan has been the guiding muse for a whole generation of poets in the later half of this century whose verses promote agonistic and fierce *tamiḻppaṟṟu,* and whose ideal devotee is the warrior willing to give up his body for Tamil (Rajendran 1985: 159–283). For did he not ask, "When harm befalls the glorious Tamil, what use is this body to us?" (Bharatidasan 1948: 9)?

In his autobiographical poem entitled "I Am King of Poetry," published late in his life in 1960, Bharatidasan takes pride in the breadth and depth of his scholarship in Tamil, in his role as a teacher of Tamil, in his various poetic creations, and in his unwavering service to his mother tongue (*tāymoḻit toṇṭu*) (Krishnamurthy 1991: viii–xii). This is not, however, the self-portrait of a militant warrior. That his militancy was largely confined to his subversive writings is also apparent from the numerous biographies of the poet, some critical but most hagiographic, that are available today. Named Subburathinam at the time of his birth in 1891, Bharatidasan was a native of Pondicherry. His father was an affluent merchant who fell upon hard times; but we are told that he nevertheless encouraged his son to pursue his love for Tamil, unprofitable though it might be. In 1909, instead of following in his father's footsteps as a businessman, Subburathinam decided to become a Tamil teacher, taking up his first job in a small village school near Karaikal. From then on up until 1946, he worked in various schools in the French colony. His son proudly mentions that his father frequently talked to him about the difficulties and the indignities of being a low-paid Tamil teacher. At the risk of jeopardizing his job, on several occasions Subburathinam protested to local French authorities over the low salaries paid to Tamil teachers and over their right to organize; over the quality of Tamil textbooks used in schools, which promoted casteism and hierarchy among young children; and so on (Mannar Mannan 1985: 31–69).

There were two important turning points in the poet's life. Around 1909, he met Subramania Bharati, who had recently arrived in Pondicherry. Over the next two decades or so, Bharatidasan's poems were dominated by the two themes that saturate Bharati's own poetry—Hinduism and Indian nationalism (Ilango 1982; Ilavarasu 1990). He wrote many passionate songs on Hindu deities and on Bhārata Mātā, wore *khadi* (homespun), and kept company with the various nationalists who were part of Bharati's coterie. This is also when he published what was perhaps his earliest prose essay on Tamil, which appeared in the nationalist daily *Cutēcamittiraṉ* in May 1914 and expounded, in a style highly reminiscent of Bharati's Indianism, on the need for a Tamil thesaurus.[23] Soon after Bharati's death in 1921, Subburathinam assumed the pseudonym Bharatidasan, "the follower of Bharati," a name that demonstrated his devotion to his mentor even as it allowed him to publish anticolonial tracts while holding a government job. Although he was chastised over the years for having adopted a name that both was Sanskritic and tied his poetic persona to that of the complex figure of Bharati, Bharatidasan steadfastly maintained that his mentor had been foremost in opposing caste oppression and hierarchy and that he was the first to write in a style of Tamil easily comprehensible to even the commoner.[24] Throughout his life, he remained publicly loyal to Bharati's memory, refusing to be daunted by those who ridiculed him for having declared himself a slave (*tācaṉ*) to a Brahman (Ilango 1982).

The second important transformation in his life came in the late 1920s when he was converted to Dravidianism, through exposure to Ramasami's fiery anti-God and anticaste writings and to his polemical weekly, *Kuṭi Aracu*. Their passionate espousal of the "self-respect" of Tamilians and fierce opposition to Brahmanism resonated with Bharatidasan's own nascent ideas on such matters (Krishnamurthy 1991: 91–92). Although he continued to publish nationalist poems in the Bharati tradition into the mid-1930s, he progressively became the poetic voice of the Dravidian movement, translating into verse many of Ramasami's rationalist, atheist, anti-Brahman, and anti-India ideas. It was during the first wave of anti-Hindi protests of the late 1930s that his writings began to reach a wider audience in the Presidency; over the next few decades, his poems were recited by protesters in anti-Hindi street marches, and his iconoclastic plays were performed at public meetings and conferences of Dravidianist parties. In contrast to many of his more militant followers, Bharatidasan himself rarely participated in such activities. He showed his devotion to Tamil primarily by writing fiery poems, plays, and movie scripts; helping local poets organize; and editing and publishing in polemical journals, such as *Putuvai Muracu* and *Kuyil,* and poetry magazines, such as *Cuppiramaṇiya Pārati Kavitā Māṇṭalam.* Fellow devotees often write with admiration that he conducted his numerous literary activities despite financial straits and political hostility. Nevertheless, when he died in 1964, his reputation as the most important Tamil poet of the post-Bharati generation was well secured, not least because of the deployment of his poetry and his plays in the political activities of the Dravidian movement in the 1940s and 1950s (Krishnamurthy 1991: 89–220).

The experiences of the poet Mudiyarasan resonate with those of Bharatidasan, his mentor and fellow Dravidianist. In his as yet unpublished reminiscences, Mudiyarasan writes that when he was a young man attending college, he heard a talk by Bharatidasan and was convinced that he too, like the famous poet, should write poems on the Tamil land, language, and community (Mudiyarasan n.d.: 151). And indeed, although not as prolific a poet or playwright as his famous mentor, beginning in the late 1940s, Mudiyarasan produced his share of verses on the beauties and glories of Tamil, which earned him the title of *kaviyaracu,* "king of poets," in 1966. Many of his poems, like Bharatidasan's, promote the image of the ideal devotee as militant warrior; his most brilliant effort, the epic *Pūṅkoṭi,* even enlists the Tamil woman in such a role. Yet, like Bharatidasan, he too rarely took an active, public part in language protests; constrained by his job as a government employee, he could spread Tamil consciousness among young Tamilians only through subversive teaching and writing.

Born in 1920 into a poor family in a small village called Periyakulam in Madurai district, he tells us that his love for Tamil was fostered by his mother, who sang sweet lullabies to him, and by a maternal uncle who, although a shopkeeper by profession, had great interest in Tamil literature. He also recalls with affection that his interest in Tamil was paradoxically further stimulated by his first Tamil teacher in primary school, who was a Brahman (Mudiyarasan n.d.: 4–5). It is clear from his reminiscences that he was struck by the urgency of the Tamil cause, growing up in an environment in which he witnessed Tamil and its speakers being demeaned everywhere, often by fellow Tamilians who were Brahman. As a student in a local college in Mayilam, he was troubled when he heard his teacher offering his prayers in Sanskrit, and he was clearly offended when he saw that Brahman students were given privileged treatment (Mudiyarasan n.d.: 21). So in 1947, when he took up his first job as Tamil teacher in Muthialpet High School in Madras, he began his classes with the invocation, "Long live Tamil." His students wrote "Long live Tamil" on the blackboard in their Sanskrit classroom, an act that, he notes, offended his Brahman colleagues (Mudiyarasan n.d.: 26–27). During the centenary celebrations of the high school, he was incensed when the invocation prayer was sung in Sanskrit; his anger only abated when his students spontaneously filled the hall with cries of "Long live Tamil" (Mudiyarasan n.d.: 31). In 1949, he moved to Karaikkudi to teach Tamil in another high school, a job that he held until his retirement in 1978; there he continued to keep vigil over Tamil. If any of his (Brahman) colleagues made fun of Tamil or Tamilians, he writes, he would pounce upon them fiercely, like a tiger (Mudiyarasan n.d.: 48).

It is apparent from his reminiscences that Mudiyarasan cherished his role as a Tamil teacher and as a molder of young minds. Although as a government employee he could not openly and publicly speak out against the state's language policies without risking his job, he practiced his devotion to Tamil subversively by encouraging his students to take pride in their language and their heritage. He was not deterred by the hostility with which such efforts were greeted by some of his senior colleagues and headmasters, who were often Brahmans. In 1966, soon after his passionate poem *Pūṅkoṭi* was proscribed, the then-Congress government tried to force him out of his job, and it was only the coming of the DMK to power in 1967 that prevented this from happening (Mudiyarasan n.d.: 57). Mudiyarasan's frustration at not being able to participate more publicly and militantly in Tamil devotional activities is apparent throughout his reminiscences. The fear of losing his job and concern over how he could take care of his large family under those circumstances clearly restrained his desire to openly espouse his Tamil devotion. Nevertheless, he proudly recalls that in 1949, his wife joined the anti-Hindi picketing launched by the women's wing of the DK. During the anti-Hindi demonstrations of the previous year, he himself, along with some of his colleagues, had picketed the high school in which they taught, just for one day. "We are Tamil teachers. Tamil is being harmed. We intend nothing more than showing our grief," Mudiyarasan told the authorities who questioned them (Mudiyarasan n.d.: 42–45).[25] In the mid-1960s, when the protests against Hindi increased in intensity and scale, he recalls being accused of antinationalist and antigovernment activities in the classroom, and he was subjected to interrogation by state officials. He laments that Tamilians are their own enemies, and he writes that only when Tamil speakers appreciate the worth of their language would Tamilnadu improve (Mudiyarasan n.d.: 76–78).

THE SCHOLAR DEVOTEE

Within the devotional community, all forms of devotion to Tamil are more or less equally valid, but a special kind of veneration and affection adheres to those who are deemed to be learned scholars (*aṟiñar*). This is quite paradoxical, for Tamil's devotees have been only too painfully aware that the world at large does not treat the Tamil scholar with any particular respect. Until recently, Tamil teachers were routinely paid less than their colleagues, were often the butt of popular jokes, and not surprisingly had a poor self-image. Yet, one model for devotion that clearly exists in the community is that of the scholar devotee who shows his passion for Tamil by pouring his life and energy into deciphering ancient manuscripts, writing books that may sell few copies but nevertheless are a labor of love, and teaching students who are largely unenthusiastic about the language. That all this he does under material conditions that range from middling to appalling is what makes the devotion of the scholar devotee particularly heroic.

Few narratives offer a more strikingly poignant portrayal of one devotee's struggle to pursue scholarship in Tamil under circumstances that were both materially daunting and socially discouraging than Swaminatha Aiyar's *Eṉ Carittiram* (My story). As a young man, Swaminathan recalls a visitor asking his father: " 'What does your son do?' My father replied, 'He reads Tamil.' Stunned, as if he had heard something incredible, he burst out, 'What? Tamil?' He did not stop there. 'He reads Tamil? Why could he not study English? And how about Sanskrit? If he studies English, he would benefit in this world. The study of Sanskrit will prepare him for the other world. Studying Tamil will bring him neither benefit' " (Swaminatha Aiyar 1982: 262). The visitor was not alone in thinking thus. Several of Swaminathan's Brahman kinsmen urged him to study either Sanskrit or the more profitable English. But for him, as he wrote later, the motto of his life had been prefigured by the anonymous author of the seventeenth-century poem *Tamiḻ Viṭutūtu:* "O preeminent Tamil! I exist because of you! / Even the ambrosia of the celestials, I do not desire!" (Swaminatha Aiyar 1991b: 127).

A native of Uthamadanapuram in Tanjavur district, Swaminathan was born in 1855 and raised as a devout Smarta Brahman. His father made his (meager) livelihood through giving music performances and religious discourses in the Tanjavur hinterlands. Although supportive in most ways, his father wished that Swaminathan would follow in his footsteps and would study music and the Telugu language that was most appropriate for a career as musician. But Swaminathan tells us, "Contrary to everyone's desires, from the time I was a young man, my mind was immersed in the beauties of the goddess Tamil (*tamiḻt teyvam*). More and more, it yearned for Tamiḻttāy's auspicious grace (*tiruvaruḷ*). Sanskrit, Telugu, English—none of these held my interest. Sometimes, I even felt a deep aversion towards them. . . . Tamil had captured my heart" (Swaminatha Aiyar 1982: 156). And Tamil had indeed captured his heart, for there appears to have been space for little else in his life, at least as it is narrativized in his reminiscences. He seems to have been attached to his parents, later even turning down an opportunity to teach in the prestigious Presidency College in Madras city so that they could spend their last days in their beloved Kaveri Valley. The birth of his first son is noted, with some joy. But in the seven-hundred-odd pages of his autobiography, his wife, Madurambikai, does not feature at all, apart from a brief mention on the occasion of their marriage in 1868. Even that important rite of passage left him unmoved. "It does not appear as if anything new has happened to me, now that I have become a householder." For a few days, before and after the occasion, he was filled with great joy, revelling in all the attention—and gifts (!)—he received. Then he soon realized that "there was little gain from all this. I have only one purpose. Tamil is my wealth. It is the food for the hunger of my mind. . . . It was true then. It is true now." So he concludes his brief discussion of his marriage (Swaminatha Aiyar 1982: 123–30).

The absence of details about his personal life is in striking contrast to the wealth of information he provides on the world of Tamil scholarship around the turn of this century. As he tells us on several occasions, he had no worldly interests other than the desire to study Tamil and to spend his time in the company of other Tamil scholars. He got ample opportunity to do so when he apprenticed himself around 1871 to Meenakshisundaram Pillai (1815–1876), perhaps the best-known Tamil savant of his time, on whom he later published a detailed biography. His relationship with his teacher, as he presents it in his reminiscences, echoes his relationship to the language; it was marked by intense reverence, devotion, even love. He recalls how he walked once, in the hot noonday sun, to another village, about two miles away, in order to procure a manuscript that he thought his master would like to see (Swaminatha Aiyar 1982: 193–94). He lapped up eagerly even the smallest word of praise that his master would throw his way, was jealous of fellow students who he feared may make their way into his master's heart, and constantly worried about falling out of favor.

By his own reckoning, Swaminathan's life took a dramatic turn on 21 October 1880, the day he met Ramasami Mudaliar, the *munsif* (civil judge) of Kumbakonam. By then, much had happened in his life. His master had died; he himself had moved to Kumbakonam, where he had secured a job teaching Tamil in the government college; he had an infant son; and he had already begun to acquire quite a name for himself in Tamil scholarly circles. Flushed with pride over his accomplishments, he set out to meet Ramasami Mudaliar, who he had heard was a Tamil enthusiast. Quizzed on the depth of his knowledge, Swaminathan tells us that he proudly rattled off the names of the numerous texts that he had learned by heart. Ramasami Mudaliar, however, was unimpressed. "What is the use of knowing all this. . . . These are all later works. Do you know any of the ancient ones?" he asked. A week later, he handed Swaminathan a manuscript of the ancient epic poem *Cīvaka Cintāmaṇi,* which he had never before seen. Humbled by the realization of how much more there was to know, he began the quest for other such old texts that changed the course of his life (Swaminatha Aiyar 1982: 528–34).

As he recalls, this of course was no easy matter. Frequently relying on word-of-mouth information about manuscript collections in remote villages, he would walk for miles down country roads, sometimes riding bullock carts which broke down, at other times taking trains (one of the few signs in his autobiography, we note, of industrial modernity). On these trips—the equivalent of other people's holy pilgrimages—he would sometimes encounter wonderful people who filled him with awe and joy because of their obvious reverence for Tamil, and because of the care with which they had maintained old Tamil manuscripts; their abodes, he writes, were "temples of the goddess Tamil (*tamil̲t teyvam*)" (Swaminatha Aiyar 1982: 636–38, 690–94). More often, he came across signs of utter callousness, and with horror he recounts stories of old manuscripts being cast into fire as fuel, or thrown into the river. Our ancients tell us that Tamil survived fire and water in the past, but not any more, he writes. In many places, he ignored discomfort as well as personal disrespect. Had he been defeated by these hardships, he could never have restored Tamil̲ttāy's jewels back to her, he writes (Swaminatha Aiyar 1982: 640–86). Until the very end of his life, he appears not to have lost his love for these manuscripts. "My body may be tiring with age, but my mind has still not lost its devotion to these palm leaves," he observes (Swaminatha Aiyar 1991b: 120).

With the acquisition of the desired manuscripts, the battle had only barely begun. He had to labor hard to read them, struggling over the meanings of archaic words that had long been in disuse, and to understand ancient worldviews quite alien to his Shaiva and Brahmanical upbringing. There were also the challenges of printing, at a time when that technology was still fairly new (Venkatachalapathy 1994a: 274–78). Unlike many later scholars, who would leave the details to the publisher and the press, Swaminathan supervised the entire printing process from start to end, from the selection of the font to the binding of the finished product. Above all, there were financial problems. Publication of these works demanded enormous outlays of money, far in excess of his modest income as a college teacher, and he had to turn to a network of patrons—some reliable, others not so. On more than one occasion, he had to borrow money to keep the printing process going. He also spent many of his waking moments worrying over potential competitors (including fellow devotee Damodaram Pillai), who might beat him to the punch, and dealing with nasty rumors that were floated about his inabilities and inadequacies. About his troubles and worries, he writes: "In the land of *ten̲r̲al* [southern breeze] and sandal, our Tamil reigns, sweet and soft. I have dedicated myself to the auspicious service (*tiruppaṇi*) of that glorious goddess Tamil. Thanks to the wondrous grace of that goddess, the waves of trouble of this world do not deluge me in misery" (Swaminatha Aiyar 1982: 657). Not surprisingly, when the first copies of his published *Cintāmaṇi* arrived from the binders, he stacked them reverentially and offered them worship. For, he writes, the text—whether published or unpublished—"appears to me as the image of a deity. My desire is only to wipe away the dust and clothe it anew so I can see it. . . . I believe that each part of it is divinity itself" (Swaminatha Aiyar 1982: 611).

Swaminathan lived his life in the high noon of empire. Yet there are few signs of colonialism, westernization, or modernity in his reminiscences. With touching candor, he confesses to the thrill of excitement he felt as a child when he learned the English alphabet. There must be something magical about it, he notes, for even mere association with it confers so much prestige (Swaminatha Aiyar 1982: 61–62). Frequently, during the course of his travels and research, he would encounter fellow devotees—Vedanayakam Pillai, Damodaram Pillai, and others—who knew English and were obviously men of influence and power. And yet it astounded him that they continued to be enthusiastic about Tamil. Swaminathan was not alone in registering such wonder, and a special affection is accorded in the devotional community to all those who had not let their knowledge of English, or their worldly affluence, get in the way of their love for Tamil. Indeed, in the early years of *tamiḻpparru,* there were quite a few "gentlemen scholars" such as J. Nallaswami Pillai and P. V. Manickam Nayakar, who, like Swaminathan, expressed their devotion to Tamil through their scholarship. But they moved in a world that appeared far removed from Swaminathan's. They had university degrees, were well-placed in the hierarchies of government, were fluent in English, and were materially well-off.

One such savant devotee whose story is told with a great deal of pride in the devotional community is Somasundara Bharati, reverentially referred to as *nāvalar,* "the eloquent." A native of Ettaiyapuram, where his father was part of the local landlord's coterie, Somasundaram was a childhood friend of Subramania Bharati with whom he would read Tamil on the sly. Unlike a majority of Tamil's devotees, Somasundaram led a life of comparative ease and affluence as a lawyer, first in Tuticorin and then in Madurai. All the same, we are told that he did not let his law practice, profitable though it was, interfere with his devotion to Tamil. Even while working as a lawyer, he earned a master's degree in Tamil in 1913, and over the next few decades he published numerous essays on the language and its literature, mostly in a compensatory classicist vein (Sambasivan 1967). In 1933, when he was asked to head the Tamil department of the newly founded Annamalai University in Chidambaram, he was faced with a difficult choice, his biographers tell us. On the one hand, he had his lucrative career as a lawyer; on the other, there was service to Tamil, hardly profitable but fulfilling in so many other ways. Somasundaram did not find it difficult to make up his mind: he gave up his law practice and headed the Tamil department for five years (Sambasivanar and Ilankumaran 1960: 57–67). This is not the only instance in which his *tamilpparru* led Somasundaram to change the course of his life. In 1937–38, when the government announced its compulsory Hindi policy, Somasundaram was one of the leading figures who spoke out against the Congress at numerous rallies; on one occasion, he even suffered a physical assault. His opposition to Hindi was all the more unusual because he had been a dedicated member of the Congress for much of his life up until then: he had organized numerous political rallies on that party's behalf and had been quite involved in nationalist politics. And yet, as he declared in his *Open Letter to the Hon. C. Rajagopalachariar,* when Tamilttāy was in danger, how could he afford to maintain his old political convictions (Somasundara Bharati 1937)?

A very different model of scholarly devotion is offered by the life of G. Devaneyan, referred to in devotional circles as *pāvāṇar,* "the poet." The author of numerous books, essays, and poems, most of which are in the contestatory classicist idiom, Devaneyan is best known for his etymological researches on Tamil, and for his attempts to prove that Tamilnadu (or Kumari Nadu, as he called it) had been the site of the birth of humanity and that Tamil speakers were the first humans (Devaneyan 1972). Most of the trials and tribulations that Devaneyan faced in practicing his *tamilpparru* followed from having to combat not just the difficulties of abject poverty, but the social stigma of hailing from a very low-caste family recently converted to Christianity. Born in 1902 in the small village of Shankaranayinarkoyil in Tirunelveli district, Devaneyan tells us that when he was a high school student, he had memorized all of Shakespeare's plays and desired to become an English professor at Oxford. And then in 1918–20, he read history and Tamil, and became devoted to the latter.[26] Poverty prevented him from pursuing his higher education, and he began to work as a Tamil schoolteacher in Ambur, North Arcot. But this did not deter him from later passing the Tamil examinations administered by the Madurai Tamil Sangam in 1924 and by the Shaiva Siddhanta Kazhagam in 1926, which gave him the title of *pulavar,* "scholar." Recognizing the value placed on formal university degrees, however, he also went on to earn a master's degree in Tamil from Madras University in 1944. Meanwhile, he held a variety of teaching jobs, mostly poorly paid in small-town schools; starting in

1944, he found a period of stable security for about twelve years, teaching Tamil in Salem.

The one theme that runs through the various biographies on him, written by fellow devotees, is the stark state of poverty in which he lived; often he did not have enough money even to feed his growing family, let alone to do research and publish his works (Tamilkudimagan 1985; Tamilmallan 1989). In his letters to fellow scholars, he frequently laments over his material conditions and writes piteously about visits to bookstores where, even after striking a hard bargain that brought the price of a book down, he still could not afford to purchase it and would have to go home empty-handed (Ilankumaran 1985: 6). Although he found an outlet for publishing his books in the Shaiva Siddhanta Kazhagam, he also published quite a few of his researches at his own expense. For, as his biographers tell us, he could never let economic considerations stand in the way of his *tamiḻpparṟu* (Tamilmallan 1989: 45–52). In a letter to a friend in 1964, Devaneyan tells him that he would go anywhere if invited to speak publicly on the linguistic problems facing Tamilians, even if he were not paid for his lecture. He was even willing to forgo being reimbursed for travel expenses, when it was Tamil's future that was at stake, for as he writes in another letter, "the life-breath of the Tamilian is Tamil" (Ilankumaran 1985: 9, 79). Such an attitude was forged fairly early in his life. For instance, in a 1937 letter to a fellow devotee, he writes, "As long as we live, we ought to not let Tamil decline" (Ilankumaran 1985: 11). On many occasions, he tells us that his duty to Tamil was to rescue it from the clutches of Sanskrit and to make the world accept what he believed to be the first principle that guided his own life: namely, that Tamil was the first language of the world and the parent of them all. It is for this purpose that he believed he had been created by God (Ilankumaran 1985: 20, 57, 80, 110).

Such statements of devotion are also interspersed with comments of despair and frustration. In 1964, he laments that if he had devoted himself as passionately to English as to Tamil, he would have been a respected professor at Oxford. "The extent to which I have grieved and suffered because of Tamil is no laughing matter" (Ilankumaran 1985: 121). On another occasion, he asked, "What does it matter if Shankaralinga Nadar fasted [to death]? What does it matter if Chinnasami immolated himself? The Tamilian will not heed or improve" (Ilankumaran 1985: 14). The despair expressed by Devaneyan echoed that of so many devotees who came to hold that a life dedicated to the Tamil cause had brought little material comfort, and even fewer social benefits. His wife's death in 1963 after a lingering illness left him both grieving and guilt-stricken, for he had had no money to buy medicines that might have saved her life. For much of his lifetime, he had few decent clothes to wear, and on occasion he survived for days on gruel and raw onions (Ilankumaran 1985: 110; Tamilmallan 1989: 48–52).

And yet, we are told that even when he was offered a way out of such abject poverty, he refused to take it, because it involved bringing humiliation to Tamil. In 1956, he was hired by Annamalai University to produce a Tamil etymological dictionary. He had to report his findings to a committee headed by Suniti Kumar Chatterjee, the well-known Bengali linguist who, despite not knowing Tamil, was put in this position of power. Devaneyan's opinions on Tamil and its relationship to Sanskrit were at odds with Chatterjee's, and when asked to change his views, he refused. "Why should we fear to tell the truth about Tamil? How long should we Tamilians live in fear and servitude in this fashion?. . . . It is the duty of every researcher to reveal the truth, whatever may be its consequences. The rescuing of Tamil from its cruel subjection to Sanskrit is the purpose of my life. This is why I have been created by God" (quoted in Tamilkudimagan 1985: 16–17). In 1961, he resigned his job (or was relieved of it, by other accounts) and returned to his former hand-to-mouth existence. In words that have been repeated many times by his fellow devotees, he is supposed to have declared, "I am poor; I have a wife and children; but I also have honor" (quoted in Tamilkudimagan 1985: 17). As his biographers tell us, rather than betray Tamil and take care of himself, he chose to live heroically, as a poor but honorable and devoted Tamilian.

THE DEVOTEE AS PUBLICIST

"In my dreams and in my thoughts, I forever think about Tamil and Shaivism. May the Lord offer me grace so that I continue to think about them" (Anbupalam Ni 1967: 56). So declared Maraimalai Adigal in a public meeting in Madras in 1949 at the end of a life dedicated to the task of publicizing the glories of Tamil. Years before, in 1912, during the early years of his career while he was travelling to numerous small towns all over the Presidency as well as Sri Lanka to spread the message of Shaivism and Tamil, he noted in his diary: "I am leading a life happier than that of a prince" (quoted in M. Tirunavukarasu 1959: 130). Service to Shaivism and to Tamil appears to have been the motto of

Maraimalai's "princely" life. A devotee with ardent faith in the power of reform, Maraimalai made full use of the modernist technologies of print, associations, and public lectures to convert his fellow speakers into devotees of Tamil.

Maraimalai's use of such technologies of publicity, which were much favored by many reformers all across colonial India, may be traced back to his early youth. Growing up in the coastal town of Nagapattinam, he founded the Intu Matāpimāṉam Caṅkam (Society for Pride in Hindu Religion) to combat missionary attacks on Hinduism in 1892 when he was sixteen. At this time, he was an ardent believer in Vedantic and Sanskritic Hinduism (Nambi Arooran 1976: 312–13). Within a few years, however, he came under the influence of the well-known scholar Somasundara Nayakar (1846–1901), on whom he subsequently wrote a biography, and was converted to the latter's philosophy of Shaiva Siddhanta. In 1897, as a young man, he had his first encounter with the power of print when he published several essays defending his mentor's version of Shaivism against Vedantic detractors (M. Tirunavukarasu 1959: 4–19). A year later, he secured regular employment as a Tamil teacher in Madras Christian College. This did not stop him from continuing with his proselytizing activities, using weekends as well as his vacation days to give public lectures on Shaivism and Tamil; to publish his researches on Caṅkam poems; and to establish reform societies such as the Caiva Cittānta Makā Samājam (Society for Shaiva Siddhanta), founded in 1905, and the Camaraca Caṉmārkka Nilaiyam (Sacred Order of Love), founded in 1911 (Nambi Arooran 1976: 319–27).

Maraimalai's diaries and letters offer interesting glimpses of the lives of those devotees who turned into publicists and reformers dedicated to the Tamil cause. They formed associations, published books and journals, and organized literary conferences to spread the message of Tamil. These conferences were festive occasions marked by religious hymns and popular songs on Tamil, speeches on the wonders of its literature, and debates about how to go about restoring the language to its former glory. Speakers like Maraimalai were treated particularly well. On one occasion, when he visited Salem, he was taken in procession around the town and greeted by local notables; he then gave a talk for about an hour and a quarter on "the nobility and antiquity of Tamil." His talk was followed by discussions and lectures by other scholars and devotees (M. Tirunavukarasu 1959: 700–702). Yet it is also clear from his son's account, as well as from the reminiscences of others, that Maraimalai was a demanding publicist for the Tamil cause. Fellow devotee K. A. P.

Viswanatham recalls that after being invited to address the annual conference of the Shaiva Siddhanta association of Tiruchirapalli in 1921, Maraimalai presented a formidable list of demands which included detailed specifications on his lodging, provisions for worship and for his food, as well as payment of two hundred silver coins. When asked, "How many will invite you if you ask so much for service to Tamil and to Shaivism?" Maraimalai acerbically replied that while his fellow Tamilians were willing to heap thousands on actors and singers, they refuse to similarly honor Tamil scholars (Viswanatham 1989: 15–17). For Maraimalai, the honoring—both materially and otherwise—of speakers like himself was the honoring of Tamil itself.

His speeches certainly appear to have influenced at least one young man to convert to the Tamil cause. R. P. Sethu Pillai, who later became professor of Tamil in Madras University and published numerous books and essays on Tamil and its literature, many of them Indianist and compensatory classicist in sentiment, recalls a public lecture on Tamil that Maraimalai gave in the small town of Palayamkottai in June 1912. Tirunavukarasu, to whom Sethu Pillai talked later about this event, describes the impact of Maraimalai's speech on the young man: "His being pulsed with the consciousness of Tamil. 'I, too, will learn this great Tamil. I, too, will spread Tamil by lecturing and by offering my services,' he thought to himself" (M. Tirunavukarasu 1959: 162–63).

Maraimalai appears to have been paid well for his speeches. Much of the money he made on these lecture tours was ploughed back into his publication and reform activities. In a 1941 letter to a friend, he observes, "I have spent an enormous amount of wealth on Tamil" (Anbupalam Ni 1967: 24–26). Yet, like the majority of Tamil's devotees, he appears to have led a life of only middling prosperity, and the prefaces to his various books as well his letters contain frequent references to the financial hardship that he faced in continuing with his publication efforts, to the lack of appreciation for his work, and so on. Nonetheless, he worked on tirelessly, beginning most days at the crack of dawn with prayers and going to bed past midnight (Anbupalam Ni 1967: 49–51).

In 1911, at the age of thirty-five and as the sole breadwinner for his family—consisting of his aged mother, his wife, and seven children—Maraimalai decided to give up his teaching career and become an ascetic instead. In doing so, his son tells us, he was following an age-old tradition: "Having dedicated himself to the cause of Shaivism and Tamil, he donned the ascetic's robes and the lifestyle of a renouncer" (M. Tirunavukarasu 1959: 128).[27] At least in his son's reckoning,

Maraimalai's act was justifiable, his dedication to the cause of Shaivism and Tamil overriding his family responsibilities. Indeed, it is as an ascetic that Maraimalai entered the most productive period of his career as Tamil devotee; these were the "golden years of his life" (Tirunavukarasu 1959: 481). He published prodigiously and his books sold well; there were numerous requests for his presence as inaugural speaker at conferences; he became a member of the local vegetarian society and led campaigns against the performance of animal sacrifices in rural and low-caste temples. Scholars and admirers thronged to visit his home in Pallavaram, a suburb of Madras where he had taken up residence after becoming an ascetic. "Ah! How many people are now filled with Tamil devotion! They are filled with pride in their community. My work has had its impact. In the future, my books will sell abundantly, and my thoughts will spread far and wide. Tamil will flourish! Shaivism will triumph!" he remarked in contentment to his son in the 1940s (M. Tirunavukarasu 1959: 836–37; Anbupalam Ni 1967: 25).[28] Above all, these were the years in which he earnestly pursued the *taṉittamiḻ* cause, republishing pure Tamil versions of his early essays and striving to create a language that would be as free of Sanskrit words as possible. He refused to lend the prestige of his name to any publication that did not conform to his notion of Tamil, and periodically he had public disputations with fellow scholars on the purity of their language. Indeed, though his livelihood partly depended on the remuneration he received from speaking at conferences, he refused (in a letter he wrote in English) "to attend any Tamil meeting which is not willing to maintain and advance pure Tamil. Of all the Cultivated ancient Languages, Tamil is the only one which is still living in all its pristine glory. I am strongly convinced that any mixture of foreign words in it will tend to vitiate its healthy life and hamper its vigorous growth. Please, therefore, excuse me for not attending your conference which does not seem to meet my ideal" (quoted in Ilankumaran 1991: 127).

In his personal life as well, his son tells us, he attempted to meet his ideals. After 1912, he refused to allow the participation of Brahman priests in the domestic rituals performed at home, deeming this a non-Tamil practice; after 1916, he attempted to speak only in pure Tamil; in the shrine that he built in his home in 1931 in Pallavaram, worship was offered only in Tamil; and he was a devout Shaivite, regularly visiting Shaiva temples where he would sing Tamil hymns to his heart's content and, we are told, would bring tears of joy to all those who heard him.

All the same, his devotion, like that of so many others, was not without its share of contradictions. Later in his life he was neutral, even hostile, to the cause of Indian nationalism, but in his early years, according to his diary entries, he composed nationalist songs, attended nationalist lectures, and even wrote in 1906 that he bought a bundle of *swadeshi* (nationalist) candles (M. Tirunavukarasu and Venkatachalapathy 1988: 25–30). On the incarceration of the nationalist leader Tilak, his diary entry in English dated 23 July 1907 reads, "Oh! Mother India! Are thy sons to suffer thus!" (Anbupalam Ni 1967: 40). At the same time, he also composed songs commemorating George V's accession in 1911 and joined the celebrations in Pallavaram marking that occasion. In 1912, noting that the government probably had him under surveillance, he comments on the stupidity of this, for he was after only a preacher, and he writes that he desired British rule to continue (M. Tirunavukarasu and Venkatachalapathy 1988: 35–36).

He may have spent much of his public life castigating Sanskrit for its evils, but unlike those in a later generation of Tamil devotees who criticized the language without any knowledge of it, Maraimalai had formally learned Sanskrit and even translated from it into Tamil a well-known play, *Shakuntala*. In his later published writings, he may have ardently preached the inherent superiority of Shaiva Siddhanta, but in his diaries he expresses admiration for Vivekananda's Vedantic teachings and even gave a public lecture in 1909 on the *Bhagavad Gītā*'s importance in modernity (M. Tirunavukarasu and Venkatachalapathy 1988: 32–33). Indeed, although in a large number his writings on Tamil he may appear a classicist, in his own personal reading habits he appreciated a good number of modern works written in other languages. His love for English offers another similar contradiction. He seems to have spent a good part of his limited funds on purchasing English books to stock his personal library, and he translated numerous English classics into Tamil. His son tells us that on his many lecture tours and pilgrimages, he would carry along with him as reading material English books, rather than Tamil. He maintained his personal diary in English. When asked about this, he told his son, "My thoughts, speech, and writing are all in Tamil. To ensure that my knowledge of English does not fade away, I write my daily diary in English" (M. Tirunavukarasu 1959: 700). Such contradictions lasted until the end; when he died in September 1950, he requested that his body be cremated rather than buried in what had been deemed the authentic Tamil style (Viswanatham 1989: 22).

THE DEVOTEE AS PATRON

Among the many grievances of the devotional community was the absence of appreciative patrons who would extend their liberality and largesse to the support of Tamil and its followers. In 1897, as a young man barely fifteen, Subramania Bharati lamented to one such patron, the landlord of Ettaiyapuram:

> In this world, surrounded by oceans and abounding with languages,
> Is our glorious and auspicious Tamil, sweeter than nectar, to which the great lord Shiva himself offered his grace;
> Yet there is no one around anymore to favor it;
> Its learners languish away, while lesser tongues flourish.
>
> (Bharati 1987: 2)

Tamil's devotees were of course not alone in colonial India in lamenting over the deteriorating state of patronage extended to traditional arts and letters. The attrition and disappearance of royal courts and religious centers of learning, the redirection of funds towards "useful" and "modern" forms of knowledge, the rise of new bourgeois forms of consumption, and a colonial state indifferent to the promotion of India's languages and literatures—all these contributed to the generalized feeling that things were no longer as they were in the past. The nostalgia for ancient Caṅkam poems that was so endemic in devotional circles was also very much a nostalgia for an age in which magnanimous kings were imagined to welcome with open arms the poor poet who wandered into their courts, lend an appreciative ear to his compositions, and shower him with food, clothing, and gold. Those were the days, its devotees sigh, when the wealthy and the notable were admirers of Tamil (and of its scholars). But today, "we lavishly heap our wealth on jewelry, cards, drinks, tobacco, entertainment . . . but would not spend even one paisa out of a hundred rupees to protect [Tamiḻttāy]. What a shame!" (Lakshmana Pillai 1892–93: 154).

Not surprisingly, when one such patron did put in an appearance at the turn of this century, and placed his considerable wealth and influence at the service of Tamil, he came to be narrated in devotional writings as a Caṅkam king reincarnate. The institution that he founded and funded in 1901, the Madurai Tamil Sangam, was itself characterized as the "Fourth" Tamil Caṅkam, thus establishing a genealogical connection with the three ancient academies that are believed to have flourished in the distant past under the patronage of successive generations of Pandyan kings. Its founder-patron, Pandithurai Thevar, named at birth in 1876 Ugrapandyan (an ancient name that recalled the glory of the Pandyan kings of the Caṅkam age), was the landlord (*zamindar*) of Palavanatham, a small estate in Ramanathapuram district. In the reckoning of his biographers and admirers, Pandithurai—unlike many of his *zamindari* cohort, who frittered away their life and wealth in wasteful activities—was an enthusiastic Tamil scholar and poet himself. He may have inherited his love for Tamil from his father, Ponnusami Thevar (1837–70), who also had been its patron, "like the Pandyan kings of yore," in the words of the famous Shaivite scholar Arumuga Navalar (M. Raghava Aiyangar 1948: 51). Indeed, distressed that so many great works of ancient Tamil had yet to find their way into print, Ponnusami, who was then the chief manager of the Ramanathapuram estate of his brother, Muthuramalinga Setupati (1841–73), commissioned Arumuga Navalar to publish texts such as the *Tirukkōvaiyār* and the *Tirukkuṟaḷ,* which he then distributed at his own expense to scholars. Ponnusami also established a much-needed printing press for the publication of Tamil books in Ramanathapuram town (M. Raghava Aiyangar 1948: 51–53).

Raised in an environment where such value was placed on Tamil learning, Pandithurai continued this tradition of extending patronage to Tamil and also prevailed upon his more influential cousin, Bhaskara Setupati (1868–1903), the *zamindar* of Ramanathapuram, to do the same. Indeed, their "courts," we are told, were like "heaven on earth." Here, from morning till late into the night, one could hear learned disquisitions on the intricacies of Kamban's *Irāmāvatāram* or the *Tirukkuṟaḷ;* poets and musicians were frequent visitors, and "forgetting hunger and thirst," they would sing their compositions and recite poetry. In addition to throwing his court open to visiting scholars, Pandithurai also financed the publication of many ancient manuscripts, including some of Swaminatha Aiyar's (M. Raghava Aiyangar 1948: 76–95). Tamil enthusiasts narrate with pride an incident from Pandithurai's life illustrating how his devotion to Tamil led him to ensure that the reading public had access to well-published and error-free editions of their ancient texts. An Anglo-Indian lawyer of Madurai had had the temerity to publish five hundred copies of the *Tirukkuṟaḷ,* "made easy." Pandithurai invited him over to his palace and asked to see the publication. He noted with anger that the lawyer had erred in the very first key verse of the text. Learning that only two hundred copies of the publication had been sold so far, Pandithurai purchased the remaining three hundred and burned the whole lot, rather than expose his fellow Tamilians to such a travesty (M. Raghava Aiyangar 1948: 105–7).

The scarcity of good published versions of Tamil literary works was what spurred Pandithurai to found his well-known Sangam. In one version of the story, when he was visiting Madurai and needed copies of the *Tirukkuṟaḷ* and Kamban's *Irāmāvatāram* to prepare a lecture, he discovered that it was impossible to procure them. If these works, the heart of Tamil literature, were unavailable in Madurai, the center of Tamil learning, what fate awaited Tamil? he lamented. Resolving to do something to change this, in 1901 he summoned together various notables and scholars and spoke of the need to create a society dedicated to the improvement of Tamil (M. Raghava Aiyangar 1948: 87–89). "The rejection of our mother tongue, Tamil, and the embracing of English mostly for the sake of greater comfort, is like the rejection of our mother in favor of our newly arrived wife," he declared in his speech urging his fellow speakers to come forward and help him in his new venture.[29]

His idea was not new. Since the 1880s, a few such societies had sprung up in the Presidency, although most were short-lived. No doubt, the Madurai Tamil Sangam's own longer and more fruitful existence was the result of a convergence of factors: the liberal funding it received from Pandithurai and Bhaskara Setupati (who also used their influence to get other notables to make contributions); the supplementing of the scholarly activities of the Sangam with the establishment of a printing press, a research center, a school that conducted exams and offered degrees in Tamil, and a library (which was started with liberal donations of books from Pandithurai's and the Setupati's own collections); and the founding of a journal, *Centamiḻ*, in late 1902. All of these attracted to the Sangam some of the finest minds in the world of Tamil learning. But not least of the reasons for the Sangam's success was the symbolic capital that accrued from its location in Madurai; from its self-representation as continuing the traditions of the ancient academies of the Tamil land; and from the persona of its founder, Pandithurai, as a true descendant of the great *vaḷḷaḷ*s, "benefactors," of yore (Rowther 1907).

A less spectacular, but no less heroic, model of patronage is offered by the life of V. Tiruvarangam Pillai, the founder of the Shaiva Siddhanta Kazhagam, perhaps the largest publishing house devoted to printing ancient Tamil literary and religious books from its inception in 1920 to this day. Tiruvarangam's life, in stark contrast to Pandithurai's, began in a humble Vellala home in Palayamkottai in Tirunelveli district, where his family ran a general merchandise store. When his father died in 1899, the young Tiruvarangam, who was then only nine years old, went to work in Tuticorin to support his family. When he was seventeen, he sailed to Colombo where he worked for a number of years in various commercial establishments. His entrepreneurial skills must have been forged in this context, for he was able to gather together enough money in 1914 to help finance the first trip to Colombo by Maraimalai Adigal (about whose skills as a speaker and reformer there was much talk). Furthermore, he was also able to put together a handsome purse which he presented to Maraimalai and which enabled the latter to continue with his work in Madras. Over the next few years, Tiruvarangam continued to help Maraimalai's reform activities by arranging for public lectures, collecting funds, and opening bookstores in Colombo and Madras to help sell the reformer's books. In 1920, he even launched a monthly journal called *Centamiḻkkaḷañciyam,* primarily for the purpose of publishing Maraimalai's commentary on the *Tiruvācakam* (Ilankumaran 1982: 1–30) .

His crowning achievement, however, was the establishment of the Kazhagam in Tirunelveli in 1920, with a branch office opening in Madras in 1921. His biographer tells us that he took the cue from Maraimalai and his circle of scholar friends, who lamented that Tamilians were quick to invest in all kinds of new ventures but none would support the publication of books of knowledge which are the very source of life (Ilankumaran 1982: 30–31). True to the spirit of *tamiḻppaṟṟu,* its admirers insist that although the Kazhagam is a business venture, it has not let economic reasons override its dedication to the cause of Tamil (Ilankumaran 1991: 183). The Kazhagam's involvement in Tamil devotional activities over the past few decades has been manifold, including the support of educational institutions as well as of Tamil libraries. Additionally, it has convened numerous public conferences on various aspects of Shaiva and Tamil literature, on the creation of Tamil technical terms, on Tamilnadu history, and the like. In 1937, Tiruvarangam and his associates played a key role in the founding in Tirunelveli of the Tamiḻp Pātukāppuk Kaḻakam (Society for the Protection of Tamil), which published several pamphlets and books promoting the cause of *taṉittamiḻ* and protesting the government's Hindi policy. In 1923, Tiruvarangam also started the *Centamiḻc Celvi,* a journal devoted to promoting the twin causes of Shaivism and Tamil that is still published today.

But over and above all this, Tiruvarangam's fame in the world of *tamilpparru* rests on the role that the Kazhagam has played in the field of publishing: under its auspices, almost every major work in Tamil and Shaiva literature, as well as several minor and hitherto unknown ones, has been printed and made available to the public. Indeed, the image of Tiruvarangam that is remembered most fondly by fellow devotees is that of a man whose voluminous coat pockets were ever stuffed with old manuscripts and galley proofs. In 1980, V. S. Manickam, then vice-chancellor of Madurai Kamaraj University, noted that if Tiruvarangam had not founded the Kazhagam, none of the following would have found their way into print: Tamil school textbooks, the Caṅkam poems, the *Tolkāppiyam,* M. Varadarajan's sparkling commentary on the *Tirukkuṟaḷ,* dictionaries and encyclopedias, and the *Centamiḻc Celvi.* Consequently, "our Tamiḻttāy, too, would have wandered around like a weakling able to carry only one child. [But, because of the Kazhagam], our Tamiḻttāy has acquired several heads and arms, her blood has been enriched with knowledge, and her nerves and sinews have been strengthened with books. She now has the capacity to go everywhere in all directions; even shouldering the burden of fifty million of her children, she flourishes happily" (quoted in Ilankumaran 1982: 2).

THE WARRIOR DEVOTEE

Increasingly from the 1930s on, especially as Dravidianist sentiments began to dominate the devotional community, the *kaviñar* (poet) and the *aṟiñar* (scholar) had to make room for a new kind of devotee, the *maṟavar* (warrior), who fiercely fought in the glorious and honorable battle for liberating Tamiḻttāy. Among the many devotees who so present themselves, perhaps none is as spectacular as Muthuvel Karunanidhi. His life, he writes, is a "battle," and he is the "warrior" who bravely and fearlessly takes it on (Karunanidhi 1989: 7). His reminiscences are sprinkled with numerous allusions to the Caṅkam past, and there are repeated comparisons between his own efforts for the Tamil cause and the heroic deeds of ancient Tamil warriors. Like those ancient *maṟavar*s who battled to maintain their honor, he writes that he, too, was prepared to battle—and had indeed done so—to maintain the honor of Tamil and the well-being of its speakers. The four most memorable days of his life, he recalls, are the day he was born; the day he got married; the day he met his beloved leader, Annadurai; and, finally, the day he was thrown into prison for the first time during "the battle to protect [his] language" (Karunanidhi 1989: 15).

Born in 1924 into a working-class family in the small village of Tirukkuvalai near Tiruvarur in Tanjavur district, Karunanidhi's involvement in the Tamil cause began very early, when he was in high school. He was fourteen when the first wave of anti-Hindi protests began to sweep across the Presidency in the late 1930s, and he recalls being impressed with the Tamilian Brigade that marched from Tiruchirapalli to Madras in 1938 and with young men like Dhalamutthu, Natarajan, and Stalin Jegadeesan who had sacrificed themselves in the battle against Hindi. Inspired by their deeds, he organized his fellow students and marched every evening through the streets of Tiruvarur carrying the Tamil banner and shouting anti-Hindi slogans. The student procession was headed by a cart bearing a giant poster of Tamilttāy being stabbed by Rajagopalachari (fig. 5). The students chanted a verse that young Karunanidhi himself had composed: "Let us all gather together and go to war! / Let us chase away and drive back that she-devil, Hindi!" (Karunanidhi 1989: 43–44). One day during their daily march, the students encountered their Hindi teacher. Karunanidhi handed him a pamphlet of anti-Hindi songs, raised the Tamil banner, and shouted, "Let Hindi die! Long live Tamil!" He writes that even though he was just a teenager, and ought to have been scared about confronting his teacher in this way, he felt no fear for his "blood and [his] breath pulse[d] with Tamil" (Karunanidhi 1989: 42–46).

His participation in these anti-Hindi protests laid the foundation for his full-scale involvement in politics. Soon after, he dropped out of high school, became actively involved in the youth wing of the Dravidian movement, and contributed essays on rationalism, atheism, and other such issues to various party newspapers. In 1942, he founded his own newspaper, the *Muracoli,* which continues to be published to this day; and by the early 1950s, he was writing scripts for plays and movies that propagated the ideals of the movement. Later in his life he wrote, "Even if I have a mother and father, wives and children and siblings, and whether they stay with me or part from me, it is the [Dravidian] movement that I think of as my family, and I think of myself as part of it" (Karunanidhi 1987b: 1). He recalls that during several crucial moments in his life, such as the deaths of his father and of his first wife, he was off making speeches for the movement rather than at their side (Karunanidhi 1989: 96, 107). He observes (with some amusement) that when he got married the second time, his wedding took place on 15 September 1948—the same day that Ramasami had called for a renewed protest against Hindi. Friends and relatives had gathered at Karunanidhi's home. He himself was standing at the entrance, greeting his guests, when an anti-Hindi procession went by on its way to picket the local school. The processors were shouting anti-Hindi slogans: "Let Hindi die! May Tamil live!" In the roar of these slogans, he notes, the music of his wedding party could hardly be heard. He, too, joined the procession, and went off to picket the nearby school. Fortunately, he writes, he was not arrested on that day and returned home to marry his bride, who had been waiting patiently through all this (Karunanidhi 1989: 113–15).

From the early 1950s, as a key member of the newly formed DMK, Karunanidhi began to participate enthusiastically in various protests launched by that party, picketing shops run by North Indian merchants and tarring over Hindi names on public billboards. He gained early fame in 1953 when he led a group of DMK volunteers in a bid to change the name of the industrial town called Dalmiapuram to its Tamil original, Kallakudi. His narration of this event offers a clear illustration of Karunanidhi's efforts to capitalize on themes drawn from ancient heroic poetry. He writes that he and twenty-four others set out on that fateful day. "Look, the herd of Tamil lions has set out to cast aside the crown of dishonor that sits on our Tamil̲ttāy's head. . . . We ran towards our mother. We erased the name Dalmiapuram. We painted on the name Kallakudi." Then, over the protests of police officials who had gathered there, he and his fellow "warriors" laid themselves down on the railroad tracks as they heard the train approaching: "One last time, I looked up at the sky! I looked around at Kallakudi; I looked to my heart's content at Tamil̲ttāy who nurtured me. I looked at all those standing around me . . . I closed my eyes. I heard the sound of the train approaching. My heart resounded with the words, 'May Tamil live long!'" Several men lost their lives or were injured at Kallakudi, and Karunanidhi himself was sentenced to six months in prison. "We received our reward for fighting for the honor of Tamilians," he concludes (Karunanidhi 1989: 196–214).[30]

This is not the only time Karunanidhi went to prison in the battle to save the honor of his language and his fellow speakers; he was imprisoned once again in 1965 for his role in the anti-Hindi protests of that year. He writes in the style of the *mar̲avar* devotee, "I will have no greater joy than if I die on the battlefield, opposing Hindi" (Karunanidhi 1989: 476). And although he has held several public and political offices—as a member of the Legislative Assembly from 1957; as a cabinet minister in the first DMK government in 1967; and then as chief minister of the state from 1969 to 1976, 1989 to 1991, and most recently beginning in May 1996—he clearly takes pride in his persona as a "warrior" for Tamil, as someone who has been ready to put his body on the line for his fellow speakers of Tamil. As he declared later in life, in a verse that admirably captures his flamboyant presentation of self:

> O Tamilians! O Tamilians!
> If you throw me into the ocean, I will float on it as a raft; you may climb aboard and ride the waves.
> If you throw me into the flames of a fire, I will be the burning log; you can use me in your hearth and cook your meals.
> If you dash me against the rocks, I will break into the flakes of a coconut; you can pick these up and eat them, and rejoice.
>
> (Karunanidhi 1987b: 229)

Another devotee who presents himself, albeit less colorfully than does Karunanidhi, as a *maṟavar* battling for Tamil is M. P. Sivagnanam. Sivagnanam's life, like Karunanidhi's, offers an illustration of how *tamiḻp-paṟṟu* can bring fame and fortune, the trials and tribulations involved in its practice notwithstanding. Born in 1906 into a very poor family of the low Gramani caste in Madras city, Sivagnanam had to drop out of school early, and he helped support his family through a variety of minor jobs: rolling tobacco for country cigarettes, working as a day laborer on construction sites, and as a printer for about eight years. In 1927, he joined the Congress and rose slowly but steadily in its ranks, in spite of his low-caste, working-class background. In 1942, he was imprisoned in Amaravati for his participation in the Quit India protests. This was a turning point in his life, for there he read Caṅkam poetry for the first time and came to believe that the Tamil country ought to be ruled only by Tamilians; that every Tamilian's credo ought to be, "Tamil everywhere, everything in Tamil"; that Tamil should be the first principle of their lives; and that the Tamil land should be restored to its original, "sacred," and "natural" frontiers (Sivagnanam 1974: 250–53).

Over the next two decades, he "battled" to make this vision a reality. In his autobiography suggestively entitled *Eṉatu Pōrāṭṭam* (My struggle), Sivagnanam writes that he had to conduct this battle on several fronts. As a Tamil devotee in the regional Congress, he struggled to ensure that Tamil interests were not compromised by that "nationalist" party. By 1953, he found that his continuing membership in the party threatened his devotion to Tamil. He writes that if he had not severed his connections with the Congress, he could have become mayor of Madras, or even a cabinet minister—no small achievement for a poor boy from the slums. But "for the sake of Tamil and Tamilnadu and Tamilians," he gave all this up (Sivagnanam 1974: 709). On another front, as a "nationalist," he also conducted a series of campaigns against the Dravidian movement in the 1950s to counter any possibility of Tamilnadu seceding from India (Sivagnanam 1974: 535–55).

His fame in Tamil devotional circles rests on his attempts to popularize the poems of the Caṅkam; on his efforts to commemorate the birthdays of great Tamil poets and nationalists like Bharati; and on a series of assaults he led from the late 1940s through the 1950s to ensure that the borders of the newly formed linguistic state of Madras conformed to what was imagined as Tamiḻakam, "the home of Tamil," in the Caṅkam age, stretching from the Tirupati hills in the north to the Cape in the south. He also fought to ensure that the city of Madras would not be lost to neighboring Andhra Pradesh, declaring in 1953, "We will save our capital if it means cutting off our heads. As long as the last Tamilian is alive, we will not surrender our rights. We will not forget our heroic heritage. Fiercely, we will rise! We will protect our Tamiḻttāy" (Sivagnanam 1974: 617). And fiercely he did rise and march, and he was detained in 1953 and in 1956 by the Congress government for his role in these border campaigns. Although by the mid-1960s Sivagnanam joined ranks with the DMK party in order to fight the common battle against Hindi and was subsequently elected to the Madras Legislative Assembly, he turned down an offer to join the DMK cabinet in 1967, wishing not to be diverted from his true service to Tamil, its land, and its people (Sivagnanam 1974: 981).

THE DEVOTEE AS MARTYR

While not minimizing the sacrifices made by these better-known luminaries, the real "warriors" of *tamiḻppaṟṟu* were the hundreds of relatively unknown, even anonymous, young men who, from the 1930s on, increasingly took to the streets, courted arrest, undertook fasts, died under police fire, and burned themselves alive for the sake of Tamil and Tamiḻttāy. Whatever each individual's intentions and motivations may have been, their deeds are remembered, textualized, and circulated by their fellow devotees to conform to the ideal of the "Tamil martyr" (*moḻi tiyāki*). Their names are invoked again and again in poem and song, in speech and writing. Since 1967, after the DMK first came to power, buildings and streets and bridges have been named after them; commemorative statues have been installed; and pensions have been given to their survivors. And since 1968, the party has routinely celebrated 25 January as "Language Martyrs' Day."[31] The memory of these martyrs is repeatedly used to spur Tamil speakers to take up the Tamil cause and, if need be, to sacrifice their lives for their language/mother.

If a populist political movement reaches its apogee when it gains its first martyrs, *tamiḻpparṟu* attained that moment in 1939. Early that year, two young men, Natarajan and Dhalamutthu, died in prison, having been arrested along with numerous others for joining the anti-Hindi picketing in front of the Hindu Theological High School in Madras city. The government was quick to point out that both men had been in poor health when they had entered the prison, and that they died of cellulitis and amebic dysentery.[32] In devotional writings, however, their deaths are presented as heroic sacrifices to the Tamil cause, and over the years these men have attained the status of devotees who selflessly gave up their lives for their language (Annadurai 1985: 34–36, 56–57; Karunanidhi 1989: 196–207; Parthasarathy 1986: 410–37). Their funeral processions in Madras city were attended by hundreds of mourners and marked by fiery speeches celebrating their martyrdom. Annadurai proclaimed that Natarajan's name and deeds had to be inscribed in gold in the history of the world. Another admirer, Kanchi Rajagopalachari, a maverick Brahman in the Justice Party and archcritic of the government, declared that never before even in the glorious history of ancient Tamilnadu had anyone sacrificed his life for his language, predicting that Natarajan's grave would become a hallowed site for all true Tamilians. Natarajan's father, we are told, declared that his son's spirit lived on in all true Tamilians and invited them to continue the battle for Tamil rights (Iraiyan 1981: 108).[33]

Government records only tell us that Dhalamutthu Nadar was a native of Kumbakonam, an illiterate who was arrested on 13 February 1939, fell ill on 6 March, and died on 11 March.[34] According to Tamil's devotees, he was married, and when he was arrested, the judge asked him if he would return to his hometown if he was released; he refused the conditions. Sentenced to six months' "rigorous imprisonment," he entered prison shouting "Down with Hindi! May Tamil flourish" (Iraiyan 1981: 107). Natarajan, government sources note in passing, was an illiterate twenty-year-old "Adi-Dravida" carpenter and a native of Madras. He was arrested on 5 December 1938, fell ill and was admitted to the hospital on 30 December, and died on 15 January 1939. The 22 January issue of the *Sunday Observer* carried an interview with K. Lakshmanan, young Natarajan's father, in which he declared that his son often sang religious and anti-Hindi songs at home. Three days prior to his arrest, his son had expressed his desire to go to jail for the sake of Tamil. Lakshmanan also said that when his son was hospitalized, he was told by the authorities that if he submitted an apology for his activities, he would be released from prison. But Natarajan refused.[35] In its editorial of 22 January, the *Nakaratūtaṉ* declared that Natarajan, filled with "love for Tamil," preferred to die a honorable death in prison rather than agree to a dishonorable release (Ilanceliyan 1986: 171–72; Visswanathan 1983: 244–47).

Along with Dhalamutthu and Natarajan, these early protests against Hindi also produced another martyr in a young man who called himself Stalin Jegadeesan. On 1 May 1938, he started a fast, demanding the cancellation of the government's Hindi legislation. He was frequently put on display at anti-Hindi meetings, and his photograph was periodically published in sympathetic newspapers. A statement issued by him, published in the *Viṭutalai,* had him declaring that he had gone on his fast to prove to Hindi supporters that Tamiḻttāy still had loyal sons: "I will return with our Tamiḻaṉṉai [Tamiḻttāy], or I will die," he concluded.[36] Following his example, another man, named Ponnusami, also went on a fast on 1 June in front of Rajagopalachari's residence, sitting under a tree and carrying the Tamil banner (with its characteristic emblems of the tiger, the bow, and the fish, signifying the ancient Tamil dynasties of the Chola, Chera, and Pandya). He is reported to have declared: "I shall fast unto death; even if released from jail I shall go and fast and die in front of the Premier's house. If Jegadeesan should die . . . [a] thousand lives should go for it."[37]

Some anti-Hindi leaders such as Ramasami rejected fasting as a form of protest; others such as Annadurai used the example of Jegadeesan to spur Tamil speakers to join the cause. At an anti-Hindi meeting in 1938, Annadurai thundered, "If Jegadeesan dies, I am ready to take his place, and die along with ten other persons. As soon as Jegadeesan dies, you should also be prepared to die."[38] Jegadeesan, however, did not die; on the contrary, it was reported that he had been stealthily eating at night all along, and his fast was called off after about ten weeks (Nambi Arooran 1980: 208–10; Visswanathan 1983: 201–5).

Stalin Jegadeesan may not have given up his life for Tamil, but Shankaralinga Nadar certainly did, in the process of demanding that

Madras state be renamed Tamilnadu. Nothing in the biography of Shankaralingam, as it has been documented by T. Sundararajan (1986) from information obtained from his grandson, offers a clear reason for why he took this course of action. A lifelong Gandhian, Shankaralingam was born in 1895. He was a social reformer and nationalist in his native Virudhunagar, but there seems to be little evidence of devotion to Tamil during his early years. The only possible explanation that Sundararajan himself obliquely offers is that by the 1940s, Shankaralingam was disillusioned with life, and perhaps the fast was one last effort to do something for his beloved Tamilnadu (Sundararajan 1986: 68–76). He died on 13 October 1956 after a fast of over seventy days; his demand for renaming the state was not granted until a decade later. Soon after Shankaralingam's death, in 1958–59, two young men named Ilavalakan and Arangarathinam fasted in front of radio stations in Tiruchirapalli and Madras demanding that the Sanskritic work for radio, *ākāṣvāṇi,* which smacked of Hindi domination, be replaced with the pure Tamil term, *vāṉoli.* Others, including K. A. P. Viswanatham, joined in their protest, and more than sixty were arrested by 1960. Arangarathinam himself was hailed as the great hero who was a direct descendant of ancient Tamil warriors like Senguttuvan and Neduncheliyan, and Bharatidasan wrote poems and editorials celebrating his heroic act (Sambandan 1976: 120–25).[39]

All these martyrs, however heroic and lauded, were soon overshadowed by Chinnasami, who set himself on fire in Tiruchirapalli on 25 January 1964, on the eve of municipal elections in the state. Chinnasami's self-immolation inaugurated a dramatic new form of expressing devotion and offered a spectacular new model of the true devotee of Tamil, as one who turns himself into ashes for his language/mother. Verses have been written on him, including a long poem which portrays him and his family as the archetypal heroic Tamilians (Puthumai Vannan 1968). During the 1964 elections, the DMK plastered the walls of Madras city with posters showing the charred body of Chinnasami, and in the 1967 campaign, the party staged a play on his life and death. In April 1967, soon after the party came to power, a memorial to Chinnasami was set up near Tiruchirapalli (Karunanidhi 1989: 698; M. S. S. Pandian 1992: 17; Ryerson 1988: 132–33).

In his memoirs, Karunanidhi tells us Chinnasami's story in a chapter entitled "Chinnasami, the Lion Tamilian" (Karunanidhi 1989: 498–501). A native of the small village of Kilpaluvur near Tiruchirapalli, Chinnasami had a primary school education up to the fifth grade and later worked as a day laborer. In his spare time, he avidly read Dravidianist literature and newspapers, and he had even named his only daughter Dravidacelvi, "Lady Dravida." A few days before he immolated himself, he had visited Madras, and on a chance meeting with Chief Minister Bhaktavatsalam, he implored the latter to do something to save Tamil. He was taken into custody. On 25 January, in the early dawn, he doused himself with kerosene and set himself ablaze in front of the railway station in Tiruchirapalli. He was twenty-seven. Karunanidhi writes that as the flames consumed him, he shouted, "Let Hindi die! May Tamil flourish!" Karunanidhi also quotes from a letter Chinnasami is believed to have written to a friend on the eve of his death in which he declared, "O Tamil! In order that you live, I am going to die a terrible death!" In a speech that Karunanidhi himself gave soon after Chinnasami's death at a public meeting, he declared, "Even when his youthful face was being scorched by the flames, from the bottom of his heart, he cried out, consumed by passion for his mother tongue, 'May Tamiḻttāy flourish! Down with Hindi.' He then surrendered his life." Karunanidhi concludes that in his death, Chinnasami gave truth to every Tamil devotee's reigning sentiment: "I want to die with Tamil on my lips! / My ashes should burn with the fragrance of Tamil!" (Karunanidhi 1989: 498). His wife Kamalam, it is reported, today takes pride in the fact that he was the first to immolate himself in the battle against Hindi. "[His] greatness is my wealth," she notes with tears.[40]

A year after Chinnasami's death, in the early months of 1965, several other young men followed in his footsteps and immolated themselves. Today, in various devotional tracts, their names are repeated, over and again, almost like a litany: Sivalingam, Aranganathan, Veerappan, Mutthu, and Sarangapani.[41] Three other young men—Dandapani, Mutthu, and Shanmugam[42]—died after consuming poison. On January 27, an eighteen-year-old college student named Rajendran, himself the son of a policeman, was killed when police opened fire on a huge anti-Hindi protest march at Annamalai University in Chidambaram. The varying stories of all these young men have been narrativized in the devotional community to conform to the image of the selfless Tamil martyr, overwriting any individual aspirations or passions they might have had. Each of them, prior to death, professed his devotion to Tamil and lamented over Tamil's fate at the hands of Hindi. Some left behind letters (which were found sometimes beside their charred bodies) in which they proclaimed their deaths to be "in protest against the imposition of Hindi, and [as] sacrifice at the altar of Tamil" (Barnett 1976: 131); others cried out "Long Live Tamil! Down with Hindi!" as their bodies were beginning to burn. When neighbors tried to save Veerappan, he reportedly told them as the flames were consuming his body that they should use their efforts to save not him, but Tamil. Young Sarangapani died in his hospital bed, saying, it is claimed, "I have given up my life for Tamiḻttāy" (Parthasarathy 1986: 412). Mallika, Aranganathan's wife, told newsmen that her husband cared for Tamil deeply, even more than for his three children and herself. For days before his death, he had been troubled about the ruin that Hindi was causing Tamil, the DMK newspaper *Muttāram* reported.[43] Many of these young men, it is claimed, were inspired by Chinnasami's example, which they read about in DMK party newspapers. Aranganathan is believed to have immolated himself after seeing the charred body of Sivalingam. Sivalingam in turn was inspired to his act by Chinnasami's.

With the exception of Veerappan, who was a schoolteacher, and Sarangapani and Dandapani, who were college students, all the others, like Chinnasami, had had only a basic education and held low-paying jobs of various kinds. Like Chinnasami again, they all came from very poor rural families, and at least in the government's reckoning, they "were also reported to be suffering from domestic troubles, illnesses, etc."[44] Finally, they all appear to have subscribed to the ideals of Dravidianism to various degrees. Like Chinnasami, they were rank-and-file members of the DMK. Some DMK leaders publicly expressed their horror over these immolations; others attended the men's funerals. The party has in general condoned devotion in this form and even celebrates such martyrs, if the hagiography it generates on these young men is any testimony. DMK newspapers routinely carried photographs of the charred bodies and the funeral processions of the dead martyrs, and, as already noted, the date of Chinnasami's self-immolation has become "Language Martyrs' Day." The speeches and essays of key DMK leaders are to this day sprinkled with celebratory allusions to these men. It is reported with pride that newspapers, both Indian and foreign, carried news of the immolations. The Tamil devotee had at last succeeded in drawing the attention of the rest of the world to the plight of his language/mother, by literally burning himself to death.

THE ANTI-DEVOTEE

Finally, I turn to the maverick figure of E. V. Ramasami, the "patriarch" (*tantai*) of the Dravidian movement, who is reverentially referred to as

Periyār (the great one) by his followers and admirers. Perhaps more than any single individual, Ramasami has had the greatest influence, by their own reckoning, on the lives of large numbers of Tamil's devotees, especially those who write in the Dravidianist idiom. Indeed, in a literary culture given to extravagant adulation and excess, praise of Ramasami is only surpassed by praise of Tamil (Pulamaidasan 1975). To quote a typical example:

> You were the courageous one
> in the group that sought
> the welfare of southern people.
>
> . . . .
>
> You mastered and embraced
> the British language
> as the language of science.
>
> You blocked the ascent of Hindi
> that had gained a place
> in the life of my people.
>
> You are the king who rises up
> if Tamils anywhere suffer.
>
> . . . .
>
> You, who always think
> about developing fair Tamil
>
> . . . .
>
> You . . . came as a son
> so fair Tamil could flourish.
> (quoted in Richman 1997: 198, 204)

It is ironic that his admirers wrote verses such as this, for the subject of all this adulation had very little patience with a literary form like poetry. Even more ironically, beginning in the 1940s if not earlier, Ramasami launched a sustained attack on the passionate attachment to Tamil that was the binding glue of the devotional community; in the 1950s, he even referred to the language as "primitive" and "barbaric" (Nannan 1993: 52, 138–50; E. V. Ramasami 1960: 10–11). This attack peaked in the early 1960s when he published a polemical pamphlet provocatively entitled *Tāyppāl Paittiyam* (Madness over mother's milk), in which he boldly satirized the hallowed figure of Tamiḻttāy (E. V. Ramasami 1962: 7–17). Nevertheless, devotees who are admirers of Ramasami strategically overlook his denial of Tamil and present him instead as its "savior"—even as one of Tamiḻttāy's true sons. Indeed, because so many of them profess to be rationalists and atheists, they can no longer call upon Hindu deities to grant protection to their adored subject, Ramasami; instead, they turn to Tamil or Tamiḻttāy to do so. Typically, praise poetry on Ramasami begins with praise of Tamil. For Tamiḻttāy's devotees, he is one of their own, and one of hers, as well.

And yet all along, Ramasami vigorously resisted being thus appropriated into the Tamil devotional community; hence my characterization of him as "anti-devotee." So, for instance, in July 1939 at a public meeting in Coimbatore, he announced:

> The chairman says I have great devotion for our mother tongue, Tamil. He also said that I toil hard for it. . . .
>
> I do not have any devotion for Tamil, either as mother tongue or as the language of the nation. I am not attached to it because it is a classical language, or because it is an ancient language, or because it was the language spoken by Shiva, or the language bestowed upon us by Agastya. . . . Such an attachment and devotion is foolish. I only have attachment to those things that have qualities that have utility. I do not praise something just because it is my language or my land or my religion or because it is something ancient.[45]

Here, in one sweep, he vigorously set himself in opposition to every assertion made by the devout, across the various regimes of *tamiḻp-paṟṟu,* over the past half century. Indeed, in contrast to its devotees who imagined Tamil as a person—their goddess, their mother, even their beloved lover—Ramasami represented it as a worldly object: an instrument (*cātaṉam*) for communicating one's thoughts, a tool (*karuvi*) for expressing ideas. The greatness of a language, he wrote, lay in the ease with which one could express thoughts in and through it, and the efficiency with which one could learn it; its usefulness lay in its appropriateness for any community's conditions for existence, its compatibility with the environment, and so on (Anaimuthu 1974: 963–69; Kothandaraman 1979). So, in his 1939 speech in Coimbatore, he conceded that if he had any affection (*aṉpu*) at all for Tamil, it is because it had some use for its speakers. Over the following decades, he became less willing to make even this concession. Mudiyarasan recalls that at the Language Teachers Conference in 1948 over which Ramasami presided, he scribbled the words "Down with Tamil" on a piece of paper lying on the table; contrary to the spirit of the conference, Ramasami declared in his own speech, "First, Tamil has to die. . . . Only English should reign. It is only then that the Tamilian will improve" (Mudiyarasan n.d.: 42–43). Ramasami himself wrote a few years later that when he made a similar point at another public meeting, some Tamil "fanatics" (*moḻi veṟiyar*) asked him whose son he was. Ramasami replied that if speaking English meant that Tamilians were children of the British, then they should also give up using other "English" products such as the radio and the telephone (E. V. Ramasami 1962: 6–7).

Indeed, in his editorials of early 1967, which were surely a commentary on recent happenings in the state, convulsed as it had been by anti-Hindi protests, he wrote: "In our land today, those who have no other means of survival invoke Tamil in order to survive. They declare in frenzy that 'Tamil has to be protected; We will labor for Tamil; We will give up our lives for Tamil.' . . . The people [of this land] should not be fooled by this. . . . How can people who live in modern times be seized by this language madness (*moḻi paittiyam*)? The madness over language is like the madness over caste and religion" (Anaimuthu 1974: 983, 1001).

"Why should we get into a frenzy over language?" This was an interesting question to raise at a time when so many had claimed, and acted on the premise, that a life without Tamil was a life not worth living. In the numerous self-reflections that Ramasami offers on his life, "service to Tamil," that driving imperative of Tamil's devotees, hardly figures at all—yet another reason for characterizing him as "anti-devotee." Instead, the burning passion of his life, as he himself declared on many occasions, was to put an end to caste exploitation: specifically, to Brahman denigration of, and domination over, the "non-Brahman," Dravidian populace (S. Chidambaranar 1971: ix–xxxi, 15–20). It is caste and religion that were his central concerns for most of his life, not language. As he declared in the 1950s, "language is not so important for man" (E. V. Ramasami 1962: 1).

Not surprisingly, unlike any of its devotees, Ramasami makes no claims to have labored for Tamil. Born in 1879 into a middle-class merchant family in Erode, by his own reckoning he was a rebellious young man, going against the wishes of his orthodox parents on more than one occasion. He dropped out of school—not driven out by poverty, as was the case with so many of Tamil's devotees, but by choice—and started working for his father. It was not until 1915, when he was in his thirties, that he began to involve himself in civic activities; and here, too, unlike many in the devotional community, his interest lay in local politics, and increasingly in anticolonial politics. By 1920, after serving for two years as chairman of the Erode municipality, he joined the Congress, and by all accounts he ardently threw himself into promoting the end of untouchability, the virtues of *khadi* (homespun) and teetotalism, and other such staples of Gandhian nationalism. In 1924, he led a campaign in Vaikom (in present-day Kerala) to demand the rescinding of rules prohibiting Untouchables from access to roads near the local temple. He received the sobriquet *Vaikkam Vīrar,* "hero of Vaikom," for his efforts, and this campaign also consolidated his growing reputation as a man who was radically opposed to Brahmanical privilege and caste exploitation (S. Chidambaranar 1971: 1–88; Visswanathan 17–66).

Soon after, in 1925–26, he parted from the Congress, dissatisfied with the party's Brahmanical predilections, the most recent illustration of which was its support of separate dining facilities for Brahman students in Subramania Aiyar's Tamil school in Sheramadevi (discussed earlier). Over the next few years, he began to drift towards the Justice Party, the premier organization that represented "non-Brahman" interests in the Presidency, although there were considerable differences between its conservative, elite agenda and Ramasami's own rationalist, atheist, iconoclastic imperatives that found expression in the Self-Respect movement he spearheaded from this time on. He also founded, and often acted as editor of, a number of controversial and radical newspapers and journals, such as the *Kuṭi Aracu, Viṭutalai, Revolt,* and so on, publications which reportedly had a transformative influence on so many of Tamil's devotees. And yet his own writings are marked by the absence of the literary flourishes and the erudite citations from ancient Tamil literature that characterize devotional writings; on the contrary, Ramasami appears to have taken an almost perverse pleasure in using colloquialisms, *koccaittamiḻ* (unrefined Tamil), even what some would consider vulgarisms. Ironically, or perhaps deliberately, the Tamil that he employed in his writings was inflected with Sanskrit, his polemical attacks against the language notwithstanding.

Ramasami's involvement in activities related to Tamil began in the 1930s (Nannan 1993: 11–14). In 1934–35, in essays he published in *Pakuttaṟivu* and *Kuṭi Aracu,* he called for reform and rationalization of the Tamil script in order to make it more serviceable in printing and typewriting. Although not the first person to call for such a reform, nevertheless he was among the earliest to demonstrate by example: his publications began to use a modified version of the script that was eventually officially adopted by the Tamilnadu state in 1978. In the 1940s and 1950s, Ramasami also supported the demand for use of Tamil in temple worship, the Tamil music (*tamiḻ icai*) movement, the call for renaming Madras state Tamilnadu, the protests over better pay for

Tamil teachers, and all other such causes that were so dear to Tamil's followers (Anaimuthu 1974: 959–63; Kothandaraman 1979; Nambi Arooran 1980: 167–68; Velu and Selvaraji 1989).

Of course, his reputation and fame as devotee of Tamil rests on his spirited opposition to Hindi and on his vigorous leadership of the anti-Hindi movement from the late 1930s through the 1960s. Indeed, as early as 1926, long before the opposition to the language had grown among scholars as well as the general populace, he insisted that Hindi was being favored politically, pedagogically, and financially by the Brahman-dominated Congress party at the expense of Tamil (E. V. Ramasami 1985). Over the next few decades, he vigorously flooded newspapers and magazines with powerful, and often colorful, arguments against the language; led numerous campaigns for picketing government offices, schools teaching Hindi, and business establishments run by North Indians; tarred over Hindi names on official boards in railway stations and post offices; burned the Constitution of India and the national map; and was arrested on numerous occasions for all his efforts. His admirers mention that in this process, not only did he instill Tamil consciousness into the hitherto "sleeping" Dravidian masses, but he was also responsible for politicizing women and drawing them into the Tamil cause.

Through all this, Ramasami paradoxically maintained that he was speaking out against Hindi not because he was a devotee of Tamil, but because he saw Hindi as an agent of continuing Aryan, Brahman, Sanskritic, North Indian imperialism. During the 1930s, he was willing to concede that given their other choices—the irrational and ritualistic Sanskrit, and the "backward" Hindi—Tamilians were much better off with Tamil (Anaimuthu 1974: 968–69, 1763–825). But from the 1940s, even as he was leading the fight against Hindi, he also attacked the enormous political, symbolic, and emotional investment in Tamil made by so many of his fellow Tamil-speaking Dravidians. He ridiculed neo-Shaiva attempts to divinize the language, declaring that if Tamil society had to progress, and if Tamil had to take its place among the modern languages of the world, its intimate ties with religion had to be severed. What use was it to declare that Tamil emerged from Shiva's drum or that it could magically create a woman out of some old bones, as some of its devotees were wont to do, when the language did not have the capacity to express rational thought? he asked with brutal realism (Anaimuthu 1974: 969, 976–77; E. V. Ramasami 1960).

While he was willing to go along with the contestatory classicist and

Dravidianist claim that Tamil was more ancient than and a superior language to Sanskrit, he questioned the wisdom of the proposition that the salvation of modern Tamil speakers lay in a return to the imagined perfect past of their Caṅkam poems. And here, his growing disparagement of Tamil was matched only by his utter scorn for its high literature, whose "classicality" its devotees had so painstakingly constructed over the past few decades. Instead, he insisted that all of Tamil literature—with the possible exception of the *Tirukkuṟaḷ*—was tainted with Sanskritic ritualism, casteism, gender inequalities, and irrational follies, arguing that it was the very means by which Tamilians had been, and would continue to be, enslaved to Aryanism (Anaimuthu 1974: 959–1002; Nambi Arooran 1980: 164–66; E. V. Ramasami 1960).

But above all, Ramasami attacked the feminization of Tamil as a mother figure, that construct so dear to the Indianist and Dravidianist imaginations. What is this "obstinacy" over the mother tongue when the language spoken by our mothers is itself so problematic? he demanded. "Having given birth to us, if our mother left us in the house of a Telugu speaker or a Muslim, would we not start to speak in Telugu or Urdu? Just because our mother spoke Tamil does that mean that Tamil will spurt from us all by itself?" Moreover, can the baby talk that mothers use with their infants be used by us as adults? Is this not utter foolishness? he asked (Anaimuthu 1974: 969).

Ramasami thus deconstructed the metaphorical construct of the "mother tongue" to reveal what it was, after all—a metaphor; and in general, there was a remarkable absence in his writings of references to Tamiḻttāy, "mother's milk," "mother tongue," and all such staples of *tamiḻppaṟṟu*. This is not surprising, for as he asked in his provocative pamphlet, *Tāyppāl Paittiyam* (Madness over mother's milk), why is it that Tamilians insist, as if they were "children," that they would only live on their mother's milk, Tamil: " 'Mother's milk is superior' only if the mother's milk has power (*cakti*) and substance (*cattu*). When the mother, Tamil, is herself without substance and diseased, how could the child who drinks her milk improve? The mother's milk will be strong only if the mother herself is well-nourished. Is Tamil well-nourished?" (E. V. Ramasami 1962: 9–10).

Contrary to so many of her devotees who proposed that imbibing Tamiḻttāy's milk cultivated in the Tamil speaker the true "Tamil" qualities of virtue and chastity, heroism and self-respect, Ramasami argued that Tamilians who had been content with drinking her milk were diseased with irrationalism, superstition, and traditionalism, so much so that one recoiled from the nasty odor of religiosity and orthodoxy that emanated from them. He went on to propose that if Tamilians took to drinking "bottled milk," that is, English, they would gain in fortitude, independence, and rationality (E. V. Ramasami 1962: 10–12). As in his antireligious and anticlassicist arguments against devotional claims, he invoked the power of modern science and rationalism to undermine the "irrational" follies of its devotees' attachment to Tamil:

> If Tamiḻttāy offers her milk for scientific examination, it will be proven that there is nothing in it that provides strength or fortitude to the body, and the reality of mother's milk will be revealed. Is it not appropriate that those who praise the virtues of mother's milk should tell us what its constituents are that supposedly contribute to our well-being? Instead of so doing, they have turned . . . mother's milk into a capital resource with which they have deluded the people.
>
> (E. V. Ramasami 1962: 12–13)

The pamphlet ends by announcing that through deploying the trope of mother's milk to stir the gullible Tamilians' devotion to their language, Tamil devotees had only succeeded in turning them into fools. This, Ramasami concluded, was "the real fruit of mother's milk."

Ramasami's most vehement statements about the "madness" over Tamiḻttāy, or the "barbarism" of Tamil, were made in the 1950s and 1960s, when the DMK was riding the crest of the popular and political wave in the state by projecting itself as the guardian of the language. In 1949, that party had split off from Ramasami's DK, which he had created in 1944 out of the ashes of the defunct Justice Party (of which he had been president since 1938). The ostensible occasion for the split was Ramasami's (second) marriage, at seventy, to Maniyammai, a party worker forty or so years younger than him; the marriage was denounced as a betrayal of Ramasami's own dearly held principles. But other ideological differences had accumulated between Ramasami and Annadurai, his able lieutenant of many years, including their varying stances on Dravidian and Indian nationalisms, Brahmanism, and electoral politics. As the DMK became more and more vigorous in its espousal of the Tamil cause, Ramasami took an alternate route. After 1953, he even backed the Congress in spite of that party's reputation as "anti-Tamil," a reputation that Ramasami himself had helped establish in earlier years (Barnett 1976: 56–84). He also called upon Tamil speakers to abandon Tamil and to embrace English, at one point even urging, "Speak with your wives and children and servants in English! Give up your infatuation with Tamil (*tamiḻp paittiyam*). . . . Try and live like human beings!" (Anaimuthu 1974: 989). Where the DMK was willing to concede the usefulness of English in the public sphere, Ramasami insisted that even in the private, intimate space of their homes, Tamilians should abandon their "mother" and adopt English—a stunning repudiation of a fundamental devotional premise.

Yet it would be a mistake to reduce Ramasami's iconoclastic pronouncements on Tamil to the shifting vagaries of electoral and party politics alone. His dismay over Tamil-speaking Dravidians' preoccupation with their language cannot be separated from his dominant ideological and political objective through much of the 1940s and early 1950s—the creation of a separate Dravidian nation, in opposition to the Indian nation (M. S. S. Pandian 1993). He argued that their ethnic/racial identity as "Dravidians" was, and should be, more important to Tamilians than their linguistic identity as speakers of Tamil. Unlike language—which he insisted could be picked up today and dropped tomorrow—the bond of blood was durable and distinctive. And yet, paradoxically, he had as encompassing a vision of Tamil as so many of its devotees, for in making his case for a "Dravidian nation," he suggested there was no distinction between Tamil and the other Dravidian languages: "Some of our pandits declare that these four languages emerged from one, that they are four sisters that were borne by one mother's womb. This is utter nonsense. There was only one daughter who was given birth to by Tirāviṭattāy [Mother Dravida], and her name is Tamil. We have given it four different names, because the language is spoken in four different places. *But in all four places, it is Tamil that is spoken*" (E. V. Ramasami 1948: 30, emphasis mine). So, for Ramasami, "Dravidian is Tamil, Tamil is Dravidian"—a sentiment that led him to deny the existence of the non-Tamil languages and their speakers as autonomous entities, and enabled his imagination of a unitary Dravidian nation.

Why did Tamil's devotees absorb Ramasami into their ranks, despite his stunning disparagement of their object of devotion? They lionized him for his leadership of the anti-Hindi struggle: since so much of *tamiḻppaṟṟu* from the 1930s defined itself in its opposition to Hindi, it follows that Ramasami's catalytic role in these protests bestowed the aura of a Tamil devotee on him. Moreover, for all his numerous slippages, contradictions, and turnabouts in politics, Ramasami consistently and fiercely opposed Brahmanism, Aryanism, and Sanskrit. Since so much of the devotional community was itself animated by such an opposition, he is seen as a fellow traveller in their own struggle against these forces.

Further, Ramasami's fundamental ideological and political commitment to restore the "self-respect" and rights of Dravidians resonated with the devotees' own efforts to reinstate the lost privileges and honor of Tamil.

But above all, I would maintain that this most undevoted "Tamilian" was ensnared by the inexorable logic of *tamilpparru*. In that logic, there is no other subject-position available to someone like Ramasami other than that of "devotee of Tamil." For, as the century progressed and especially as the Dravidianist idiom came to hold sway over the devotional community, a "Tamilian" or "Dravidian" had to be, by definition, a devotee of Tamil; no other ways of being were possible. As one of the founding fathers of the Dravidian movement, Ramasami's status as paradigmatic "Tamilian" was sacrosanct; it could not, and indeed should not, be interrogated. Inevitably, this meant that if he had to retain that status, he had to be converted into a *tamil anpar,* a devotee of Tamil. His protests notwithstanding, the devotional community appropriated this maverick individual and rendered him, like many others, into a subject of Tamil.

CHAPTER SIX

Conclusion

Tamil Subjects

With the analytic of devotion based on the Tamil word *paṟṟu,* and with the help of Tamilttāy, I set out to write the language question in colonial and post-colonial Tamil India differently, as a history that is not a rehearsal of Europe's linguistic nationalism(s). My attempt to write such a history, organized around the concept of language devotion with attention to notions of love, labor, and life at the service of Tamil, has certainly followed my desire not to hastily empty the culturally specific and contingent into a ready-made narrative of language-and-nationalism. But just as surely, I *had* to attempt a different history, because Tamil's own devotees have insisted from the turn of the century that there is literally nothing else in the world like their language; there is no one else like their Tamilttāy. Yet, in so insisting, and in conducting a whole range of activities around such a conviction, they recast their language in a manner that robs it of its putative exceptionalism. Tamil's singularity and uniqueness are constituted by demonstrating that it is a "divine" language, like Sanskrit, and just as "classical" as Greek and Latin. Most important, Tamil is presented to its speakers, for the first time in its long history, as a "mother tongue," just like the languages of modern Europe. Despite considerable effort to endow her with a distinctive and different persona, even their beloved Tamilttāy seems like other modern icons of the nation such as Bhārata Mātā and Britannia, when she does not resemble the mother-goddesses of conventional Hinduism.

Which is why this history of Tamil devotion is almost the same even when it is not quite, to paraphrase Homi Bhabha: in the process of talking and writing eloquently about their love and devotion for their language, Tamil's devotees, who were colonial subjects after all, began to subscribe to the reigning certitudes of linguistic nationalism. In their narratives, as in those of Herder or Fichte, the state of the language mirrors the state of its speakers; language is the essence of their culture, the bearer of their traditions, and the vehicle of their thoughts from time immemorial. It holds the key to their social solidarity and to their political health and fortunes:

> National life and national progress depend upon the development of the language of a people. A study of the language of a nation reveals to us their social status, their moral and intellectual progress, their inner life, their spiritual and religious advancement, their political problems and aspirations, their love of science and arts, their commercial intercourse, their assimilation of foreign ideas and ideals, and finally, among other things, their place in the scale of nations. . . . [T]he future salvation of our country entirely depends upon our improving our vernacular tongue.[1]

It is clear from this statement that Tamil's devotees also become subscribers to the patrimonial imagination ushered in by colonial modernity, in which language is constituted as a tangible, material possession of its speakers. Like other kinds of property, its value and worth could be enhanced by not allowing it to decline, by continuing to develop it, and by preventing others from encroaching upon it. The life of Tamil and the lives of its speakers as a community are now imagined as inextricably intertwined in a way that they had never been before in the land in which the language had been spoken for at least two thousand years. Not least, in Tamil India as well as in Europe, this patrimonial imagination was supplemented by the conviction that language is "the improver no less than the improved" (Spadafora 1990: 196). As in other parts of colonial India, many literate Tamil speakers were convinced that their society was in a state of total decline. Taking the cue from their colonial masters, they offered numerous solutions for its "improvement": most notably, the rationalization of religion; the abolition of caste consciousness; the spread of modern, scientific education; and the "reform" of women. For its devotees, subjects of the modern linguistic imagination, the primary solution lay in their language, identified through their discursive practices as the source of antiquity, autonomy, and authenticity of its speakers, who are imagined as a singular community and a potential nation unto themselves. So, from the turn of this century, Tamil's adherents offered *tamiḻpparṟu* as a liberating force to their fellow speakers. Energized by their devotion to their language, its speakers would be able to right all wrongs and set themselves on the road to prosperity and well-being.

Though conducted around a language bearing the singular name "tamiḻ," *tamiḻpparṟu* nevertheless produces an entity that is multiply imagined and contrarily fashioned. In certain contexts, Tamil is constituted in religious terms as a "divine" language favored by the gods themselves; in other cases, it is secularly imagined as a "classical" tongue, the parent of the languages of the world and the progenitor of one of its most ancient "civilizations," if not the oldest. For the devotional community as a whole, however, Tamil is increasingly "mother tongue"—the language of their mothers, their homes, and their childhood. Even here, there are differences between those who imagine Tamil as part of a larger "family" of "mother tongues," harmoniously coexisting within the framework of the Indian nation, and those who emphatically assert that it is the one and only mother/tongue to which its speakers owe total and unconditional allegiance, the language of their (Tamil) nation.

Given these varying conceptions, what appeared as a relatively straightforward agenda for "reviving" the language in order to "improve" its speakers splintered into various projects at odds with each other. Thus the "community" of devotees is shot through with difference: there were those who invested their efforts in forming associations, convening revivalist conferences, and running journals that disseminated knowledge about "divine" and "classical" Tamil among the populace; there were others who pragmatically focused on promoting its study as "mother tongue" in schools and colleges, and on its adoption as the language of government, politics, and public communication; and finally, there were the "warriors" in the trenches, willing to give up their lives to protect the integrity of their beloved language. I have also suggested that these varying devotional imaginings about the language frequently clashed with the imperatives of the modern state. In the latter's bureaucratic-rationalist perspective, Tamil is an instrument and tool for governing a modern populace. But as we have seen, for its ardent followers Tamil is not merely an inanimate object but a near and dear person, their personal goddess, their compassionate mother, and their beloved lover. Increasingly from the 1950s, as many of its devotees gained political power, and even held the highest political office in the state by the late 1960s, these very contrary imaginations about Tamil came to a head, producing a series of language policies that can claim some success but are also marked by numerous contradictions, even failure.

The vast scholarly literature on language, nationalism, and modernity has rightly recognized the various strategies through which languages have been linguistically transformed through rationalization and standardization, especially through the interventions of the state and its agencies. But much less attention has been paid to the structures of sentiments in which languages come to be embedded in the new people-centered ideologies of modernity. With the analytic of devotion, I have tracked the myriad ways in which Tamil came to be subjected to the love, loyalty, and reverence of those who claimed to be its devotees. Instead of assuming, as its speakers (and scholars) are wont to do, that attachment to a language, imagined in primordial terms as the "mother tongue," is natural and inevitable, I have argued that it is produced under specific historical conditions, and as such is subject to negotiation and change. Correspondingly, the power that a language exercises over its speakers, as indeed the passions that it elicits, is ideologically produced and historically contingent. Unless we pay attention to such structures of sentiment and regimes of love that coalesce around languages, it is very difficult, even impossible, to explain why and how they acquire the ability to arouse their speakers to rally around their cause, to the point of surrendering body, life, and spirit.

The linchpin in the ideologies of devotion which emerged around Tamil is the construct of "mother tongue," a label that was appropriated for the language for the first time in the closing decades of the nineteenth century and is an expression of the regimes of mimicry spawned by colonial rule everywhere. And yet, as this most European of terms played itself out in Tamil India, it was subversively taken apart not just to reveal the convergence between "language" and "motherhood" that went into its constitution in the first place, but also to mobilize all the emotive and sentimental powers that had come to be associated with the mother figure by the end of the nineteenth century. Thus one of its devotees asked of his fellow speakers in 1918, "Do you love your own mother? Then you must surely love your mother tongue" (Devasikhamani 1919: 26–27). Another, speaking to other women in 1938, reminded them that "forgetting [our] mother tongue is akin to forgetting [our] mother" (Nilambikai n.d.: 21). Such statements are not surprising, for Tamil's adherents insist that they did "not refer to their language as mother tongue for rhetorical reasons" (K. Appadurai 1944:

20); rather, "my knowledge of Tamil is my mother's gift. For that reason, Tamil is my mother tongue" (Sivagnanam 1974: 868). In the writings of Tamil's devotees, *tamiḻ*, *tāymoḻi* (mother tongue), *tāyppāl* (mother's milk), and *tāy* (mother) all shade into each other. It is in this context that the figure of Tamiḻttāy assumes significance. Neither ubiquitous nor routinized in their discourses, her devotees strategically deployed Tamiḻttāy at crucial moments to draw the attention of speakers of Tamil to the plight of their language: to elicit their passions, filial and otherwise, to cajole them to place their bodies and lives at the service of Tamil. And all such deployments, once again, drew upon the new emotive powers that had come to be invested in motherhood. For, while her devotees may insist that she is an ancient and time-honored figure, I have argued that Tamiḻttāy is essentially a modern being, erupting within the regimes of *tamiḻppaṟṟu* as a consequence of laminating the domain of "motherhood" onto that of "language" in late colonial India.

As the figure of the mother came to be reconfigured as a sign of the authentic, pure community, and as a metonym for "the people," and as the language they spoke was configured as the bearer of the true soul, spirit, and genius of the "community" of its speakers within the ideologies of modernity, the motherhood of language was fashioned into a weapon to contend with both British colonialism *and* Indian nationalism. In repeated circulation through the discursive activities of *tamiḻppaṟṟu,* the motherness of Tamil acquires a material presence in the lifeworld of Tamil speakers that has rendered it natural, and hence inviolable. As recently as 1990, schoolchildren in Tamilnadu were told in an essay entitled "Devotion to Mother Tongue," which appears in their seventh-grade textbook published by the government:

> "Motherland" and "mother tongue" are concepts that have a relationship to "mother." Our mother tongue captures our inner sentiments and shows them to us. It is language that distinguishes humans from animals. The mother tongue is the language with which one speaks with the mother who rears and raises us from the time of birth. The mother is the first acquaintance of the child, and it is through her that the child recognizes others as well. *Just as the child has great devotion towards its mother, similarly, all of us, too, must have devotion towards our mother tongue.*
>
> (Government of Tamilnadu 1990: 49, emphasis mine)

Statements like these serve to remind its speakers of Tamil's status as their mother, lest they forgot this in its naturalization as "mother tongue." *Tamiḻppaṟṟu* constitutes the motherness of Tamil within a context in which both their mothers and their language had been rendered foundational for the very existence of Tamil speakers as a community.

Today, there are many who continue to lament that a century of devotional activities notwithstanding, Tamil has not "improved" and is far from being the language of prestige, profit, and power that *tamiḻp-paṟṟu* intends for it. In the words of a contemporary poet, Tamiḻttāy continues to wear feathers, not ornaments (Kailasapathy 1986: 49). The rhetoric of decline that marked so many a devotional narrative in the colonial period continues to plague post-colonial discourses as well, as does the lament of critics who insist that Tamil devotion is misplaced to start with, and that "wallowing in sentimentalism" about Tamil is not really going to bring about fundamental transformations in the lives of its speakers (Ramaswamy 1992b: 421–28). And yet, if Tamil's devotees had accompanied the anthropologist Jacob Pandian in the early 1970s to a high school in Pulicat, outside Madras city, they would have undoubtedly been pleased with the responses of the teenage students there to his questions about their allegiance to Tamil. Early in the century, few had studied Tamil or known much about its history or culture; but these students echoed many of the ideas that the devotional community had been circulating over the past few decades. One of them, a young man of seventeen, even proclaimed, "There is everything in Tamil, and learning Tamil will make me possess everything I require. If any danger threatens my mother tongue, I will give my life to protect it. My life is interwoven with my mother tongue." Another, age sixteen, maintained that "more than caste, religion, and country I love Tamil. Tamil is one of the greatest languages." A Brahman student, whose mother tongue was officially Telugu, nevertheless insisted, "I consider Tamil as my mother tongue. . . . The culture of India is better than any other cultures of the world. . . . Tamil culture is the greatest in India." A sixteen-year-old Muslim student similarly said, "I know a little Urdu which is considered the language of Muslims, but I like only Tamil and my love for Tamil is increasing day by day. . . . [T]he ancient Tamil kings, Chera, Chola, and Pandya protected Tamil as though Tamil was their mother" (J. Pandian 1987: 151–64).

In addition to these young voices, there are other signs that Tamil has left its mark on the political and cultural landscape of contemporary Tamilnadu. Since Indian independence, and especially since the late 1960s, the state has pursued policies that are informed, if only rhetorically, by the devotional belief that Tamil is everything. Districts, cities, urban streets, state corporations, and the like have been renamed over the past decades after Tamil historical figures, litterateurs, and devotees, inspired by Bharatidasan's lament that "in the Tamil streets of the Tamil land, there is no Tamil," as well as by Bharati's demand that "the sound of Tamil ought to thunder in its streets." Grand state-sponsored architectural projects have recreated scenes from the Tamil literary and historical past. Statues of famous poets and devotees adorn city squares, public buildings, and beachfronts. Efforts to Tamilize, following normative models drawn from literature and history, are not limited to the physical landscape of Tamilnadu. In their private lives as well, many Tamil speakers have taken to adopting personal names, conducting marriages and funerals, and celebrating festivals and rituals in what is identified as the authentic Tamil way. Such activities supplement other efforts to Tamilize the public domain: today, the language of government is Tamil; the medium of education in state schools and colleges is Tamil; and television, radio, and other technologies of mass communication are in Tamil. Admittedly, the language does not have sole reign in public—it shares space with both English and Hindi; nevertheless, its presence is by no means insignificant.

Statistics generated by the colonial government in the first half of the century show a steady increase in the volume of Tamil print activity, especially in fields such as literature, religion, and the sciences. The post-colonial state in its annual administrative reports has regularly carried announcements of the steady progress of Tamil in educational and administrative domains; of the establishment of Tamil universities and academies; of the publication of new scientific and administrative glossaries, dictionaries, encyclopedias, and school and college textbooks; and so forth. Indeed, no less a critic than Annadurai was able to declare in 1945 at a public meeting held in Annamalai University: "Today, Tamilnadu welcomes all those poets who labor for Tamil, and sing for it. . . . [W]herever one goes, one hears Tamil. . . . Even those who vowed that they would only speak English, now claim that they will only speak in Tamil, write in Tamil, think in Tamil. . . . [W]e can see Tamil literature, Tamil plays, Tamil music everywhere. Even those who yesterday refused are beginning today to declare that they are 'Tamilian' (*tamiḻar*)" (Annadurai 1968: 12–13).

Why is Annadurai so pleased that speakers of Tamil are at last declaring themselves "Tamilian"? A year later, K. A. P. Viswanatham wrote in an editorial: "Westerners refer to the Tamilian as 'Black Man.' His neighbors refer to him as 'Indian.' Aryans call him 'Dravidian,' and Brahmans, 'Shudra.' At the time of the *Veda*s, he was referred to as '*arakkar*' [demon]. Members of the Justice Party called him 'non-Brahman,' and for the Government, he is a 'non-Muslim.' . . . When there is no one to refer to the Tamilian as 'Tamilian,' will at least the Tamilian call himself 'Tamilian'?"[2] Why was this so important for Viswanatham? And why is it that one of the chief government buildings in Madras city carries the message, boldly emblazoned across its facade, "Declare yourself a Tamilian! Stand proudly, your head held high!"? What is at stake in making such a claim?

My attempt to answer this question begins with the proposition that as the language they speak becomes subject to the discourse(s) of *tamiḻp-paṟṟu,* its speakers become subjects of Tamil, their state of subjection reflected in the terms *tamiḻ-aṉ,* "Tamilian" (lit., "he-of-Tamil"), or *tamiḻ-ar,* "Tamilians" (lit., "they-of-Tamil"). Admittedly the category of *tamiḻaṉ* is an old one, and its presence in literary sources has been traced back by some scholars to at least the late first millennium (Krishnan 1984: 145–46). Nevertheless, I would insist that it assumes significance in political and social discourses only with the consolidation of the people-centered and patrimonial ideologies of language ushered in by modernity. From the turn of this century, discussions of what to do about improving Tamil have been invariably accompanied by the question, "Who is a Tamilian?" or "Who are the Tamilians?" The question is repeatedly posed, and answers repeatedly sought, because at stake is the production and definition of the modern Tamil subject. Today, in the various human sciences, not only is the concept of subject widely deployed, but there is a proliferating literature on what it means to be a subject, on the various processes of subjection, on subjectivity or the state of being a subject, and so on. Paul Smith comments on this state of affairs:

> Over the last ten or twenty years [these] discourses have adopted this term, the "subject," to do multifarious theoretical jobs. In some instances the "subject" will appear to be synonymous with the "individual," the "person." In others—for example, in psychoanalytical discourse—it will take on a more specialized meaning and refer to the unconsciously structured illusion of plenitude which we usually call "the self." Or elsewhere, the "subject" might be understood as the specifically subjected *object* of social and historical forces and determinations.
>
> (Smith 1988: xxvii)

It is this last sense of the "subject"—as the "specifically subjected object of social and historical forces"—that I draw upon here in my discussion of the notion of the "Tamilian" in Tamil devotional discourses. *Tamilpparru,* I suggest, divides the world into two: those who are Tamilians and those who are not. Speakers of Tamil are evaluated, and then transformed—*if* they qualify—through the discursive practice(s) of *tamilpparru* into *tamilar,* "Tamilians," their beings and subjectivities inevitably and necessarily bound to the language. This process of subjection, moreover, proceeds categorically, epistemologically, and ontologically.

Categorically speaking, the *tamilan* is the entity who is cajoled, even compelled, into being, as we see in the statements of Annadurai and Viswanatham, by *tamilpparru.* He—and it is always "he"; the term itself is gendered masculine—is the principal addressee and interlocutor in all its regimes. Minimally, a *tamilan* is one whose "mother tongue" is Tamil. But it is a measure of the multiplicity of conceptions about the language that reigns among its devout that no single definition of the *tamilan* prevails, either. For radical neo-Shaivism, all those Tamil speakers adhering to a (reformed) Shaiva religion and who are not Brahman are the true Tamilians; in classicism, Tamilians are those who are racially Dravidian and historically "the lineal descendants of the original and highly civilized Tamils of pre-Aryan times" (Maraimalai Adigal 1974b: 14). Dravidianism admits into the category all those who claim Tamil as their "mother tongue" and disavow attachment to any other language, especially to Sanskrit and Hindi. Indianism has perhaps the most ambitious logic of subjection at work and admits, like Dravidianism, that Tamilians are those who claim Tamil as their "mother tongue". All the same, it also insists that those who maintain that the Tamil land is their home—"even though their mother tongue may be another"—are also Tamilians (Kalyanasundaranar 1935: 37; Ramalinga Pillai 1953: 55–56; Sivagnanam 1974: 387). Indeed, for some devotees of Tamil, one does not even have to be born a Tamil speaker to become "Tamilian": all those who show desire for Tamil are Tamilians; all those who are devoted to it are also transformed into subjects of Tamil. Thus K. Appadurai refers to the missionary devotees, Caldwell and Pope, as *vellait tamilar* (white Tamilians), and writes:

> I wish to declare that all those who show devotion to Tamil ought to be considered *tamilar.* It gives me great pleasure to include amongst Tamilians all those who come to the Tamil land and learn and use Tamil and turn into devotees of Tamil. . . . If asked who are the Tamilians, we could easily say

> that they are those who reverence Tamiḻttāy. If asked who are the friends of Tamilians, they are the speakers of other languages who wish they could have been borne by Tamiḻttāy's womb.
>
> (K. Appadurai 1944: 11–21)

By the same token, one could be born a speaker of Tamil yet spurn the language, chasing after Sanskrit, English, or Hindi, and hence be disqualified as a Tamilian. This is the plight, of course, of the Brahman, who is not reckoned to be a Tamilian by neo-Shaivism, contestatory classicism, and Dravidianism, which chastise him for not being devoted to Tamil.

Categorically speaking, the modern Tamil subject has also been produced through a disavowal of alternate selves, contrary allegiances, and prior commitments. Tamil's devotees repeatedly insist that a *tamiḻaṉ* is one who, regardless of whether he is Hindu, Muslim, or Christian, claims Tamil as his mother tongue:

> Wherever you may be, whether in Burma, Malaya, Durban, Lanka, or Fiji, you are a Tamilian. Your mother tongue is Tamil. You may be a Hindu, a Muslim, or a Christian at home, in your temples and mosques and churches. There is no objection to that. But in public and on the streets, when asked, "Who are you?," do not say that you are a Brahman or Vellalan or Pillai or Mudaliar or Naidu or Servai, or that you belong to this or that religion. Do not speak with a sectarian mind. "I am a Tamilian. Tamilnadu is mine. Wherever I am, I belong to the Tamil populace." Say so proudly with your head held high!
>
> (Suddhananda Bharati 1938: 111–12)

Thus, in the process of producing the *tamiḻaṉ,* preexisting allegiances are recognized and set aside—in some sectors of the devotional community, even discredited—in favor of declaring one's primary loyalty to Tamil. As Kalyanasundaram reminded his fellow speakers in 1928, "If we wish to bind the people born in this [Tamil] nation into the net of unity, there is only one instrument, and that is the Tamil language. . . . We may be attached to different religions but we cannot forget we are all Tamilians" (Kalyanasundaranar 1935: 25–26). Similarly, a decade later, Shaktidasan Subramanian, a Brahman devotee and who also edited the nationalist newspaper *Navacakti,* insisted: "There is only one *jāti* [lit., "caste"] in Tamilnadu, and that is the Tamil *jāti.* Think of yourself as *tamiḻaṉ*" (S. Subramanian 1939: 5).

As all manner of differences are thus dissolved, and other allegiances rendered illegitimate, the name of the collectivity—*tamiḻar*—becomes one's name, *tamiḻaṉ;* individualities are collapsed into a shared linguistic identity: "If they ask me 'Who are you?,' instead of referring to myself in terms of this or that caste, or this or that religion, I will declare proudly, 'I am a Tamilian.' I will not hate any other Tamilian. Even if another Tamilian hates me, I will transform him through my love" (Suddhananda Bharati 1938: 103–4).

But a *tamiḻaṉ* is a being who is asked not just to set aside his individuality, and contrary allegiances, in favor of being a part of the collectivity of Tamilians; he is also asked to submit himself to the regime of *tamiḻppaṟṟu,* to become a devotee of Tamil. Suddhananda Bharati invited the Tamilian to take the following oath:

> I am a Tamilian; Tamil is my mother tongue. I live only for the betterment of Tamil, of Tamilians, and of Tamilnadu. All my deeds will contribute to the glory of Tamil, of Tamilians, and of Tamilnadu. I will oppose and conquer anything that harms Tamil, Tamilians, and Tamilnadu. I may forget my life, but I will not forget Tamil. They may destroy my body, but I will not forsake Tamil. . . . I live so that I may restore my mother back on her throne as the queen of languages.
>
> (Suddhananda Bharati 1938: 103)

The Tamil speaker thus (re)emerges in this discourse with his entire life project rewritten in terms of Tamil. He is repeatedly called into being, told to arouse himself from his "sleep" and serve his mother/language by Tamilizing himself: by adopting a Tamil name, by speaking and writing and thinking only in Tamil, by marrying only a Tamil woman, by raising his children as true *tamiḻar.* His life is the life of Tamil and, correspondingly, Tamil's life is his life. For, as Bharatidasan reminded his fellow speakers in 1945:

> The progress of our glorious Tamiḻttāy is your progress.
> You should realize this and arouse yourself!
> O young Tamilian, open your eyes!
> . . . .
> Every victory that she attains is your victory!
> . . . .
> Know this! The evil that befalls Tamiḻttāy befalls you as well!
>
> (Bharatidasan 1969: 9–10)

Thus, as far as the ardent devotee of Tamil is concerned, the *tamiḻaṉ* has no existence outside and beyond his mother/tongue, a point I will return to shortly.

The transformation of speakers of Tamil into subjects of Tamil, *tamiḻar,* also takes place epistemologically, as they come under the scrutiny of various modern knowledge practices which provide them with their "history," tell them about their true "culture," find a place for them in the evolution of human "civilization," establish their relationship to other language speakers of the world, and so on. The discourses of *tamilpparru,* as I noted earlier, liberally draw upon the various human sciences of philology, history, ethnology, and archaeology in constructing their structures of devotion to the language. In recent years, there has been considerable discussion of the part played by these sciences in transforming men and women into objects of knowledge, and of the complicity between these (European) knowledge practices and the exercise of colonial power and control (Said 1978). In India, with colonialism came not just the English language and new linguistic habits and cultural dispositions, but new concepts for imagining the world and for securing one's place in that world. At the same time, there was a vigorous renewal of the ancient and the authentic, a revamping of "tradition" which accompanied what Thomas Metcalf (1994) has adroitly characterized as the complex interplay between essential similitude and the enduring difference between themselves and the "natives" that the colonial masters stressed in their various ideologies and institutions of rule. The colonized subject's being is in turn shot through with traces of the archaic and the new, of the "West" and the "Orient," of "tradition" and "modernity."

In producing the Tamil subject who is similarly a melange of the old and the new, Tamil devotionalism thus continues and extends a process already well under way under colonialism. In the (colonizing) knowledges which Tamil's devotees inherited (or appropriated, as the case may be), the Tamilian had already been incorporated into an European and colonial economy of significations that assigned him a linguistic label and a racial category, decided whether he possessed a "history," and determined whether his "culture" was worthy of being classified as a "civilization." In engaging such knowledge practices, if only to counter their assertions, *tamilpparru* further ensnared the Tamilian in this colonial economy of meanings in which it mattered—politically, economically, and psychologically—whether one's language was a "classical" tongue or a mere "vernacular"; whether one's religion was "rational" or "idolatrous"; and whether one possessed "civilization" or was "primitive."

Perhaps nothing illustrates this process of ensnarement better than the troubling category of "Dravidian" to which the *tamilan* has been subjected in colonial ideologies, as well as in the discourse(s) of Tamil devotionalism. As I noted earlier, not all of Tamil's devotees agree to the use of the term "Dravidian" to refer to the Tamilian—and it is important to register the resistance, if only scattered and muted, to the global hegemony of European meanings. Some worried over it because of the negative connotations it had picked up in colonial usage; others insisted that the *tamiḻaṉ* should be identified by a term that indicated his attachment to his language; still others protested that this was not a "Tamil" term at all and that it was foisted on the Tamilian by his colonial masters. Such protests notwithstanding, the notion that the "Tamilian" is a "Dravidian," and distinct from the Sanskrit-speaking "Aryan," has had a long and enduring life in the cultural and political discourses of the region up until today. Most ironically, this has meant that for much of this century, the *tamiḻaṉ* has been subjected to a category that is a Europeanization of a Sanskrit term used in pre-colonial times to refer, often in a derogatory sense, to the peoples of southern India, Brahmans included (M. Srinivasa Aiyangar 1914: 1–6). To paraphrase Kwame Appiah, the overdetermined course of cultural nationalisms in India has been to make real the many imaginary identities to which Europe has subjected it (Appiah 1992: 62). The Dravidianization of the *tamiḻaṉ,* however much it may have been a strategy of empowerment for the disenfranchised and the marginalized, is very much an instance of such an overdetermination.

Last but not least, the *tamiḻaṉ* has been transformed into a subject of Tamil ontologically as well, his very being suffused with the language. Tamil is not just a language that determines his categorical existence and life project from without, but it is also the very life force (*uyir*) that animates him from within. So, Shaktidasan addresses the young *tamiḻaṉ* and asks him to remember: "My mind is filled with Tamil; my life is Tamil; my pulse is Tamil; my veins are Tamil; my blood is filled with Tamil; all my flesh is Tamil" (S. Subramanian 1939: 4). Another devotee echoes this sentiment in verse:

> Tamil abides in me,
> as my flesh
> as my life
> as my life force.
> (quoted in K. Appadurai 1944: 29)

As the language itself is thus corporealized, its speakers come to be Tamilized. The *tamiḻaṉ* is (re)produced substantially as the language becomes part of his very life essence, feeding his consciousness and his spirit. Incorporated as it has been into the body of the *tamiḻaṉ,* and blended as it has with his very life and consciousness, it is impossible to separate Tamil from his being:

> We can turn mountains into pits;
> We can dry up the ocean bed;
> We can fly speedily through the skies.
> . . . .
> We can even bring the dying back to life.
>
> The Tamilian cannot be separated from Tamil
> Even for a moment, by anyone.[3]

This incorporation of the language into the very being of the *tamiḻaṉ* carries tremendous consequences, for in its most passionate moments, *tamiḻpparṟu* certainly instructs Tamil speakers that devotion to their language should supersede devotion to their parents, their spouses, and children; but it also tells them that devotion to their language should transcend attachment to their own bodies and to their own lives. Even when thrown into prison for his participation in the anti-Hindi protests in 1965, the poet Perunchitran was willing to declare:

> When they tell me that
> This body, and all the blood and sinews and feelings that it contains, belongs to Tamiḻttāy and to other *tamiḻar,*
> I lose all my fatigue!
>
> (Perunchitranar 1979: 66)

And decades earlier, the mystic poet Suddhananda Bharati insisted, "I may forget my own life, but I will not forget Tamil. They may destroy my body, but I will not forsake Tamil" (Suddhananda Bharati 1938: 103).

The subjection of the *tamiḻaṉ* to Tamil is complete when he willingly agrees thus to surrender his body, his life, and his soul to his mother/language. And so it came about that in the cool dawn of a January morning in 1964, young Chinnasami burned himself alive, leaving behind a letter in which he declared, "O Tamil! In order that you live, I am going to die a terrible death!" In order to enable Tamil to live and flourish, *tamiḻpparṟu* transforms its speakers, who ought to have been masters of the language, into its subjects, a critical reversal of the patrimonial imagination it inherited from European modernity. Their dearest possession, their language, ends up by possessing its devotees, compelling them to sacrifice to it their body, life, and spirit. It is only fitting that one of Tamil's own has the last word:

There is nothing more precious than life.
However, if any evil befalls you, my glorious Tamiḻttāy!
I will not think that life is precious;
To put an end to your suffering,
I will give up my life.

(Pulavar Kulanthai 1972: 21)

Notes

ABBREVIATIONS

MLAD	*Madras Legislative Assembly Debates*
MLCD	*Madras Legislative Council Debates*
NNR	*Native Newspaper Reports, Madras Presidency*
LSD	*Lok Sabha Debates*
RSD	*Rajya Sabha Debates*
TNLAD	*Tamilnadu Legislative Assembly Debates*

CHAPTER ONE. INTRODUCTION

1. On the cultural politics of language in the colonial period, see Cohn 1985; Kaviraj 1992; Sudhir 1993; and Washbrook 1991. Surveys of language issues in independent India may be found in Ram Gopal 1966 and Brass 1990. For the role of caste, class, and religion in linguistic politics, see Brass 1974; Harrison 1960; and Karat Prakash 1973. The emergence of Hindi to sociopolitical prominence and the crisis of India's national and official language policies are discussed in Dasgupta 1970; King 1994; K. Kumar 1990; Lelyveld 1993; and Nayar 1969.

2. Barnett 1976; Irschick 1969, 1986; Nambi Arooran 1976, 1980; Ramaswamy 1992b; Washbrook 1989.

3. In 1899, Sabapathy Navalar (1844–1903) published his *Tirāviṭa Pirakācikai Eṉṉum Tamiḻ Varalāṟu* (History of Tamil: The Dravidian light), but this work did not explicitly draw upon comparative philology or historical linguistics. It begins with a treatment of Tamil's divine origins, and then surveys its grammatical and literary works on the basis of Tamil's own traditions. Sabapathy's *varalāṟu* is more a "story" of Tamil litterateurs and their work than a

secular "history" of the language, its title notwithstanding (Sabapathy Navalar 1976).

4. Government of Tamilnadu Order No. 1393 (Public), 17 June 1970. Decades before the hymn was authorized as the state prayer song, it was sung at the gatherings of literary societies and revivalist conferences, and included in textbooks. In 1929, M. S. Purnalingam Pillai (1866–1947), a devotee of Tamil who taught English at Madras Christian College and other institutions, and founded and edited the monthly journal *Ñāṉapōtiṉi,* declared (perhaps too enthusiastically) that the hymn "has become a household word among the Tamils and is recited in every Tamil Society [*sic*]" (Purnalingam Pillai 1985: 343). Thaninayagam observes, "The burden of these lines has been a recurrent theme during the last sixty years and has not been superseded even now as the main undertone of patriotic Tamil writing" (Thaninayagam 1963: 3).

5. Some argued that Tamiḻttāy was nothing more than a minor deity and that it was sacrilegious to subordinate the great gods of Hinduism to her. Others wondered whether the state's new prayer song would signal Tamilnadu's intention to separate from the Indian union, and commented on the inappropriateness of singing about Tamiḻttāy in gatherings where there would be non-Tamilians present. There was even concern that Sundaram Pillai's poem ridiculed other languages in its extravagant praise of Tamil. "Is it necessary to praise our own language by debasing others? Is this Tamil culture?" (Karunanidhi 1987: 233–36; Vimalanandam 1971).

CHAPTER TWO. ONE LANGUAGE, MANY IMAGININGS

1. Neo-Shaiva claims to the contrary, the Theosophical Society published large numbers of books and journals in Tamil relating to religion, philosophy, and national regeneration (Nambi Arooran 1980: 58). The Tamil that was promoted, however, was closely linked to Sanskritic and Brahmanical Hinduism. The society also ran Sanskrit schools and had grand plans for initiating a "national Sanskrit movement" (Suntharalingam 1974: 303).

2. For different interpretations of the rise of the "non-Brahman" movement, see Irschick (1969), who presents it as "the articulation of a pre-existing social rivalry between Brahman and non-Brahman" in the context of the spread of western education and competition for jobs; Barnett (1976), who traces it to the social strains and sense of "relative deprivation" suffered by rural "non-Brahman" elites as they moved to colonial cities; Washbrook (1976), who locates it as a direct product of governmental policy and action which interpellated various social groups as "Brahman," "non-Brahman," and the like; and Subramanian, who extends Washbrook to emphasize transformations in the "pre-colonial profile and logic of power and status" which shifted the delicate balance of power in the late colonial period in favor of Brahmans. This, he suggests, produced a reaction among "non-Brahman elites" who had hitherto exercised considerable dominance and privilege, but who now found their new "lowered status in the emergent public sphere defined by colonial law and bureaucracy galling" (N. Subramanian 1993: 114, 104).

3. See also *Centamiḻc Celvi* 41 (1966–67): 457–63.

4. *Centamiḻc Celvi* 46 (1971–72): 153.

5. Tirunelveli South India Shaiva Siddhanta Works Publishing Society; henceforth Shaiva Siddhanta Kazhagam.

6. Indeed Damodaram Pillai's editorial prefaces to these publications between 1881 and 1892, using Western modes of textual criticism, contain some of the earliest gendered conceptions of Tamil, including *tamiḻmātu,* "Lady Tamil"; *tamiḻaṇaṅku,* "Goddess Tamil"; *kaṉṉittamiḻ,* "virgin Tamil"; and more rarely, *tāymoḻi,* "mother tongue." He even suggested that medieval and modern Tamil are the products of the (incestuous) "marriage" between the "virgin" Tamil and the "hero" Sanskrit (Damodaram Pillai 1971: 6, 12, 19, 69, 93–94).

7. In a series of essays written between 1890 and 1895, T. Chelvakesavaroya Mudaliar (1864–1921), who taught Tamil at Pachaiyappa College in Madras, dismissed as fable, and contrary to the truths of philology (*pāṣātattuvaccāttiram*), the belief that Shiva created Tamil (Chelvakesavaroya Mudaliar 1929: 15–16). In another narrative cast in the form of a "dramatic interlude," a philologist (*pāṣainuṟppulavar*) attempts to convince traditional pandits that the belief that the languages of the world emerged from different parts of the lord's body is nothing but fabrication. "God is not necessary for creating a language" (Namasivaya Mudaliar 1910: 60–61).

8. Or consider how the nationalist historian Romesh C. Dutt's much-cited treatise on Indian history, *Ancient India* (1893), was received by one Tamil devotee: "From his work, it is clear, that he has not studied much about the southern people, their condition, civilisation, literature, and language. Thus his work may be fitly entitled 'the Ancient Aryans' rather than 'the Ancient India.' Every step that the migrating Aryans took in the Bharata land [India] is described by him as an *Aryan Conquest*—an expression which has an agreeable sound, but no meaning" (Savariroyan 1900–1901: 106).

9. *The Light of Truth or Siddhanta Deepika* 6 (1902–03): 117–19.

10. *NNR* 11 (1913): 428; 41 (1916): 1739.

11. *NNR* 35 (1917): 2257–58. Another editorial in the same daily (11 February 1916) also insisted that English education "only leads our girls to take to foreign ways of thinking and dressing, and that therefore, instruction should be given to them only through the vernacular" (*NNR* 8 [1916]: 296). See also exchange of views on this issue in *Āṉantapōtiṉi* 8, no. 7 (1923): 263–66; 9, no. 6 (1923): 233–235.

12. *MLCD* 45 (1928): 80–81. The *Madras Mail,* a pro-government newspaper, responded that "the adjective 'vernacular' always meant 'one's own' and to extend it to mean 'a slave's language' or even to 'belonging to a slave' would be gratuitous" (quoted in Nambi Arooran 1980: 109). In 1934, the Madras Presidency Tamilians Conference passed a resolution which declared, "Instead of referring to Tamil—the preeminent language of the world, fully equipped to transmit all kinds of scholarship—as a 'vernacular,' a derogatory term of slavery, we request the university authorities and the government to use the term 'mother tongue' (*Centamiḻc Celvi* 12 [1934–35]: 579). In February 1939, the government of India finally abandoned the term for official use (Nambi Arooran 1980: 109). Barely a month later, when a member in the Madras Legislative Assembly used the term to refer to Indian languages, he was chastised by

the Speaker: "There is no question of vernacular. The word is tabooed on the floor of this House" (*MLAD* 11 [1939]: 597).

13. Devaneyan Pavanar, a devotee whose works are contestatory classicist, lists the following reasons to account for the "Anti-Tamil" biases of the Tamilnadu Congress: "1) Re-Brahmanization of staff in public offices . . . ; 2) Introduction of compulsory Hindi in Tamil Nad against the will of the Tamils; 3) Misrepresentation of Tamil language, literature, and culture by Brahman authors and historians; 4) Rewarding of Sanskrit scholars and promotion of Sanskrit studies at the expense of Tamil; 5) Suppression of Tamil with the help of betrayers and venal professors of Tamil in all ways possible; 6) Prevention of orthodox and genuine Tamil scholars from being appointed to responsible posts in the Tamil department, either of Government or of a University" (Devaneyan 1967: 25–26).

14. Government of Madras Order No. 562 (Education and Public Health), 5 March 1938; Order No. 2438 (Education), 21 November 1960; *MLAD* 44 (1961): 545–614, 63 (1965): 627–28.

15. *MLAD* 29 (1960): 268–80.

16. That the "common man" in Tamilnadu in the 1960s also came increasingly to believe that only the followers of the Dravidian movement "loved" Tamil is clear from Barnett (1976: 161–236).

17. *Kuyil,* 6 December 1960, 6.

18. English transcription of Tamil speech. Government of Madras Order No. 4068 (Home), 23 August 1938.

19. *Kuyil,* 15 April 1962, 1.

20. *Kuyil,* 21 June 1960, 3.

21. *Kuyil,* 17 June 1958, 13.

22. *Kuyil,* 19 May 1959, 5.

23. *Kuyil,* 8 December 1959, 1.

24. Government of Tamilnadu Order No. 1393 (Public), 17 June 1970.

25. *Mālai Maṇi* (*Inti Etirppu Malar*), 7 August 1960, 12 (emphasis mine).

26. *Nam Nāṭu,* 25 February 1967; *Muracoli,* 25 February 1967.

27. *Nam Nāṭu,* 7 April 1967; see also *Nam Nāṭu,* 24 February 1967.

CHAPTER THREE. FEMINIZING LANGUAGE

1. I am indebted here to the marvellous analysis by Helen Hackett of Elizabeth I of England as both "virgin mother" and "maiden queen" (see Hackett 1995).

2. Prior to this, in 1881, Damodaram Pillai had already referred to Tamil as *aṇaṅku* (Damodaram Pillai 1971: 12, 19), and in 1879, Vedanayakam Pillai had invoked her as *araci,* "queen" (Vedanayakam Pillai 1879: 285).

3. *Centamiḻc Celvi* 6 (1928–29): 236–43.

4. See *Centamiḻc Celvi* 4 (1926–27): 296–300; 29 (1954–55): 474–76.

5. *Kuyil,* 2 August 1960, 16.

6. *Intippōr Muracu* 1985: 59.

7. As far back as 1881, Damodaram Pillai made a similar suggestion in his analysis of the historical development of Tamil (1971: 19).

8. *Viṭutalai,* 18 May 1938, 3; *Kuṭi Aracu,* 22 May 1938, cover; *Pakuttaṟivu* 4, no. 2 (June 1938). In his memoirs, Karunanidhi recalls that as a young boy growing up in the Tanjavur suburb of Tiruvarur, he mounted this cartoon on a placard and took it around his small town in a daily procession an effort to mobilize his fellow speakers (1989: 44).

9. *Aṟappōr,* 8 September 1961, 1; *Tiruviḷakku,* 12 February 1965; *Muracoli,* 19 and 29 January, 3 February 1965; *Muttāram,* 15 March 1966; *Kaḻakakkural,* 15 January 1976.

10. *Kuṭi Aracu,* 19 December 1937, 15. The inspiration behind this cartoon appears to have been K. A. P. Viswanatham, a devotee whose writings are a melange of radical neo-Shaivism, contestatory classicism, and Dravidianism. A native of Tiruchirapalli, Viswanatham inherited his father's flourishing tobacco business but dedicated himself from his early youth to *tamiḻppaṟṟu,* playing a leading role in anti-Hindi protests into the early 1990s, in the demand for Tamil as liturgical language as well for as for changing the name of Madras state, and in numerous other such causes (Sambandan 1976).

11. Bharatidasan made a similar suggestion in the 1920s (1955: 25–29).

12. *Viṭutalai,* 27 December 1938, 4. In the *Mahābhārata,* Dushasana is the principal Kaurava prince responsible for disrobing Draupadi.

13. *Kuyil,* 15 August 1948, 29.

14. An oblique exception to this is a speech made by V. Balakrishnan in the Madras Legislative Assembly in December 1956, when he compared the efforts of government officials to coin Tamil neologisms for English bureaucratic words to the "rape of virgin Tamil" (*kaṉṉittamiḻai kaṟpaḻittatu pōl ākum*); *MLAD* 37 (1956): 637–38.

15. *Kuyil,* 15 August 1948, 29.

16. *Tamiḻ Muracu* (Pondicherry), 14 January 1960, 27.

17. *Nam Nāṭu,* 28 January 1979, 8.

18. *Kuṭi Aracu,* 28 May 1939, 16.

19. See also the essay entitled "Sahōtaratuvam" (Fraternity), *Intiyā,* 11 December 1909; and the editorial entitled "Vantē Mātaram" (Homage to [our] mother), *Intiyā,* 22 January 1910.

20. *NNR* 13 (1913): 816. Such equations between language and mother's milk are not limited to the Indian context. For instance, a sixteenth-century Spanish theologian, Luis de Leon, also likened "vernacular" languages to the "milk that children drink from their mother's breast" (Rafael 1988: 25). Similarly, David Laitin, in his study of language politics in contemporary Somalia, cites Somalian poetry in which an explicit equation is made between Somali, mother's breast, and mother's milk (1977: 115, 133–34). See also Faust's exhortation that the mother "must be an educator" because "the child sucks in its first ideas with the mother's milk" (Kittler 1990: 55).

21. *MLAD* 37 (1956): 628. Here, as in other instances, the term "bottled milk" refers to English. For other comparisons between Tamil as mother's milk and English as "bottled" milk, see Maraimalai Adigal (1967b: 82) and his daughter Nilambikai's speech to Tamilnadu Women's Conference in 1938 (*Viṭutalai,* 15 November 1938, 1; Nilambikai n.d.: 3).

22. See also *Kuyil,* 1 September 1947, 6.

23. See also *Kuyil,* 15 July 1948, 12.

24. *Viṭutalai,* 26 November 1938; see also *Muracoli,* 26 January 1965, 1.

25. *Ñāṉapāṉu* 3, no. 9 (1915): 222.

26. *Muttāram,* 15 March 1966, cover. The same cover was reprinted years later in the DMK party magazine on the occasion of the celebration of the "Language Martyrs' Day" in January 1976 with a verse celebrating the young men (*Kaḻakakkural,* 15 January 1976).

27. *Camanīti* 1965, February 12: 5.

28. English transcript of Tamil speech. Government of Madras Order No. 4818–4819 (Home Confidential), 5 October 1938.

29. *Teṉmoḻi* 2, no. 8 (1964): 69.

30. *Kumari Malar* 29, no. 7 (1972): 71–72.

31. The noun *kaṉṉi* in this compound means, among other things, virgin-maiden, youthfulness, freshness, and everlastingness. So, from at least the 1880s, Tamil's modern devotees refer to their language as *kaṉṉittamiḻ,* which in various contexts could mean "virgin Tamil," "youthful Tamil," "eternal Tamil," and so on.

32. *Kumari Malar* 4 (1943): 11–12.

33. *Tiṉappurаṭci,* 21 January 1993, 2.

34. *MLAD* 37 (1956): 637–68.

35. *Kuyil,* 19 August 1958, 1; *Teṉmoḻi* 2, no. 5 (1964): 7–9. See also *Kuyil,* 15 July 1948, 3–5, for a poem titled "The Pleasure (*iṉpam*) That Comes in Serving the Dravidian Nation."

36. Nineteenth-century mystics like Ramalinga Adigal and Dandapanisami characterized Tamil as "father tongue" to assert its superiority over Sanskrit, described as "mother" (Krishnan 1984: 197–99). In recent years, the domination of the feminized Tamiḻttāy notwithstanding, occasionally some verses personify Tamil as king, father, son, and male lover (Mudiyarasan 1976: 32–33, 40–41; Nagarajan 1980: 3–8, 13–15, 17–25, 39–31).

37. *Intippōr Muracu* 1985: 52.

38. A historically nuanced study of motherhood in colonial India has yet to be written, though a beginning has been made in "Ideology of Motherhood," a special issue of the *Economic and Political Weekly* 25, nos. 42–43 (1990).

39. *Viṭutalai,* 18 May 1938, 3; and *Kuṭi Aracu,* 22 May 1938, cover page.

40. To the best of my knowledge, living women have not played Tamiḻttāy in public processions. For comparative examples of real women representing female icons of the nation in other parts of the world, see Hunt (1984: 63–66) for eighteenth-century France; and Ryan (1990: 26–37) for the nineteenth-century United States.

41. *Pōrvāḷ,* 7 August 1948, 10.

42. *Tamiḻaracu* 11, no. 13 (1981): 1–12. I thank Paula Richman for bringing these poems to my attention. See also Richman 1997.

43. *Aṟappōr,* 8 September 1961, 1; *Muracoli,* 19 and 29 January, 3 February 1965; *Muttāram,* 15 March 1966; *Kaḻakakkural,* 25 January 1976.

44. *Tiruviḷakku,* 12 February 1965.

45. *Muttāram,* 1 December 1968, cover; *Maṟavaṉ Maṭal,* 3 May 1970, cover.

46. *Nakkīraṉ,* 15 January 1960; *Camanīti,* January 1968.
47. *Muracoli,* 19 and 29 January, 13 March 1965.
48. See cover of Kandiah Pillai (1958) and illustration accompanying the essay "Intikku tāymoḻi Tamiḻē" (Tamil is the mother tongue of Hindi), *Kaḻakak-kural,* 19 January 1975, 19.
49. *Muracoli,* 18, 19, 21, April 1993; *Mālai Muracu,* 17 April 1993; *Indian Express,* 18 April 1993.

CHAPTER FOUR. LABORING FOR LANGUAGE

1. *Kuyil,* 8 December 1959, 1; see also *Tamiḻppaṇi* 1950.
2. The term *aruccaṉai* refers to a particular, personalized form of worship in which the (Brahman) priest recites, generally in Sanskrit, the traditional names of the deity in the presence of the devotee, who then receives its blessings. Many of Tamil's devout demanded, however, that not just the *aruccaṉai* but the entire ritual of *vaḻipāṭu* (worship) be performed in Tamil.
3. See also *Centamiḻc Celvi* 29 (1954–55): 437–44, 501–16; 44 (1969–70): 237.
4. It is not surprising that Shaiva rather than Vaishnava reformers spearheaded the demand for *tamiḻ aruccaṉai,* for it is in Shaiva temples, rituals of worship, and festival processions that the doctrinal and ritual subordination of Tamil to Sanskrit, and of the social subordination of "non-Brahman" functionaries to Brahman priests, is more marked (Cutler 1987: 187–93).
5. *Centamiḻc Celvi* 46 (1971–72): 159–60.
6. See also *Tamiḻaṉ Kural* 1, no. 11 (1955): 12–15.
7. *Kuyil,* 15 August 1948, 3–5; 9 August 1960, 10.
8. Quoted in Government of Madras Order No. 2128 (Public Secret), 11 July 1957. See also Order No. 4330 (Public Confidential), 28 December 1956.
9. *Centamiḻc Celvi* 29 (1954–55): 437–39; 43 (1968–69): 31–32.
10. *Centamiḻc Celvi* 46 (1971–72): 113.
11. *MLCD* 17 (1956): 407.
12. *MLCD* 33 (1959): 179–81. In his memoirs, Bhaktavatsalam, who went on to be chief minister of the state from 1963 until the DMK takeover in 1967, writes, "In the worship of god, there ought to be no language hatred. If we go to Tirupati or Simhachalam in Andhra, or to Brindavan in the north, we can hear the *Tiruvāymoḻi* being recited there. Just because it is in Tamil, it is not hated. They do not start an agitation saying that they do not want to worship in a language they do not understand." He went on to note, in a manner reminiscent of orthodox Indianism, that both Hindu and Indian culture show the intertwining of Sanskrit and Tamil, Aryan and Dravidian, to an extent that makes it impossible to pry them apart. The *Veda*s, he declared, are a fount of great wisdom, and much appreciated by everybody all over the world. "Why should we demean their greatness?" he asked (Bhaktavatsalam 1971: 246–48).
13. *MLCD* 33 (1959): 181; see also Harrison 1960: 130.
14. *MLCD* 33 (1959): 180.
15. Bhaktavatsalam indeed later wrote in his memoirs that the demand for Tamil *aruccaṉai* was motivated less by love for Tamil than by hatred for

Sanskrit. Just as there ought to be no opposition to worship being offered through Tamil if desired, by the same token there ought to be no opposition to Sanskrit as language of worship when desired. Language hatred, bad enough in any area, was especially dangerous in the domain of religion and worship, he insisted (Bhaktavatsalam 1971: 245–48).

16. *TNLAD* 7 (1971): 21–22.

17. *Centamiḻc Celvi* 44 (1969–70): 239; 46 (1971–72): 63. I am also indebted to Franklin Presler's field notes here.

18. Subsequent to the Supreme Court stay order, the government moderated its stand, declaring that the "Tamil *aruccaṉai* only" order had been an overzealous interpretation and that the government had only tried to establish Tamil's legitimate place in acts of worship, with no intention of excluding Sanskrit (Presler 1987: 117–18).

19. *Centamiḻc Celvi* 46 (1971–72): 112. See also *Maṟavaṉ Maṭal,* 7 November 1971, 9; 14 November 1971, 11; 2 January 1972, 1.

20. *Centamiḻc Celvi* 46 (1971–72): 112.

21. See also *Centamiḻc Celvi* 29 (1954–55): 437–39.

22. *TNLAD* 7 (1971): 22.

23. Nor was it the first time he did this. In 1897, he published a series of articles under the pure Tamil pseudonym "Murukavēḷ" (Tirumaran 1992: 139).

24. Maraimalai Adigal's son Tirunavukarasu remembers that if he and his brother uttered any Sanskrit words at home, they agreed to pay a penalty (M. Tirunavukarasu 1959: 324).

25. *Ñāṉapānu* 3 (1915): 102, 181–84, 190–91, 197–198. See also Chidambaram Pillai 1989.

26. *Ñāṉapānu* 3 (1915): 200.

27. See also *Centamiḻc Celvi* 12 (1934–35): 337–39, 563–80; 15 (1937–38): 92–102, 149–55; Government of Madras Order No. 773 (Public), 27 February 1956; Order No. 2207 (Public), 22 February 1956.

28. *MLAD* 5 (1957): 164.

29. *MLCD* 17 (1956): 415; see also Kumaramangalam 1965: 96–97.

30. *MLAD* 37 (1956): 651.

31. *MLCD* 30 (1959): 34.

32. *MLAD* 2 (1957): 48; 15 (1958): 606; 35 (1960): 111–13. See also Sambasivanar and Ilankumaran 1960: 104; Visswanathan 1983: 239.

33. See also *Tamiḻp Pātukāppu Nūṟṟiraṭṭu* 1967.

34. The We Tamils claimed, *pace* the Dravidian movement, that even within a "Dravidian" nation, Tamil speakers would remain a minority. The only solution was therefore the creation of a linguistically homogeneous Tamil-speaking nation. So enthusiastic was Adithan in his vision of Tamilizing everything that he named his party's headquarters Tamiḻaṉ Illam, "The Home of the Tamilian"; the publications unit of the party was named after Tamiḻttāy; party workers wore clothes made of cotton grown in Tamilnadu, spun by Tamil-speaking workers on looms manufactured in Tamilnadu; and so on (Kuppusami 1969: 33–34). The party eventually merged in 1967 with the DMK. For Adithan's views on Tamil and nationalism, see his *Tamiḻp Pēraracu* (The Tamil empire). Published originally in 1942, it was updated and reprinted several times over

the next two decades. It made a vigorous case against "North Indian" economic and political imperialism, and it called for the creation of an independent Tamilnadu comprising the Tamil-speaking areas of India and Sri Lanka (Adithanar 1965). In the Rajya Sabha, T. S. Pattabhiraman, a Congress member, declared the We Tamils to be "a virulent type of Tamilians [*sic*]. They say that Tamil Nad must be only for people who speak Tamil and all that" (*RSD* 43 [1963]: 1970).

35. Government of Madras Order No. 2551 (Public), 15 September 1959; Order No. 1327 (Public Confidential), 19 August 1960.

36. See also *MLAD* 38 (1961): 33; 5 (1967): 658.

37. "The DMK has got nothing to do with fasting [*sic*]. The fasting was undertaken by a non-party man, in fact a relative of the Chief Minister of Madras, Mr. Shankaralinga Nadar" (*RSD* 43 [1963]: 2012). Despite this declaration by Annadurai in 1963 in the Parliament, in 1968 he reminded his colleagues in the Madras Legislative Assembly that he had visited Shankaralingam and had requested that he give up his fast (*MLAD* 14 [1968]: 211). Earlier, in 1956, the DMK also celebrated "Shankaralinganar Day" and invoked him as a Tamil hero in its publications (N. Subramanian 1993: 205).

38. See also the obituary in *Tīcuṭar* 1, no. 24 (1956): 3–4.

39. *MLAD* 14 (1968): 211.

40. Indeed, in 1960 the Madras Corporation, now under DMK control, was Tamilized as "Ceṉṉai Mānakarāṭci," a gesture which confirmed that party's *tamiḻppaṟṟu* even as it showed up the Congress's deficiency in this regard (Karunanidhi 1989: 369).

41. *MLAD* 38 (1961): 122–27; *MLCD* 41 (1961): 559–60.

42. *RSD* 43 (1963): 1921–2053.

43. *MLCD* 55 (1964): 383–89.

44. *LSD* 21 (1968): 232–61.

45. *RSD* 43 (1963): 2045; *MLAD* 36 (1956): 170.

46. *MLAD* 36 (1956): 169.

47. *RSD* 43 (1963): 1972.

48. *MLCD* 55 (1964): 384; *MLAD* 5 (1967): 656–58; *RSD* 43 (1963): 2005–6.

49. *RSD* 43 (1963): 1979–80.

50. *MLCD* 55 (1964): 388.

51. *RSD* 43 (1963): 1973.

52. *MLCD* 55 (1964): 388.

53. *RSD* 43 (1963): 2025.

54. *MLCD* 55 (1964): 387; see also *RSD* 43 (1963): 1975.

55. *MLAD* 5 (1967): 650.

56. *RSD* 43 (1963): 1936.

57. *RSD* 43 (1963): 1969.

58. *RSD* 43 (1963): 2023, emphasis mine.

59. *RSD* 43 (1963): 2043.

60. *RSD* 43 (1963): 2011–7.

61. *MLAD* 5 (1967): 656.

62. *MLAD* 37 (1956): 633, 636–38.

63. *MLCD* 10 (1955): 757.

64. References to Tamilttāy may be found in *MLAD* 37 (1956): 619, 622, 638, 639–41, 643–44, 647, 651, 656; *MLCD* 17 (1956): 393–94, 397, 402, 407, 422.

65. *MLAD* 37 (1956): 619–20, 656–57.

66. *MLAD* 37 (1956): 618; *MLCD* 17 (1956): 394.

67. *MLAD* 37 (1956): 631–32.

68. *MLAD* 37 (1956): 619.

69. *MLAD* 37 (1956): 639.

70. *MLCD* 10 (1955): 757; 22 (1957): 336–7; It was not until January 1968 that a time limit of five years was set for the complete Tamilization of government.

71. *MLAD* 5 (1957): 162.

72. In November 1957, one government report claimed that there were only forty Tamil typewriters available for official use, as opposed to more than four thousand English typewriters (Government of Madras Order No. 1027 [Public], 31 March 1958).

73. *MLCD* 22 (1957): 336–37; *MLAD* 28 (1960): 608–12.

74. *MLAD* 37 (1956): 620–22.

75. The collector of Tiruchirapalli district wrote to the government in 1952, "Regarding the experiment of conducting the official proceeding and correspondence in the regional language in this district, I submit that on the whole the system cannot be said to be working satisfactorily. Much difficulty is experienced in writing drafts in Tamil in the absence of appropriate terms in Tamil. Further, a draft in Tamil does not always convey the spirit of the expressions correctly and in full, which may involve even legal complications in the long run" (Government of Madras Order No. 2225 [Public], 12 September 1952). See also *MLAD* 31 (1956): 460–61.

76. *MLAD* 11 (1939): 609.

77. *MLAD* 11 (1939): 542, 597–617, 804–8; 23 (1955): 633–35.

78. *MLAD* 37 (1956): 625, 647; *MLCD* 33 (1959): 12–13.

79. *MLAD* 37 (1956): 629, 631, 656; 5 (1957): 163; *MLCD* 17 (1956): 394; 30 (1959): 30.

80. *MLAD* 16 (1958): 396.

81. *MLAD* 37 (1956): 622–23; see also *MLCD* 30 (1959): 23–27.

82. *MLCD* 30 (1959): 27.

83. *MLCD* 33 (1959): 13.

84. *TNLAD* 30 (1970): 561–63.

85. *MLCD* 49 (1963): 217.

86. *MLCD* 49 (1963): 199.

87. Government of Madras Order No. 911 (Education), 21 April 1938.

88. Government of Madras Order No. 1343 (Education and Public Health), 14 June 1938.

89. Government sources conceded that on 26 January alone, more than two thousand were taken into custody, of whom thirty-two were DMK legislators; police opened fire in at least thirty-six places and 50 were killed, 130 wounded

(*MLAD* 28 [1965] 90–92; *MLCD* 63 [1965] 87–89). DMK sources give larger numbers for the dead and the wounded.

90. *India Today,* 31 March 1992, 92; *Aside,* 15 May 1993, 23–25; *The Week,* 25 July 1993, 25–26.

91. *Intippōr Muracu* 1985.

92. See also the interview in *Poṉṉi (Poṅkal Malar)* 1951: 36–41.

93. *Intippōr Muracu* 1985: 34–36.

94. Maraimalai Adigal thus noted in his diary: "My son Tirunavukarasu has been sent to prison for six months for speaking out against Hindi in order to protect Tamiḻttāy. May Shiva punish all those who harm Tamil" (M. Tirunavukarasu and Venkatachalapathy 1988: 83).

95. *Centamiḻc Celvi* 17 (1939–40): 55; see also 16 (1938–39): 407–16; 18 (1940–41): 191–92.

CHAPTER FIVE. TO DIE FOR

1. *Paṉmoḻippulavar Kā. Appātturaiyār Maṇiviḻā Malar* (Polyglot scholar Appadurai's sixtieth birthday commemorative souvenir), 1967: n.p.

2. *MLCD* 17 (1956): 406.

3. See also *Kuyil,* 16 August 1960, 5.

4. See also *Tēca Cēvakaṉ,* 26 June 1923, 2.

5. For some critical and favorable contemporary responses to Nilambikai's efforts, see *Āṉantapōtiṉi* 9 (1924): 372–75, 423–25; *Kuṭi Aracu,* 31 January 1926, 5–9.

6. *Viṭutalai,* 15 November 1938, 1–4.

7. *Viṭutalai,* 22 November 1938, 3; 29 November 1938, 3.

8. *Intippōr Muracu* 1985: 75.

9. See also *NNR* 13 (1913): 506–7.

10. *The Light of Truth or Siddhanta Deepika* 6 (1906–07): 193.

11. Ironically, in the 1870s, Pope was one of the few European philologists who insisted that "the differences between the Dravidian tongues and the Aryan are not so great" and argued that "the place of the Dravidian dialects is . . . with the Aryan than with the Turanian family of languages" (Pope 1876: 158). His essay showed the various deep-seated affinities between Tamil and Sanskrit.

12. English transcription of Tamil speech. Government of Madras Order No. 4818–4819, (Home Confidential), 5 October 1938.

13. English transcription of Tamil speech. Government of Madras Order No. 4818–4819, (Home Confidential), 5 October 1938.

14. Reprinted in *Kumari Malar* 29, no. 12 (1973): 24–27; quotation on 25.

15. See also his 1924 essay, "tamiḻil vaṭamoḻi pataṅkaḷ" (Sanskrit words in Tamil), reprinted in *Mañcari* 24, no. 4 (1971): 6–9.

16. For contemporary discussions, see also *Āṉantapōtiṉi* 19 (1933): 94–96, 163–66, 403–7; 19 (1934): 483–87, 563–66; 20 (1934): 60–63; *Centamiḻc Celvi* 12 (1934–35): 337–39, 531–37, 563–80.

17. He was also described as a "pimp" who married his daughter off to the North Indian, Gandhi's son: "This ungrateful Rajagopalachari who is baser

than a dog, who was born in the coterie which came to beg, who is wearing dark spectacles and who has become a minister by playing the pimp of his daughter, is trying to play the pimp for his [Brahman] community" (English transcription of Tamil speech; Government of Madras Order No. 549 [Public], 1 April 1939).

18. *Kuṭi Aracu,* 26 June 1938, 1.

19. *Kuyil,* 28 October 1958, 11–12.

20. See also *Kuyil,* 21 April 1959, 10–12.

21. *Tīcuṭar,* 10 May 1956, 4–5.

22. In his reminiscences on Bharati, however, Bharatidasan refers to an encounter that his mentor poet had with a North Indian named Ishwarlal in Benaras who apparently asked, "Is there a language called Tamil? Is not Tamil the child of Sanskrit? . . . Are there even books in Tamil? . . . In pure Tamil?" Furious with the North Indian's arrogance, Bharati instantaneously composed a poem—his first and only in a Tamil free of Sanskrit (Ilango 1992: 55–59). The overt antagonism towards Sanskrit expressed here is rather rare in Bharati, the one other striking exception being his short story called "Ciṉṉa Caṅkaraṉ Katai" (The story of Chinna Shankaran; c. 1913).

23. "Tamiḻp pāṣaikku ōr putiya nikaṇṭu vēṇṭum" (Need for a new thesaurus for Tamil), reprinted in *Kumari Malar* 15, no. 9 (1968): 36–39.

24. *Kuyil,* 9 September 1960, 13–14.

25. See also Government of Madras Order No. 3141 (Education), 9 December 1948.

26. *Tamiḻiyakkam* 1 (1980): 9–12.

27. His son also notes that Maraimalai resigned from his job in protest over Madras University's language policies, which treated Tamil as an optional rather than a compulsory subject of study beginning in 1906 (M. Tirunavukarasu 1959: 124–26).

28. For a contrary sentiment expressed in his private diaries, see M. Tirunavukarasu and Venkatachalapathy 1988: 76–77.

29. *Cutēcamittiraṉ,* 27 June 1901, 3.

30. Dalmiapuram was renamed Kallakudi only after Karunanidhi became chief minister of the state in 1969.

31. *Kaḻakakkural,* 25 January 1976, 12.

32. *MLAD* 11 (1939): 512–17; *MLCD* 6–8 (1939): 250; Government of Madras Order No. 334 (Public General), 21 February 1939.

33. Government of Madras Order No. 334 (Public General), 21 February 1939.

34. *MLAD* 11 (1939): 512–17; Government of Madras Order No. 2070 (Public Confidential), 27 November 1939.

35. Government of Madras Order No. 334 (Public General), 21 February 1939.

36. *Viṭutalai,* 31 May 1938, editorial; Government of Madras Order No. 2070 (Public Confidential), 27 November 1939.

37. English transcription of Tamil speech. Government of Madras Order No. 4068 (Home), 23 August 1938. Maraimalai Adigal, who went to see both men while they were fasting, noted in his diary that their sacrifice stoked the

sleeping consciousness of Tamilians (M. Tirunavukarasu and Venkatachalapathy 1988: 82).

38. Government of Madras Order No. 4861 (Home), 7 October 1938.

39. *Kuyil,* 3 February 1959, 1; 10 February, 16. See also *Kuyil,* 6 January 1959, 3; 24 February, 5; 26 May, 5; 30 June, 4–5; Government of Madras Order No. 938 (Public), 9 June 1960. In response to these protests, the Congress government in Madras did petition the central government in 1958 to adopt the Tamil term; the latter demurred. The state government however instructed that both terms were to be used in broadcasts in Madras. Not till the DMK came to power in 1967 was the term *vāṉoli* officially adopted (*MLAD* 19 [1959]: 212–13).

40. *Tīyil Venta Tamiḻp Pulikaḷ* n.d: 11. The same source notes that on the recent marriage of his daughter Dravidacelvi, Karunanidhi gave her a sizeable gift.

41. Sivalingam immolated himself on the morning of 26 January, exactly a year after Chinnasami. A native of Kodambakkam, Madras, he was twenty-two. It is reported that he frequently told his family and friends that unless at least ten Tamilians gave up their lives, there was no hope for Tamil. Telling his sister that she and the rest of the family should stay indoors, as he anticipated trouble, Sivalingam apparently set out for the railway station to join in an anti-Hindi demonstration, saying he would be back later. He left at dawn but did not return (*Tīyil Venta Tamiḻp Pulikaḷ* n.d: 12). A report in another newsmagazine notes that Sivalingam was born in 1939 into a large indigent family in a small village called Devanur in South Arcot district. He studied up to the fifth grade in Devanur, then walked two miles every day to attend middle school in the neighboring village of Chattanpatti. His Tamil teacher, a Dravidianist poet named Ponni Valavan, nurtured his love for Tamil. Unable to continue with his education, Sivalingam followed his father and elder brother to Madras, where he worked as a laborer on construction sites. He also got involved with the DMK in the city (*Ilaṭciyappātai,* 28 March 1993, 20–21). The DMK newspaper, *Muracoli,* carried a front-page photograph of Sivalingam and reported on his funeral procession (28 January 1965, 1).

A native of Chingelput district, Aranganathan set himself on fire, we are told, at 2:00 A.M. on 27 January in front of the local theater in Virugambakkam. Born in 1931, he was one of three sons. According to one version of his story, although he was employed in the central government's telephone company, he was interested in various martial arts which he taught to local youngsters. He also took upon himself the task of educating the youth of Virugambakkam in the literature of the Dravidian movement. At the time of his death, he was married, with three children, the youngest six months old (*Tīyil Venta Tamiḻp Pulikaḷ* n.d: 13). The *Muracoli* reported that prior to his death, he wrote letters to Chief Minister Bhaktavatsalam and others informing them of his intention. The paper also carried a photo of his mother, wife, and three children grieving over the charred remains of his body (*Muracoli,* 28 January 1965, 1; 29 January, 1; see also *Ilaṭciyappātai,* 28 March 1993, 21–22). Today, a road in Madras city is named after him.

A native of the village of Udaiyampatti in Tiruchi district, Veerappan immolated himself on 11 February in neighboring Ayyampalaiyam. He was twenty-seven and not married. A teacher who taught at several schools before moving to Ayyampalaiyam, he spent most of his spare time absorbed in Tamil scholarship. He was also an ardent DMK follower and attended many of its events in his area. He organized a number of youth gatherings where he would read aloud from DMK newspapers, and he taught his students about the wonders of Tamil. He even led his students in anti-Hindi protests prior to his death and also wrote letters of protest to the government. In 1980, a memorial was set up for him (*Tīyil Venta Tamiḻp Pulikaḷ* n.d: 13; *Deccan Herald,* 13 February 1965, 1).

Mutthu burned himself alive on 11 February. A native of Satyamangalam in Coimbatore district, he was, according to the *Deccan Herald,* a forty-year-old farmer who was disgusted with the police firing on anti-Hindi protesters (13 February 1965, 1). Another version, however, notes that he was born in 1943, had studied up to the fifth grade, and worked in a truck shop. He was reportedly inspired to burn himself on reading stories of other immolations in the newspapers. He had great love for Tamil, we are told, and was an avid follower of the DMK. The DMK, in turn, commemorated his memory by naming the hall in which they held their annual meeting in Madurai in 1966 after him (*Tīyil Venta Tamiḻp Pulikaḷ* n.d: 18–19).

A native of Marutavamcheri in Tanjavur district, Sarangapani set himself on fire on the grounds of his college campus in Mayiladuthurai on 15 March. He was a student studying for his bachelor's degree in commerce. He was twenty (*Tīyil Venta Tamiḻp Pulikaḷ* n.d: 25).

42. Dandapani was a student of the Coimbatore Institute of Technology who died on 28 February in Peelamedu. Born in 1944 in Kulathupalaiyam in Coimbatore district, he was the first in his indigent family to go to college. Though he realized that his family depended on him to finish his education and secure a job, Dandapani, we are told, was more inspired by the stories of other students who participated in anti-Hindi protests and by the immolations of Chinnasami and others. So he gave up his own dreams for the sake of Tamil (*Tīyil Venta Tamiḻp Pulikaḷ* n.d: 15–16).

Mutthu died in February in Keeranur near Pudukottai where he was working at a local restaurant. Born in 1943, his friends remember that even as a teenager in the 1950s in the small village of Cinnasanayakadu in Pudukottai district, he was fired with the zeal of Tamil devotion and plastered the walls of local buildings and temples with slogans such as "Down with Hindi!" "Long live Tamil!" Reading the stories of fellow Tamilians who had suffered in the anti-Hindi protests, he was filled with anger. Before he died, he wrote letters to Bhaktavatsalam, Annadurai, and others, expressing his anger. These letters were found on his body (*Tīyil Venta Tamiḻp Pulikaḷ* n.d: 21).

A native of Nartamalai in Pudukottai, Shanmugam died in a Tiruchirapalli hospital on 25 February, two days after consuming poison. Born in 1943, he worked for a local grocery store in Viralimalai to support his poor family. Prior to his death, he was filled with Tamil consciousness, gave public lectures against Hindi in DMK meetings, set fire to Hindi books, burned an effigy of Hindi, and wrote letters to his relatives urging them to join the Tamil cause. His elder brother founded the still-existing Society for the Language Martyrs of 1965 (*Tīyil Venta Tamiḻp Pulikaḷ* n.d: 22–25; *Deccan Herald,* 1 March 1965, 5).

43. *Muttāram,* 15 March 1966, 11.
44. *MLCD* 26 (1965): 169–71.
45. *Kuṭi Aracu,* 6 August 1939, 1–2.

CHAPTER SIX. CONCLUSION

1. *The Light of Truth or Siddhanta Deepika* 6 (1902–03): 93.
2. *Tamiḻar Nāṭu* 2 (1946): 3.
3. *Kuyil,* 21 June 1960, 3.

References

Abdul Karim, M. 1982. *Islāmum Tamiḻum* (Islam and Tamil). Madras: SISSW.

Abu-Lughod, Lila. 1986. *Veiled Sentiments: Honor and Poetry in a Bedouin Society.* Berkeley: University of California Press.

Adithanar, S. B. 1965. *Tamiḻp Pēraracu* (The Tamil empire). 12th rev. ed. Madras: Muttamil Patippakam. [1st ed. 1942]

Agulhon, Maurice. 1980. *Marianne into Battle: Republican Imagery and Symbolism in France, 1789–1880.* Cambridge: Cambridge University Press.

Alarmelmankai. 1914. *Tirāviṭa Matam* (Dravidian religion). Palamcottah: [The Shaiva Sabha].

Alter, Robert. 1994. *Hebrew and Modernity.* Bloomington: Indiana University Press.

Amirtham Pillai, A. K. 1906. *Tamiḻviṭutūtu* (Tamil as messenger). Tiruchirapalli: A. Subramaniyapillai.

Anaimuthu, V. 1974. *Periyār Ī. Vē. Rā Cintaṉaikaḷ* (Periyar EVR's thoughts). 3 vols. Tiruchirapalli: Periyar Self-Respect Publications.

Anandhi, S. 1991a. "Representing Devadasis: 'Dasigal Mosavalai' as a Radical Text." *Economic and Political Weekly (Annual Number)* 26(11–12): 739–46.

———. 1991b. "Women's Question in the Dravidian Movement, c. 1925–1948." *Social Scientist* 19: 24–41

Anbupalam Ni, comp. 1967. *Maṟaimalai Aṭikaḷār Kaṭitaṅkaḷ* (Letters of Maraimalai Adigal). 3rd ed. Madras: Pari Nilayam.

Anderson, Benedict. 1983. *Imagined Communities: Reflections on the Origin and Spread of Nationalism.* London: Verso.

Annadurai, C. N. 1948. *People's Poet (Barathiar).* Madras: New Justice.

———. 1968. *Ē, Tāḻnta Tamiḻakamē!* (O, downtrodden Tamilnadu!). 10th ed. Madras: Pari Nilayam. [1st ed. 1945]

———. 1969. *Āriya Māyai* (Aryan illusion). 9th ed. Tiruchirapalli: Dravida Pannai. [1st ed. 1947]

———. 1974. *Viṭutalaip Pōr* (War of Independence). 4th ed. Madras: Pari Nilayam. [1st ed. c. 1947]

———. 1985. *Aṟappōr* (Righteous war). 5th ed. Madras: Pari Nilayam. [1st ed. c. 1948]

———. 1989 [c. 1948]. *Iṉpat Tirāviṭam* (Sweet Dravidian land). Reprint, Madras: Poompukar.

Annamalai, E. 1979. "Movement for Linguistic Purism: The Case of Tamil." In *Language Movements in India,* edited by E. Annamalai, 35–59. Mysore: Central Institute of Indian Languages.

Appadurai, Arjun, 1981. *Worship and Conflict under Colonial Rule: A South Indian Case.* Cambridge: Cambridge University Press.

———. 1990. "Topographies of the Self: Praise and Emotion in Hindu India." In *Language and the Politics of Emotion,* edited by Catherine A. Lutz and Lila Abu-Lughod, 92–112. Cambridge: Cambridge University Press.

Appadurai, K. 1944. *Tamiḻ Vāḻka!* (May Tamil flourish!). Konapattu, Pudukottai: Tamilannai Nilayam.

———. 1975 [1941]. *Kumarik Kaṇṭam Allatu Kaṭal Koṇṭa Teṉṉāṭu* (Kumarikkaṇṭam, or the southern land seized by the ocean). Reprint, Madras: SISSW.

Appiah, Kwame A. 1992. *In My Father's House: Africa in the Philosophy of Culture.* New York: Oxford University Press.

Arangasami. [1977]. *Tirukkuṟaḷvēḷ Varatarācar Tamiḻviṭu Tūtu* (Tamil as messenger to Varadarajar). Lalgudi: Kanakasabhai.

Arulsami, M. S. 1966. *Kātalikku* (For my beloved). 2nd ed. Madras: Pari Nilayam. [1st ed. 1961]

Arunagirinathar. 1937. *Tamiḻttāy Pulampal* (Lamentations of Tamiḻttāy). Madras: Senguntha Mittran Printing Press.

Asher, Ronald. 1968. "The Contribution of Scholars of British Origin to the Study of Tamil in Britain." In *Tamil Studies Abroad: A Symposium,* edited by X. S. Thaninayagam, 43–80. Kuala Lampur: International Association of Tamil Research.

Badinter, Elisabeth. 1981. *Mother Love, Myth and Reality: Motherhood in Modern History.* New York: Macmillan.

Balibar, Etienne. 1989. "Racism as Universalism." *New Political Science* 16/17: 9–22

Barnett, Marguerite. 1976. *The Politics of Cultural Nationalism in South India.* Princeton: Princeton University Press.

Baskaran, S. Theodore. 1981. *The Message Bearers: The Nationalist Politics and the Entertainment Media in South India, 1880–1945.* Madras: Cre-A.

Bhabha, Homi. 1994. *The Location of Culture.* London: Routledge.

Bhaktavatsalam, M. 1971. *Eṉatu Niṉaivukaḷ* (My reminiscences). Madras: Jananayaka Seva Sangam.

Bharati, Subramania. 1937. *Essays and Other Prose Fragments.* Madras: Bharati Prachur Alayam.

———. 1987. *Pārati Pāṭalkaḷ: Āyvu Patippu* (Songs of Bharati: A research compendium). Tanjavur: Tamil University.

———. 1988. *Pāratiyār Kaṭṭuraikaḷ* (Essays of Bharati). Madras: Poompukar.

Bharatidasan. 1948. *Inti Etirppup Pāṭṭu* (Anti-Hindi songs). Pondicherry: Bharatidasan Patippakam.

———. 1955 [1930]. *Tēciya Kītam: Katar Irāṭṭiṉap Pāṭṭu* (National songs: Song of the Khadi wheel). Reprint, Turaiyur: Kalaiccolai.

———. 1958. *Tāyiṉ Mēl Āṇai* (An oath on my mother). Madras: Tamilttay Patippakam.

———. 1969. *Tamiḻiyakkam* (The resurgence of Tamil). 6th ed. Ramachandrapuram: Centamil Nilayam. [1st ed. 1945]

———. 1978. *Tamiḻukku Amuteṉṟa Pēr* (Tamil, verily, is ambrosia). Madras: Poompukar.

———. 1986. *Pāratitācaṉ Kavitaikaḷ* (Poems of Bharatidasan). Vol. 1. 26th ed. Ramachandrapuram: Centamil Nilayam. [1st ed. 1938]

———. 1992. *Tamiḻiyakkam* (The resurgence of Tamil). Reprint, Madras: Bharati.

Bower, H. 1855. "Tamil Language and Literature." *Calcutta Review* 25: 158–96.

Braidotti, Rosi. 1994. *Nomadic Subjects: Embodiment and Sexual Difference in Contemporary French Theory.* New York: Columbia University Press.

Brass, Paul. 1974. *Language, Religion, and Politics in North India.* London: Cambridge University Press.

———. 1990. "Language Problems." In *The Politics of India Since Independence,* 157–91. Cambridge: Cambridge University Press.

Caldwell, Robert. 1856. *A Comparative Grammar of the Dravidian or South-Indian Family of Languages.* London: Harrison.

———. 1875. *A Comparative Grammar of the Dravidian or South-Indian Family of Languages.* 2nd ed., rev. and enlarged. London: Trubner.

———. 1881. *A Political and General History of the District of Tinnevelly in the Presidency of Madras.* Madras: Government Press.

Cameron, Deborah, ed. 1990. *The Feminist Critique of Language: A Reader.* London: Routledge.

Chakrabarty, Dipesh. 1992. "Postcoloniality and the Artifice of History: Who Speaks for the 'Indian' Pasts?" *Representations,* no. 37: 1–26.

———. 1995. "The Time of History and the Time of Gods." Unpublished typescript.

Chatterjee, Partha. 1986. *Nationalist Thought in the Colonial World: A Derivative Discourse?* London: Zed.

———. 1989. "Colonialism, Nationalism, and Colonized Women: The Contest in India." *American Ethnologist* 16: 622–33.

———. 1993. *The Nation and Its Fragments: Colonial and Postcolonial Histories.* Princeton: Princeton University Press.

Chelvakesavaroya Mudaliar, T. 1929 [1906]. *Tamil: An Essay.* Reprint, Madras: Diocesan Press.

Chidambaram Pillai, V. O. 1989 [1915]. "Tamiḻ." In *Va. U. Ci. Kaṭṭuraikaḷ* (Essays of V. O. Chidambaram), edited by M. R. Arasu, 75–83. Reprint, Madras: Pari Nilayam.

Chidambaranar, Sami. 1971. *Tamil̠ar Talaivar: Periyār Ī. Vē. Rā Val̠kkai Varalāṟu* (The leader of Tamilians: Periyar EVR's life story). 6th ed. Tiruchi: Periyar Self-Respect Publications. [1st ed. 1939]

Chidambaranar, Thudisaikizhar A. 1938. *The Antiquity of the Tamils and Their Literature.* Coimbatore: Krishna Vilas Press.

Cohn, Bernard S. 1985. "The Command of Language and the Language of Command." In *Subaltern Studies IV,* edited by Ranajit Guha, 276–329. New Delhi: Oxford University Press.

Curtin, Philip. 1964. "Language, Culture, and History." In *The Image of Africa: British Ideas and Action, 1780–1850,* 388–413. Madison: University of Wisconsin Press.

Cutler, Norman. 1987. *Songs of Experience: The Poetics of Tamil Devotion.* Bloomington: Indiana University Press.

Damodaram Pillai, C. W. 1971. *Tāmōtaram: C. W. Tāmōtarappil̤l̤ai El̠utiya Patippuraikal̤in̠ Tokuppu* (Prefaces written by C. W. Damodaram Pillai). Jaffna: Jaffna Cooperative Tamil Books Publications.

Dasgupta, Jyotirindra. 1970. *Language Conflict and National Development: Group Politics and National Language Policy in India.* Berkeley: University of California Press.

Davin, Anna. 1978. "Imperialism and Motherhood." *History Workshop* 5: 9–65.

Derrett, J. Duncan. 1968. *Religion, Law, and the State in India.* London: Faber and Faber.

Devaneyan, G. 1966. *The Primary Classical Language of the World.* Katpadi: Nesamani.

———. 1967. *The Language Problem of Tamil Nad and Its Logical Solution.* [Katpadi]: n.p.

———. 1972. *Tamil̠ar Varalāṟu* (History of Tamilians). Katpadi: Nesamani.

Devasikhamani, S. K. 1919. *The Tamils and Their Language.* Tiruchirapalli: Young Men's Tamilian Association.

Diehl, Anita. 1977. *E. V. Ramaswami Naicker-Periyar: A Study of the Influence of a Personality in Contemporary South India.* Lund: Esselte Studium.

Dirks, Nicholas B. 1995. "The Conversion of Caste: Location, Translation, and Appropriation." In *Conversion to Modernities: The Globalization of Christianity,* edited by Peter van der Veer, 115–36. New York: Routledge.

———. 1996. "Recasting Tamil Society: The Politics of Caste and Race in Contemporary Southern India." In *Caste Today,* edited by Christopher Fuller, 263–95. Delhi: Oxford University Press.

Duara, Prasenjit. 1995. *Rescuing History from the Nation: Questioning Narratives of Modern China.* Chicago: University of Chicago Press.

Eck, Diana. 1985. *Darśan: Seeing the Divine Image in India.* Rev. ed. Chambersburg, Pa.: Anima Books.

Ellis, Francis. 1816. "Notes to the Introduction." In *A Grammar of the Teloogoo Language,* by Alexander Campbell, 1–32. Madras: College Press.

Elmore, Wilber T. 1915. *Dravidian Gods in Modern Hinduism: A Study of the Local and Village Deities of Southern India.* Hamilton, N.Y.: Wilber T. Elmore.

Erndl, Kathleen. 1993. *Victory to the Mother: The Hindu Goddess of Northwest India in Myth, Ritual, and Symbol.* New York: Oxford University Press.

Fabian, Johannes. 1986. *Language and Colonial Power: The Appropriation of Swahili in the Former Belgian Congo, 1880–1938.* Berkeley: University of California Press.

Ferguson, Charles. 1968. "Myths about Arabic." In *Readings in the Sociology of Language,* edited by Joshua Fishman, 375–81. The Hague: Mouton.

Fishman, Joshua A., Charles Ferguson, and Jyotirindra Dasgupta, eds. 1968. *Language Problems of Developing Nations.* New York: John Wiley and Sons.

Foucault, Michel. 1972. *The Archaeology of Knowledge and the Discourse on Language,* translated by A. M. Sheridan Smith. New York: Pantheon.

Gnanambal. 1936. "Tamil̲arkaḷukku Kar̲pillaiya?: Tōl̲ar Mū. Irākavaiyaṅkār Tavar̲u" (Are Tamilians unchaste? Comrade M. Raghava Aiyangar's mistake). *Pakuttar̲ivu* 1(11): 16–20.

Gover, Charles, 1871. *The Folk-Songs of Southern India.* Madras: Higginbotham.

Government of India. 1893. *Census of India, 1891: General Report.* London: Printed for the Indian Government by Eyre and Spottiswoode.

———. 1903. *Census of India, 1901.* Vol. 1, part 1, *Report.* Calcutta: Office of the Superintendent of Government Printing.

———. 1912. *Census of India, 1911.* Vol. 12, part 1, *Madras.* Madras: Government Press.

———. 1932. *Census of India, 1931.* Vol. 14, part 1, *Report.* Madras: Government of India Central Publication Branch.

———. 1933. *Census of India, 1931.* Vol. 1, part 1, *Report.* Delhi: Manager of Publications.

Government of Tamilnadu. 1990. "Tāymol̲ippar̲r̲u" (Devotion to mother tongue). In *Tamil̲p Pāṭanūl: Ēl̲ām Vakuppu* (Tamil textbook for grade seven), 49–55. Madras: Tamilnadu Pada Nul Niruvanam.

Govindarajan, M. 1988. *Tamil̲uṇarvu* (Tamil consciousness). Madras: Saraswati Patippakam.

Grierson, George A. 1906. *Linguistic Survey of India.* Vol. 4, *Munda and Dravidian Languages.* Calcutta: Office of Superintendent of Government Printing.

Guha-Thakurta, Tapati. 1991. "Women as 'Calendar-Art' Icons: Emergence of Pictorial Stereotype in Colonial India." *Economic and Political Weekly (Review of Women Studies)* 26(43): 91–99.

Gutwirth, Madelyn. 1992. *The Twilight of the Goddesses: Women and Representation in the French Revolutionary Era.* New Brunswick, N.J.: Rutgers University Press.

Hackett, Helen. 1995. *Virgin Mother, Maiden Queen: Elizabeth I and the Cult of the Virgin Mary.* New York: St. Martin's Press.

Halbfass, Wilhelm. 1988. *India and Europe: An Essay in Understanding.* Albany: SUNY Press.

Handler, Richard. 1988. *Nationalism and the Politics of Culture in Quebec.* Madison: University of Wisconsin Press.

Harrison, Selig. 1960. *India: The Most Dangerous Decades.* Princeton: Princeton University Press.

Hunt, Lynn. 1984. *Politics, Culture, and Class in the French Revolution.* Berkeley: University of California Press.

———. 1989. "Introduction: History, Culture, and Text." In *New Cultural History,* edited by Lynn Hunt, 1–22. Berkeley: University of California Press.

Ibrahim, A. Mohamad, 1920. "Tamiḻiṉ Perumai" (The greatness of Tamil). *Āṉantapōtiṉi* 5(9): 349–51.

Ilakuvanar, S. 1971. *Eṉ Vālkkaippōr* (My life's battle). Madurai: Kuralneri.

Ilanceliyan, M. 1986. *Tamiḻaṉ Toṭuttap Pōr* (The war fought by Tamilians). 2nd ed. Madras: Periyar Self-Respect Publications.

Ilango, S. S. 1982. *Pāratitācaṉ Pārvaiyil Pārati* (Bharati in Bharatidasan's eyes). Sivagangai: Annam.

———, ed. 1992. *Pāratiyāroṭu Pattāṇṭukaḷ* (Ten years with Bharati). Madras: Pari Nilayam.

Ilankumaran, R. 1982. *Kaḻaka Amaiccar Tiruvaraṅkaṉār Varalāṟu* (Life story of Tiruvarangam, founder of the Kazhagam). Madras: SISSW.

———, comp. 1985. *Pāvāṇar Kaṭitaṅkaḷ* (Letters of Devaneyan). Madras: SISSW.

———. 1991. *Taṉittamiḻ Iyakkam* (Pure Tamil movement). Madras: Manivacagar Patippakam.

Ilantiraiyan, S. 1981. *Aintāvatu Tamiḻ Māṉāṭu* (Fifth international Tamil conference). New Delhi: Salai Publications.

Ilavarasu, R. 1990. *Intiya Viṭutalai Iyakkattil Pāratitācaṉ* (Bharatidasan and the Indian national movement). Tiruchi: Marutam.

Inden, Ronald. 1990. *Imagining India.* Oxford: Basil Blackwell.

Intippōr Muracu (The Hindi war drum). 1985 [1948]. Reprint, Madras: Vidutalai.

Iraiyan, A., comp. 1981. *Cuyamariyātaic Cuṭarolikaḷ* (Leading lights of self-respect). Madras: Periyar Self-Respect Publications.

Irschick, Eugene F. 1969. *Politics and Social Conflict in South India: The Non-Brahman Movement and Tamil Separatism, 1916–1929.* Berkeley: University of California Press.

———. 1986. *Tamil Revivalism in the 1930s.* Madras: Cre-A.

———. 1994. *Dialogue and History: Constructing South India, 1795–1895.* Berkeley: University of California Press.

Iyarkaiselvan. 1959. *Malarkkāṭu Allatu Tamiḻā Eḻu!* (Forest of flowers, or Rise, O Tamilian!). Madras: [Shanti].

Jernudd, Bjorn, and Michael Shapiro, eds. 1989. *The Politics of Language Purism.* Berlin: Mouton.

Jones, Kenneth. 1989. *Socio-Religious Reform Movements in British India.* Cambridge: Cambridge University Press.

———, ed. 1992. *Religious Controversy in British India: Dialogues in South Asian Languages.* Albany: SUNY Press.

Jones, R. F. 1953. *The Triumph of the English Language: A Survey of Opinions*

Concerning the Vernacular from the Introduction of Printing to the Restoration. Stanford: Stanford University Press.

Joseph, John E., and Talbot J. Taylor, eds. 1990. *Ideologies of Language*. London: Routledge.

Kailasapathy, K. 1970. "Kālantōrum Kaṭavuḷ Vāḻttu" (Divine invocations through the ages). In *Aṭiyum Muṭiyum* (Essays on literature), 64–119. Madras: Pari Nilayam.

———. 1986. *On Art and Literature*. Madras: New Century Book House.

Kalyanasundaranar, T. V. 1919. *Tēcapaktāmirtam* (Nectar of the *Tēcapaktaṉ*). Madras: n.p.

———. 1935. *Tamiḻccōlai Allatu Kaṭṭuraittiraṭṭu* (Garden of Tamil, or Collection of essays). Vol. 1. Madras: Sadhu Publications.

———. 1949. *Pattu Āṇṭukaḷil Tirāviṭa Nāṭu* (Dravidian nation in ten years). Dharapuram: Cintanai Patippakam.

———. 1982 [1944]. *Vāḻkkaik Kuṟippukkaḷ* (Notes on life). Reprint, Madras: SISSW.

Kanakasabhai, V. 1966 [1904]. *The Tamils Eighteen Hundred Years Ago*. Reprint, Madras: SISSW.

Kandiah Pillai, N. S. 1947. *Tamiḻk Kaṭavuḷukku Āriya Pāṭalā?* (Aryan songs for Tamil gods?). Madras: Muttamil Nilayam.

———. 1958. *Namatu Tāy Moḻi* (Our mother tongue). Madras: Asiriyar Nul Patippu Kazhagam.

Kannadasan, 1968. *Kaṇṇatācaṉ Kavitaikaḷ* (Poems of Kannadasan). Vol. 3. Madras: Vanati Patippakam.

Kannappan, R., comp. 1995. *Kaviñar Kaṇṇatācaṉ Naṭattiya Ilakkiya Yuttaṅkaḷ* (Poet Kannadasan's literary battles). Madras: Kannadasan Publications.

Karat Prakash. 1973. *Language and Nationality Politics in India*. Bombay: Orient Longman.

Karthikeyan, V. 1965–66. "Tamiḻnāṭṭu Aracāṅkattiṉ Tamiḻ Vaḷarcci Paṇikaḷ" (Tamil development work of the government of Tamilnadu). *Centamiḻc Celvi* 40: 72–76.

Karunanidhi, M. 1987a. *Caṅkat Tamiḻ* (Sangam Tamil). Madras: Rockfort.

———. 1987b. *Neñcukku Nīti* (Justice for the heart). Vol. 2. Madras: Tirumakal Nilayam.

———. 1989. *Neñcukku Nīti* (Justice for the heart). 3rd ed. Vol. 1. Madras: Tirumakal Nilayam. [1st ed. 1975]

Kathiresan Chettiar, M. 1959–60. "Tamiḻaṉṉai" [Tamiḻttāy]. *Centamiḻc Celvi* 34: 169–75.

Kaviraj, Sudipto. 1992. "Writing, Speaking, Being: Language and the Historical Formation of Identities in India." In *Nationalstaat und Sprachkonflikte in Süd- und Südostasien*, edited by Dagmar Hellmann-Rajanayagam and Dietmar Rothermund, 25–68. Stuttgart: Franz Steiner Verlag.

———. 1993. "The Imaginary Institution of India." In *Subaltern Studies VII: Writings on South Asian History and Society*, edited by Partha Chatterjee and Gyanendra Pandey, 1–39. Delhi: Oxford University Press.

Kedourie, Elie. 1961. *Nationalism*. Rev. ed. New York: F. A. Praeger.

Kejariwal, O. P. 1988. *The Asiatic Society of Bengal and the Discovery of India's Past, 1784–1838*. Delhi: Oxford University Press.

Kelly, John D. 1991. *A Politics of Virtue: Hinduism, Sexuality, and Countercolonial Discourse in Fiji*. Chicago: University of Chicago Press.

King, Christopher. 1992. "Images of Virtue and Vice: The Hindi-Urdu Controversy in Two 19th-Century Hindi Plays." In *Religious Controversy in British India: Dialogues in South Asian Languages*, edited by Kenneth W. Jones, 123–48. Albany: SUNY Press.

———. 1994. *One Language, Two Scripts: The Hindi Movement in Nineteenth Century North India*. Bombay: Oxford University Press.

Kittler, Friedrich. 1990. "The Mother's Mouth." In *Discourse Networks 1800/1900*, 25–69. Stanford: Stanford University Press.

Kolodny, Annette. 1975. *The Lay of the Land: Metaphor as Experience and History in American Life and Letters*. Chapel Hill: University of North Carolina Press.

Kopf, David. 1969. *British Orientalism and the Bengal Renaissance: The Dynamics of Indian Modernization, 1775–1835*. Berkeley: University of California Press.

Kothandaraman, P. 1979. "Periyāriṉ Moḻik Koḷkai" (Periyar's thoughts on language). *Pulamai* 5: 230–39.

———. 1986. *Tamiḻ Uṇarcci, Tamiḻ Vaḷarcci, Tamiḻ Āṭci* (Tamil consciousness, Tamil improvement, Tamil rule). Madras: Ambuli.

Krishnamurthy, G. 1991. *Pāratitācaṉ Vāḻkkai Varalāṟu* (Life story of Bharatidasan). Madras: Tamilnadu Araciyal Arivayvu Kazhagam.

Krishnan, P. 1984. *Tamiḻ Nūlkaḷil Tamiḻ Moḻi, Tamiḻ Iṉam, Tamiḻ Nāṭu* (Tamil language, Tamil community, and Tamilnadu in Tamil texts). Madras: Ilantamilar Patippakam.

Kumar, Krishna. 1990. "Quest for Self-Identity: Cultural Consciousness and Education in the Hindi Region, 1880–1950." *Economic and Political Weekly* 25: 1247–55.

Kumar, Radha. 1993. *The History of Doing: An Illustrated Account of Movements for Women's Rights and Feminism in India, 1800–1900*. London: Verso.

Kumaramangalam, Mohan. 1965. *India's Language Crisis: An Introductory Study*. Madras: New Century Book House.

Kuppusami, K. 1969. *Amaiccar Ātittaṉār: Vāḻkkai Varalāṟu* (Minister Adithanar: Life story). Madras: Rani.

Laitin, David. 1977. *Politics, Language, and Thought: The Somali Experience*. Chicago: University of Chicago Press.

Lakshmana Pillai, T. 1892–93. "Tamiḻ Moḻi Vaḷarttal Allatu Tamiḻ Pāṣaiyai Apivirtti Ceyyum Mārkkaṅkaḷ" (Nurturing the Tamil language or ways to improve the Tamil language). *Vivēkacintāmaṇi* 1: 41–45, 83–88, 119–24, 152–54, 184–86.

Lakshmi, C. S. 1984. *The Face behind the Mask: Women in Tamil Literature*. Delhi: Shakti.

———. 1990. "Mother, Mother-Community, and Mother-Politics in Tamilnadu." *Economic and Political Weekly (Review of Women's Studies)* 25(42–43): 72–83.

Lelyveld, David. 1993. "Colonial Knowledge and the Fate of Hindustani." *Comparative Studies in Society and History* 35: 665–82.

Leopold, Joan. 1970. "The Aryan Theory of Race." *Indian Economic and Social History Review* 7: 271–97.

Mamani, Mugam. 1992. *Aṟivuccuraṅkam Appātturaiyār* (The treasure trove of knowledge, Appadurai). Madras: Narmada.

Mani, P. S. 1990. *Irāmakiruṣṇar Iyakkamum Tamiḻnāṭum* (The Ramakrishna movement and Tamilnadu). Madras: Poonkodi.

———. 1993. *Va. Vē. Cu. Aiyar Araciyal-Ilakkiya Paṇikaḷ* (The political and literary works of V. V. S. Aiyar). Madras: International Institute of Tamil Studies.

Manickam Nayakar, P. V. 1985 [1917]. *The Tamil Alphabet and Its Mystic Aspect.* Reprint, New Delhi: Asian Educational Services.

Mannar Mannan. 1985. *Kaṟuppukkuyiliṉ Neruppukkural* (The fiery voice of the black cuckoo). Villupuram: Mutthu Patippakam.

Maraimalai Adigal. 1930a. English preface to *Māṇikkavācakar Varalāṟum Kālamum* (Life and times of Manikavasagar), v–xxvi. Pallavaram: T. M. Press.

———. 1930b. *Paḻantamiḻkkoḷkaiyē Caivacamayam: Saivism the Tamils' Ancient Religion.* Pallavaram: T. M. Press

———. 1930c. Preface to *Paḻantamiḻkkoḷkaiyē Caivacamayam: Saivism the Tamils' Ancient Religion,* iii–ix. Pallavaram: T. M. Press.

———. 1934. English preface to *Ciṟuvarkkāṉa Centamiḻ* (Pure Tamil reader for the young), 3–12. Pallavaram: T. M. Press.

———. 1936a. *Muṟkāla Piṟkālat Tamiḻppulavōr* (Ancient and modern Tamil poets). Pallavaram: T. M. Press.

———. 1936b. *The Tamilian and Aryan Forms of Marriage.* Pallavaram: T. M. Press.

———. [1948]. Introduction to *India's Language Problem,* by K. Appadurai, vi–xxxxii. Madras: Tamil India Publications.

———. 1963 [1923]. *Vēḷāḷar Nākarikam* (Civilization of the Vellalas). Reprint, Madras: SISSW.

———. 1966 [1906]. *Paṇṭaikkālat Tamiḻarum Āriyarum* (Ancient Tamilians and Aryans). Reprint, Madras: SISSW.

———. 1967a [1931]. "Tamiḻnāṭṭavarum Mēlnāṭṭavarum," (Southerners and westerners). In *Aṟivuraikkottu* (Anthology of thoughts), 125–54. Madras: Pari Nilayam.

———. 1967b [1918]. "Tamiḻttāy." In *Aṟivuraikkottu* (Anthology of thoughts), 80–87. Madras: Pari Nilayam.

———. 1974a [1941]. "English Preface to the Tamilian Creed." In *Tamiḻar Matam* (Tamilian creed), 11–46. Reprint, Madras: SISSW.

———. 1974b [1941]. *Tamiḻar Matam* (Tamilian creed). Reprint, Madras: SISSW.

———. 1980 [1925]. "Preface to the Second Edition." In *Cintaṉaik Kaṭṭuraikaḷ* (Philosophical essays), 9–40. Reprint, Madras: SISSW.

Margolis, Maxine L. 1984. *Mothers and Such: Views of American Women and Why They Changed.* Berkeley: University of California Press.
Metcalf, Thomas R. 1994. *Ideologies of the Raj.* Cambridge: Cambridge University Press.
Montrose, Louis. 1992. "The Work of Gender and Sexuality in the Elizabethen Discourse of Sexuality." In *Discourses of Sexuality: From Aristotle to AIDS,* edited by Donna C. Stanton, 138–84. Ann Arbor: University of Michigan Press.
More, J. B. P. 1993. "Tamil Muslims and Non-Brahmin Atheists, 1925–40." *Contributions to Indian Sociology,* n.s., 27: 83–104.
Mosse, George L. 1985. *Nationalism and Sexuality: Middle-class Morality and Sexual Norms in Modern Europe.* Madison: University of Wisconsin Press.
Mudaliar, Chandra. 1974. *The Secular State and Religious Institutions in India: A Study of the Administration of the Hindu Public Religious Trusts in Madras.* Wiesbadan: Steiner.
Mudiyarasan. 1964. *Pūṅkoṭi: Moḻikkoru Kāppiyam* (Poonkodi: An epic poem for language). Pudukottai: Valluvar Patippakam.
———. 1976. *Kāviyap Pāvai* (Lady of poetry). 3rd ed. Pudukottai: Valluvar. Patippakam. [1st ed. 1961]
———. n.d. "Pāṭṭupparavaiyiṉ Vāḻkkaip Payaṇam" (The life voyage of a singing bird). Unpublished manuscript.
Mutthu, P. 1938. "Tāy Moḻi Kaṭital" (Reproof of the mother tongue). *Āṉantapōtiṉi* 24(5): 334–36.
Nagarajan, K. 1980. *Tamiḻē Ellām* (Tamil is everything). Madras: Tamil Patippakam.
Nair, Janaki. 1994. "On the Question of Agency in Indian Feminist Historiography." *Gender and History* 6: 82–100.
Nallaswami Pillai, J. M. 1898–99. "Ancient Tamil Civilization." *The Light of Truth or Siddhanta Deepika* 2: 109–13.
———. 1906–07. "Ourselves." *The Light of Truth or Siddhanta Deepika* 7: 25–31.
Namasivaya Mudaliar, C. R. 1910. "The Tamil Tongue." In *Tamil Dramatic Interludes, First Book,* 51–64. Madras: C. Coomaraswami Naidu and Sons.
Nambi Arooran, K. 1976. "Tamil Renaissance and Dravidian Nationalism 1905–1944, with Special Reference to the Works of Maraimalai Adigal." Ph.D. diss., University of London.
———. 1980. *Tamil Renaissance and Dravidian Nationalism, 1905–1944.* Madurai: Koodal Publishers.
Nannan, M. 1993. *Periyāriyal: Moḻi* (Periyar's writings: Language). Madras: Gnayiru Patippakam.
Navanitakrishnan, A. K. 1952. *Tamiḻ Vaḷarnta Katai* (The story of Tamil's growth). Madras: SISSW.
Nayar, Baldev R. 1969. *National Communication and Language Policy in India.* New York: F. A. Praeger.
Nilambikai, T. 1952 [1937]. *Vaṭacoṟṟamiḻ Akaravaricai* (Sanskrit-Tamil Dictionary). Reprint, Madras: [SISSW].

———. 1960 [1925]. *Tan̲ittamil̲ Kaṭṭuraikaḷ* (Essays on pure Tamil). Reprint, Madras: SISSW.

———. n.d. [1938]. *Tamil̲ Nāṭum Tamil̲ Mol̲iyum Mun̲n̲ēr̲uvateppaṭi?* (How can Tamilnadu and Tamil improve?). Reprint, [Madras]: T. Nilambikai.

Niranjana, Tejaswani. 1992. *Siting Translation: History, Post-Structuralism, and the Colonial Context.* Berkeley: University of California Press.

Nuhman, M. A. 1984. *Pāratiyin̲ Mol̲ic Cintan̲aikaḷ: Oru Mol̲iyiyal Nōkku* (Bharati's thoughts on language: A linguistic view). Jaffna: Jaffna University.

Ong, Walter. 1977. *Interfaces of the Word: Studies in the Evolution of Consciousness and Culture.* Ithaca: Cornell University Press.

Padmanabhan, R. A., ed. 1982a. *Pārati Putayal Perun Tiraṭṭu* (Bharati's treasure: Giant compendium). Madras: Vanati.

———. 1982b. *Cittira Pārati* (Bharati in pictures). 2nd ed. Madras: Bharatiyar Sangam.

Pancanathan, M. [196?]. *Tamil̲ An̲n̲ai Collukir̲āḷ* (Tamil̲ttāy speaks). Ponneri: Tamilcelvi Nilayam.

Pandian, Jacob. 1982. "The Goddess Kannagi: A Dominant Symbol of South Indian Tamil Society." In *Mother Worship: Themes and Variations,* edited by James Preston, 177–91. Chapel Hill: University of North Carolina Press.

———. 1987. *Caste, Nationalism, and Ethnicity: An Interpretation of Tamil Cultural History and Social Order.* Bombay: Popular Prakashan.

Pandian, M. S. S. 1992. *The Image Trap: M. G. Ramachandran in Film and Politics.* New Delhi: Sage.

———. 1993. " 'Denationalising the Past': 'Nation' in E. V. Ramasamy's Political Discourse." *Economic and Political Weekly* 28: 2282–89.

Pandian, M. S. S., S. Anandhi, and A. R. Venkatachalapathy. 1991. "Of Maltova Mothers and Other Stories." *Economic and Political Weekly* 26: 1059–64.

Parantama Mudaliar, A. K. 1926. *Tamil̲p Peruntēvi Tirupaḷḷiyel̲ucciyum, Tamil̲makaḷ Ār̲r̲uppaṭaiyum, Tamil̲ccir̲appum* (Song for awakening the great Queen Tamil from her sleep and the guide poem to Lady Tamil and the excellence of Tamil). Madras: Ten India Kalvi Sangam.

Parthasarathy, T. M. 1986. *Ti. Mu. Ka. Varalār̲u* (History of the DMK). 5th ed. Madras: Bharati Nilayam.

Pekan. 1986. *Tamil̲ttāyp Piḷḷaittamil̲* (Tamil̲ttāy as extraordinary child). 3rd ed. Madras: SISSW. [1st ed. 1979]

Perunchitranar. 1979. *Peruñcittiran̲ār Pāṭalkaḷ* (Songs of Perunchitran). Vol. 1. Madras: Tenmoli.

Peterson, Indira. 1989. *Poems to Śiva: The Hymns of the Tamil Saints.* Princeton: Princeton University Press.

Pillai, K. K., et al., eds. 1957. *Professor P. Sundaram Pillai Commemoration Volume.* Tirunelveli: SISSW.

Poovey, Mary. 1988. *Uneven Developments: The Ideological Work of Gender in Mid-Victorian England.* Chicago: University of Chicago Press.

Pope, George U. 1876. "Notes on the South-Indian or Dravidian Family of Languages." *The Indian Antiquary* 5: 157–58

———. 1979 [1900]. *The Tiruvacagam or "Sacred Utterances" of the Tamil Poet, Saint, and Sage Māṇikka-Vācagar.* Reprint, Madras: University of Madras.

Presler, Franklin. 1987. *Religion under Bureaucracy: Policy and Administration for Hindu Temples in South India.* Cambridge: Cambridge University Press.

Pulamaidasan, comp. 1975. *Kaviñar Pōṟṟum Periyār* (Poets praise Periyar). Madras: Pakuttarivu Ilakiya Manram.

Pulavar Kulanthai. 1958. "Tamiḻ Kolai" (The murder of Tamil). *Muttāram* 2(7): 19–26.

———. 1971. *Irāvaṇa Kāviyam* (Epic poem on Ravana). 2nd ed. Erode: Vela. [1st ed. 1946]

———. 1972. *Pulavar Kuḻantai Pāṭalkaḷ* (Songs of Pulavar Kulanthai). Erode: Vela.

Purnalingam Pillai, M. S. 1930. *Kaṭṭuraikkaḷañciyam* (Collection of essays). Tirunelveli: Meeraniya Press.

———. 1945 [1927]. *Tamil India.* Reprint, Madras: SISSW.

———. 1985 [1929]. *Tamil Literature, Revised and Enlarged Edition.* Reprint, Tanjavur: Tamil University.

Puthumai Vanan, M. 1968. *Tīkkuḷitta Cemmal Ciṉṉacāmi* (The warrior Chinnasami who immolated himself). [Madurai]: n.p.

Puttoli. 1977. *Tamiḻttāyiṉ Kaṇṇīr* (The tears of Tamiḻttāy). Accuveli: Damayanti.

Rafael, Vicente L. 1988. *Contracting Colonialism: Translation and Christian Conversion in Tagalog Society under Early Spanish Rule.* Ithaca: Cornell University Press.

Raghava Aiyangar, M. 1948. *Centamiḻ Vaḷartta Tēvarkaḷ* (The Thevars who nurtured Tamil). Tiruchirapalli: T. G. Gopala Pillai

———. 1986 [1911]. "Heroic Mothers of Ancient Tamilagam: Vīrattāymār." *Tamilian Antiquary* 1(9): 73–85.

Raghava Aiyangar, R. 1979. *Tamiḻ Varalāṟu* (History of Tamil). 3rd ed. [Chidambaram]: Annamalai University. [1st ed. 1941]

Rajagopalachari, C. 1937. *Tamiḻil Muṭiyumā?* (Can it be done in Tamil?). Madras: Rockhouse and Sons.

———. 1956 [1916]. "The Place of English in Indian Education." *Tamil Culture* 5: 16–29.

———. 1962. *The Question of English.* Madras: Bharatan Publications.

Rajagopalan, T. 1989. *Perumaikkuriya Peṇṭir* (Honorable women). Madras: T. Rajagopalan.

Rajendran, C. 1985. *Tamiḻk Kavitaiyil Tirāviṭa Iyakkattiṉ Tākkam* (Impact of the Dravidian movement on Tamil poetry). Madras: Poomani Patippakam.

Ram Gopal. 1966. *Linguistic Affairs of India.* Bombay: Asia Publishing House.

Ramalinga Pillai, V. 1947. *Āriyarāvatu Tirāviṭarāvatu* (Aryan or Dravidian). Madras: Tamil Pannai.

———. 1953. *Tamiḻ Moḻiyum Tamiḻ Aracum* (Tamil language and Tamil rule). Madras: Inba Nilayam.

———. 1988. *Nāmakkal Kaviñar Pāṭalkaḷ* (Songs of Namakkal Ramalinga Pillai). 2nd ed. Madras: Lifco. [1st ed. 1960]

Ramanujam, K. S. 1971. *Challenge and Response: An Intimate Report of Tamil Nadu Politics, 1967–1971.* Madras: Sundara.

Ramasami, E. V. 1948. *Moḻiyāraycci* (Thoughts on language). Erode: Valluvar.

———. 1960. *Tamiḻum Tamiḻilakkiyaṅkaḷum* (Tamil and Tamil literature). Madras: Pakkutarivu.

———. 1961. *Cutantarat Tamiḻnāṭu Ēṉ?* (Why an independent Tamilnadu?). 2nd ed. Erode: Kudiyarasu Publications.

———. 1962. *Moḻiyum Aṟivum* (Language and reason). Tiruchirapalli: Periyar Self-Respect Publications.

———. 1985 [1926]. "Intiyiṉ Rakaciyam" (Secret of Hindi). In *Intippōr Muracu* (The Hindi war drum), 76–84. Reprint, Madras: Viduthalai Publications.

Ramasami, M. S. 1947. *Tirāviṭa Nāṭu Piriviṉaip Pāṭalkaḷ* (Songs of separation of the Dravidian nation). Aruppukotai: n.p.

Ramaswamy, Sumathi. 1992a. "Daughters of Tamil: Language and the Poetics of Womanhood in Tamilnadu." *South Asia Research* 12(1): 38–59.

———. 1992b. "En/gendering Language: The Poetics and Politics of Tamil Identity, 1891–1970." Ph.D. diss., University of California, Berkeley.

———. 1993. "En/gendering Language: The Poetics of Tamil Identity." *Comparative Studies in Society and History* 35: 683–725

———. 1994. "The Nation, the Region, and the Adventures of a Tamil 'Hero.' " *Contributions to Indian Sociology,* n.s., 28: 295–322.

———. 1996. "Language of the Gods in the World of Men: Ideologies of Tamil before the Nation." Unpublished typescript.

———. Forthcoming. "Battling the Demoness Hindi: The Culture of Language Protests in Tamilnadu." In *Culture as Contested Site: Popular Participation and the State in the Indian Subcontinent,* edited by Sandria B. Frietag.

Ravindiran, V. 1996. "The Unanticipated Legacy of Robert Caldwell and the Dravidian Movement." *South Indian Studies* 1: 83–110.

Richman, Paula. 1997. *Extraordinary Child: Poems from a South Indian Devotional Genre.* Honolulu: University of Hawaii Press.

Roberge, Paul. 1992. "Afrikaans and the Ontogenetic Myth." *Language and Communication* 12: 31–52.

Rocher, Ludo. 1963. "South Indian 'Letters to the Editor' and the Indian Language Problem." *Revue du Sud-Est Asiatique* 3: 126–82.

Rowther, M. K. M. Abdul Kadir. 1907. *Maturait Tamiḻccaṅka Māṉmiyam* (The majesty of the Madurai Tamil Academy). Madurai: Vivekabanu.

Ryan, Mary. 1990. *Women in Public: Between Banners and Ballots, 1825–1880.* Baltimore: Johns Hopkins University Press.

Ryerson, Charles. 1988. *Regionalism and Religion: The Tamil Renaissance and Popular Hinduism.* Madras: Christian Literature Society.

Sabapathy Navalar. 1976 [1899]. *Tirāviṭap Pirakācikai Eṉṉum Tamiḻ Varalāṟu* (History of Tamil: Dravidian light). Reprint, Madras: SISSW.

Said, Edward. 1978. *Orientalism.* New York: Pantheon.

Sambandan, M. S. 1976 [1954]. *Tirucci Vicuvanātam* (Tiruchi Viswanatham). Reprint, Madras: Pari Nilayam.

Sambasivan, S., ed. 1967. *The Papers of Dr. Navalar Somasundara Bharatiar.* Madurai: Navalar Puthaka Nilayam.

Sambasivanar, S. 1974. *Tamiḻavēḷ Umāmakēcuvaraṉār* (Great hero of Tamil, Umamakeswaram). 3rd ed. Madurai: Valavan. [1st ed. 1964]

Sambasivanar, S., and R. Ilankumaran. 1960. *Nāvalar Pāratiyār* (The learned Bharati). Madras: SISSW.

Saravana Mutthu, T. 1892. *Tamiḻpāṣai* (The Tamil language). Madras: Srinilayam Press.

Sarkar, Tanika. 1987. "Nationalist Iconography: Image of Women in 19th Century Bengali Literature." *Economic and Political Weekly* 22: 2011–15.

Savariroyan, D. 1899–1900. "A Tamil Philology." *The Light of Truth or Siddhanta Deepika* 3: 39–42.

———. 1900–1901. "The Admixture of Aryan with Tamilian." *The Light of Truth or Siddhanta Deepika* 4: 104–8, 157–61, 218–20, 241–44, 269–71.

Sesha Iyengar, T. R. 1989 [1925]. *Dravidian India.* Reprint, New Delhi: Asian Educational Services.

Seshagiri Sastri, M. 1884. *Notes on Aryan and Dravidian Philology.* Vol. 1. Madras: Christian Knowledge Society's Press.

Sethu Pillai, R. P. 1964. *Kirustavat Tamiḻt Toṇṭar* (Christian devotees of Tamil). 5th ed. Tirunelveli: S. R. Subramania Pillai. [1st ed. 1946]

———. 1968. *Tamiḻiṉpam* (Sweetness of Tamil). 15th ed. Madras: Palaniappa. [1st ed. 1948]

Seton-Watson, Hugh. 1977. *Nations and States: An Enquiry into the Origins of Nations and the Politics of Nationalism.* Boulder, Colo.: Westview Press.

Sharif, K. M. 1990. *Kavikāmuṣerīp Kavitaikaḷ* (The poetry of poet K. M. Sharif). Madras: Tamil Mulakkam Patippakam.

———. 1992. *Kavikāmuṣerīp Talaiyaṅkaḷ, 1948–56* (Editorials of poet K. M. Sharif). Madras: Tamil Mulakkam Patippakam.

Shulman, David. 1980. *Tamil Temple Myths: Sacrifice and Divine Marriage in the South Indian Śaiva Tradition.* Princeton: Princeton University Press.

Singh, Ram Adhar. 1969. *Inquiries into the Spoken Languages of India from Early Times to Census of India 1901: Census of India 1961, Vol. 1, pt. 11–100 (1).* New Delhi: Office of the Registrar General.

Sinha, Mrinalini. 1995. *Colonial Masculinity: The "Manly Englishman" and the "Effeminate Bengali" in the Late Nineteenth Century.* Manchester: Manchester University Press.

Sivagnanam, M. P. 1960. *Tamiḻum Kalapaṭamum* (Tamil and its adulteration). Mylapore: Inba Nilayam.

———. 1970. *Viṭutalaip Pōril Tamiḻ Vaḷarnta Varalāṟu* (The history of the growth of Tamil during the Indian War of Independence). Madras: Inba Nilayam.

———. 1974. *Eṉatu Pōrāṭṭam* (My struggle). Madras: Inba Nilayam.

———. 1978. *Viṭutalaikkuppiṉ Tamiḻ Vaḷarnta Varalāṟu* (History of growth of Tamil after independence). Madras: Poonkodi Patippakam.

———. 1979. *Tamiḻakattil Piṟamoḻiyiṉar* (Speakers of other languages in the Tamil land). 2nd ed. Madras: Poonkodi.

———. 1981. *Ma. Po. Si. Paṭaittap Putiya Tamiḻakam* (The new Tamil land created by M. P. Sivagnanam), edited by Sundaram. Madras: Sekhar Patippakam.

Sivalinga Nayanar, P. 1940. "Tamiḻaṉṉaiyiṉ Taricaṉam" (The vision of Tamiḻttāy). *Āṉantapōtiṉi* 25(10): 695–700.

Sivananda Adigal. 1937–38. "Taṉakkuvamai Illātatu Tamiḻ Moḻi" (Incomparable Tamil). *Centamiḻc Celvi* 15: 601–4.

Sivathamby, K. 1978. "The Politics of a Literary Style." *Social Scientist* 6(8): 16–33.

———. 1979. *Taṉittamiḻ Iyakkattiṉ Araciyaṟ Piṉṉaṇi* (Political underpinnings of the pure Tamil movement). Madras: Cennai Book House.

Sivathamby, K., and A. Marx. 1984. *Pārati: Maṟaivu Mutal Makākavi Varai* (From the death of Bharati to the birth of the great poet). Madras: New Century Book House.

Smith, Paul. 1988. *Discerning the Subject.* Minneapolis: University of Minnesota Press.

Somasundara Bharati. 1912. *Tamil Classics and Tamilakam.* Tuticorin: n.p..

———. 1937. *An Open Letter to the Hon. C. Rajagopalachariar.* N.p.

Somasundara Pulavar, K. n.d. *Nāmakaḷ Pukaḻmālai* (A garland of praises for "Lady Tongue"). Jaffna: C. J. Iliathamby and Pandit S. Ilamurukanar.

Spadafora, David. 1990. "Language and Progress." In *The Idea of Progress in Eighteenth-Century Britain,* 179–210. New Haven: Yale University Press.

Srinivasa Aiyangar, M. 1914. *Tamil Studies: Essays on the History of the Tamil People, Language, Religion, and Literature.* Madras: Guardian Press.

Srinivasa Aiyangar, P. T. 1985 [1928]. *Pre-Aryan Tamil Culture.* Reprint, New Delhi: Asian Educational Services.

Steinberg, Jonathan. 1987. "The Historian and the *Questione della Lingua.*" In *The Social History of Language,* edited by Peter Burke and Roy Porter, 198–209. Cambridge: Cambridge University Press.

Subbarayan, P. 1956. "Minute of Dissent." In *Report of the Official Language Commission,* 315–30. New Delhi: Government of India.

Subramania Aiyar, V. V. 1981 [1914]. "Tamiḻ". In *Va. Vē. Cu. Aiyar Kaṭṭuraikaḷ* (Essays of V. V. S. Aiyar), edited by P. S. Mani, 9–21. Tirunelveli: S. N. Somayajulu.

Subramania Pillai, E. M. 1951–52. "Tamiḻttāyk Kolai" (The murder of Tamiḻttāy). *Centamiḻc Celvi* 26: 18–23, 161–71, 209–16.

Subramania Pillai, K. 1940. *Tamiḻar Camayam* (Religion of Tamilians). Madras: SISSW.

———. n.d. *A Note on the Madras Hindu Religious Endowments Bill, 1922.* Madras: n.p.

Subramania Siva. 1915. "Nāṉum Cutēcamittiraṉum" (We and *Swadeshamitram*). *Ñāṉapāṉu* 3: 196–202.

Subramaniam, C. 1962. *Tamiḻāl Muṭiyum* (Tamil can do it). Madras: Valluvar Pannai.

Subramaniam, C. S., ed. 1986. *Pārati Taricaṉam: Pāratiyāriṉ "Intiyā" Pattirakaik Kaṭṭuraikaḷ* (Glimpses of Bharati: Bharati's essays from *Intiyā*). Part 1. 2nd ed. Madras: New Century Book House.

Subramanian, N. [1950]. *Vi. Kō Cūryanārāyaṇa Castiriyār* (V. G. Suryanarayana Sastri). Madurai: V. S. Swaminathan.

Subramanian, Narendran. 1993. "Ethnicity, Populism, and Pluralist Democracy: Mobilization and Representation in South India." Ph.D. diss., Massachusetts Institute of Technology.

Subramanian, Shaktidasan. 1939. *Tamil̲ Ver̲i* (Passion for Tamil). Madras: Sadhu Accukuttam.

Suddhananda Bharati. 1936. *Paintamil̲c Cōlai* (Garden of evergreen Tamil). Singapore: Anbu Nilayam.

———. 1938. *Tamil̲uṇarcci: Essays on the Tamil Renaissance.* Ramachandrapuram: Anbu Nilayam.

———. [1950]. *Ātma Cōtan̲ai* (Self-Experiments). Madras: Shudha Nilayam.

Sudhir, P. 1993. "Colonialism and the Vocabularies of Dominance." In *Interrogating Modernity: Culture and Colonialism in India,* edited by Tejaswani Niranjana, P. Sudhir, and Vivek Chareshwar, 334–47. Calcutta: Seagull.

Sundara Shanmugan. 1948. *Tan̲ittamil̲kkiḷarcci* (Excitement of unique Tamil). Pondicherry: Paintamil.

———. 1951. *Centamil̲ Ār̲r̲up Paṭai* (Guide poem to glorious Tamil). Pondicherry: Kalvi Kazhagam.

Sundaram Pillai, P. 1922 [1891]. *Man̲ōn̲maṇīyam,* edited by S. Vaiyapuri Pillai. Reprint, Trivandrum: n.p.

Sundararajan, T. 1986. *Tamil̲ Nāṭu Peyar Mār̲r̲a Varalār̲u* (History of the change of name of Tamilnadu). Madras: Valanarasu.

Sundaresan, D. 1986. *Tamil̲ Āṭci Mol̲i—Oru Varalār̲r̲u Nōkku, 1921–1956* (Tamil as official language—a historical look). Tanjavur: Tamil University.

Suntharalingam, R. 1974. *Politics and Nationalist Awakening in South India, 1852–1891.* Tuscon: University of Arizona Press.

Suryanarayana Sastri, V. G. 1903. *Tamil̲mol̲iyin̲ Varalār̲u* (History of the Tamil language). Madras: G. A. Natesan.

———. n.d. [1922]. *Tamil̲ Viyācaṅkaḷ* (Tamil essays). Reprint, Madurai: V. S. Swaminathan.

Swaminatha Aiyar, U. V. 1982. *En̲ Carittiram* [My story]. 2nd ed. Madras: U. V. Swaminatha Aiyar Library. [1st ed. 1940–42]

———. 1991a [1941]. "Etu Tamil̲ Marapu?" (What is Tamil tradition?). In *Nin̲aivu Mañcari* (Collection of reminiscences), 2:76–85. Madras: U. V. Swaminatha Aiyar Library.

———. 1991b [1938]. "In̲n̲um Ar̲iyēn!" (I still do not know!). In *Nalluraikkōvai* (Collection of fine essays), 3:119–27. Madras: U. V. Swaminatha Aiyar Library.

———. 1991c [1940]. "Kaṭal Kaṭantuvanta Tamil̲" (Tamil across the seas). In *Nin̲aivu Mañcari* (Collection of reminiscences), 1:1–16. Madras: U. V. Swaminatha Aiyar Library.

———. 1991d [1933]. "Tamil̲ Vaḷarcci" (The growth of Tamil). In *Nalluraikkōvai* (Collection of fine essays), 2:48–58. Madras: U. V. Swaminatha Aiyar Library.

Swaminatha Upatiyayan, M. 1921. *Caivacamayamum Tamilppāṭaiyum* (Shaivism and Tamil language). Mannargudi: Bharati.

Tambiah, Stanley. 1985. "The Magical Power of Words." In *Culture, Thought, and Social Action: An Anthropological Perspective*, 17–59. Cambridge: Harvard University Press.

Tamilkudimagan, M. 1985. *Pāvāṇarum Taṉittamiḻum* (Devaneyan and pure Tamil). Madras: International Institute of Tamil Studies.

———. 1990. *Pāventar Kaṉavu* (Bharatidasan's dream). Madras: Tirumakal Nilayam.

Tamilmallan, K., ed. 1984. *Taṉittamiḻ Vaḷarcci* (The growth of pure Tamil). Pondicherry: Tanittamil Kazhagam.

———. 1989. *Pāvāṇar Perumai* (The majesty of Devaneyan). Pondicherry: Tanittamil Patippakam.

Tamiḻp Pātukāppu Nūṟṟiraṭṭu (Compilation of books for protecting Tamil). 1967 [1938]. Reprint, Madras: Tamil Pathukappu Kazhagam.

Tamiḻppaṇi (Service to Tamil). 1950. Tiruchirapalli: Tamilakam.

Thamaraikanni, V. P. 1938. *Puṉitavati Allatu Tamiḻar Viṭutalaip Pōr* (Punithavathi, or the Tamilian fight for freedom). Madras: Sakthi.

Thaninayagam, Xavier S. 1963. "Regional Nationalism in Twentieth-Century Tamil Literature." *Tamil Culture* 10(1): 1–23.

Thomas, George, 1991. *Linguistic Purism*. London: Longman.

Thomas, Nicholas. 1994. *Colonialism's Culture: Anthropology, Travel, and Government*. Princeton: Princeton University Press.

Thooran, P., ed. 1986 [1953]. *Pārati Tamiḻ* (Bharati's Tamil). Reprint, Madras: Vanati.

Tirumaran, K. 1992. *Taṉittamiḻiyakkam* (The pure Tamil movement). Tiruchi: Marutam.

Tirunavukarasu, K. 1991. *Tirāviṭa Iyakka Vērkaḷ* (Roots of the Dravidian movement). Madras: Manivacagar.

Tirunavukarasu, M. 1945. *Nīlāmpikai Ammaiyār* (Nilambikai). Madras: SISSW.

———. 1959. *Maṟaimalai Aṭikaḷ Varalāṟu* (Life story of Maraimalai Adigal). Madras: SISSW.

Tirunavukarasu, M., and A. R. Venkatachalapathy, eds. 1988. *Maṟaimalaiyaṭikaḷār Nāṭkuṟippukaḷ, 1898–1950* (Diaries of Maraimalai Adigal). Madras: SISSW.

Tīyil Venta Tamiḻp Pulikaḷ: Inti Etirpput Tiyākikaḷ Varalāṟu (The Tamil tigers who immolated themselves: The story of anti-Hindi martyrs). n.d. Salem: Kuyil Pannai.

Trawick, Margaret. 1990. *Notes on Love in a Tamil Family*. Berkeley: University of California Press.

Uberoi, Patricia. 1990. "Feminine Identity and National Ethos in Indian Calendar Art." *Economic and Political Weekly (Review of Women Studies)* 25(17): 41–48.

Ulakanathan, M. 1969. *Viṭutalai Muḻakkam* (Thunder of freedom). Madurai: Mutthu Chidamabaranar.

Vaiyapuri Pillai, S. 1989. *Tamiḻiṉ Maṟumalarcci* (The renaissance of Tamil), edited by K. Sivathamby. Madras: New Century Book House.
Varadananjaiya Pillai, A. [1938]. *Tamiḻaracik Kuṟavañci* (Fortune-teller song on Queen Tamil). Karanthai: n.p.
Varadarajan, M. 1966. *Moḻi Varalāṟu* (History of language). 3rd ed. Madras: SISSW.
Vasudeva Sharma, R. 1928. *Tamiḻ Moḻi Vaḷarcci* (Improvement of Tamil). Tirucirapuram: n.p.
Vedanayakam Pillai, S. 1879. *Piratāpam Eṉṉum Piratāpamutaliyār Carittiram* (The life and adventures in Tamil of Pradapa Mudaliar). Mayavaram: [S. Vedanayakam Pillai].
Velayutam Pillai. 1971 [1947]. *Moḻiyaraci* (Queen language). Reprint, Madras: SISSW.
Velu, K., and K. Selvaraji, comps. 1989. *Tamiḻ Eḻuttuc Cīrtiruttam: Uṇmai Varalāṟu* (Tamil script reform: True history). Velur: Kuttusi Gurusami Patippakam.
Venkatachalapathy, A. R. 1990. "Cuyamariyātai Iyakkamum Caivarum" [Self-Respect movement and the Shaivites). *Nāvāviṉ Ārāycci* 35: 63–78.
———. 1994. "Reading Practices and Modes of Reading in Colonial Tamil Nadu." *Studies in History,* n.s., 10: 273–90.
Venkatesvara Ayyar, V. 1918. *Tamiḻum Ataṉ Perumaiyum* (Tamil and its glory). Pudukottai: V. Venkatesvara Ayyar.
Vimalanandam, M. 1971. "Maṉōṉmaṇīya Vāḻttil Oru Maṟu" (A defect in the *Maṉōṉmaṇīyam*'s prayer). *Mañcari* 24(8): 75–80.
Visswanathan, E. S. 1982. "The Emergence of Brāhmaṇs in South India: With Special Reference to Tamil Nadu." In *India: History and Thought,* edited by S. N. Mukherjee, 282–325. Calcutta: Subarnalekha.
———. 1983. *The Political Career of E. V. Ramasami Naicker.* Madras: Ravi and Vasanth.
Viswanatham, K. A. P. 1941. "Etu Tamiḻ Marapu?" (What is Tamil tradition?). *Āṉantapōtiṉi* 27(6): 360–62.
———. 1989. *Eṉatu Naṇparkaḷ* (My friends). 2nd ed. Madras: Pari.
Visweswaran, Kamala. 1990. "Family Subjects: An Ethnography of the 'Women's Question' in Indian Nationalism." Ph.D. diss., Stanford University.
Warner, Marina. 1985. *Monuments and Maidens: The Allegory of the Female Form.* New York: Atheneum.
Washbrook, David. 1976. *The Emergence of Provincial Politics: The Madras Presidency, 1870–1920.* Cambridge: Cambridge University Press.
———. 1989. "Caste, Class, and Dominance in Modern Tamil Nadu: Non-Brahmanism, Dravidianism, and Tamil Nationalism." In *Dominance and State Power in Modern India: Decline of a Social Order,* edited by Francine R. Frankel and M. S. A. Rao, 1:204–65. Delhi: Oxford University Press.
———. 1991. " 'To Each a Language of His Own': Language, Culture, and Society in Colonial India." In *Language, History, and Class,* edited by Penelope J. Corfield, 179–203. Oxford: B. Blackwell.
Whitehead, Henry. 1921. *The Village Gods of South India.* Rev. 2nd ed. London: Oxford University Press.

Wolf, Eric R. 1958. "The Virgin of Guadalupe: A Mexican National Symbol." *Journal of American Folklore* 71: 34–39.

Woolard, Kathryn, and Bambi Schiefflin. 1994. "Language Ideology." *Annual Review of Anthropology* 23: 55–82.

Zvelebil, Kamil. 1974. *Tamil Literature*. Weisbaden: Otto Harrasowitz.

———. 1992. *Companion Studies to the History of Tamil Literature*. Leiden: Brill.

Index

Abu-Lughod, Lila, 84
Adithan, S. B., 154, 155, 168, 266n.34; and Tamilttāy, 180, 266n.34. *See also* Madras state: renaming
Agastya: and Tamil, 51, 87, 90, 133, 235. *See also* Potiyam
Ākāśvāṇi. See *Vāṉoli* (radio) agitation
Alagappan, A., 127
Anderson, Benedict, 5, 22, 113–14
Āṅkilattāy ("Mother English"), 50, 104. *See also* English
Annadurai, C. N., 45, 249, 251; and anti-Hindi protests, 62, 173, 229–30, 272n.42; and Dravidianism, 65, 71, 73, 102–3, 201–2, 224; and Dravidian movement, 46, 64, 71, 74, 148, 224, 240; and "Tamilnadu" agitation, 156–58, 161, 267n.37; and Tamilttāy, 73, 102–3. *See also* DMK
Annamalai University: and Tamil, 45, 91, 127, 184, 212, 215, 232, 249
Anti-Hindi protests, 32, 39, 110–11, 157, 158, 168–78; arrests in, 35, 111, 127, 170, 173, 174, 177, 187–88, 226, 231, 238, 256, 268n.89, 269n.94; in cartoons, 73, 101–103, 130, 131, 225, figs. 5, 6, 10; deaths during, 1, 109, 112, 198, 226, 228–33, 268n.89, 271n.41, 272n.42; and Dravidianism, 46, 62, 68, 196, 198, 199, 206, 207–8, 225–26, 233; and hunger fasts, 170, 176, 230–31, 270n.37; and 1948 conference, 100, 122, 173, 189; phases of, 169–70; self-immolations during, 1, 73, 131, 170, 231–33, 271n.41, 272n.42, fig. 7; Tamil Muslim participation, 174–76; and Tamilttāy, 65, 100–102, 104, 108–9, 110–11, 113, 122, 127, 130, 131, 177, 213, 225, 226, 230, 232–33, 269n.94; Tamil women in, 102, 176, 182, 185, 186, 187–89, 207
Appadurai, Arjun, 82
Appadurai, K., 44; and Hindi, 174, 180; and Tamilttāy, 125, 180, 251–52
Appiah, Kwame, 255
Aranganathan: death of by self-immolation, 108, 131, 232, 233, 271n.41, fig. 7
Arankarathinam, 231
Arumuga Navalar, 190, 221
Aryan(s): and British colonialism, 25–26, 29, 31, 36, 41–42, 269n.11; in classicism, 36, 43–44, 251, 261n.8; and Dravidian(s), 14, 26–31, 33, 38, 40, 42, 43–44, 239, 255, 269n.11; and Dravidianism, 46, 67–69, 74, 196, 241; and Hindi, 68, 111, 172, 238; and Hinduism, 26–27, 29, 33, 53; and India, 25–26, 28, 33, 36; and Indianism, 48–49, 51, 53, 201; and neo-Shaivism, 25–34; and Sanskrit, 14, 25, 138–39, 150, 201, 265n.12; and Tamil, 28–29, 37–38, 194–95. *See also* Brahmans; Dravidian(s)

Compositor: Maple-Vail Manufacturing Group
Text: 10/13 Sabon
Display: Sabon
Printer and binder: Maple-Vail Manufacturing Group